# NEGIMA!? NEO

## MAGISTER NEGI MAGI

## 6

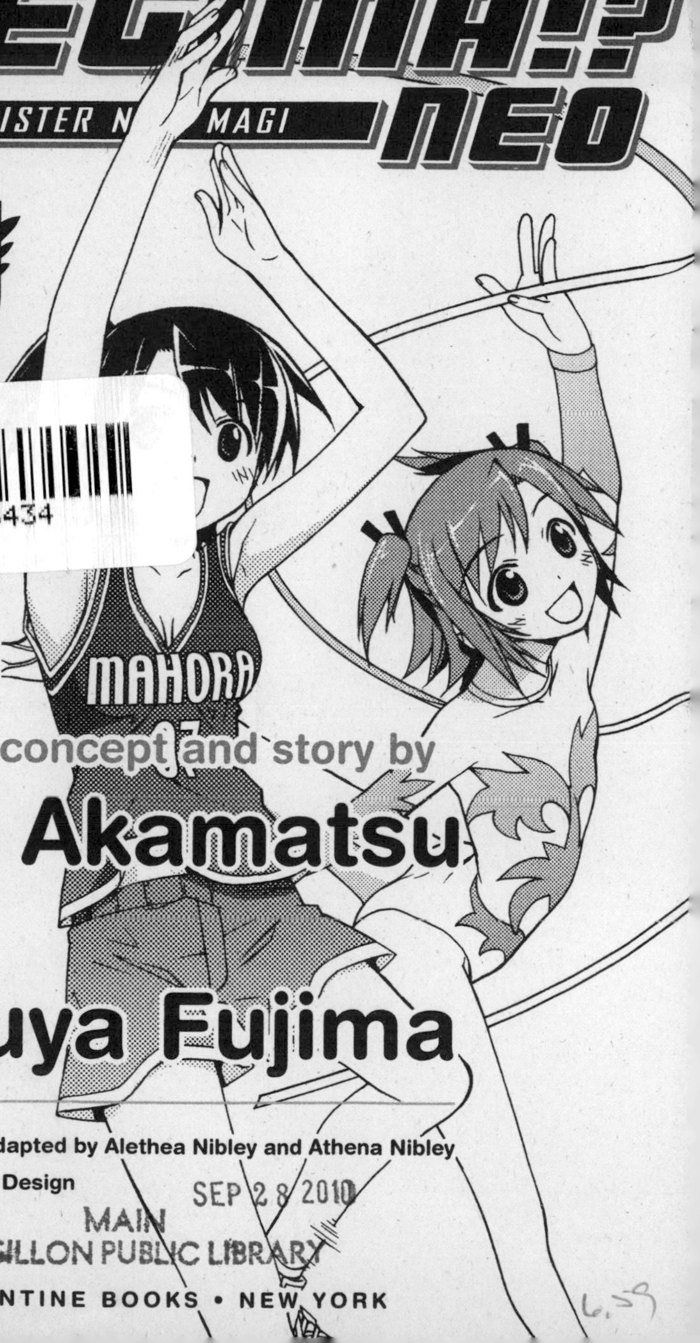
MAHORA
MAHORA



Original concept and story by

**Ken Akamatsu**

Art by

**Takuya Fujima**

---

Translated and adapted by Alethea Nibley and Athena Nibley
Lettered by Foltz Design



DEL REY
BALLANTINE BOOKS • NEW YORK

A Del Rey Manga/Kodansha Trade Paperback Original

*Negima!? neo* volume 6 copyright © 2009 Takuya Fujima © Ken Akamatsu © KODANSHA/
Kanto Maho Association/TV Tokyo. All rights reserved.
English translation copyright © 2010 Takuya Fujima © Ken Akamatsu
© KODANSHA/Kanto Maho Association/TV Tokyo. All rights reserved.

Based on the manga *Mahoh Sensei Negima!* by Ken Akamatsu,
originally serialized in the weekly *Shonen Magazine* published by Kodansha Ltd.

Published in the United States by Del Rey, an imprint of
The Random House Publishing Group, a division of Random House, Inc., New York.

DEL REY is a registered trademark and the Del Rey colophon
is a trademark of Random House, Inc.

Publication rights arranged through Kodansha Ltd.

First published in Japan in 2009 by Kodansha Ltd., Tokyo

ISBN 978-0-345-52059-3

Printed in the United States of America

www.delreymanga.com

1 2 3 4 5 6 7 8 9

Translators/adapters: Alethea Nibley and Athena Nibley
Lettering: Foltz Design

# CONTENTS

# A Word from the Artist

Hello, this is Fujima.
Thank you for buying *Negima!? neo* volume six.

We started releasing limited editions with volume two,* but
the time between this one and the last volume was so short
that for now, we're skipping a volume. (Unfortunately.)

This volume reveals Eva's shocking past, and has *that* scene
with Akira, and *this* scene with Makie and Yūna, and then
Kono-Setsu do XXX! It's full of must-read moments, so I hope
that you will enjoy reading all the way through. ^^

—Takuya Fujima

*Fujima is referring to Japan-only limited editions of the series.

# Honorifics Explained

Throughout the Del Rey Manga books, you will find Japanese honorifics left intact in the translations. For those not familiar with how the Japanese use honorifics and, more important, how they differ from American honorifics, we present this brief overview.

Politeness has always been a critical facet of Japanese culture. Ever since the feudal era, when Japan was a highly stratified society, use of honorifics—which can be defined as polite speech that indicates relationship or status—has played an essential role in the Japanese language. When you address someone in Japanese, an honorific usually takes the form of a suffix attached to one's name (example: "Asuna-san"), is used as a title at the end of one's name, or appears in place of the name itself (example: "Negi-sensei," or simply "Sensei!").

Honorifics can be expressions of respect or endearment. In the context of manga and anime, honorifics give insight into the nature of the relationship between characters. Many English translations leave out these important honorifics and therefore distort the feel of the original Japanese. Because Japanese honorifics contain nuances that English honorifics lack, it is our policy at Del Rey not to translate them. Here, instead, is a guide to some of the honorifics you may encounter in Del Rey Manga.

**-san:**  This is the most common honorific and is equivalent to Mr., Miss, Ms., or Mrs. It is the all-purpose honorific and can be used in any situation where politeness is required.

**-sama:**  This is one level higher than "-san" and is used to confer great respect.

**-dono:**  This comes from the word "tono," which means "lord." It is an even higher level than "-sama" and confers utmost respect.

**-kun:**  This suffix is used at the end of boys' names to express familiarity or endearment. It is also sometimes used by men among friends, or when addressing someone younger or of a lower station.

**-chan:** This is used to express endearment, mostly toward girls. It is also used for little boys, pets, and even among lovers. It gives a sense of childish cuteness.

**Bôzu:** This is an informal way to refer to a boy, similar to the English terms "kid" and "squirt."

**Sempai/
Senpai:** This title suggests that the addressee is one's senior in a group or organization. It is most often used in a school setting, where underclassmen refer to their upperclassmen as "sempai." It can also be used in the workplace, such as when a newer employee addresses an employee who has seniority in the company.

**Kohai:** This is the opposite of "sempai" and is used toward under-classmen in school or newcomers in the workplace. It connotes that the addressee is of a lower station.

**Sensei:** Literally meaning "one who has come before," this title is used for teachers, doctors, or masters of any profession or art.

**-[blank]:** This is usually forgotten in these lists, but it is perhaps the most significant difference between Japanese and English. The lack of honorific, known as *yobisute,* means that the speaker has permission to address the person in a very inti-mate way. Usually, only family, spouses, or very close friends have this kind of permission. It can be gratifying when some-one who has earned the intimacy starts to call one by one's name without an honorific. But when that intimacy hasn't been earned, it can be very insulting.

# NEGIMA!? neo

MAGISTER N MAGI

6

MAHORA

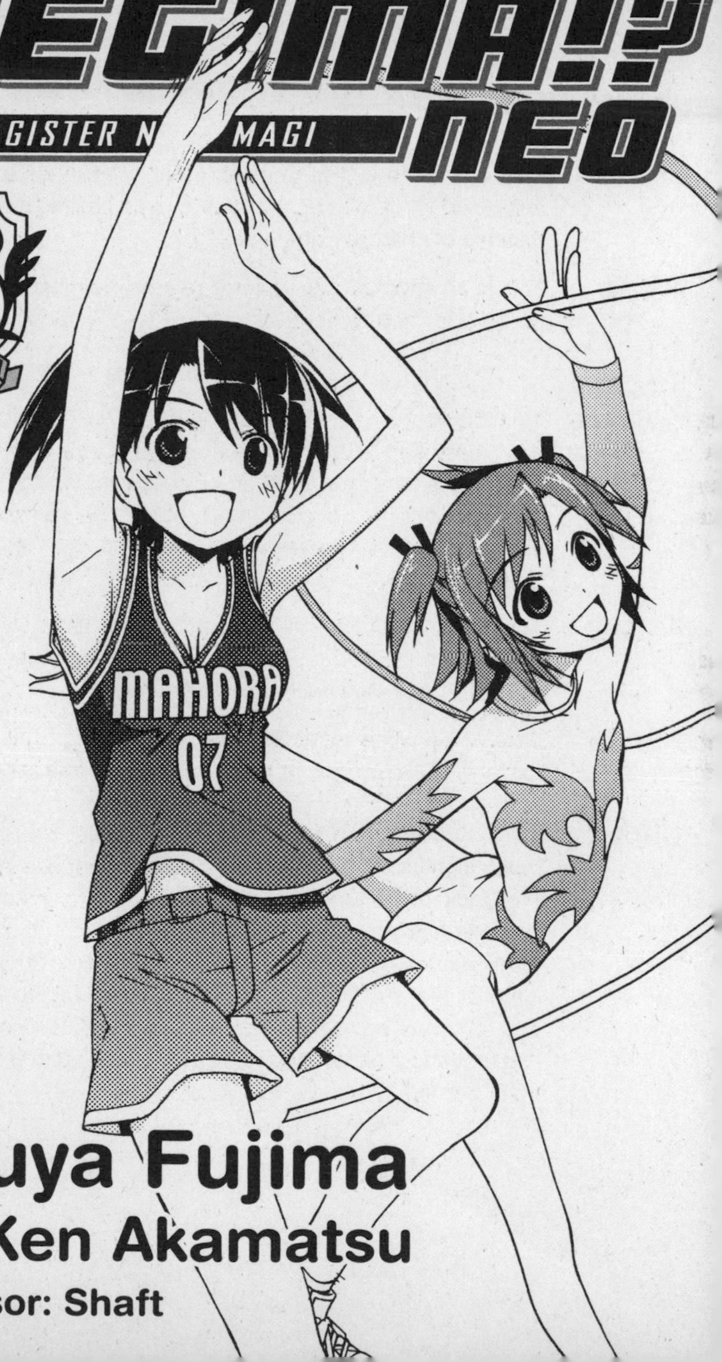
MAHORA
07

**Takuya Fujima**

**Original Story: Ken Akamatsu**

**Supervisor: Shaft**

SPLASH

# NEGIMA!? NEO

## MAGISTER NEGI MAGI

# Volume ⑥ Contents

KISS

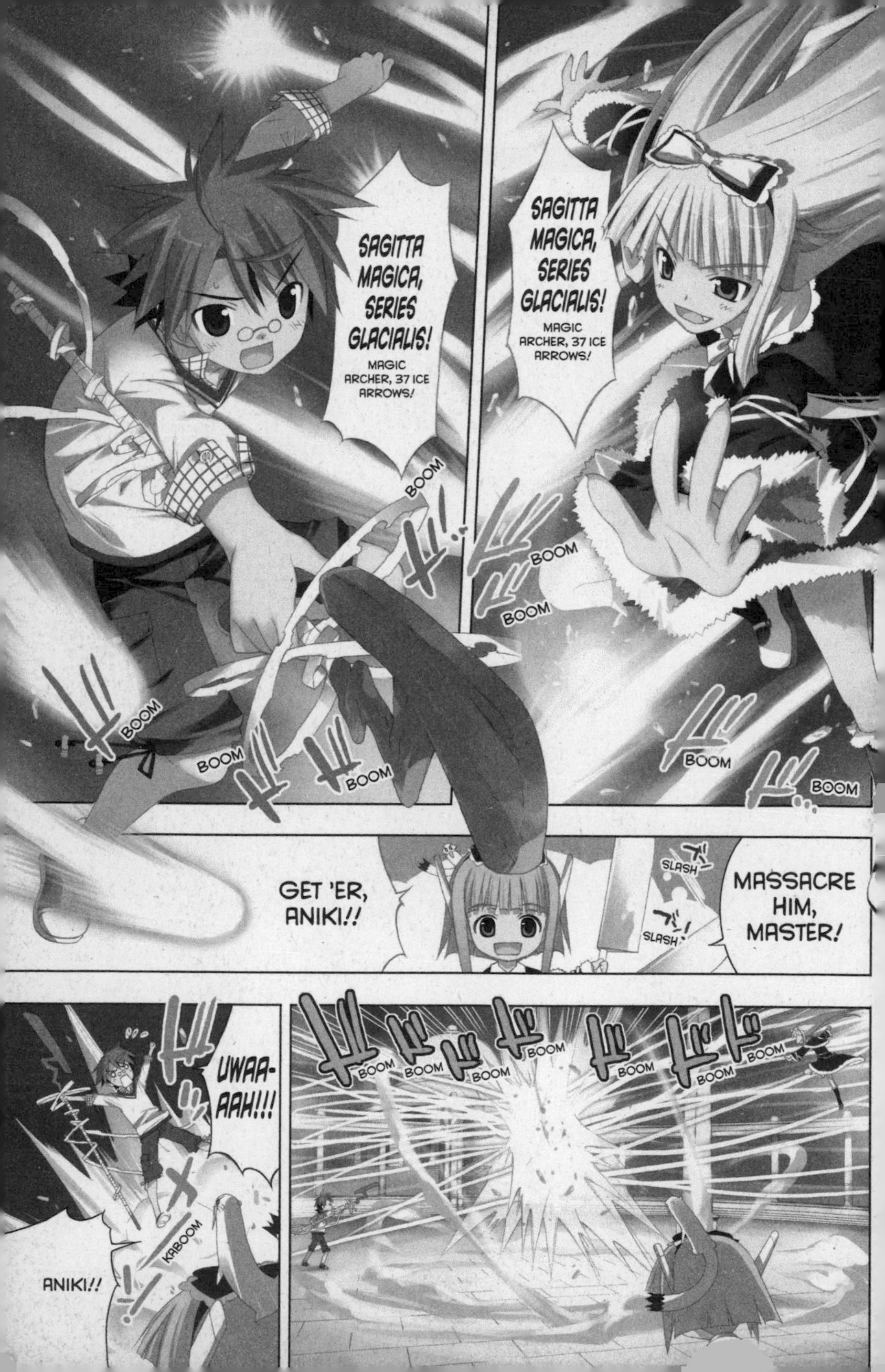
SAGITTA MAGICA, SERIES GLACIALIS!
MAGIC ARCHER, 37 ICE ARROWS!
BOOM
BOOM
BOOM
BOOM
SAGITTA MAGICA, SERIES GLACIALIS!
MAGIC ARCHER, 37 ICE ARROWS!
BOOM
BOOM
BOOM
BOOM
MASSACRE HIM, MASTER!
SLASH
SLASH
GET 'ER, ANIKI!!
BOOM
BOOM
BOOM
BOOM
BOOM
BOOM
BOOM
UWAA-AAH!!!
KABOOM
ANIKI!!

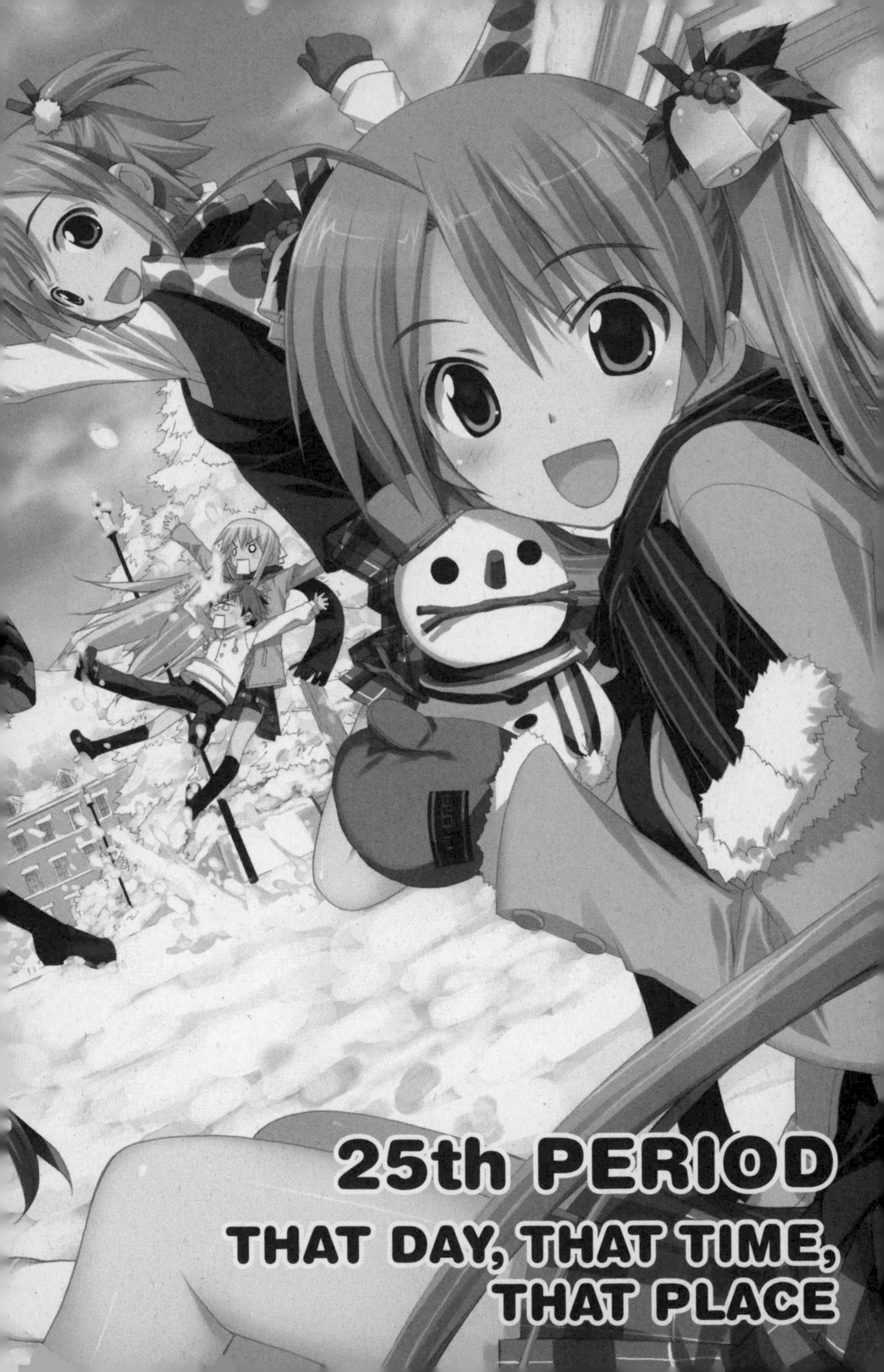

# 25th PERIOD

## THAT DAY, THAT TIME, THAT PLACE

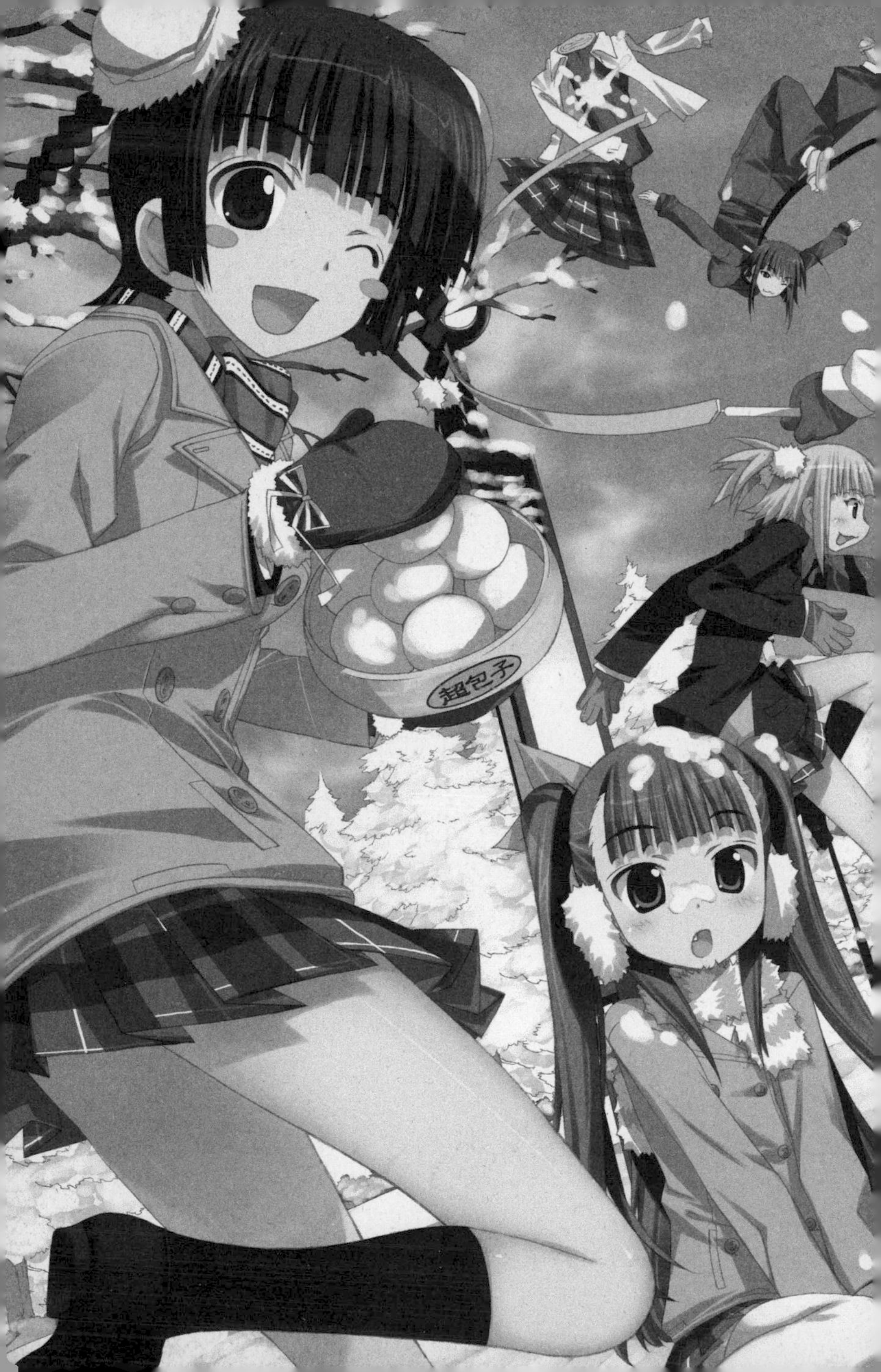
超包子

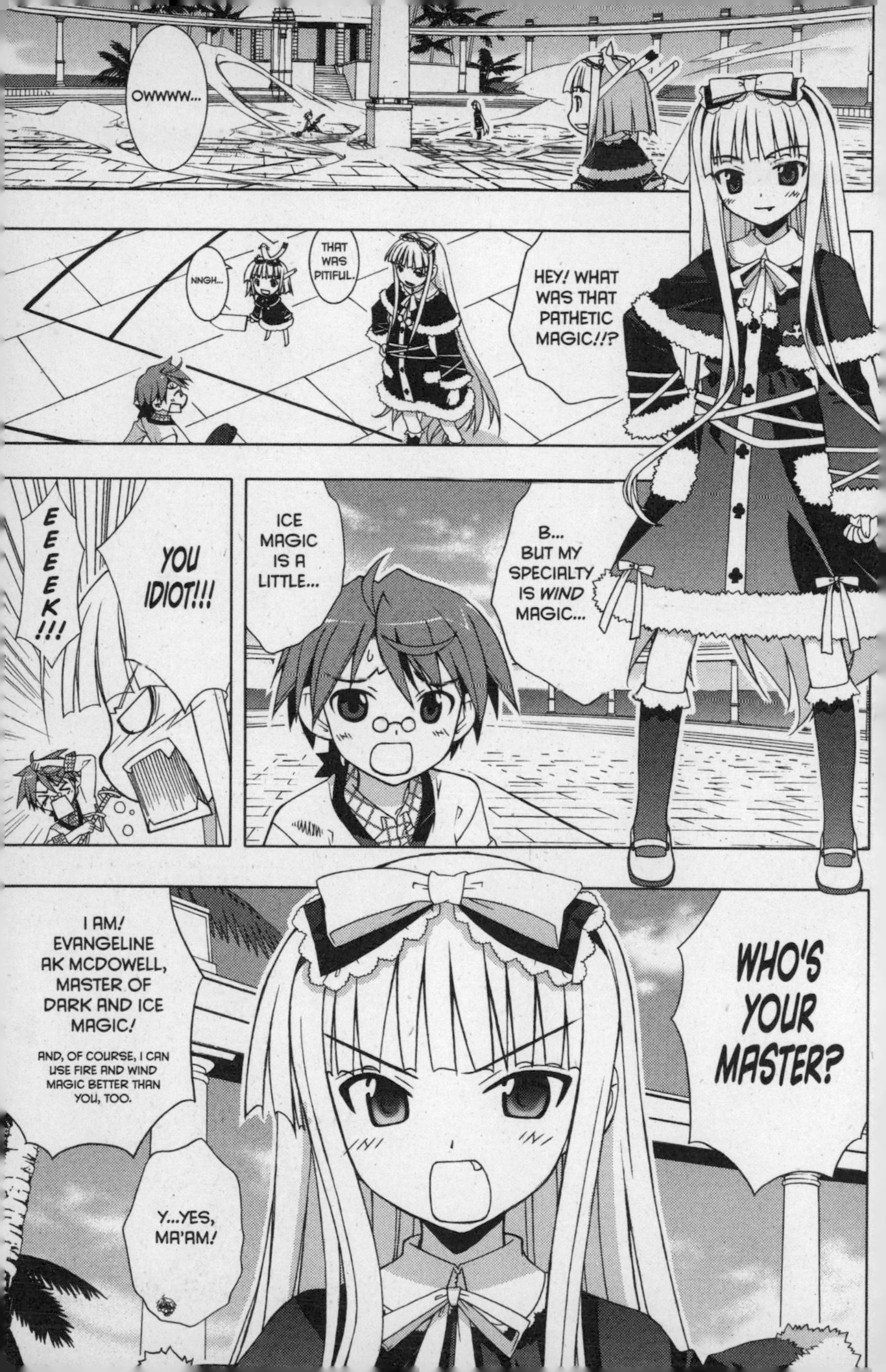
OWWWW...
HEY! WHAT WAS THAT PATHETIC MAGIC!!?
THAT WAS PITIFUL.
NNGH...
B... BUT MY SPECIALTY IS WIND MAGIC...
ICE MAGIC IS A LITTLE...
YOU IDIOT!!!
EEEEEK!!!
WHO'S YOUR MASTER?
I AM! EVANGELINE AK MCDOWELL, MASTER OF DARK AND ICE MAGIC!
AND, OF COURSE, I CAN USE FIRE AND WIND MAGIC BETTER THAN YOU, TOO.
Y...YES, MA'AM!

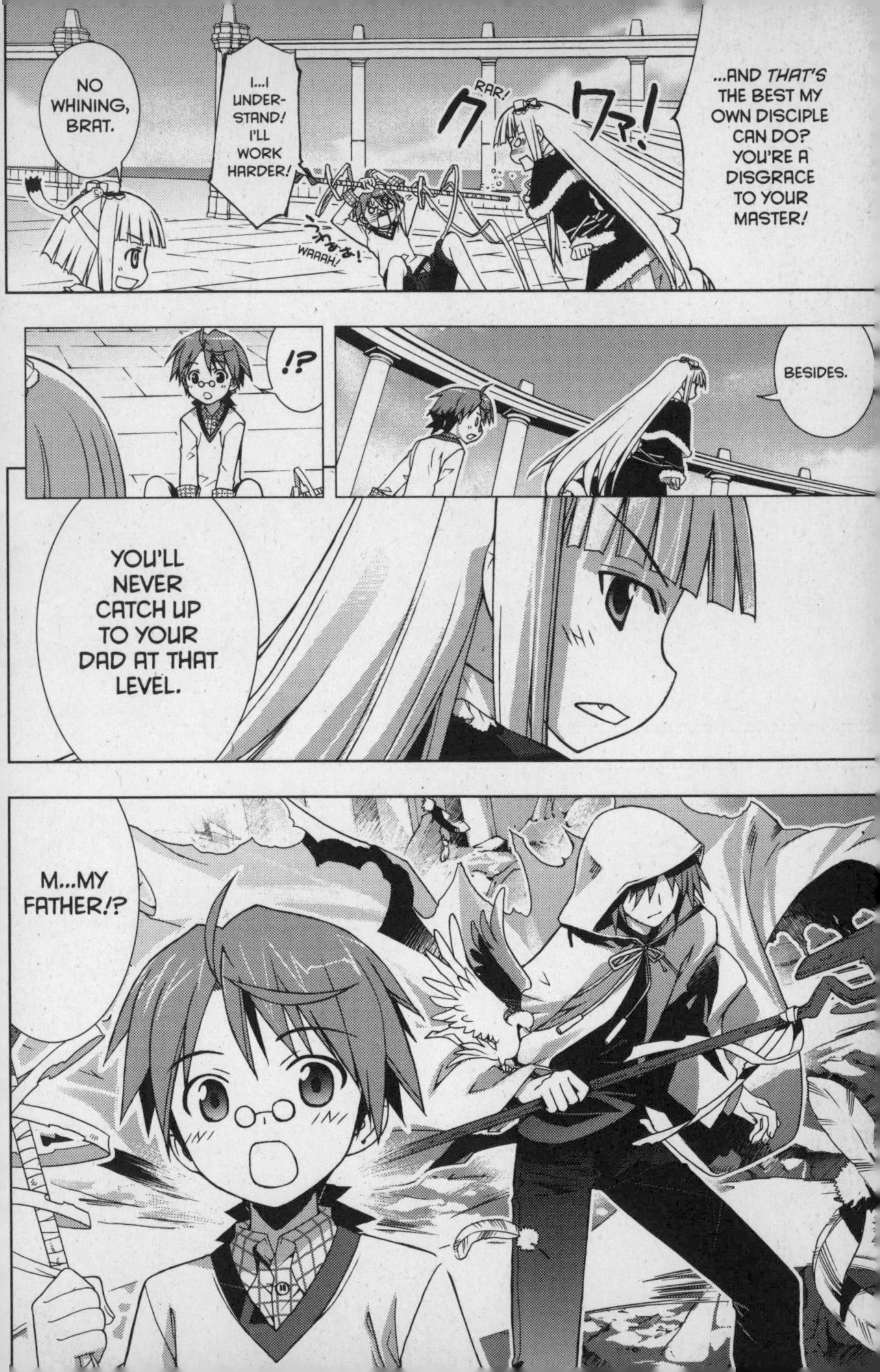
...AND *THAT'S* THE BEST MY OWN DISCIPLE CAN DO? YOU'RE A DISGRACE TO YOUR MASTER!
RAR!
WAAAH!
I...I UNDERSTAND! I'LL WORK HARDER!
NO WHINING, BRAT.
BESIDES.
!?
YOU'LL NEVER CATCH UP TO YOUR DAD AT THAT LEVEL.
M...MY FATHER!?

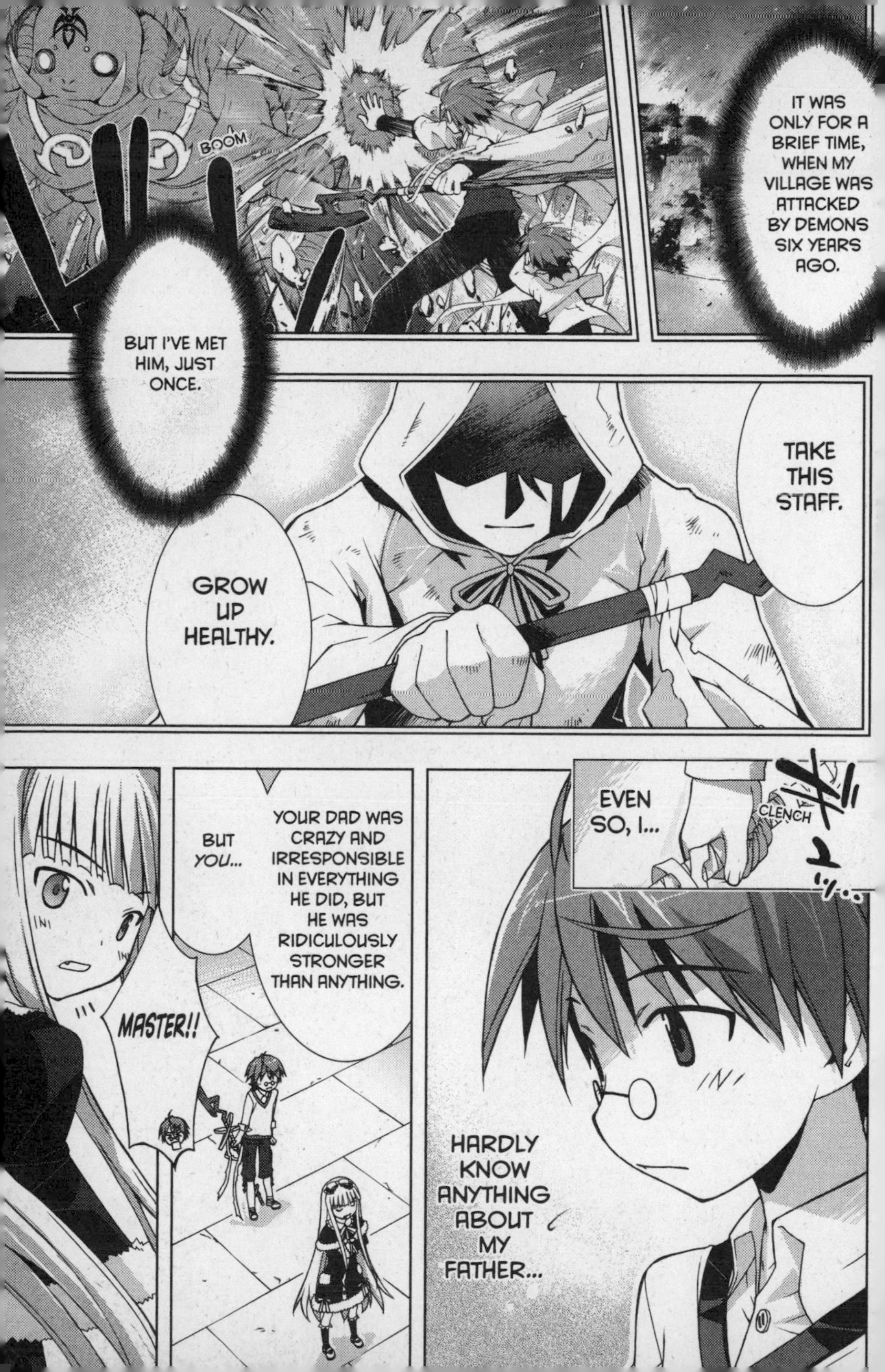
IT WAS ONLY FOR A BRIEF TIME, WHEN MY VILLAGE WAS ATTACKED BY DEMONS SIX YEARS AGO.
BOOM
BUT I'VE MET HIM, JUST ONCE.
TAKE THIS STAFF.
GROW UP HEALTHY.
EVEN SO, I...
CLENCH
HARDLY KNOW ANYTHING ABOUT MY FATHER...
YOUR DAD WAS CRAZY AND IRRESPONSIBLE IN EVERYTHING HE DID, BUT HE WAS RIDICULOUSLY STRONGER THAN ANYTHING.
BUT *YOU*...
*MASTER!!*

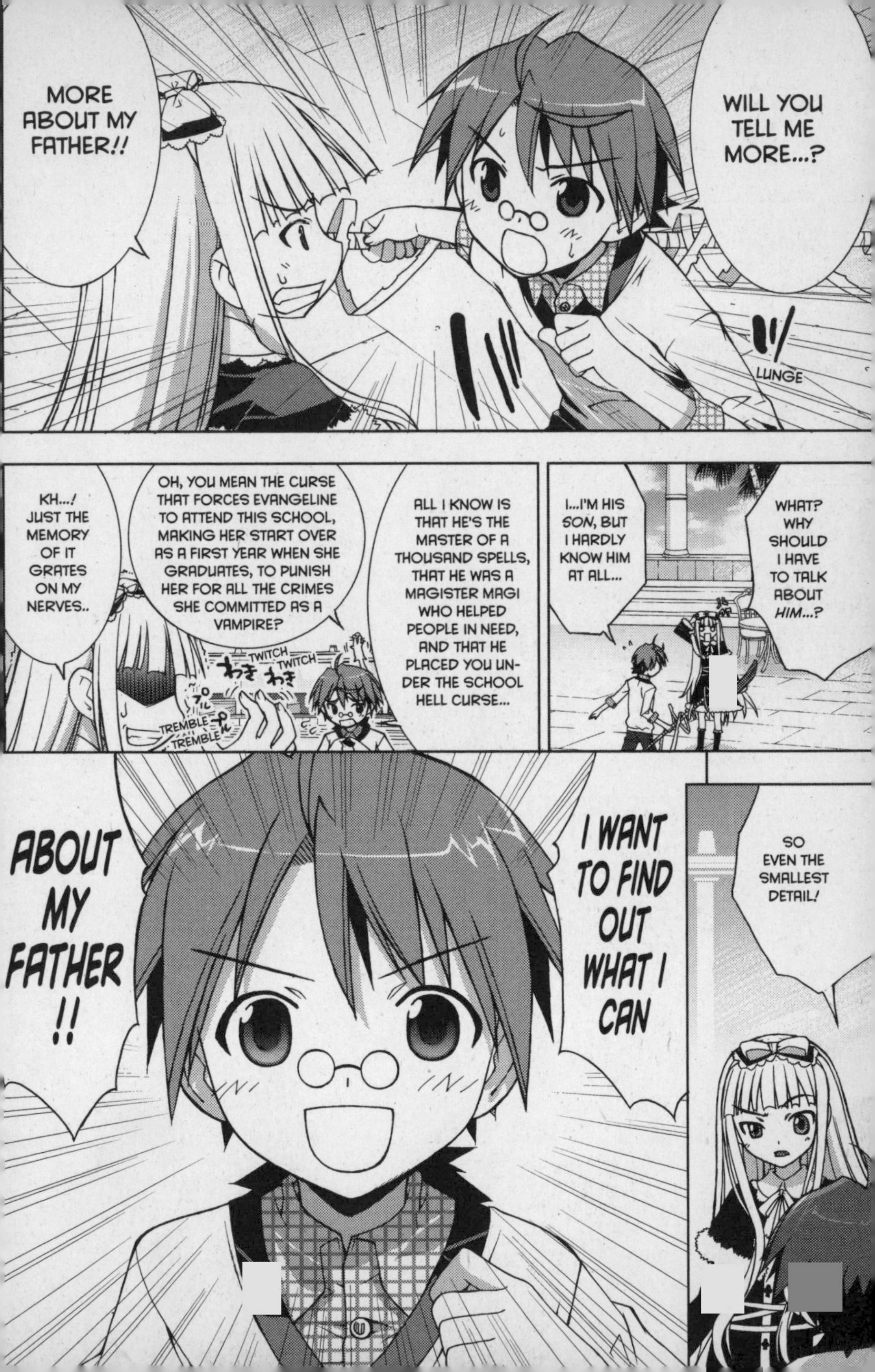
WILL YOU TELL ME MORE...?
LUNGE
MORE ABOUT MY FATHER!!
WHAT? WHY SHOULD I HAVE TO TALK ABOUT *HIM*...?
I...I'M HIS *SON*, BUT I HARDLY KNOW HIM AT ALL...
ALL I KNOW IS THAT HE'S THE MASTER OF A THOUSAND SPELLS, THAT HE WAS A MAGISTER MAGI WHO HELPED PEOPLE IN NEED, AND THAT HE PLACED YOU UNDER THE SCHOOL HELL CURSE...
OH, YOU MEAN THE CURSE THAT FORCES EVANGELINE TO ATTEND THIS SCHOOL, MAKING HER START OVER AS A FIRST YEAR WHEN SHE GRADUATES, TO PUNISH HER FOR ALL THE CRIMES SHE COMMITTED AS A VAMPIRE?
わき わき
TWITCH TWITCH
TREMBLE TREMBLE
KH...! JUST THE MEMORY OF IT GRATES ON MY NERVES..
SO EVEN THE SMALLEST DETAIL!
I WANT TO FIND OUT WHAT I CAN
ABOUT MY FATHER!!

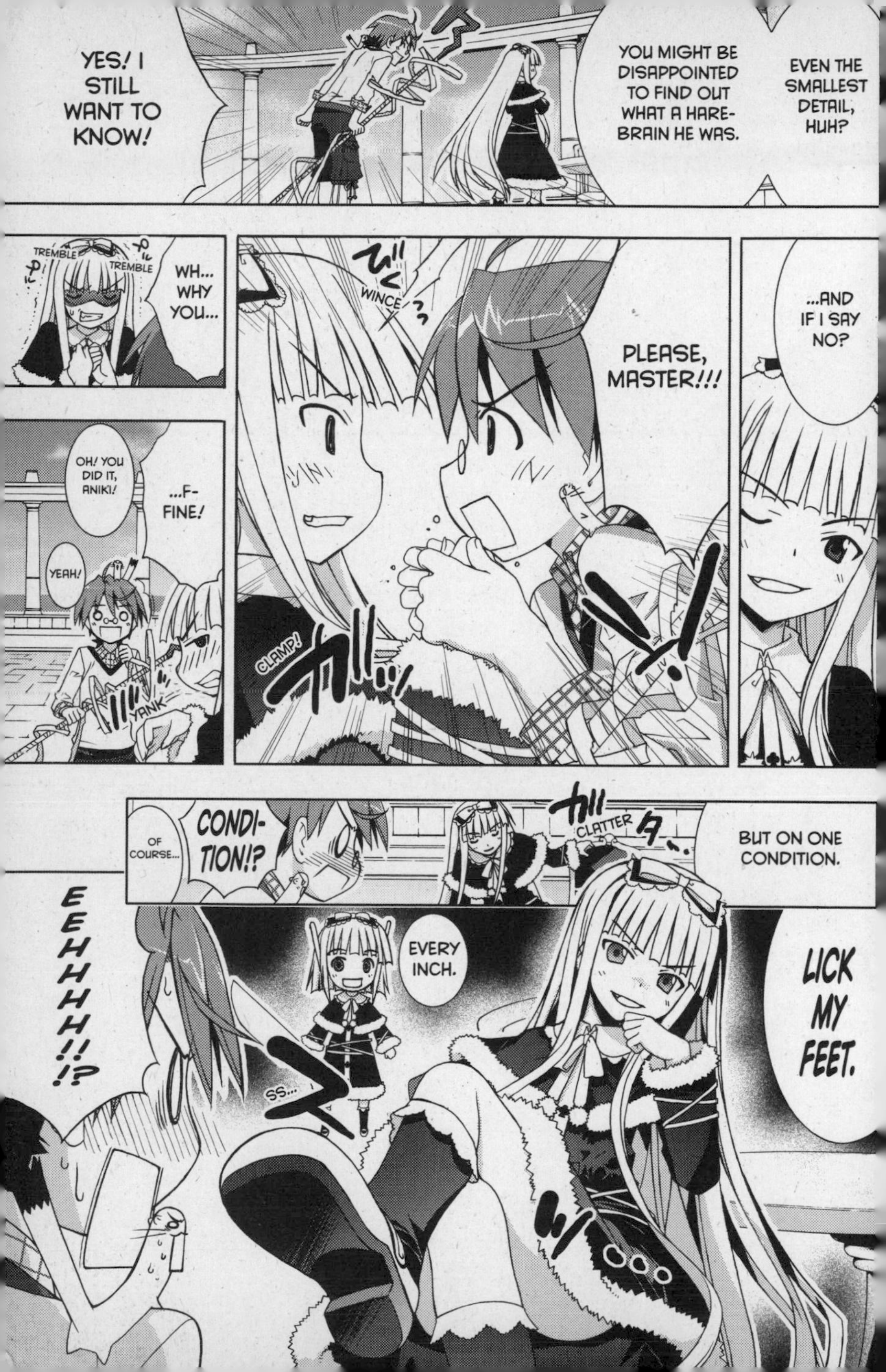
EVEN THE SMALLEST DETAIL, HUH?
YOU MIGHT BE DISAPPOINTED TO FIND OUT WHAT A HARE-BRAIN HE WAS.
YES! I STILL WANT TO KNOW!
...AND IF I SAY NO?
WINCE
PLEASE, MASTER!!!
CLAMP!
TREMBLE
TREMBLE
WH... WHY YOU...
...F-FINE!
OH! YOU DID IT, ANIKI!
YEAH!
YANK
BUT ON ONE CONDITION.
CLATTER
CONDI-TION!?
OF COURSE...
LICK MY FEET.
EVERY INCH.
SS...
EEHHHHH!!!?

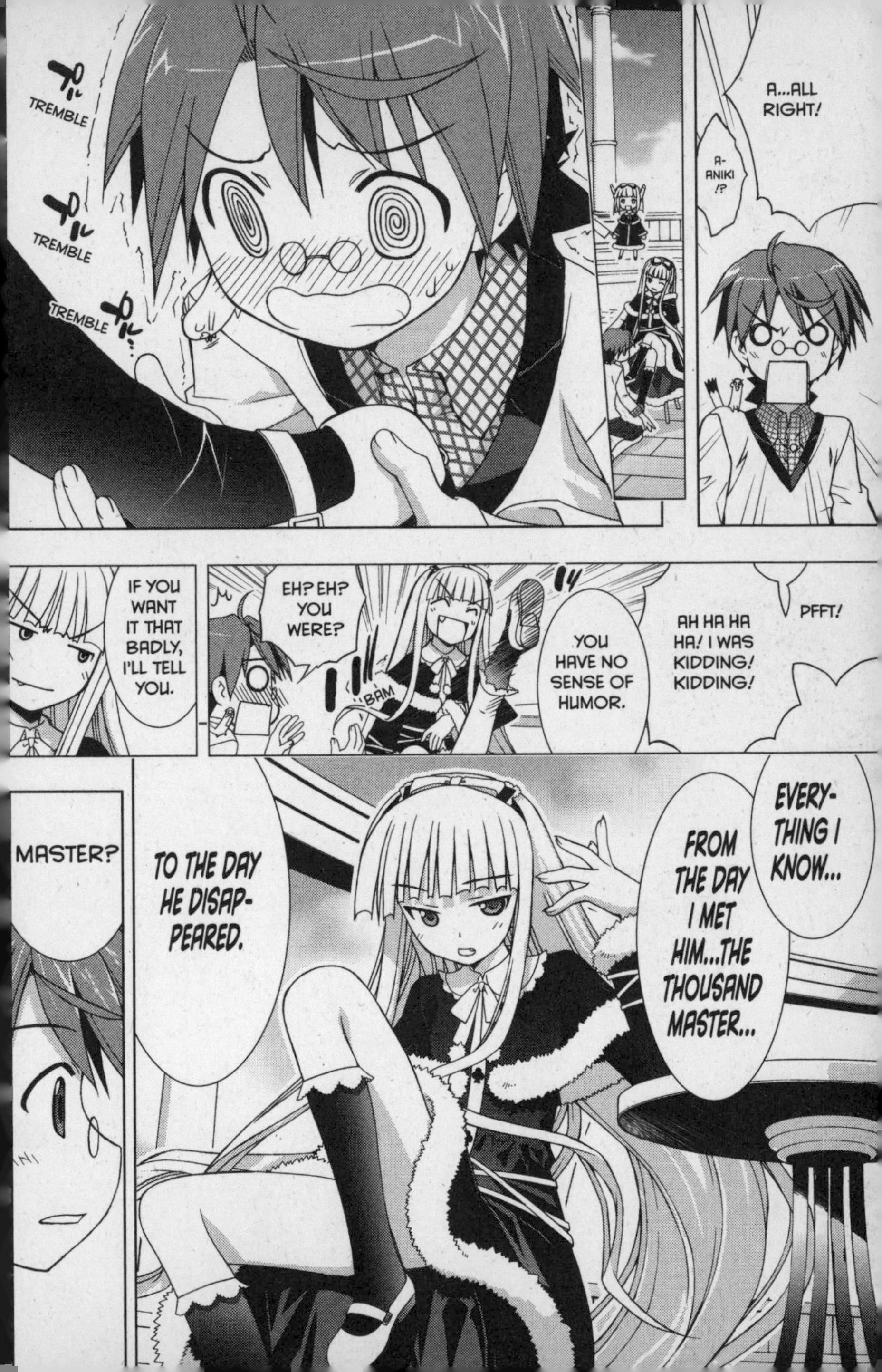
A...ALL RIGHT!
A-ANIKI!?
TREMBLE
TREMBLE
TREMBLE
PFFT!
AH HA HA HA! I WAS KIDDING! KIDDING!
YOU HAVE NO SENSE OF HUMOR.
BAM
EH? EH? YOU WERE?
IF YOU WANT IT THAT BADLY, I'LL TELL YOU.
EVERY-THING I KNOW...
FROM THE DAY I MET HIM...THE THOUSAND MASTER...
TO THE DAY HE DISAP-PEARED.
MASTER?

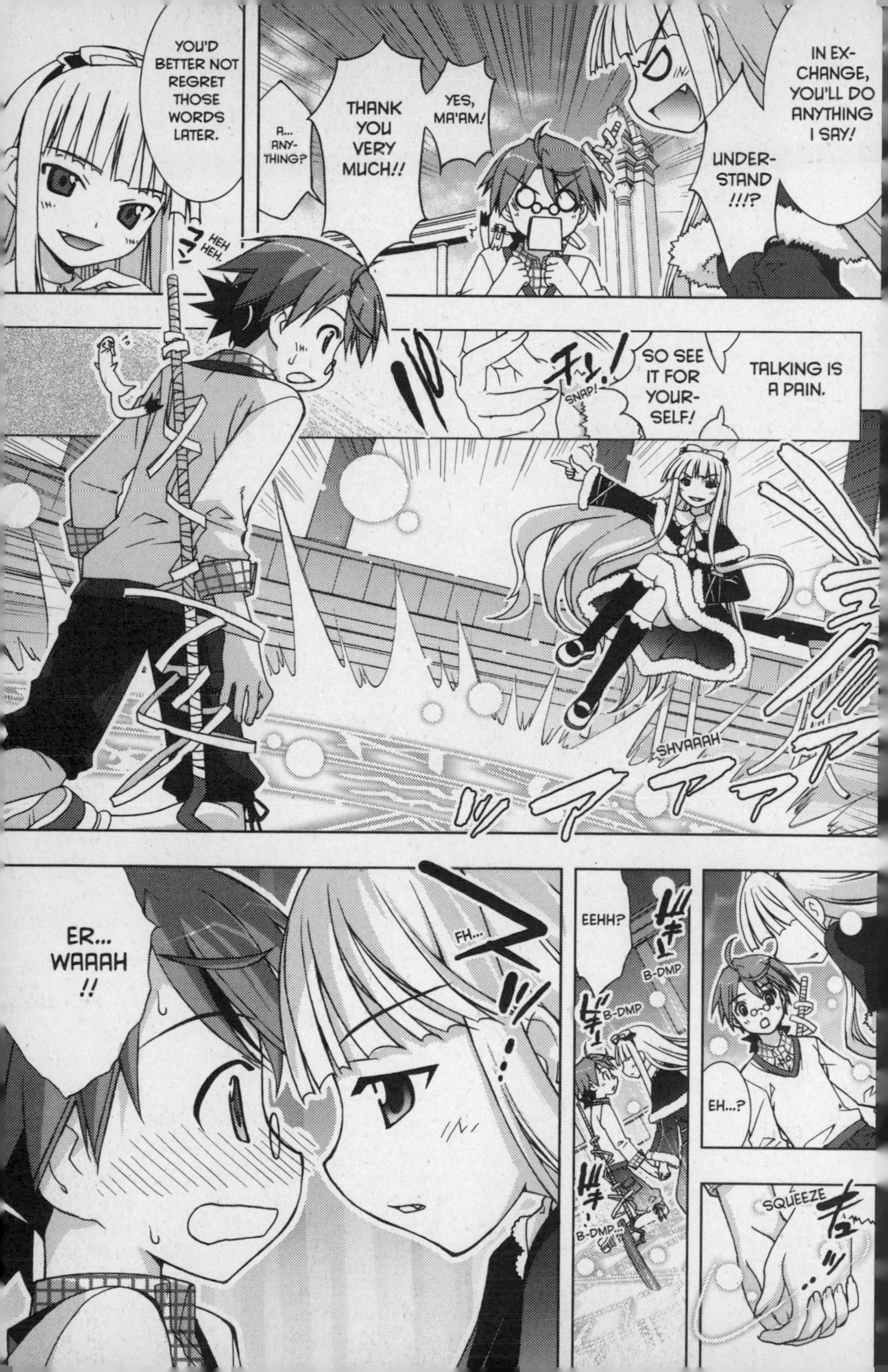
IN EX-CHANGE, YOU'LL DO ANYTHING I SAY!
UNDER-STAND!!!?
YES, MA'AM!
THANK YOU VERY MUCH!!
A... ANY-THING?
YOU'D BETTER NOT REGRET THOSE WORDS LATER.
HEH HEH.
TALKING IS A PAIN.
SO SEE IT FOR YOUR-SELF!
SNAP!
SHVAAAH
EH...?
SQUEEZE
EEHH?
B-DMP
B-DMP
B-DMP...
FH...
ER... WAAAH!!

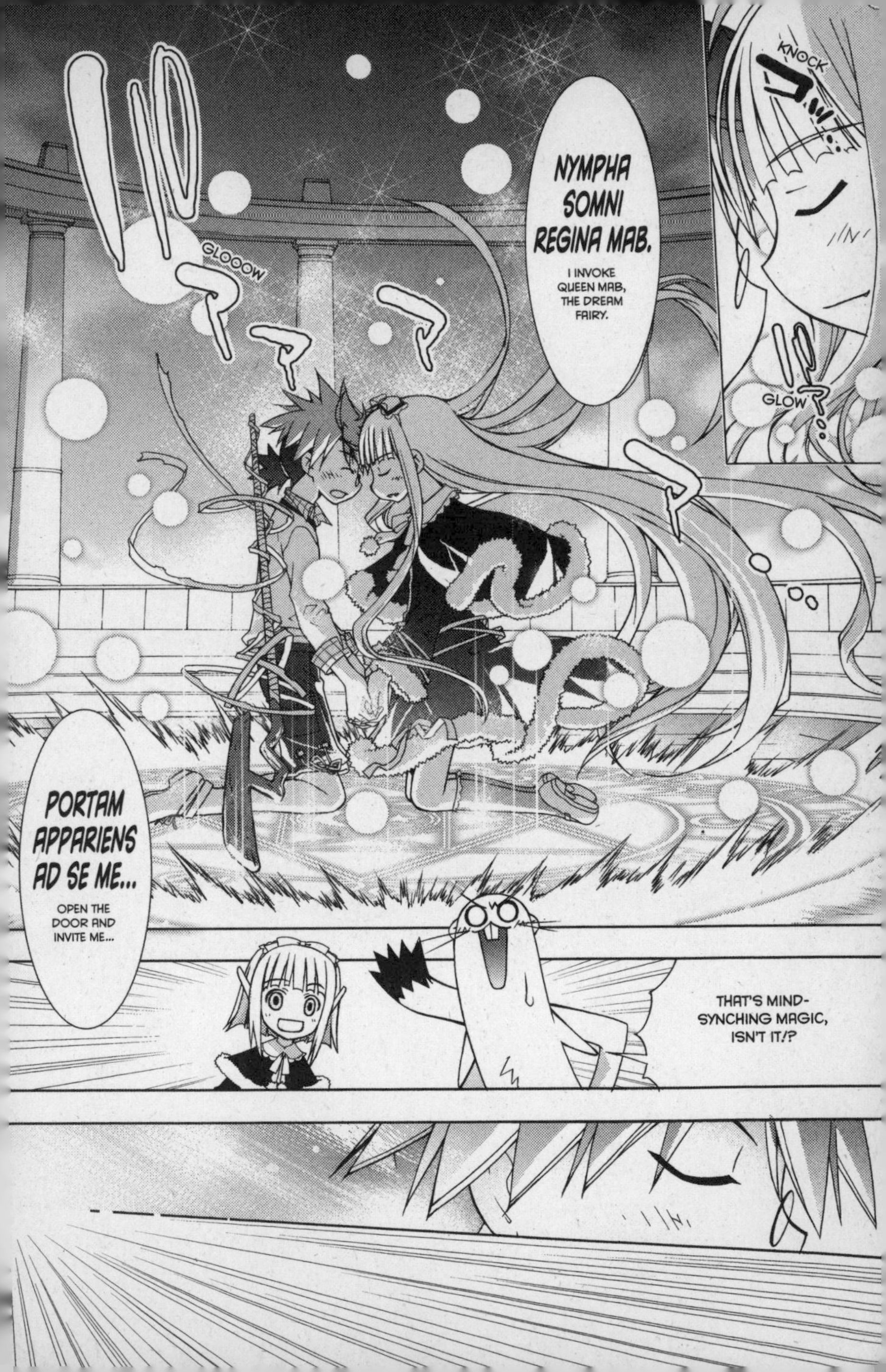
KNOCK
GLOW
NYMPHA SOMNI REGINA MAB.
I INVOKE QUEEN MAB, THE DREAM FAIRY.
GLOOOW
PORTAM APPARIENS AD SE ME...
OPEN THE DOOR AND INVITE ME...
THAT'S MIND-SYNCHING MAGIC, ISN'T IT!?

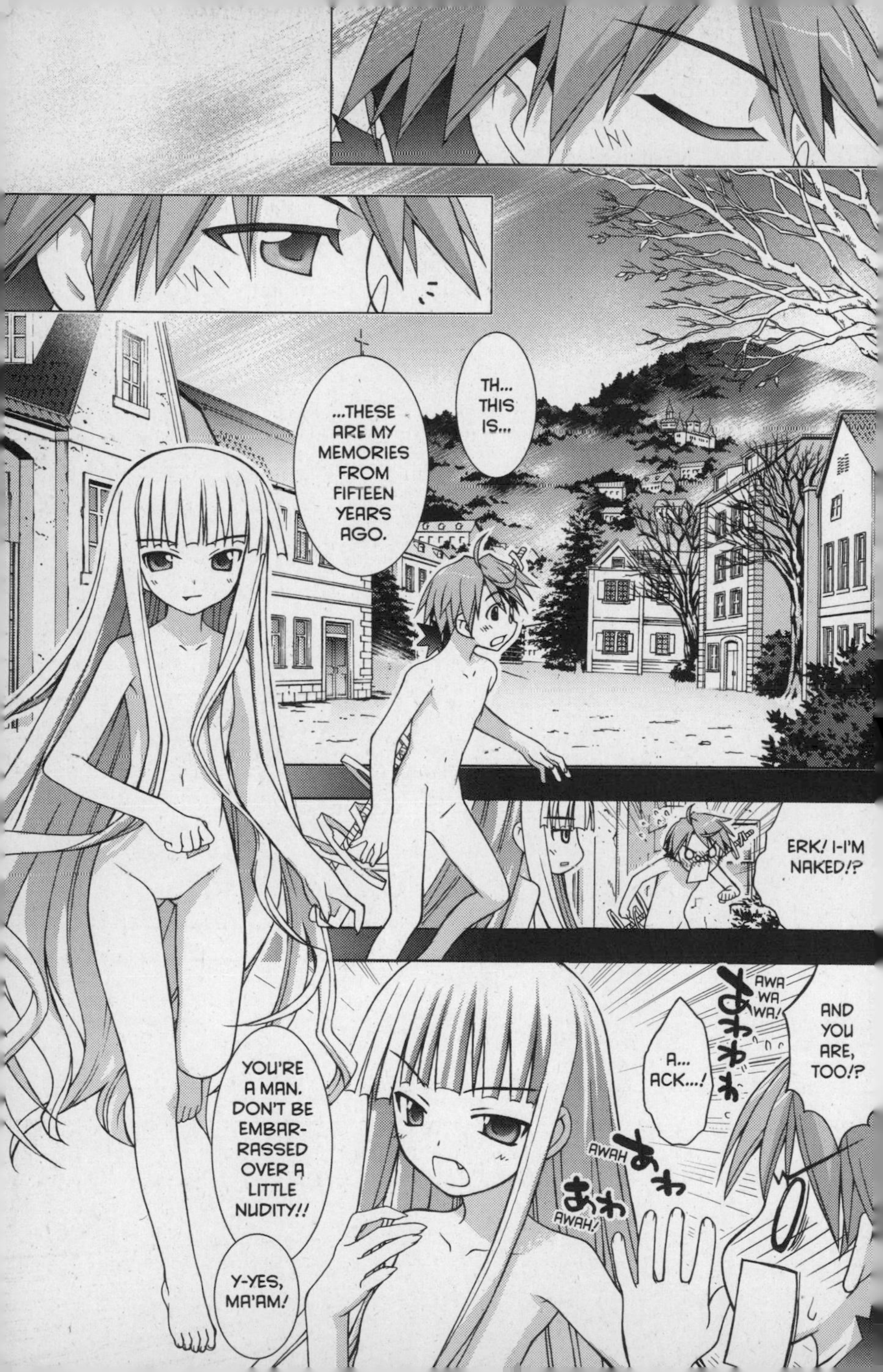
TH... THIS IS...
...THESE ARE MY MEMORIES FROM FIFTEEN YEARS AGO.
ERK! I-I'M NAKED!?
AND YOU ARE, TOO!?
AWA WA WA!
A... ACK...!
AWAH
AWAH!
YOU'RE A MAN. DON'T BE EMBARRASSED OVER A LITTLE NUDITY!!
Y-YES, MA'AM!

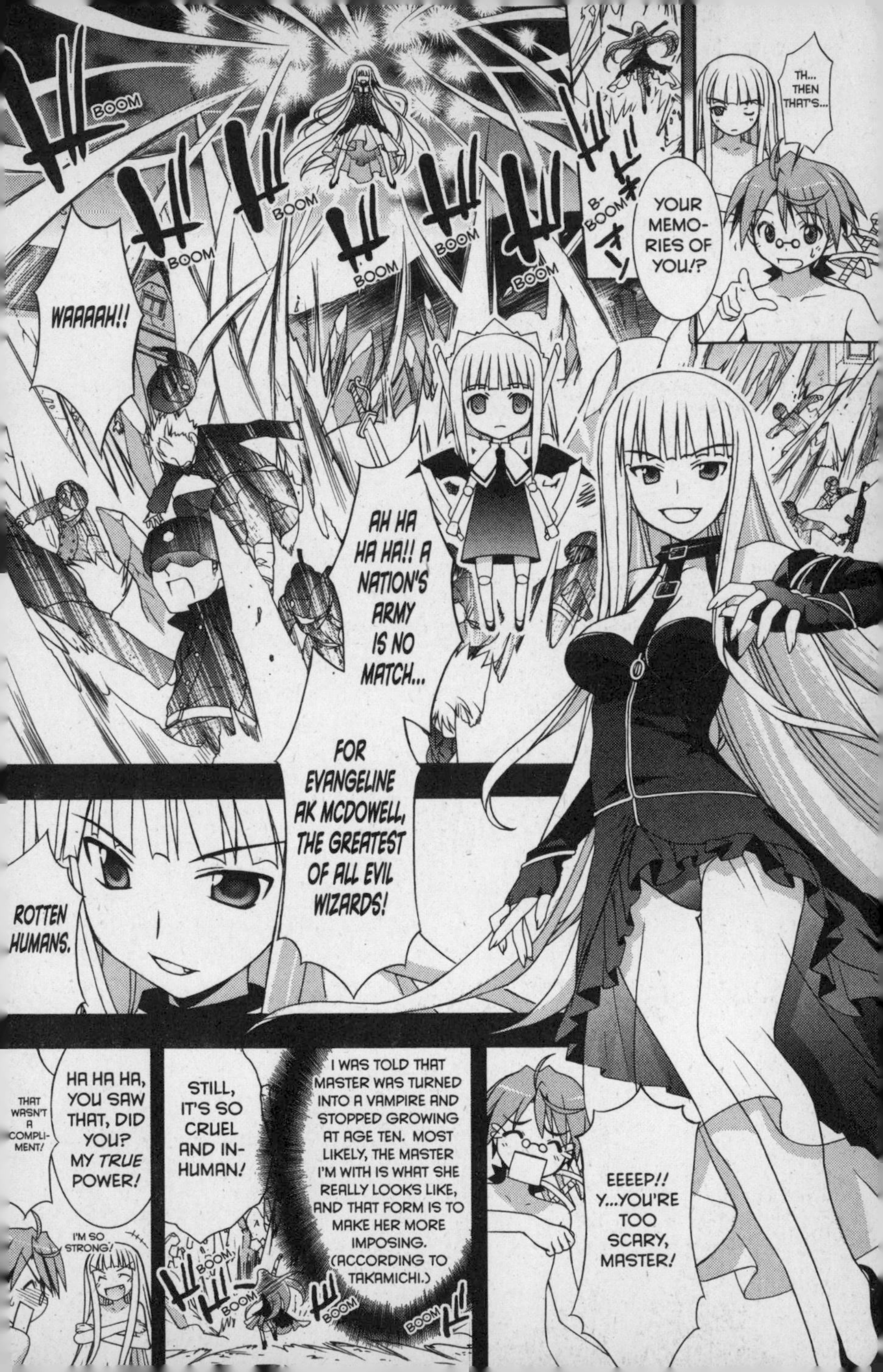
TH... THEN THAT'S...
YOUR MEMORIES OF YOU!?
BOOM
BOOM
BOOM
BOOM
BOOM
B-BOOM
BOOM
WAAAAH!!
AH HA HA HA!! A NATION'S ARMY IS NO MATCH...
FOR EVANGELINE AK MCDOWELL, THE GREATEST OF ALL EVIL WIZARDS!
ROTTEN HUMANS.
EEEEP!! Y...YOU'RE TOO SCARY, MASTER!
I WAS TOLD THAT MASTER WAS TURNED INTO A VAMPIRE AND STOPPED GROWING AT AGE TEN. MOST LIKELY, THE MASTER I'M WITH IS WHAT SHE REALLY LOOKS LIKE, AND THAT FORM IS TO MAKE HER MORE IMPOSING. (ACCORDING TO TAKAMICHI.)
STILL, IT'S SO CRUEL AND IN-HUMAN!
BOOM
BOOM
BOOM
BOOM
HA HA HA, YOU SAW THAT, DID YOU? MY *TRUE* POWER!
I'M SO STRONG!
THAT WASN'T A COMPLIMENT!

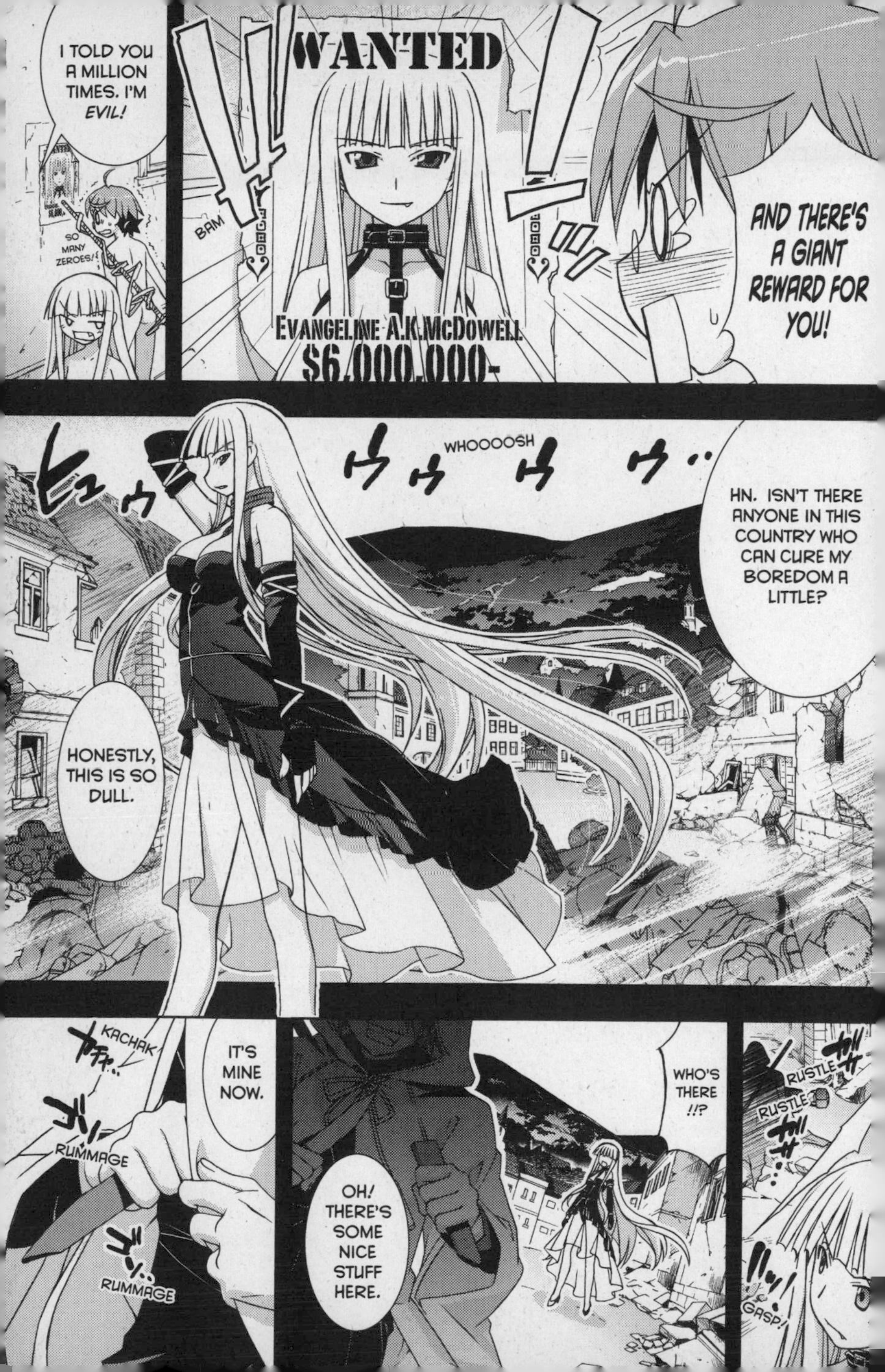
AND THERE'S A GIANT REWARD FOR YOU!
WANTED
BAM
EVANGELINE A.K.McDOWELL
$6,000,000-
I TOLD YOU A MILLION TIMES. I'M *EVIL!*
SO MANY ZEROES!
WHOOOOSH
HN. ISN'T THERE ANYONE IN THIS COUNTRY WHO CAN CURE MY BOREDOM A LITTLE?
HONESTLY, THIS IS SO DULL.
RUSTLE
RUSTLE
GASP!
WHO'S THERE !!?
OH! THERE'S SOME NICE STUFF HERE.
IT'S MINE NOW.
KACHAK
RUMMAGE
RUMMAGE

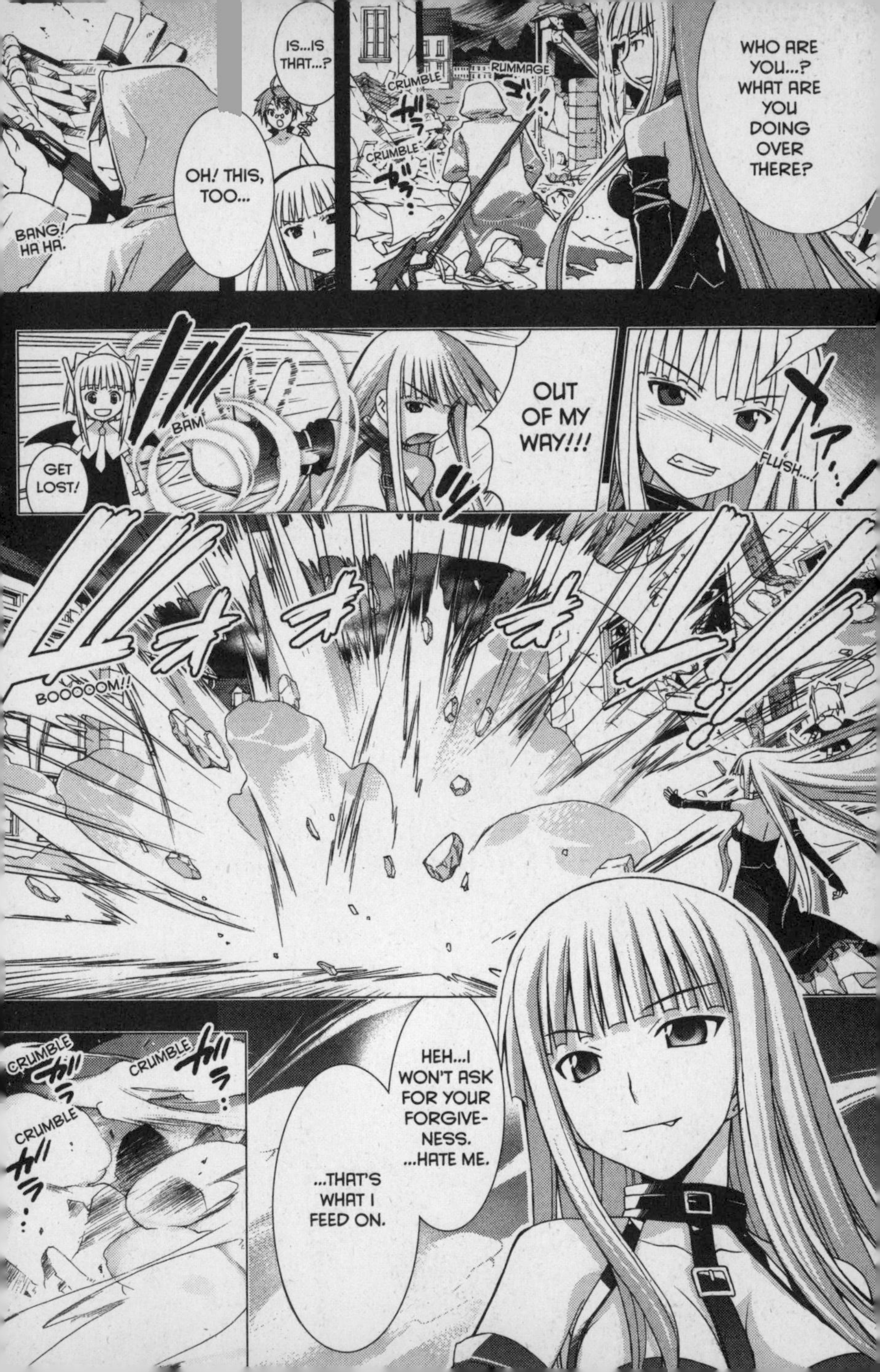
RUMMAGE
CRUMBLE
CRUMBLE
WHO ARE YOU...? WHAT ARE YOU DOING OVER THERE?
IS...IS THAT...?
OH! THIS, TOO...
BANG! HA HA.
FLUSH...!
OUT OF MY WAY!!!
BAM
GET LOST!
BOOOOOM!!
HEH...I WON'T ASK FOR YOUR FORGIVE-NESS. ...HATE ME.
...THAT'S WHAT I FEED ON.
CRUMBLE
CRUMBLE
CRUMBLE

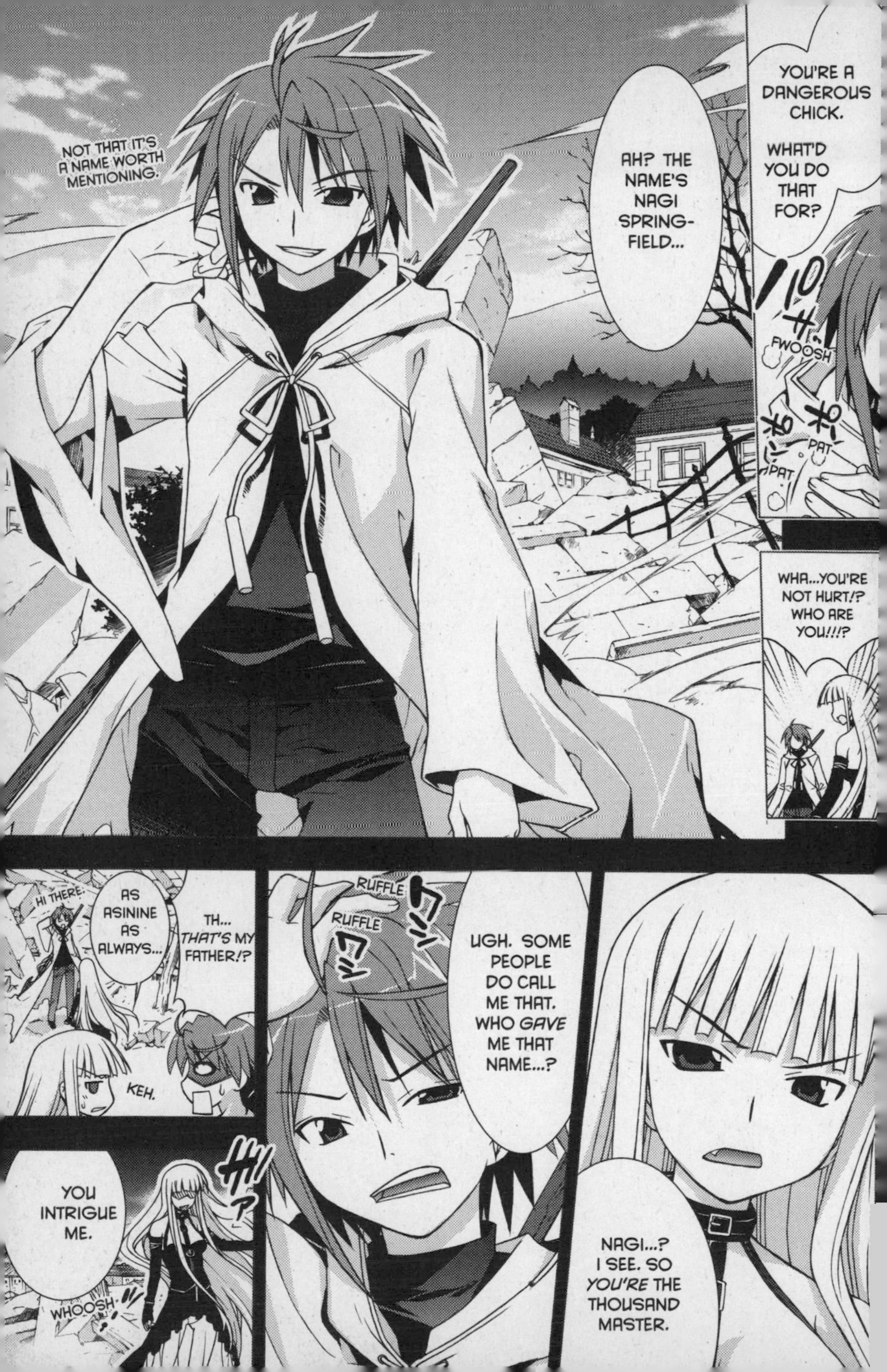
YOU'RE A DANGEROUS CHICK.
WHAT'D YOU DO THAT FOR?
FWOOSH
PAT
PAT
WHA...YOU'RE NOT HURT!? WHO ARE YOU!!!?
AH? THE NAME'S NAGI SPRING-FIELD...
NOT THAT IT'S A NAME WORTH MENTIONING.
NAGI...? I SEE. SO *YOU'RE* THE THOUSAND MASTER.
RUFFLE
RUFFLE
UGH. SOME PEOPLE DO CALL ME THAT. WHO *GAVE* ME THAT NAME...?
TH... *THAT'S* MY FATHER!?
AS ASININE AS ALWAYS...
HI THERE.
KEH.
YOU INTRIGUE ME.
WHOOSH

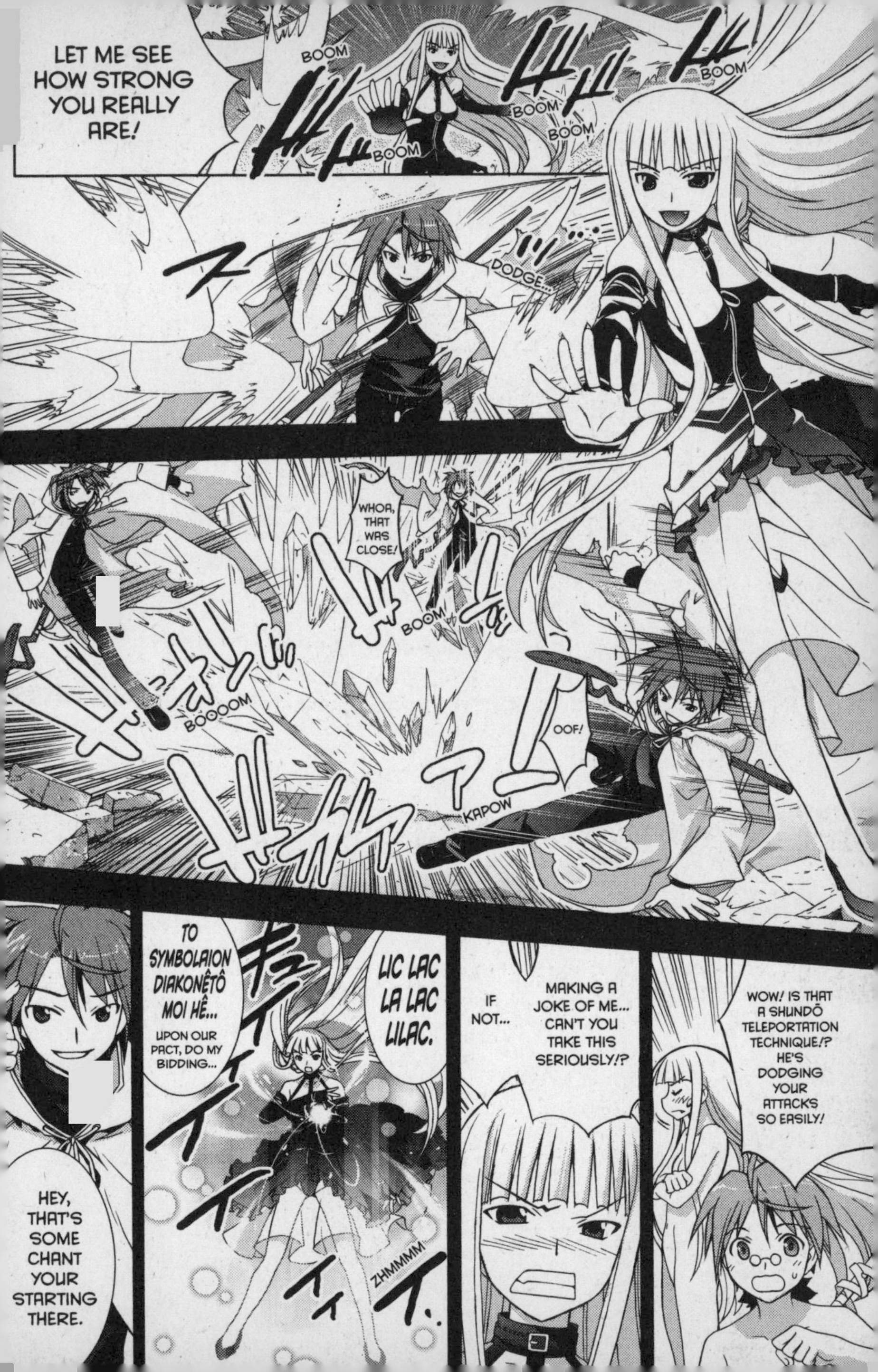
LET ME SEE HOW STRONG YOU REALLY ARE!
BOOM
BOOM
BOOM
BOOM
BOOM
DODGE...
WHOA, THAT WAS CLOSE!
BOOM!
OOF!
BOOOOM
KAPOW
WOW! IS THAT A SHUNDŌ TELEPORTATION TECHNIQUE!? HE'S DODGING YOUR ATTACKS SO EASILY!
MAKING A JOKE OF ME... CAN'T YOU TAKE THIS SERIOUSLY!?
IF NOT...
LIC LAC LA LAC LILAC.
TO SYMBOLAION DIAKONÊTÔ MOI HÊ...
UPON OUR PACT, DO MY BIDDING...
ZHMMMM
HEY, THAT'S SOME CHANT YOUR STARTING THERE.

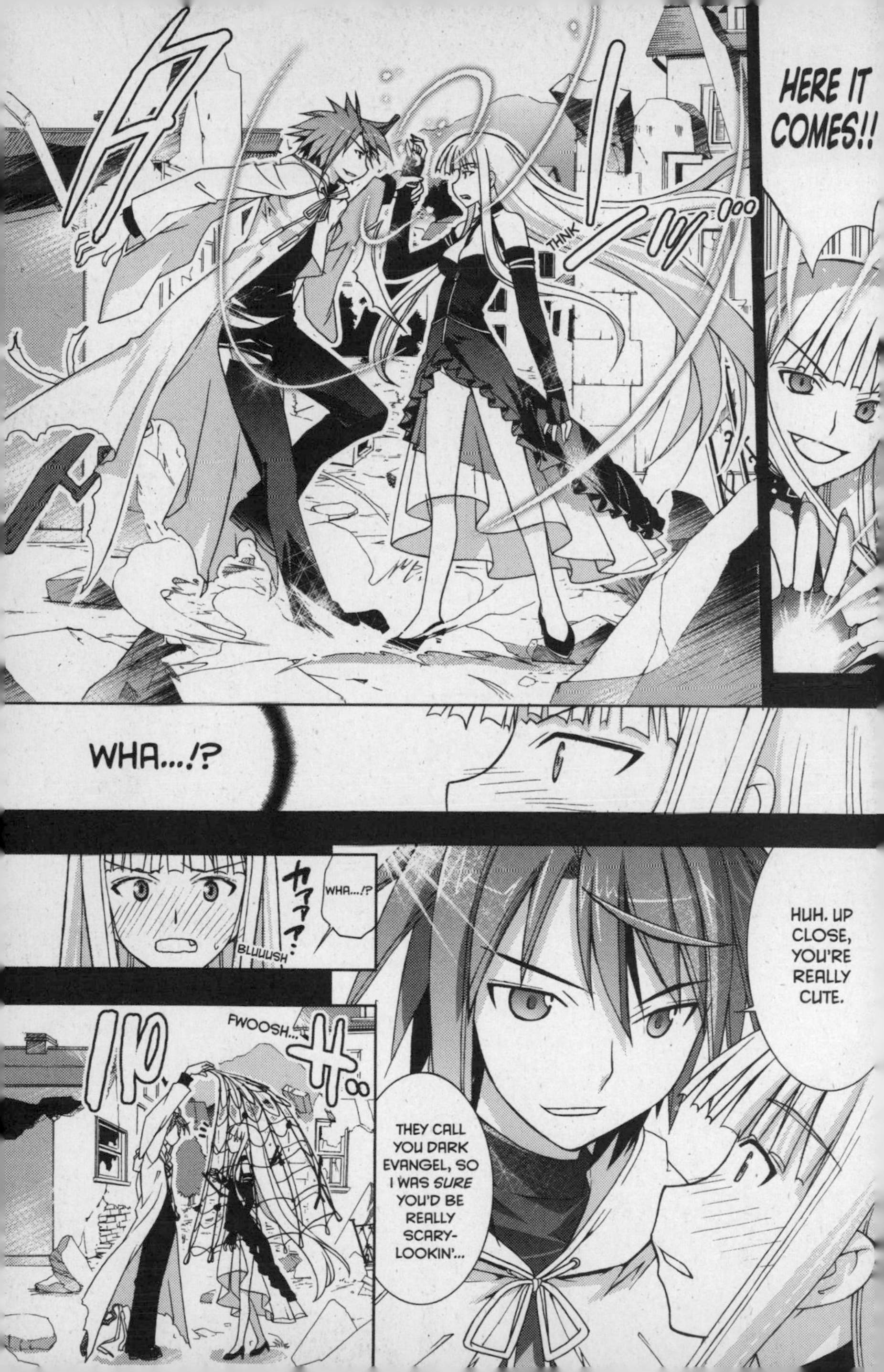
HERE IT COMES!!
THNK
WHA...!?
HUH. UP CLOSE, YOU'RE REALLY CUTE.
THEY CALL YOU DARK EVANGEL, SO I WAS *SURE* YOU'D BE REALLY SCARY-LOOKIN'...
WHA...!?
BLUUUSH
FWOOSH...

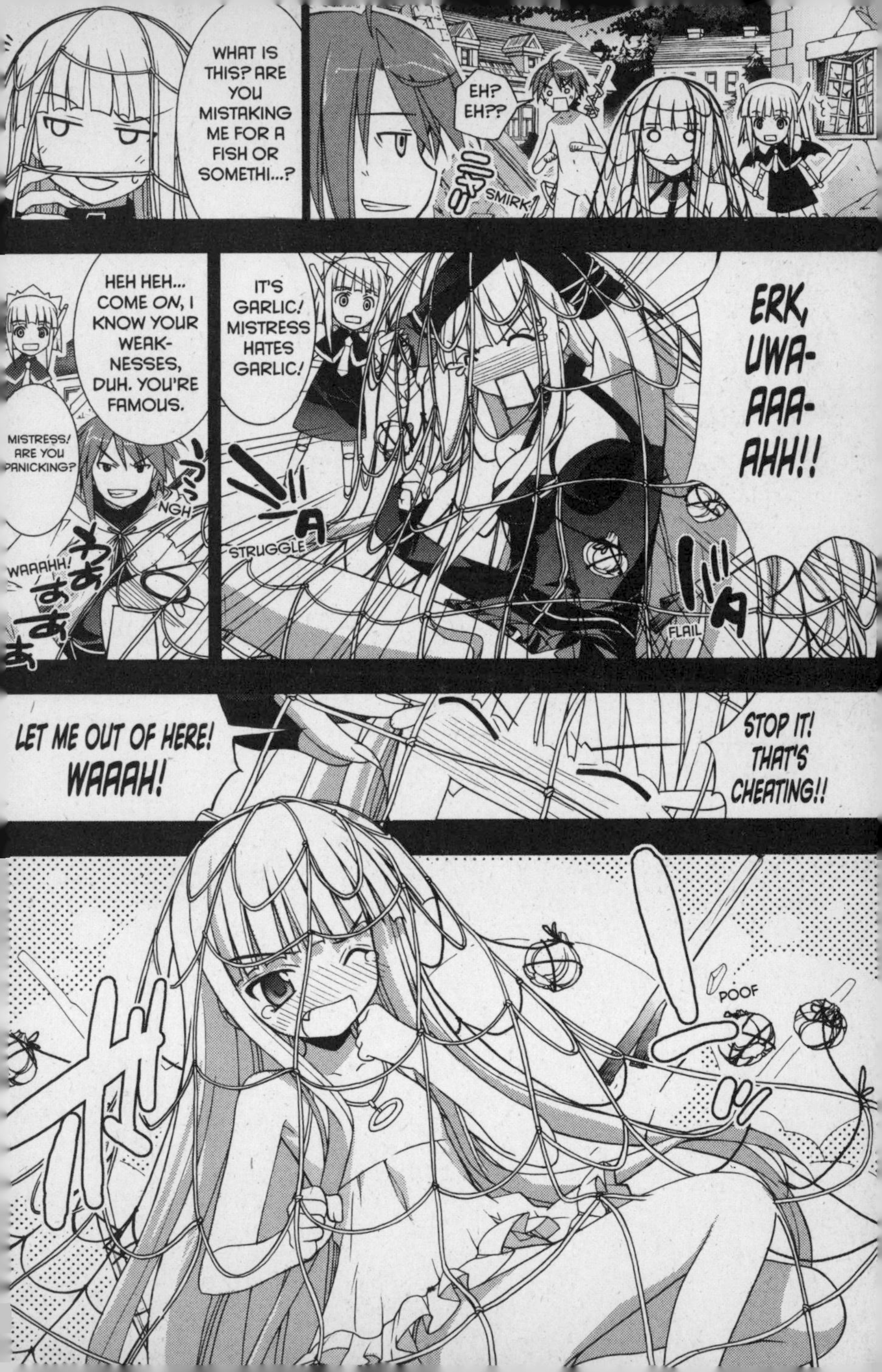
EH? EH??
SMIRK
WHAT IS THIS? ARE YOU MISTAKING ME FOR A FISH OR SOMETHI...?
ERK, UWA-AAA-AHH!!
FLAIL
IT'S GARLIC! MISTRESS HATES GARLIC!
STRUGGLE
HEH HEH... COME ON, I KNOW YOUR WEAK-NESSES, DUH. YOU'RE FAMOUS.
NGH
MISTRESS! ARE YOU PANICKING?
WAAAHH!
STOP IT! THAT'S CHEATING!!
LET ME OUT OF HERE! WAAAH!
POOF

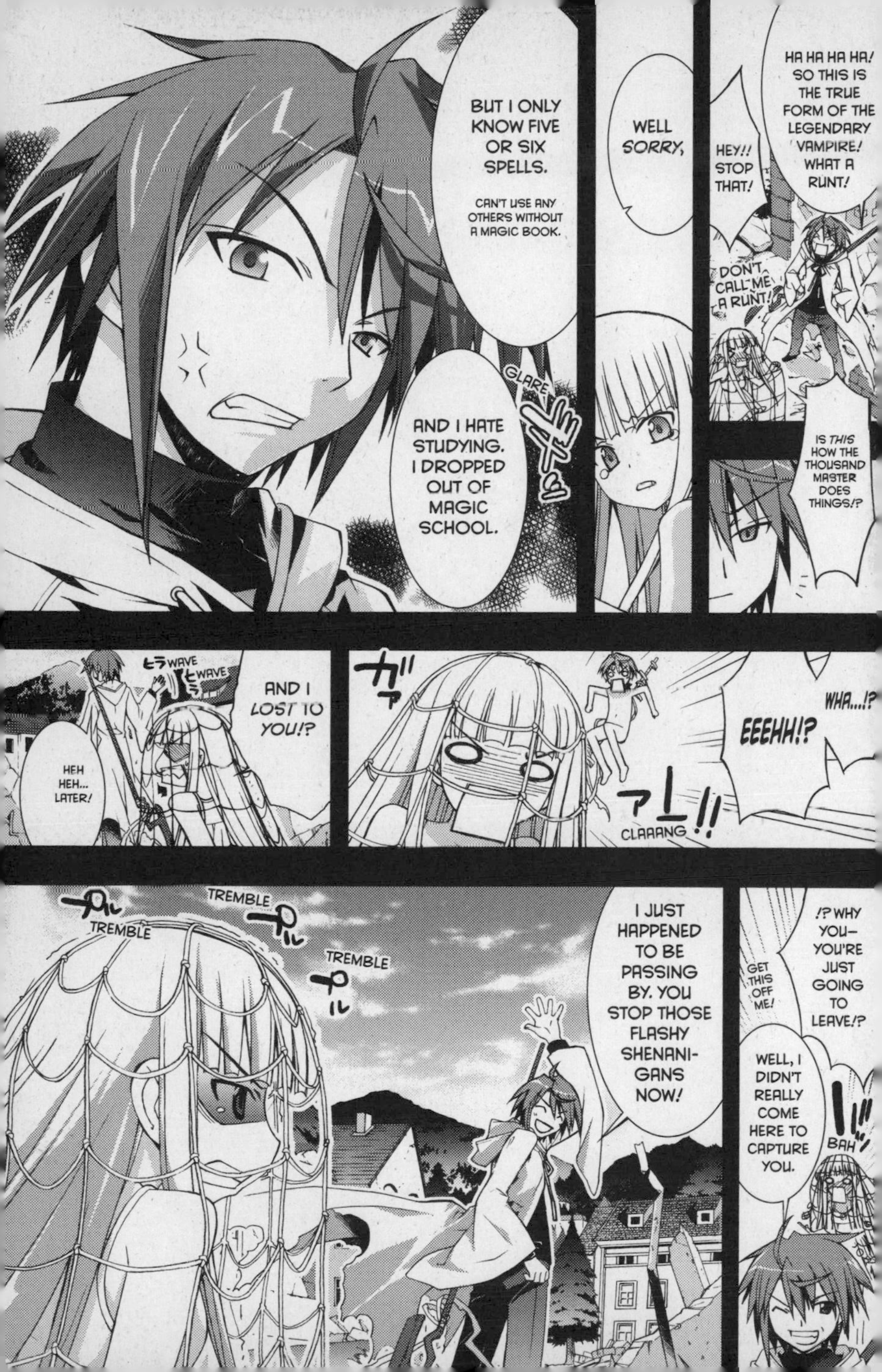
HA HA HA HA! SO THIS IS THE TRUE FORM OF THE LEGENDARY VAMPIRE! WHAT A RUNT!
HEY!! STOP THAT!
DON'T CALL ME A RUNT!
IS *THIS* HOW THE THOUSAND MASTER DOES THINGS!?
WELL *SORRY,*
BUT I ONLY KNOW FIVE OR SIX SPELLS.
CAN'T USE ANY OTHERS WITHOUT A MAGIC BOOK.
GLARE
AND I HATE STUDYING. I DROPPED OUT OF MAGIC SCHOOL.
WHA...!?
EEEHH!?
CLAAANG!!
AND I *LOST* TO *YOU!?*
WAVE WAVE
HEH HEH... LATER!
!? WHY YOU— YOU'RE JUST GOING TO LEAVE!?
GET THIS OFF ME!
WELL, I DIDN'T REALLY COME HERE TO CAPTURE YOU.
BAH
I JUST HAPPENED TO BE PASSING BY. YOU STOP THOSE FLASHY SHENANI-GANS NOW!
TREMBLE
TREMBLE
TREMBLE

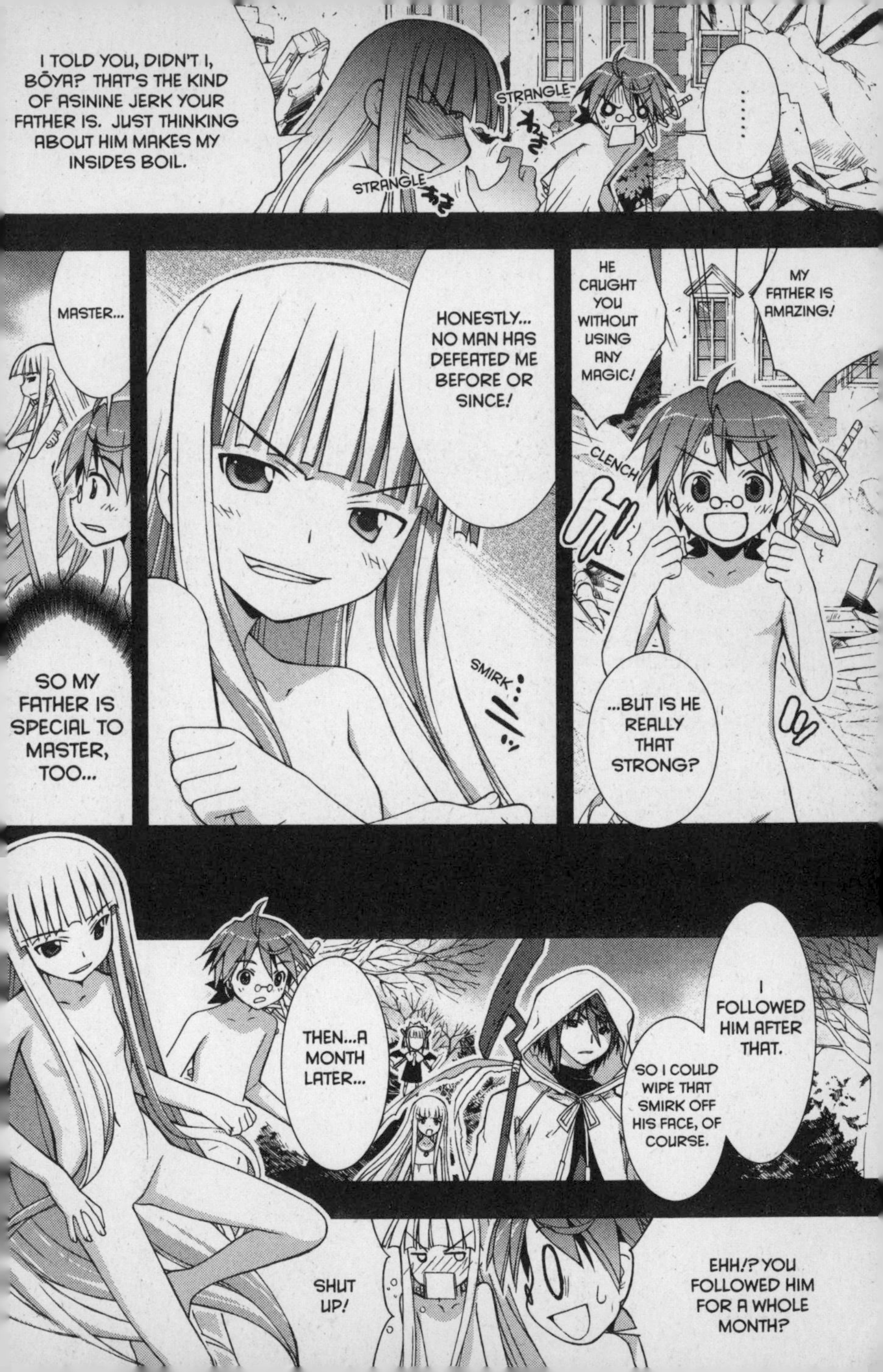
......
STRANGLE
I TOLD YOU, DIDN'T I, BŌYA? THAT'S THE KIND OF ASININE JERK YOUR FATHER IS. JUST THINKING ABOUT HIM MAKES MY INSIDES BOIL.
STRANGLE
MY FATHER IS AMAZING!
HE CAUGHT YOU WITHOUT USING ANY MAGIC!
CLENCH
...BUT IS HE REALLY THAT STRONG?
HONESTLY... NO MAN HAS DEFEATED ME BEFORE OR SINCE!
SMIRK...
MASTER...
SO MY FATHER IS SPECIAL TO MASTER, TOO...
I FOLLOWED HIM AFTER THAT.
SO I COULD WIPE THAT SMIRK OFF HIS FACE, OF COURSE.
THEN...A MONTH LATER...
EHH!? YOU FOLLOWED HIM FOR A WHOLE MONTH?
SHUT UP!

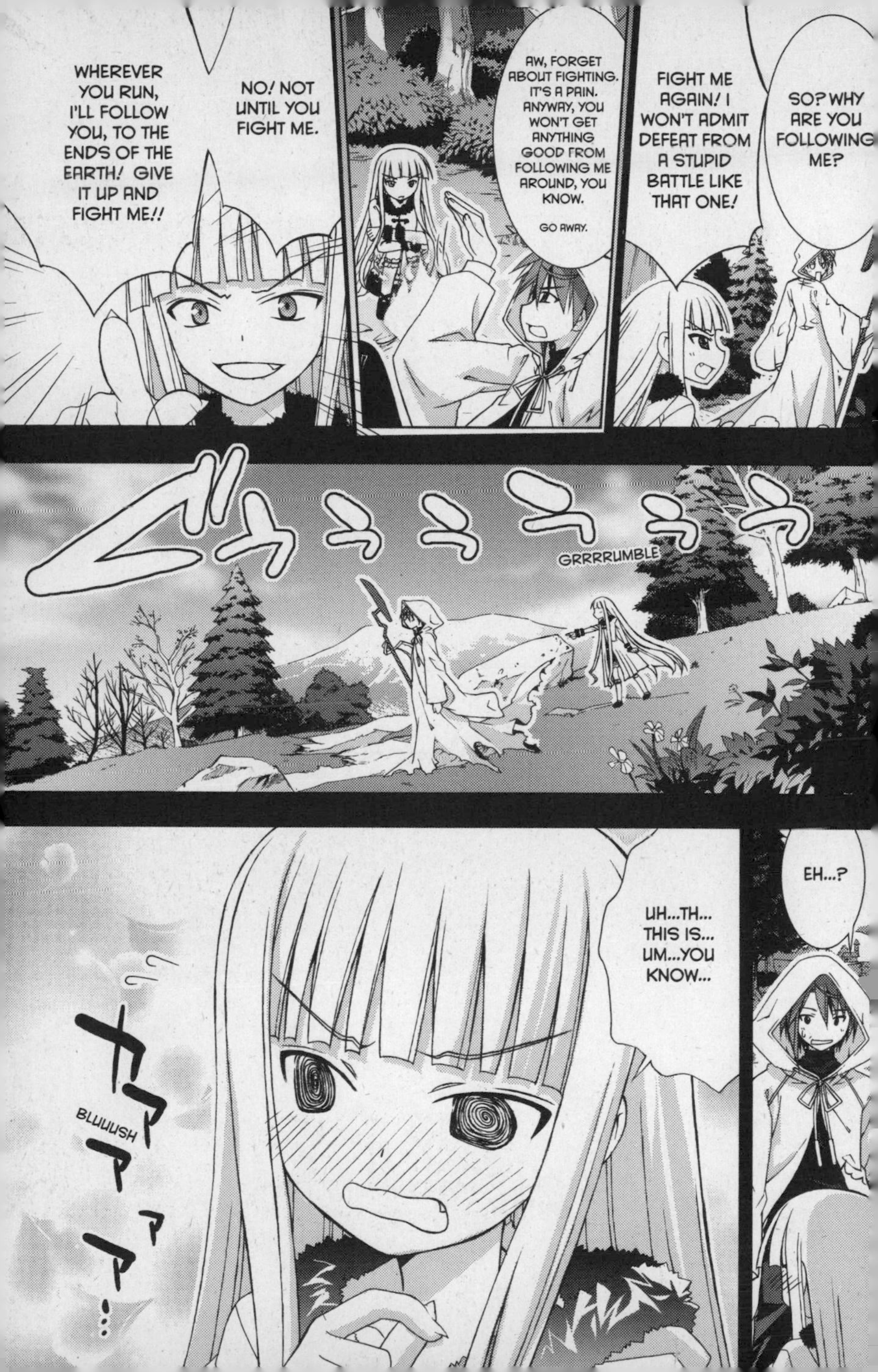
SO? WHY ARE YOU FOLLOWING ME?
FIGHT ME AGAIN! I WON'T ADMIT DEFEAT FROM A STUPID BATTLE LIKE THAT ONE!
AW, FORGET ABOUT FIGHTING. IT'S A PAIN. ANYWAY, YOU WON'T GET ANYTHING GOOD FROM FOLLOWING ME AROUND, YOU KNOW.
GO AWAY.
NO! NOT UNTIL YOU FIGHT ME.
WHEREVER YOU RUN, I'LL FOLLOW YOU, TO THE ENDS OF THE EARTH! GIVE IT UP AND FIGHT ME!!
GRRRRUMBLE
EH...?
UH...TH... THIS IS... UM...YOU KNOW...
BLUUUSH

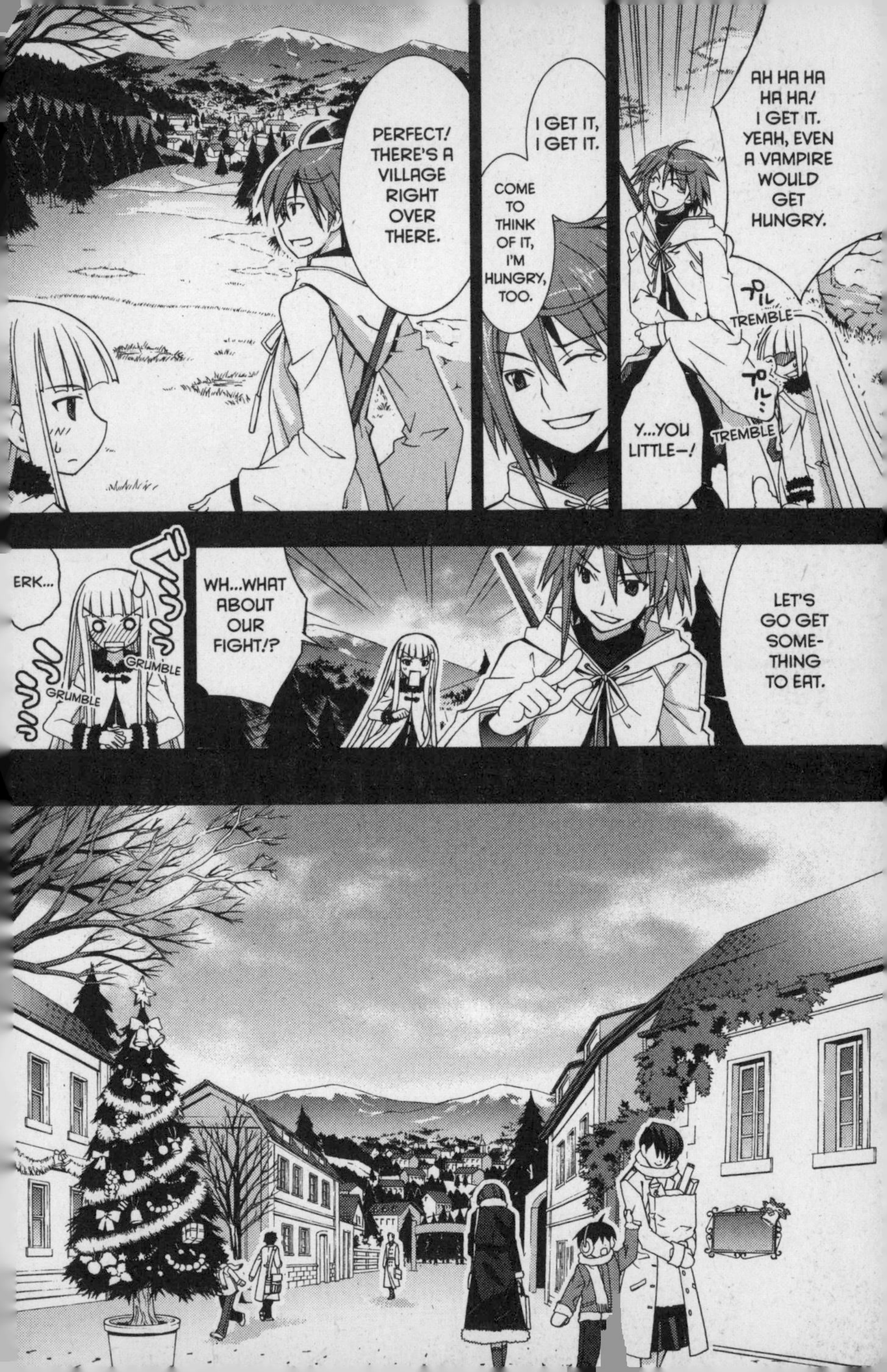
AH HA HA HA HA! I GET IT. YEAH, EVEN A VAMPIRE WOULD GET HUNGRY.
TREMBLE
TREMBLE
Y...YOU LITTLE—!
I GET IT, I GET IT.
COME TO THINK OF IT, I'M HUNGRY, TOO.
PERFECT! THERE'S A VILLAGE RIGHT OVER THERE.
LET'S GO GET SOME-THING TO EAT.
WH...WHAT ABOUT OUR FIGHT!?
ERK...
GRUMBLE
GRUMBLE

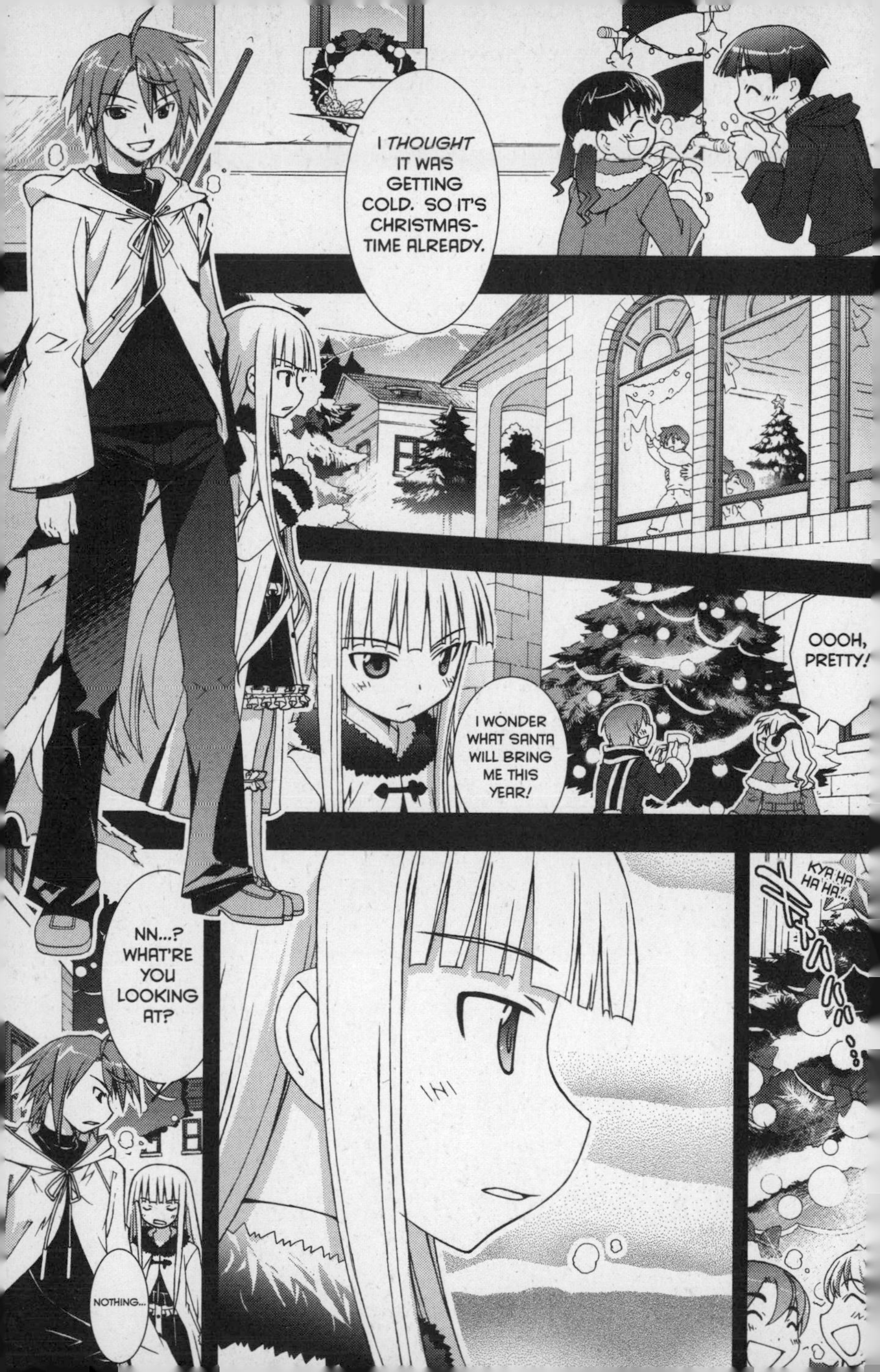
I *THOUGHT* IT WAS GETTING COLD. SO IT'S CHRISTMAS-TIME ALREADY.
OOOH, PRETTY!
I WONDER WHAT SANTA WILL BRING ME THIS YEAR!
KYA HA HA HA...
NN...? WHAT'RE YOU LOOKING AT?
NOTHING...

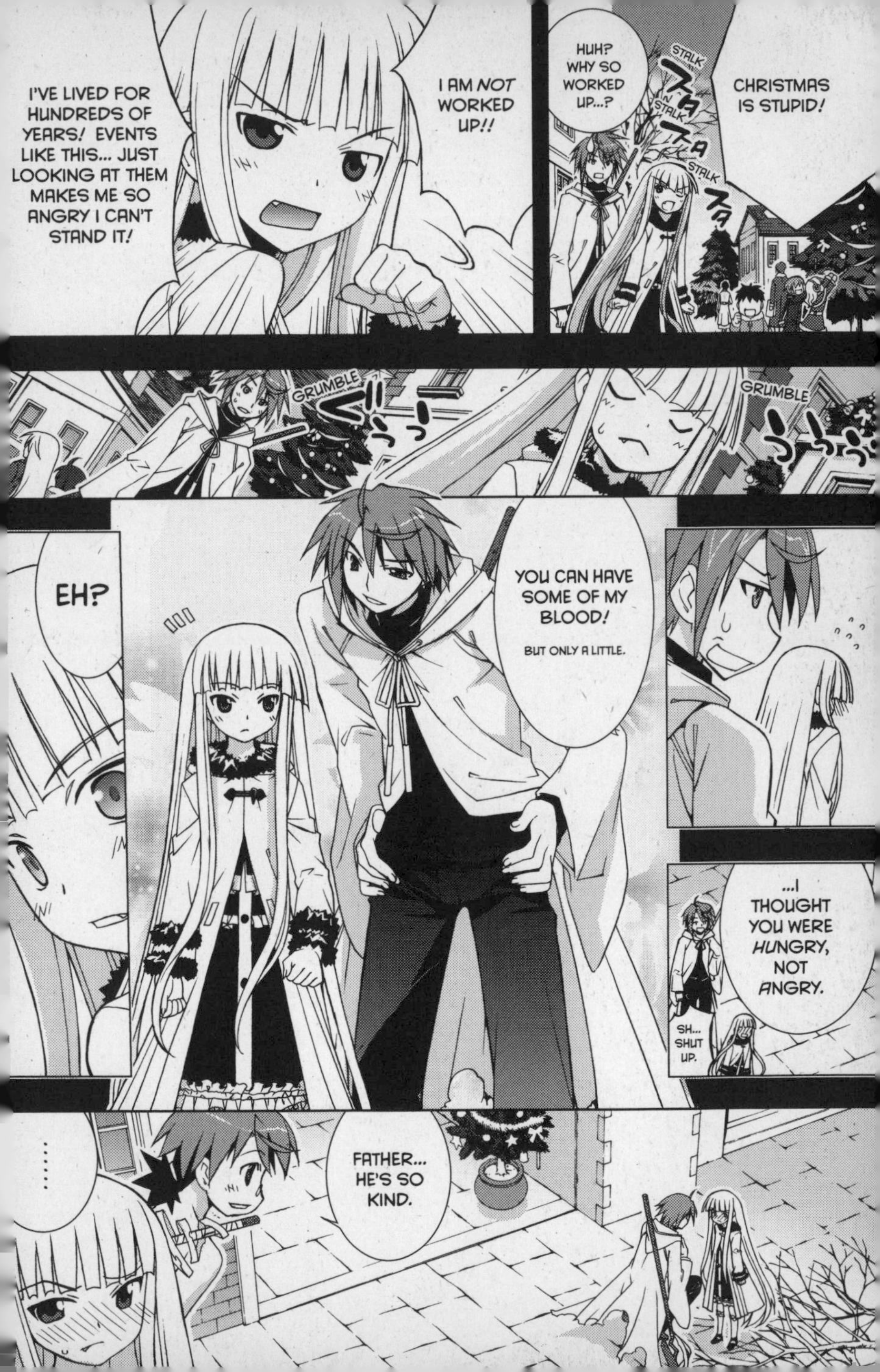
CHRISTMAS IS STUPID!
HUH? WHY SO WORKED UP...?
STALK
STALK
STALK
I AM *NOT* WORKED UP!!
I'VE LIVED FOR HUNDREDS OF YEARS! EVENTS LIKE THIS... JUST LOOKING AT THEM MAKES ME SO ANGRY I CAN'T STAND IT!
GRUMBLE
GRUMBLE
...I THOUGHT YOU WERE *HUNGRY*, NOT *ANGRY*.
SH... SHUT UP.
YOU CAN HAVE SOME OF MY BLOOD!
BUT ONLY A LITTLE.
EH?
FATHER... HE'S SO KIND.
......

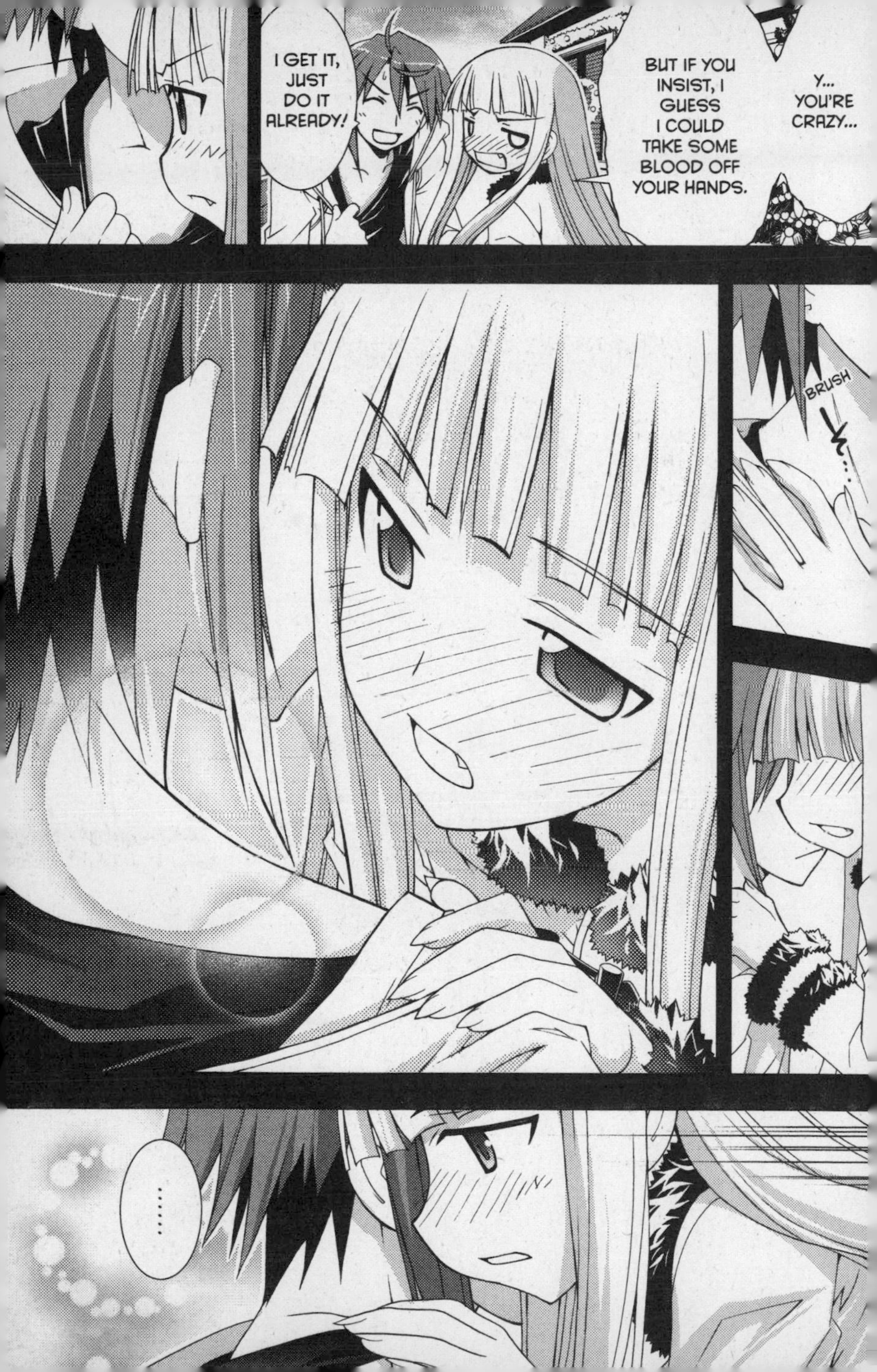
Y... YOU'RE CRAZY...
BUT IF YOU INSIST, I GUESS I COULD TAKE SOME BLOOD OFF YOUR HANDS.
I GET IT, JUST DO IT ALREADY!
BRUSH
......

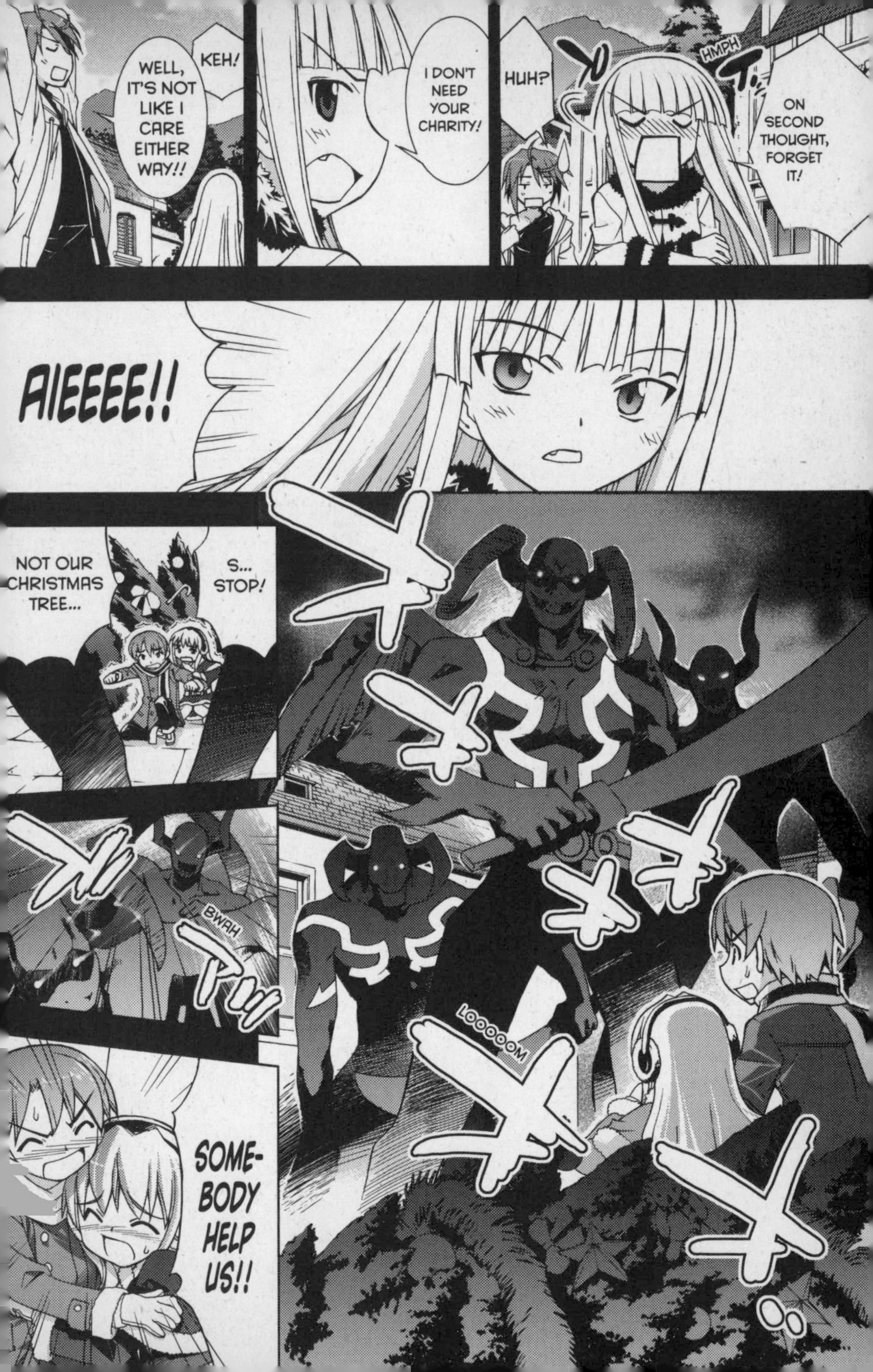
HMPH
ON SECOND THOUGHT, FORGET IT!
HUH?
I DON'T NEED YOUR CHARITY!
KEH!
WELL, IT'S NOT LIKE I CARE EITHER WAY!!
AIEEEE!!
LOOOOOM
S... STOP!
NOT OUR CHRISTMAS TREE...
BWAH
SOME-BODY HELP US!!

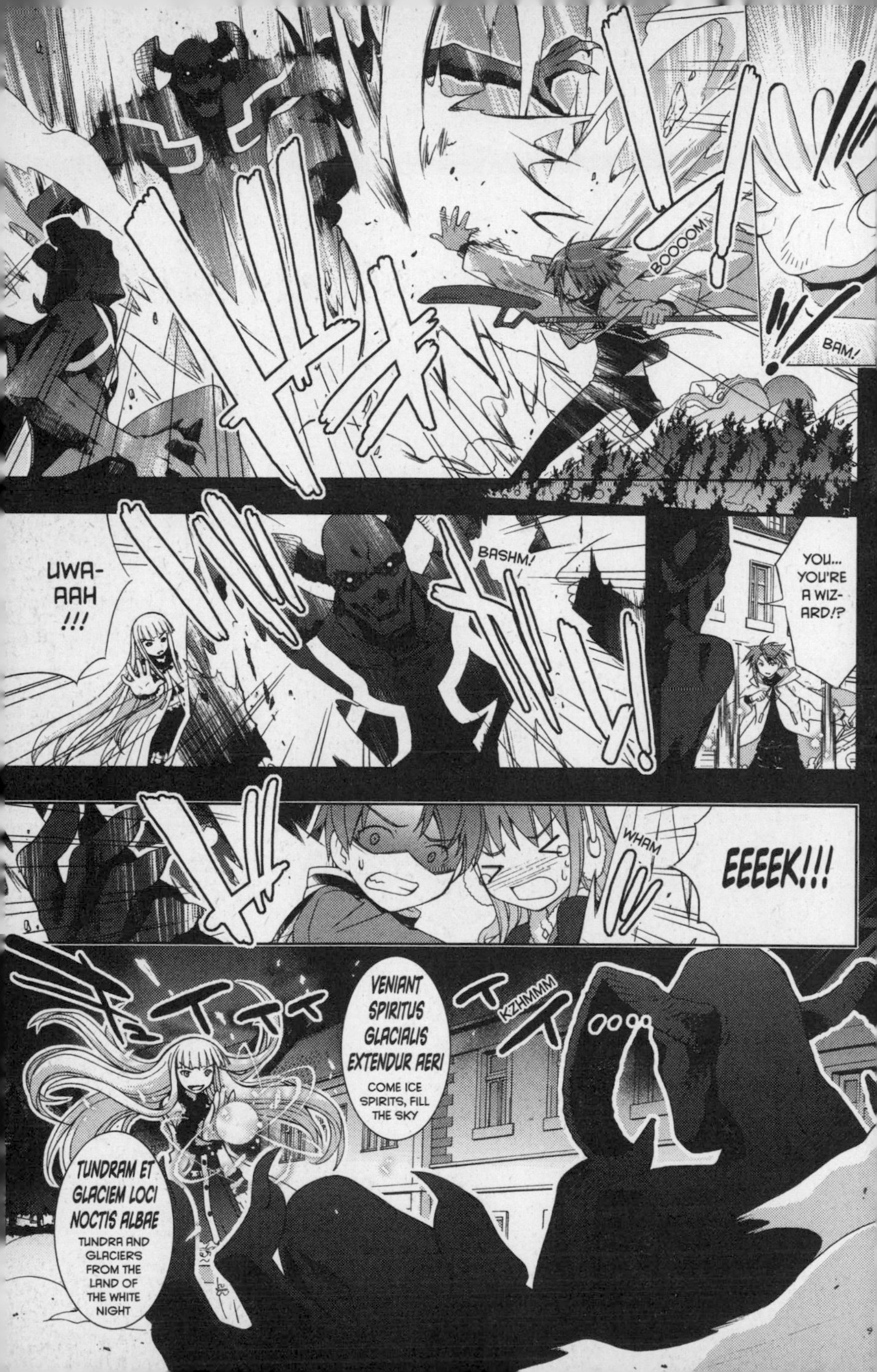
BOOOOM!
BAM!
YOU... YOU'RE A WIZ-ARD!?
BASHM!
UWA-AAH!!!
EEEEK!!!
WHAM
KZHMMM
...
VENIANT SPIRITUS GLACIALIS EXTENDUR AERI
COME ICE SPIRITS, FILL THE SKY
TUNDRAM ET GLACIEM LOCI NOCTIS ALBAE
TUNDRA AND GLACIERS FROM THE LAND OF THE WHITE NIGHT

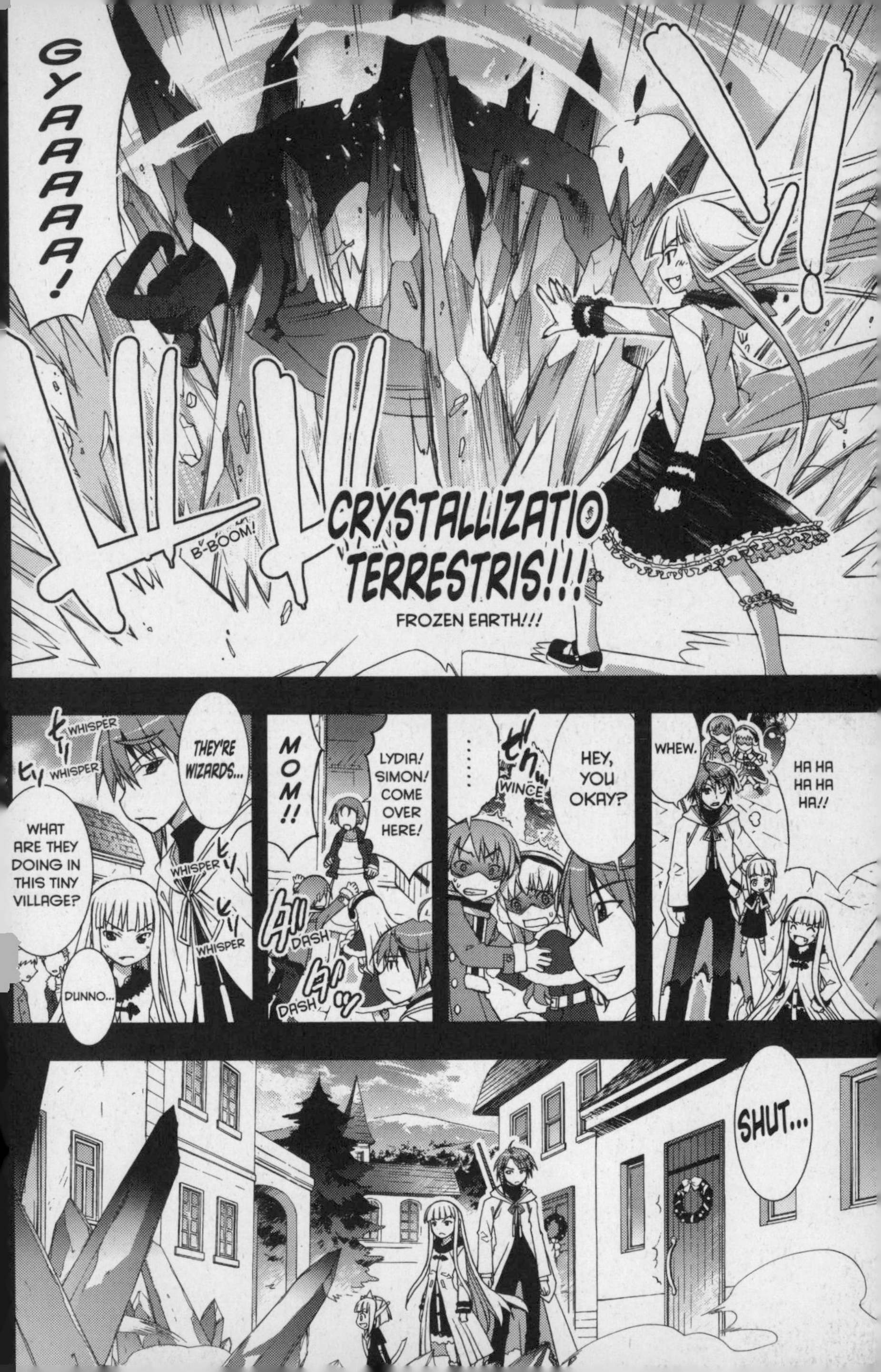
CRYSTALLIZATIO TERRESTRIS!!!
FROZEN EARTH!!!
GYAAAAAA!
B-BOOM!
WHEW.
HA HA HA HA HA!!
HEY, YOU OKAY?
......
WINCE
LYDIA! SIMON! COME OVER HERE!
MOM!!
DASH
DASH
THEY'RE WIZARDS...
WHISPER
WHISPER
WHISPER
WHISPER
WHAT ARE THEY DOING IN THIS TINY VILLAGE?
DUNNO...
SHUT...

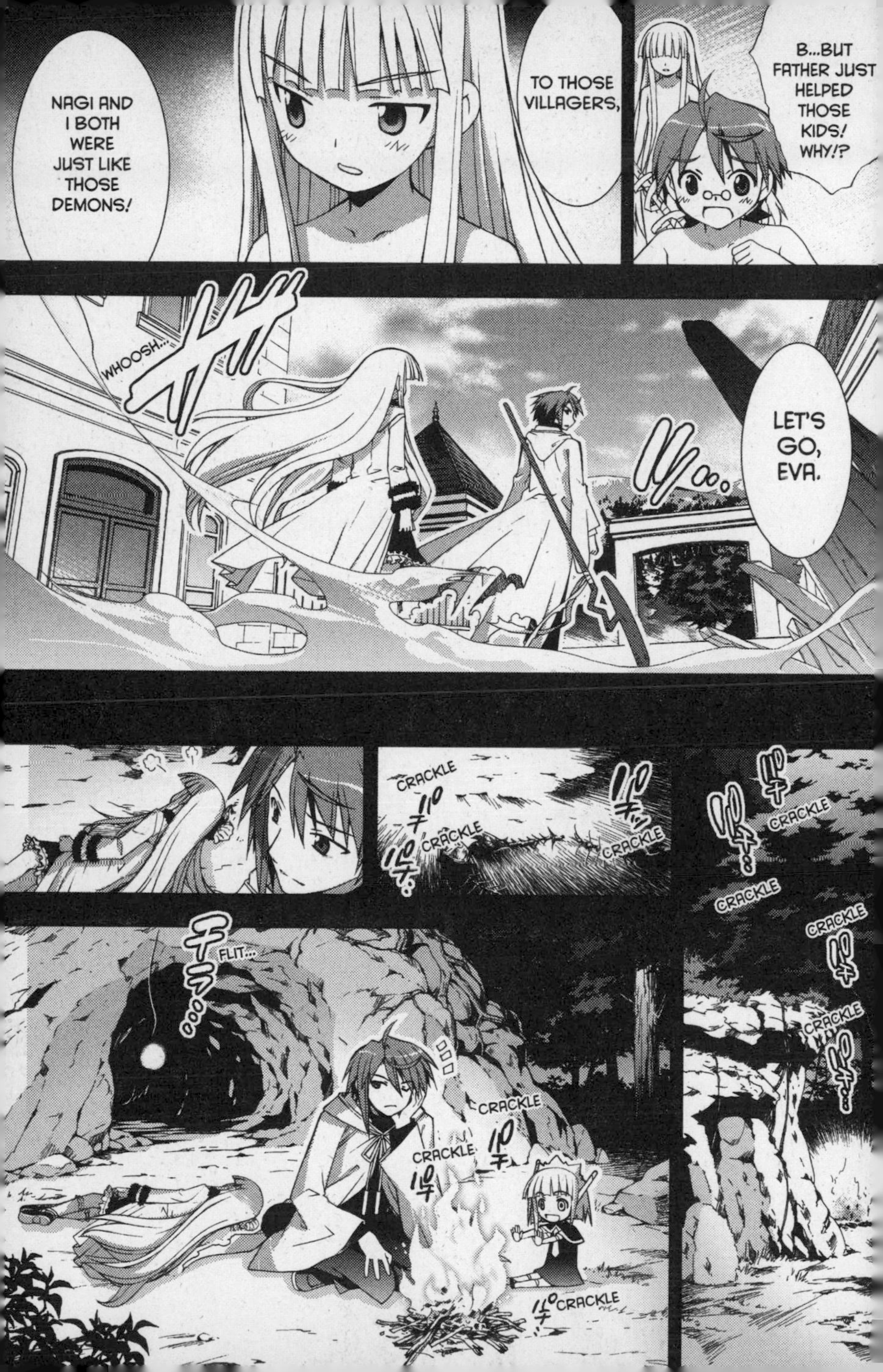
B...BUT FATHER JUST HELPED THOSE KIDS! WHY!?
TO THOSE VILLAGERS,
NAGI AND I BOTH WERE JUST LIKE THOSE DEMONS!
LET'S GO, EVA.
WHOOSH...
CRACKLE
CRACKLE
CRACKLE
CRACKLE
CRACKLE
CRACKLE
CRACKLE
CRACKLE
FLIT...
CRACKLE
CRACKLE
CRACKLE

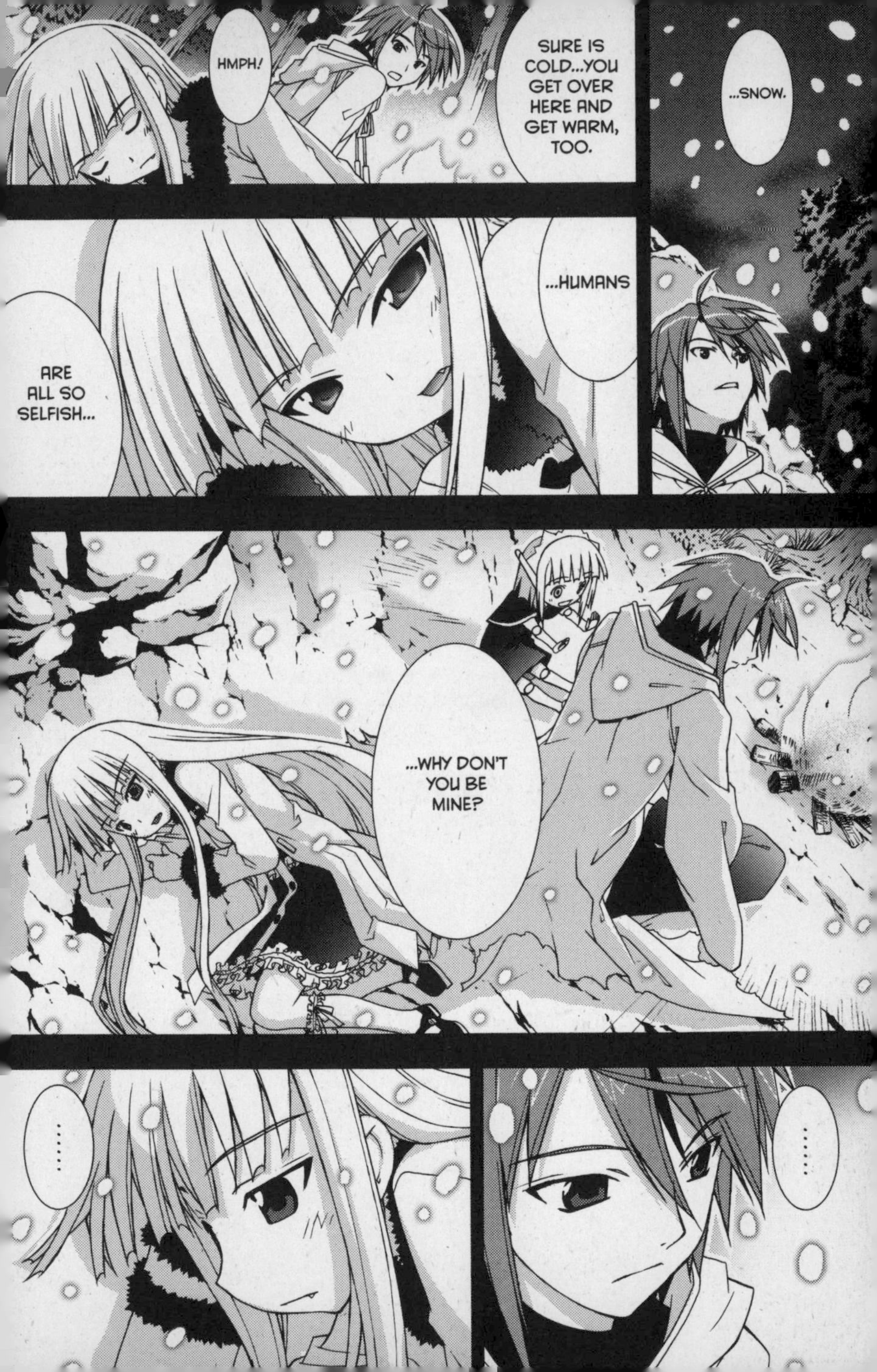
...SNOW.
SURE IS COLD...YOU GET OVER HERE AND GET WARM, TOO.
HMPH!
...HUMANS
ARE ALL SO SELFISH...
...WHY DON'T YOU BE MINE?
......
......

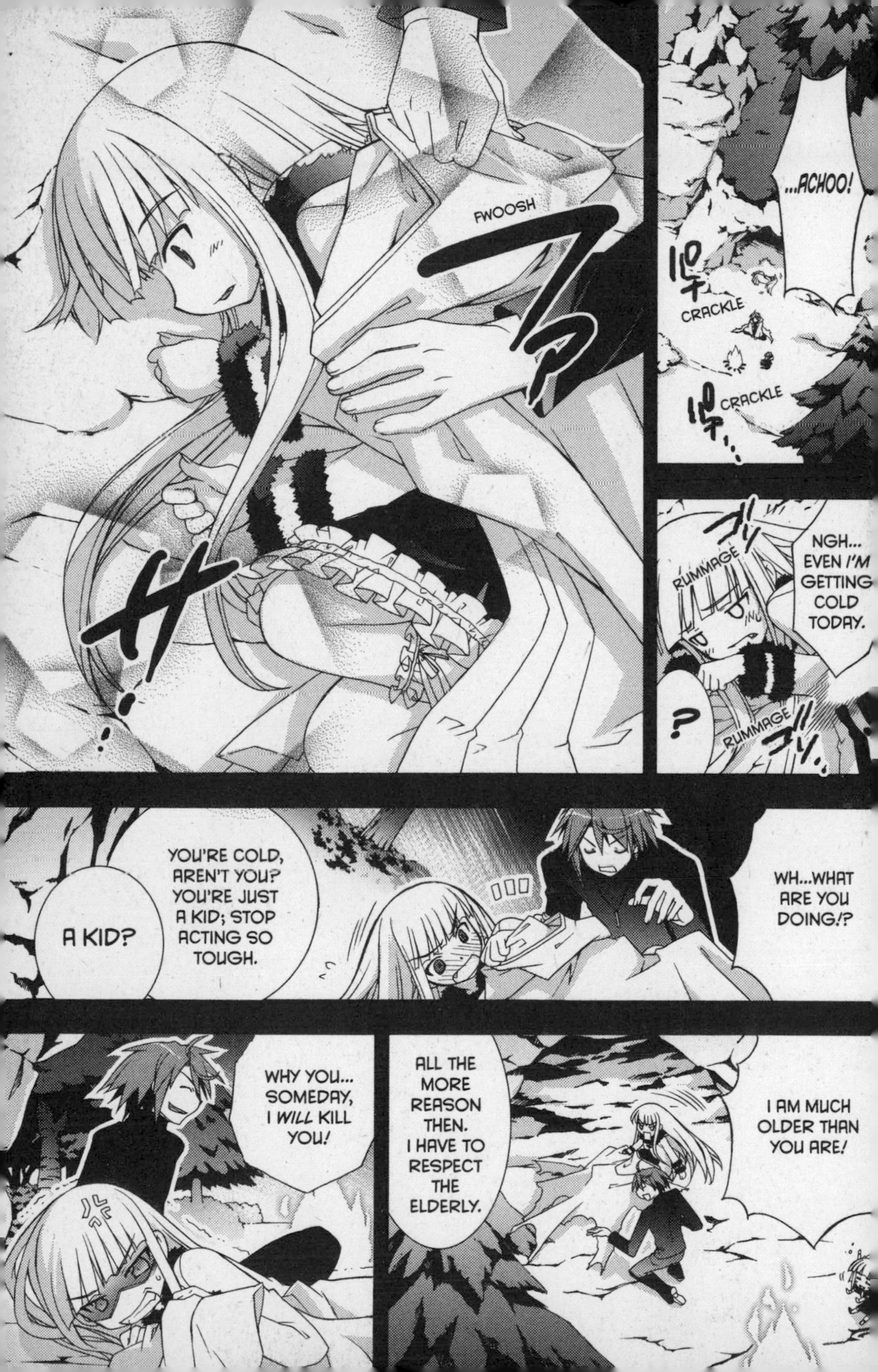
...ACHOO!
CRACKLE
CRACKLE
NGH... EVEN *I'M* GETTING COLD TODAY.
RUMMAGE
?
RUMMAGE
FWOOSH
WH...WHAT ARE YOU DOING!?
YOU'RE COLD, AREN'T YOU? YOU'RE JUST A KID; STOP ACTING SO TOUGH.
A KID?
I AM MUCH OLDER THAN YOU ARE!
ALL THE MORE REASON THEN. I HAVE TO RESPECT THE ELDERLY.
WHY YOU... SOMEDAY, I *WILL* KILL YOU!

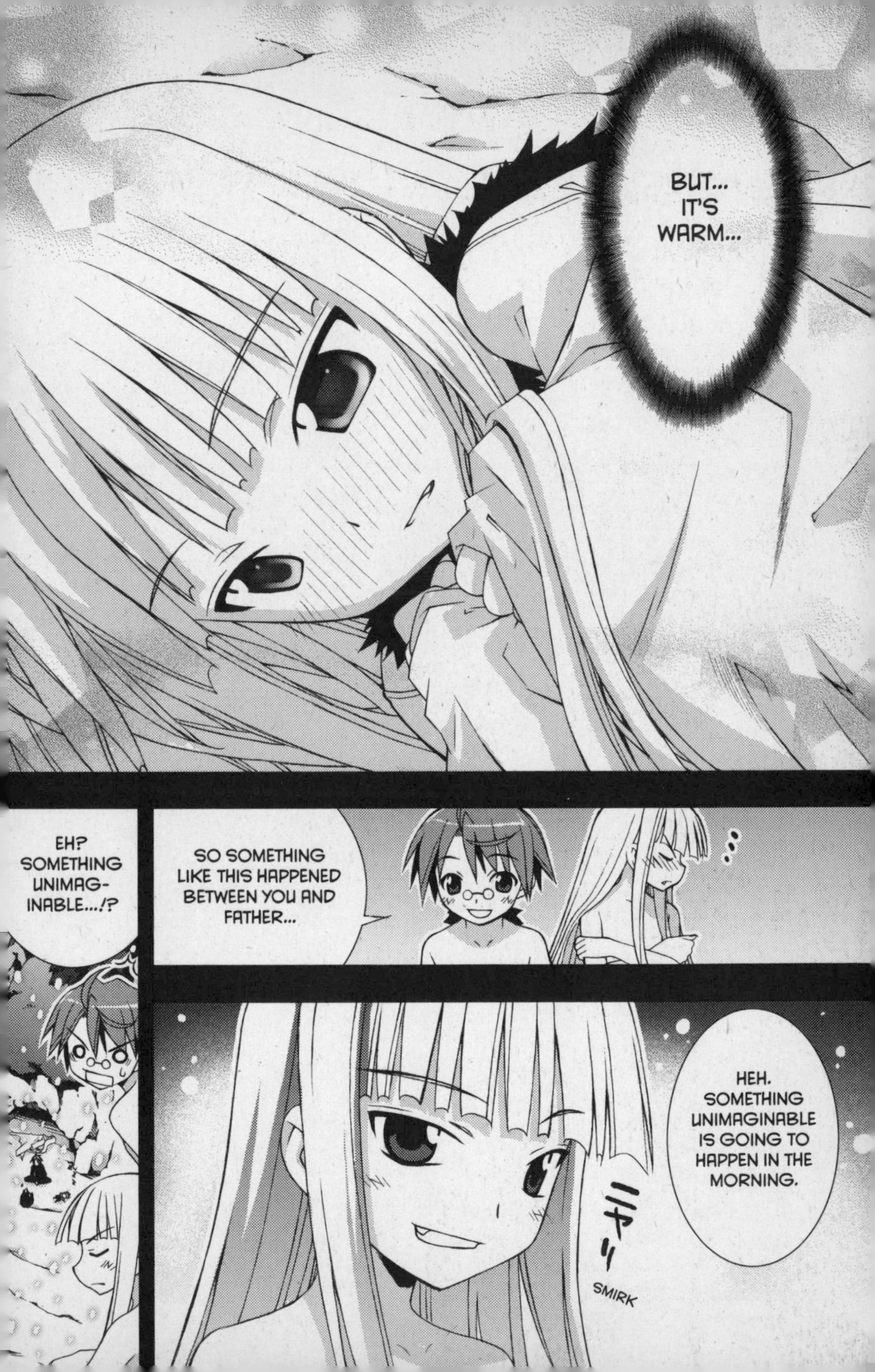
BUT... IT'S WARM...
...
SO SOMETHING LIKE THIS HAPPENED BETWEEN YOU AND FATHER...
HEH. SOMETHING UNIMAGINABLE IS GOING TO HAPPEN IN THE MORNING.
ニヤリ
SMIRK
EH? SOMETHING UNIMAG-INABLE...!?

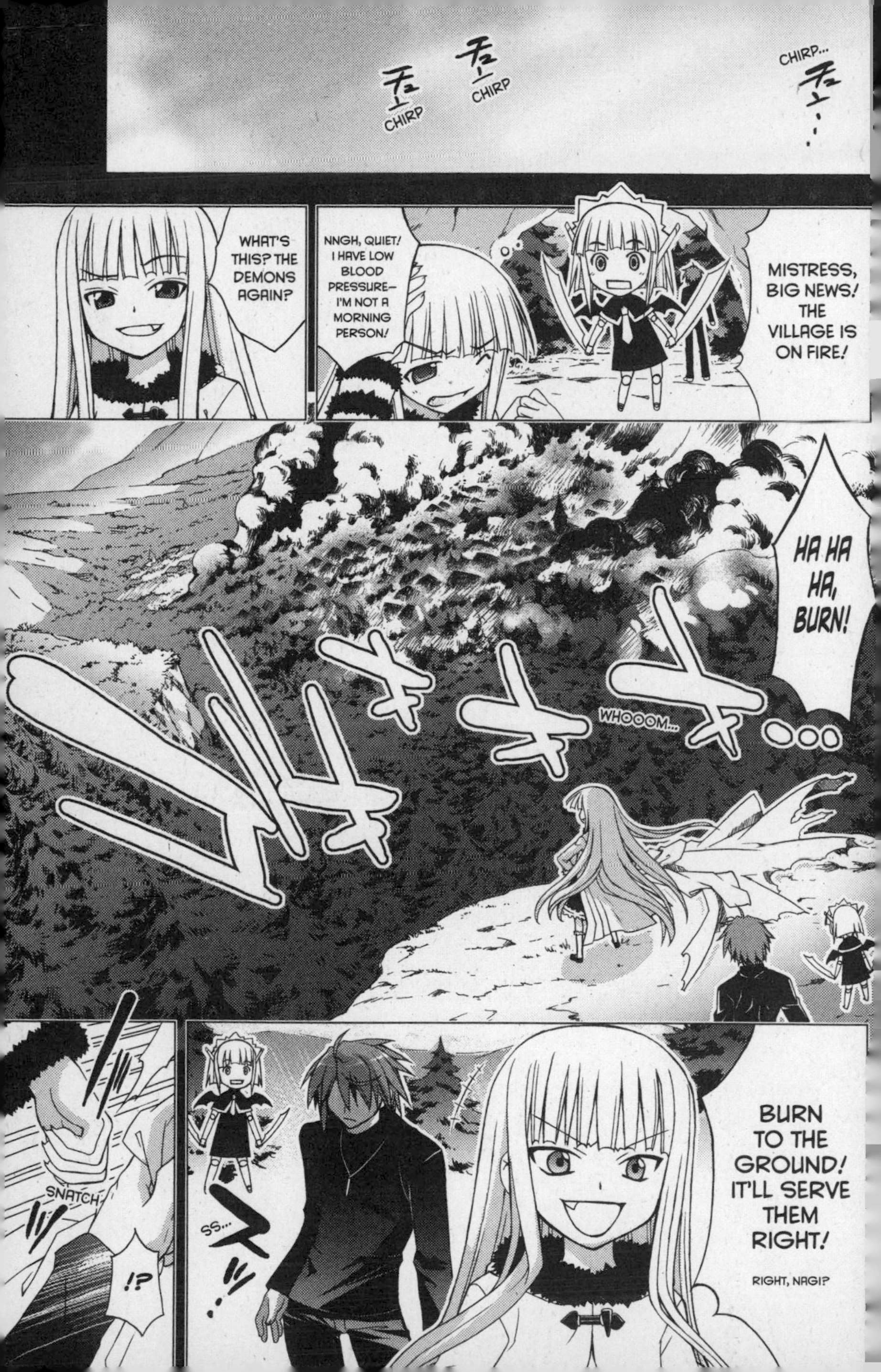
CHIRP...
CHIRP
CHIRP
MISTRESS, BIG NEWS! THE VILLAGE IS ON FIRE!
NNGH, QUIET! I HAVE LOW BLOOD PRESSURE—I'M NOT A MORNING PERSON!
WHAT'S THIS? THE DEMONS AGAIN?
HA HA HA, BURN!
WHOOOM...
BURN TO THE GROUND! IT'LL SERVE THEM RIGHT!
RIGHT, NAGI?
SS...
SNATCH
!?

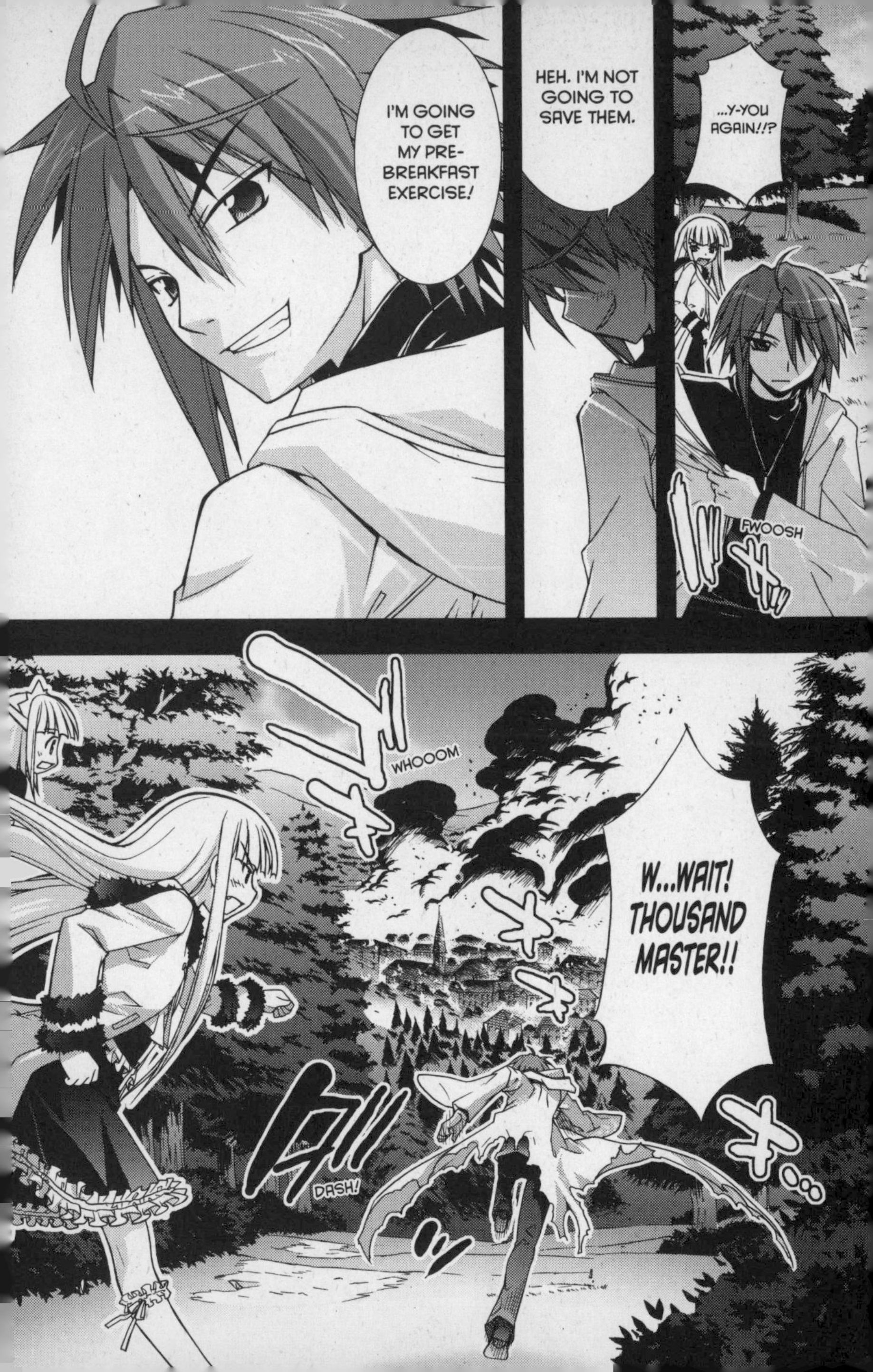
...Y-YOU AGAIN!!?
FWOOSH
HEH. I'M NOT GOING TO SAVE THEM.
I'M GOING TO GET MY PRE-BREAKFAST EXERCISE!
W...WAIT! THOUSAND MASTER!!
WHOOOM
DASH!

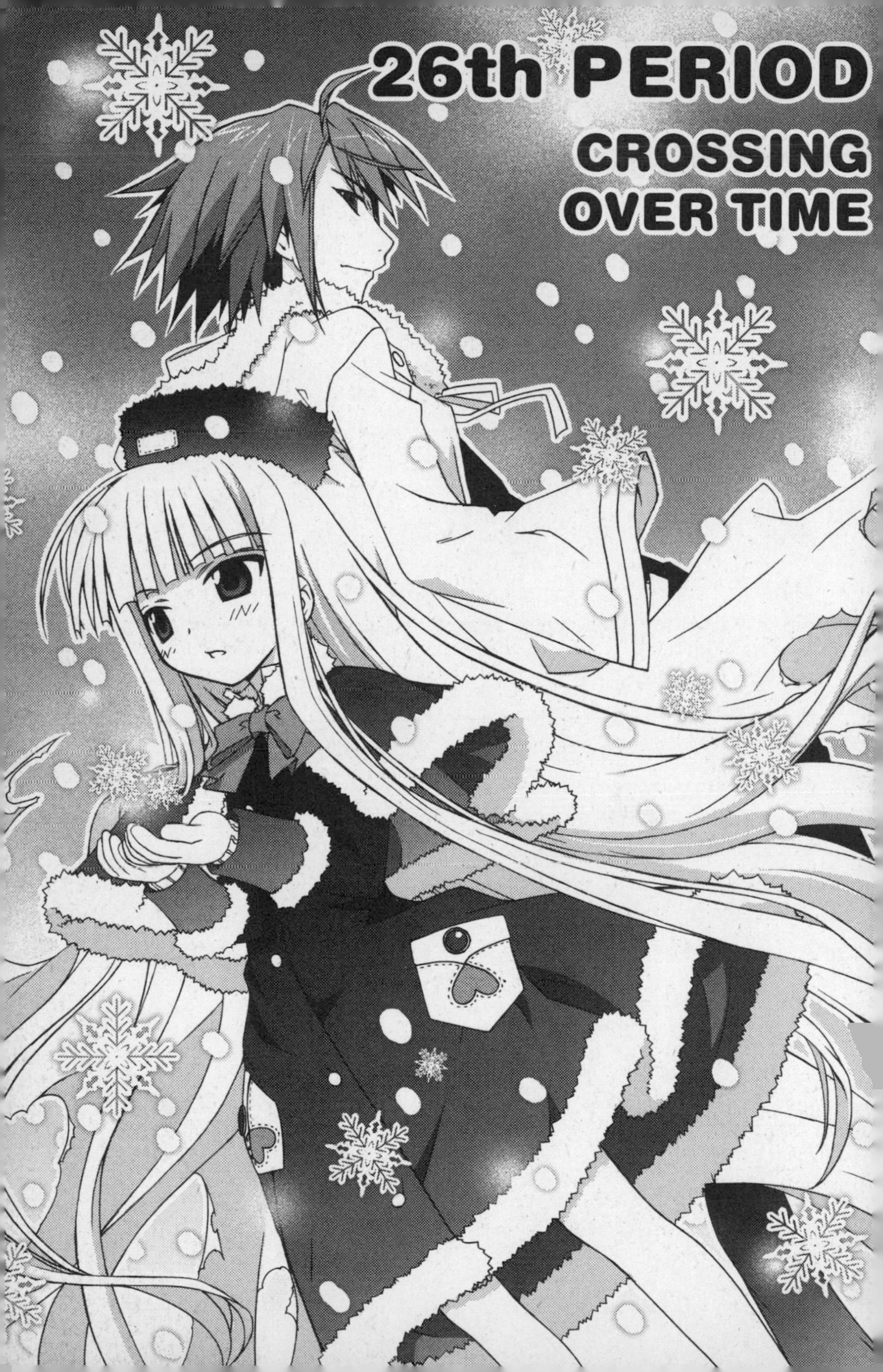
26th PERIOD
CROSSING OVER TIME

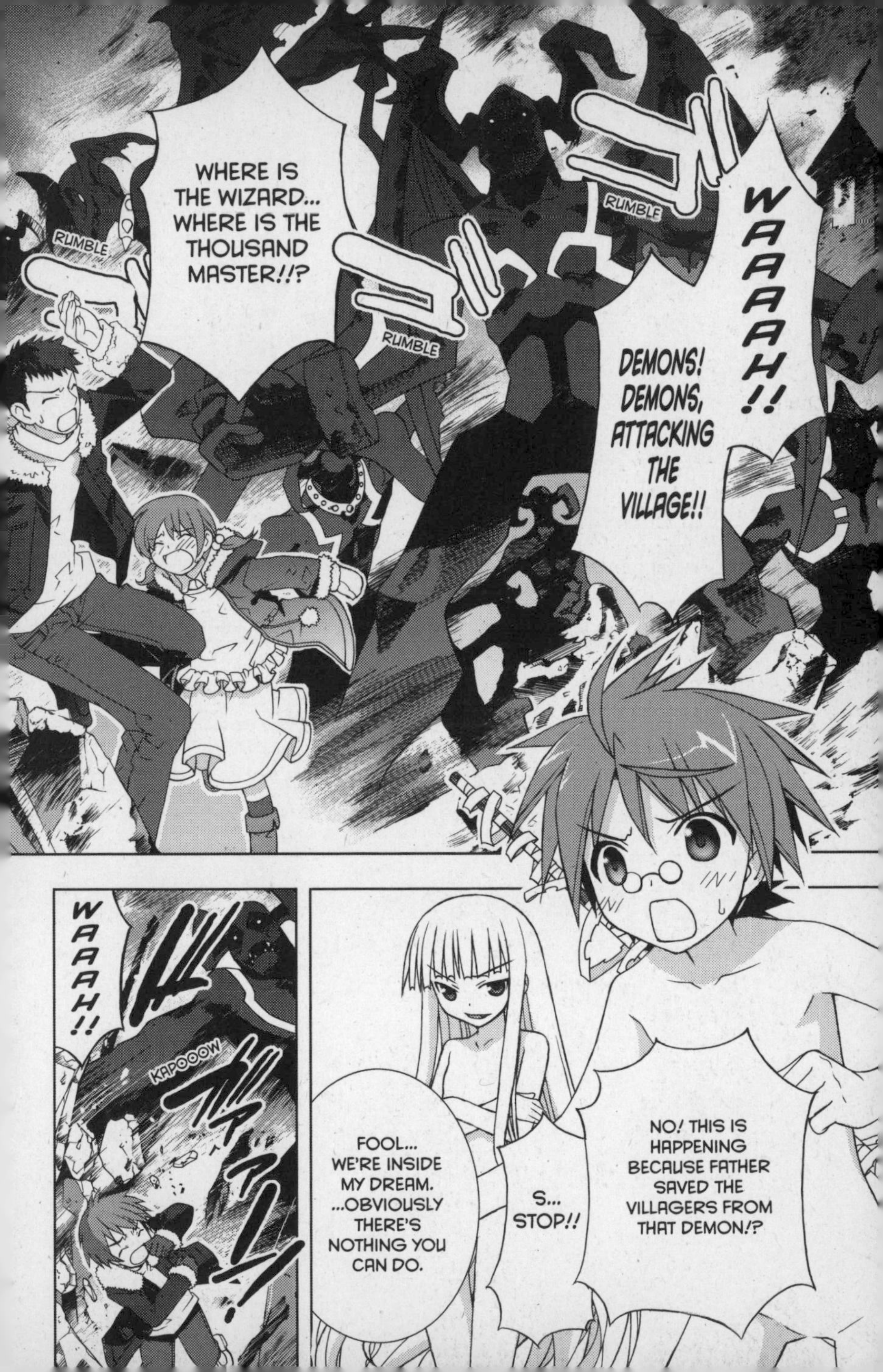
WAAAAAH!!
DEMONS! DEMONS, ATTACKING THE VILLAGE!!
RUMBLE
RUMBLE
WHERE IS THE WIZARD... WHERE IS THE THOUSAND MASTER!!?
RUMBLE
NO! THIS IS HAPPENING BECAUSE FATHER SAVED THE VILLAGERS FROM THAT DEMON!?
S... STOP!!
FOOL... WE'RE INSIDE MY DREAM. ...OBVIOUSLY THERE'S NOTHING YOU CAN DO.
WAAAAH!!
KAPOOOW

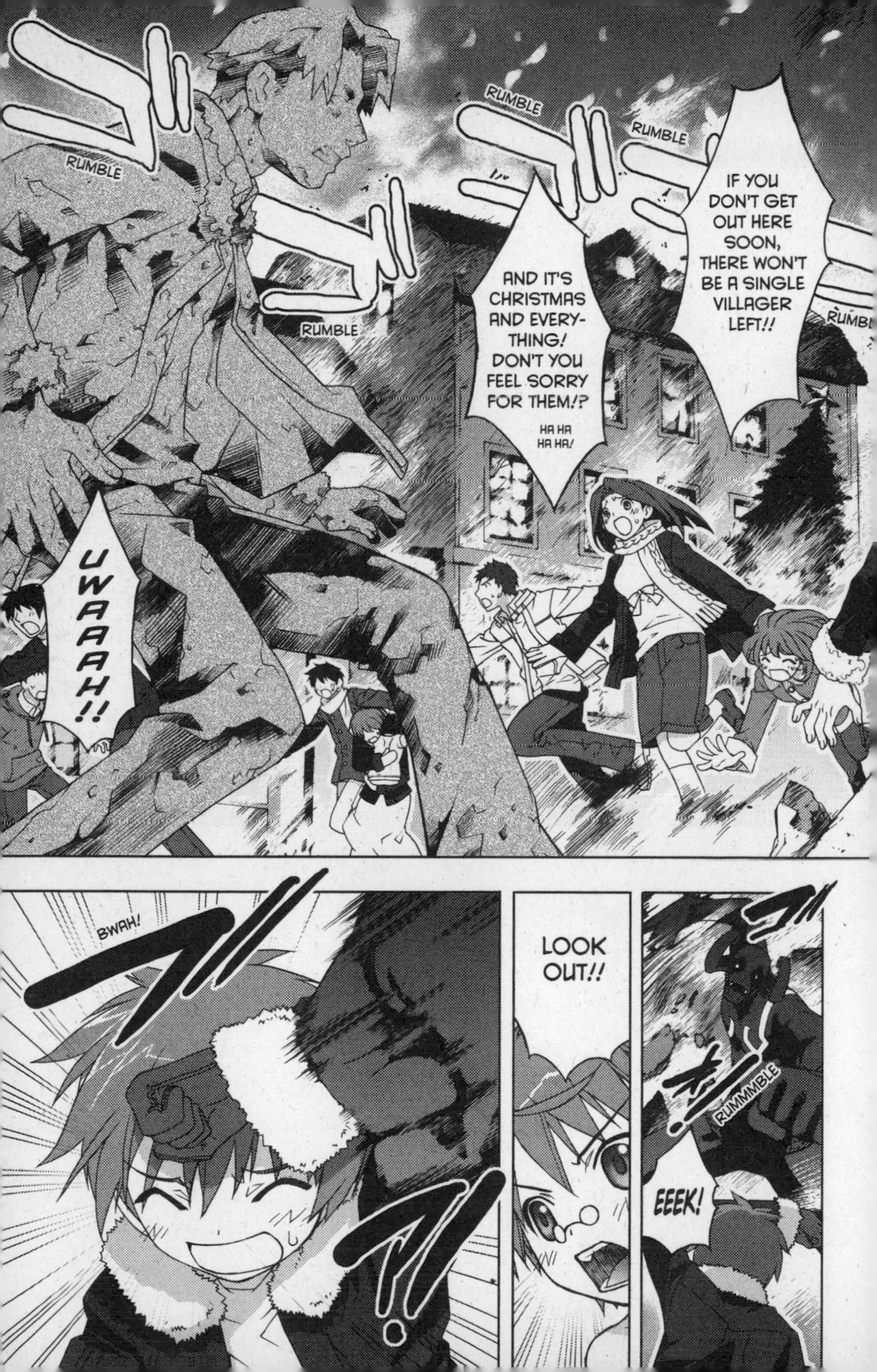
RUMBLE
IF YOU DON'T GET OUT HERE SOON, THERE WON'T BE A SINGLE VILLAGER LEFT!!
RUMBLE
RUMBLE
AND IT'S CHRISTMAS AND EVERY-THING! DON'T YOU FEEL SORRY FOR THEM!?
HA HA HA HA!
RUMBLE
RUMBLE
UWAAAAH!!
RUMMMBLE
EEEK!
LOOK OUT!!
BWAH!

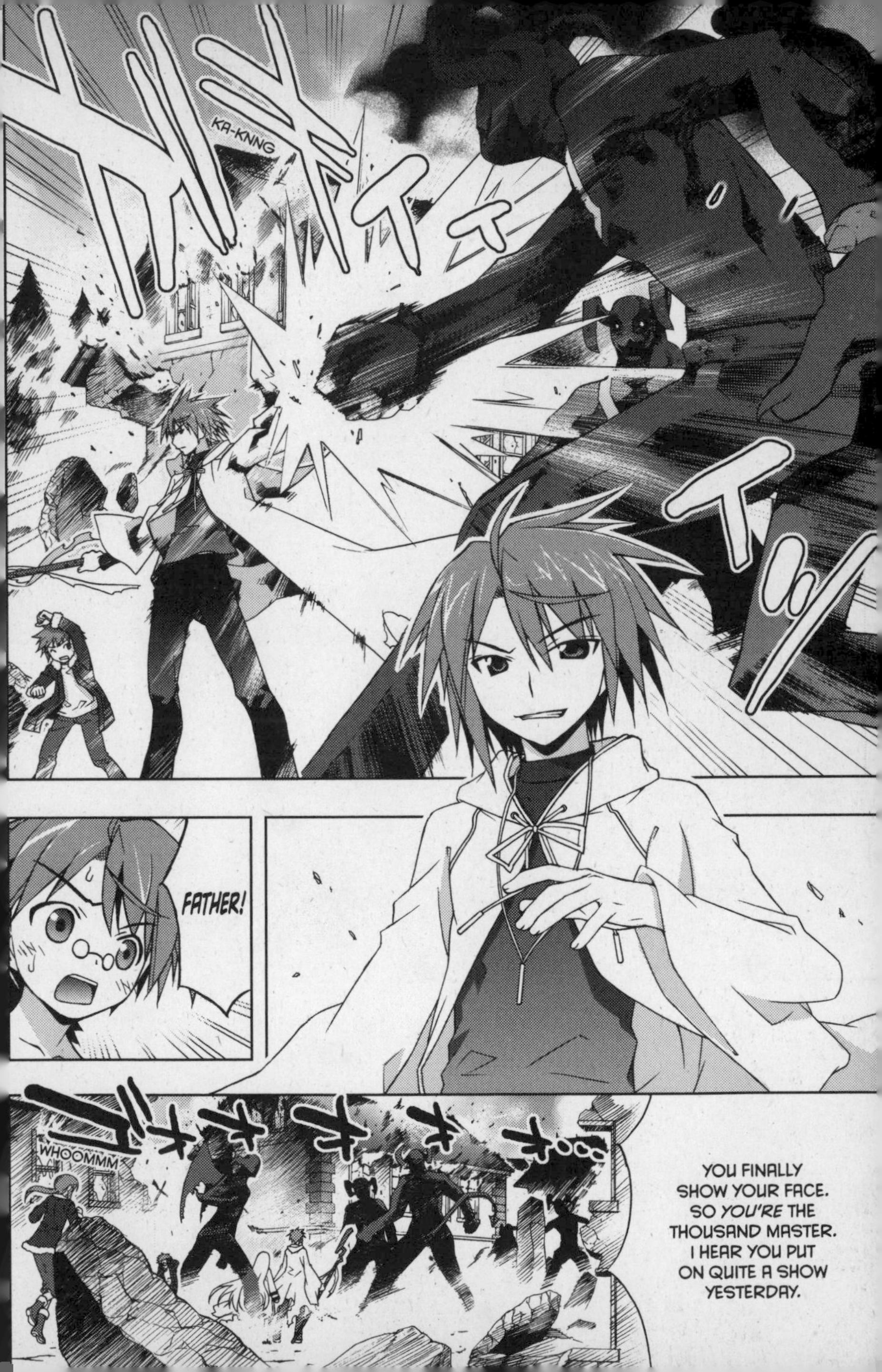
KA-KNNG
FATHER!
YOU FINALLY SHOW YOUR FACE. SO *YOU'RE* THE THOUSAND MASTER. I HEAR YOU PUT ON QUITE A SHOW YESTERDAY.
WHOOMMM

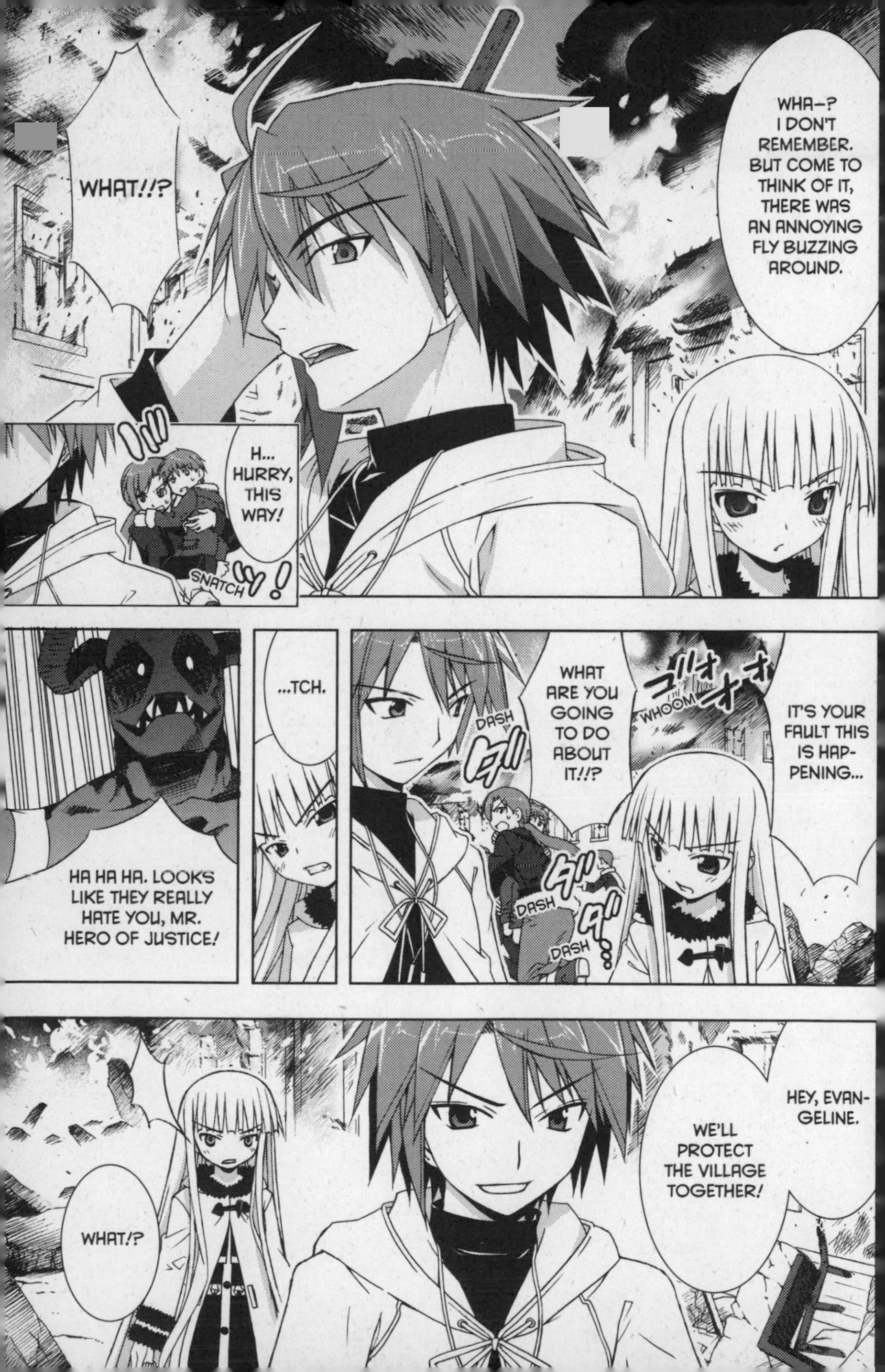
WHA–? I DON'T REMEMBER. BUT COME TO THINK OF IT, THERE WAS AN ANNOYING FLY BUZZING AROUND.
WHAT!!?
H... HURRY, THIS WAY!
SNATCH
IT'S YOUR FAULT THIS IS HAP-PENING...
WHOOM
WHAT ARE YOU GOING TO DO ABOUT IT!!?
DASH
DASH
DASH
...TCH.
HA HA HA. LOOKS LIKE THEY REALLY HATE YOU, MR. HERO OF JUSTICE!
HEY, EVAN-GELINE.
WE'LL PROTECT THE VILLAGE TOGETHER!
WHAT!?

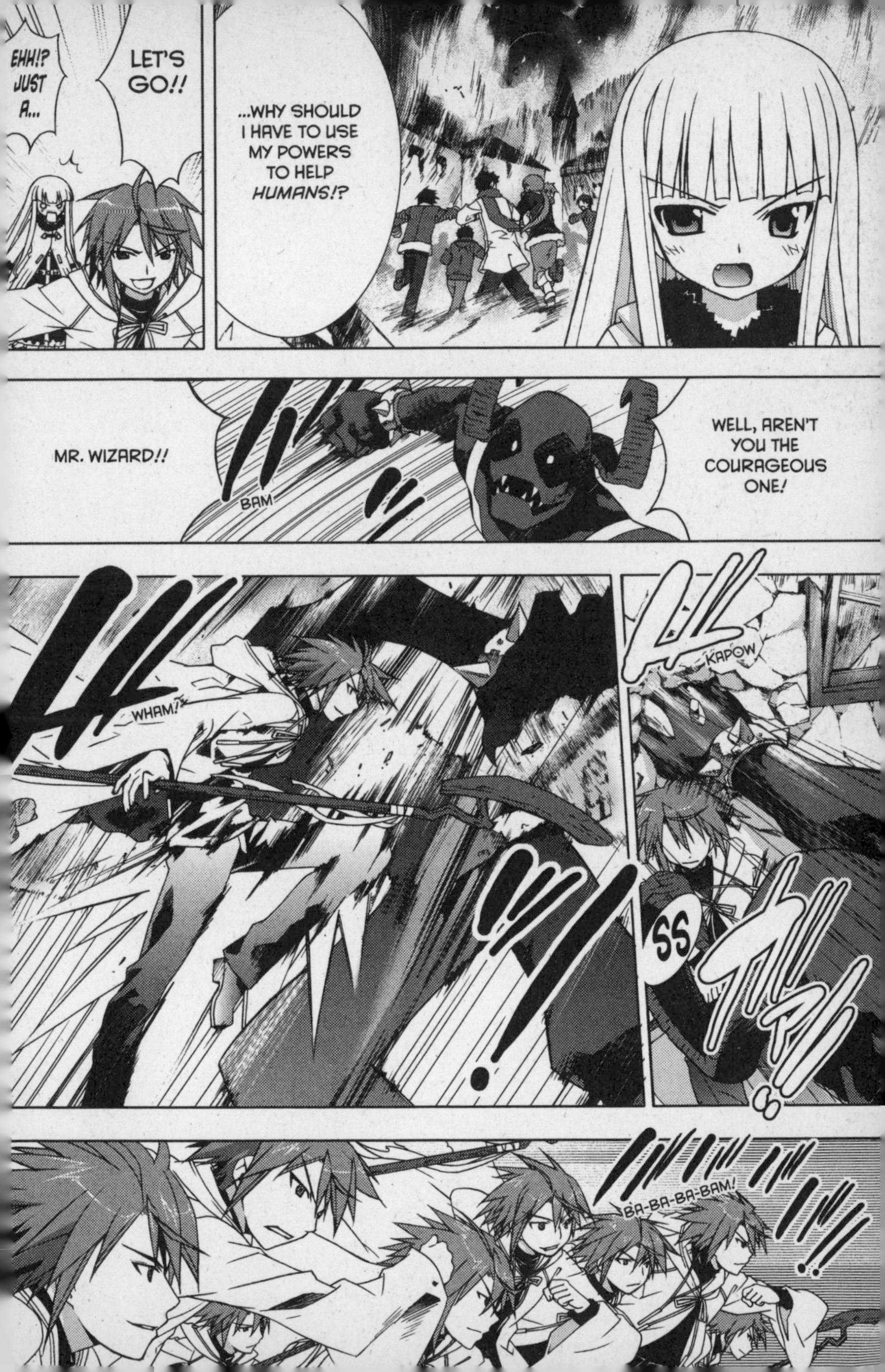
...WHY SHOULD I HAVE TO USE MY POWERS TO HELP HUMANS!?
LET'S GO!!
EHH!? JUST A...
WELL, AREN'T YOU THE COURAGEOUS ONE!
BAM
MR. WIZARD!!
KAPOW
SS
WHAM!
BA-BA-BA-BAM!

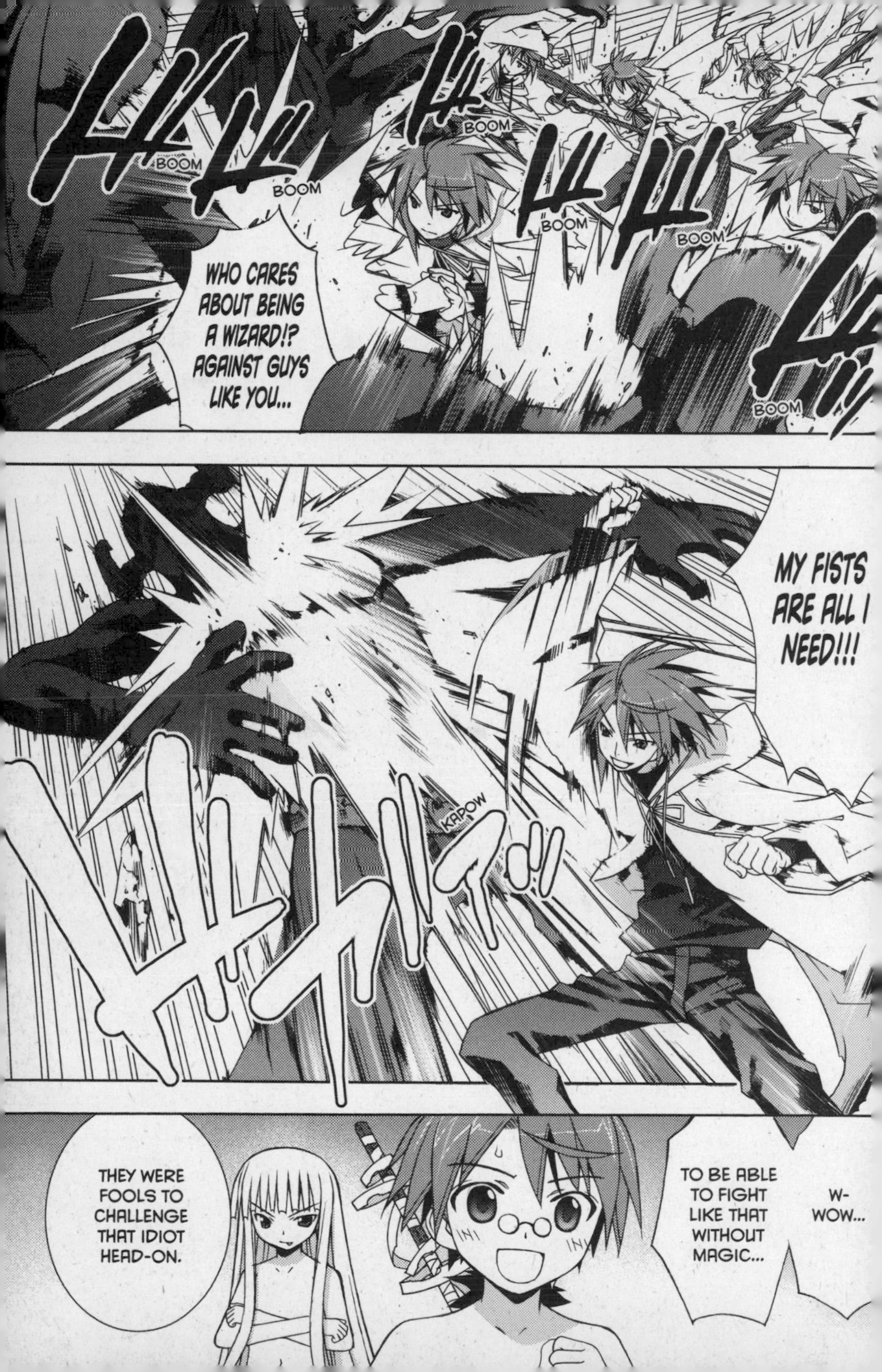
BOOM
BOOM
BOOM
BOOM
BOOM
BOOM
BOOM
WHO CARES ABOUT BEING A WIZARD!? AGAINST GUYS LIKE YOU...
MY FISTS ARE ALL I NEED!!!
KAPOW
W- WOW...
TO BE ABLE TO FIGHT LIKE THAT WITHOUT MAGIC...
THEY WERE FOOLS TO CHALLENGE THAT IDIOT HEAD-ON.

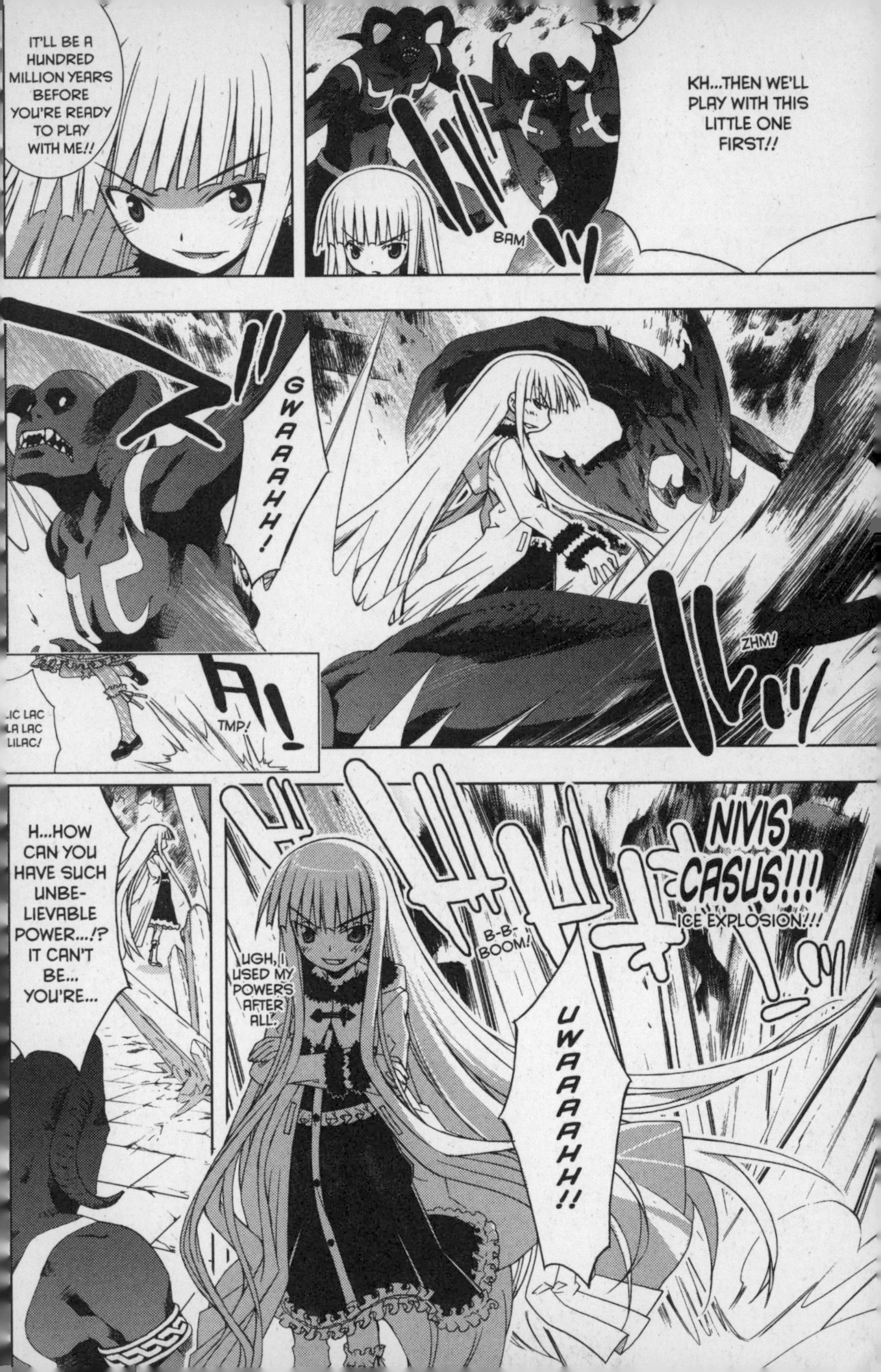
IT'LL BE A HUNDRED MILLION YEARS BEFORE YOU'RE READY TO PLAY WITH ME!!
KH...THEN WE'LL PLAY WITH THIS LITTLE ONE FIRST!!
BAM
GWAAAAHH!
ZHM!
LIC LAC LA LAC LILAC!
TMP!
NIVIS CASUS!!!
ICE EXPLOSION!!!
B-B-BOOM!
UWAAAAAHH!!
UGH, I USED MY POWERS AFTER ALL.
H...HOW CAN YOU HAVE SUCH UNBE-LIEVABLE POWER...!? IT CAN'T BE... YOU'RE...

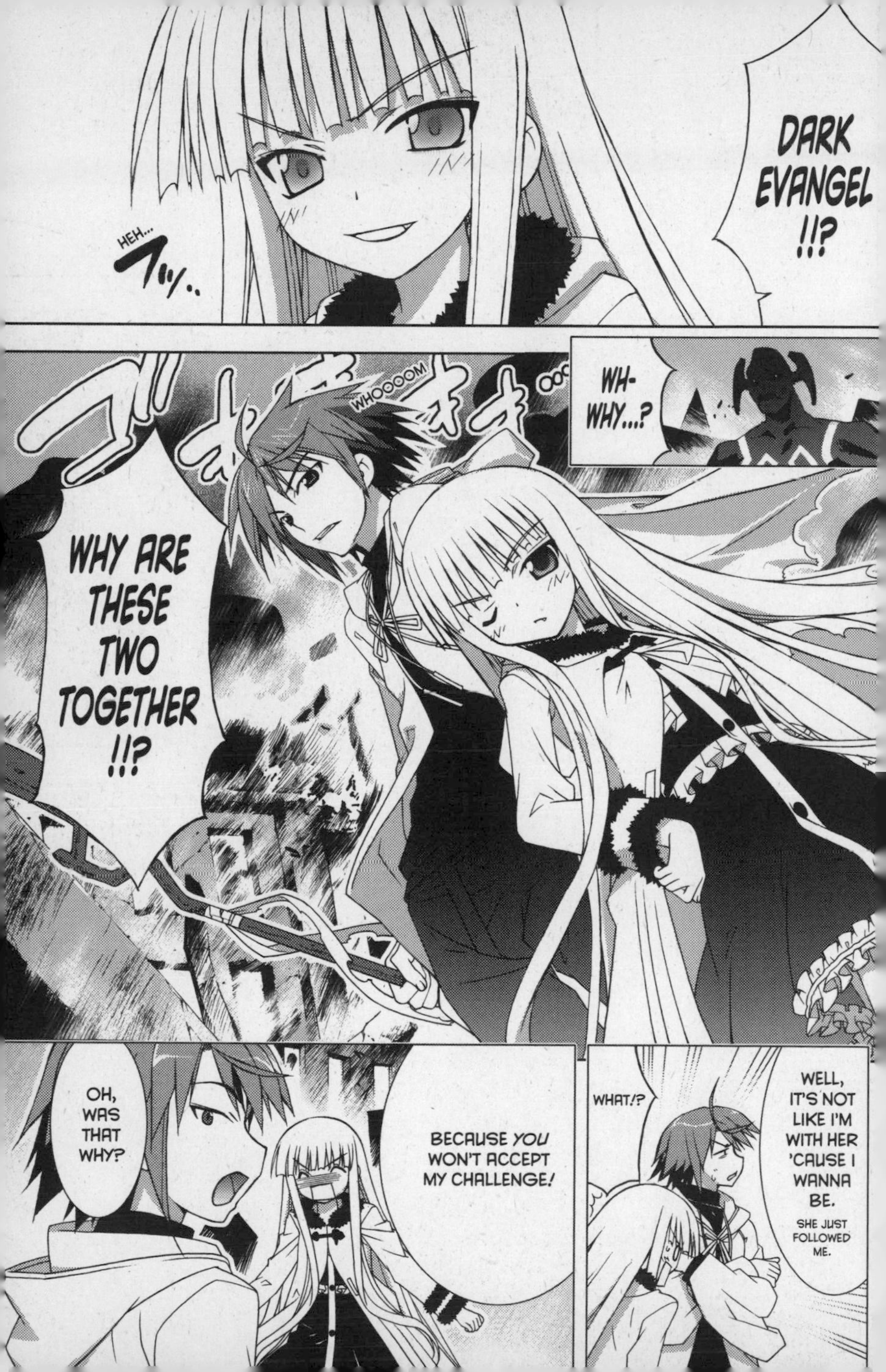
DARK EVANGEL !!?
HEH...
WH- WHY...?
WHOOOOM
WHY ARE THESE TWO TOGETHER !!?
WELL, IT'S NOT LIKE I'M WITH HER 'CAUSE I WANNA BE.
SHE JUST FOLLOWED ME.
WHAT!?
BECAUSE *YOU* WON'T ACCEPT MY CHALLENGE!
OH, WAS THAT WHY?

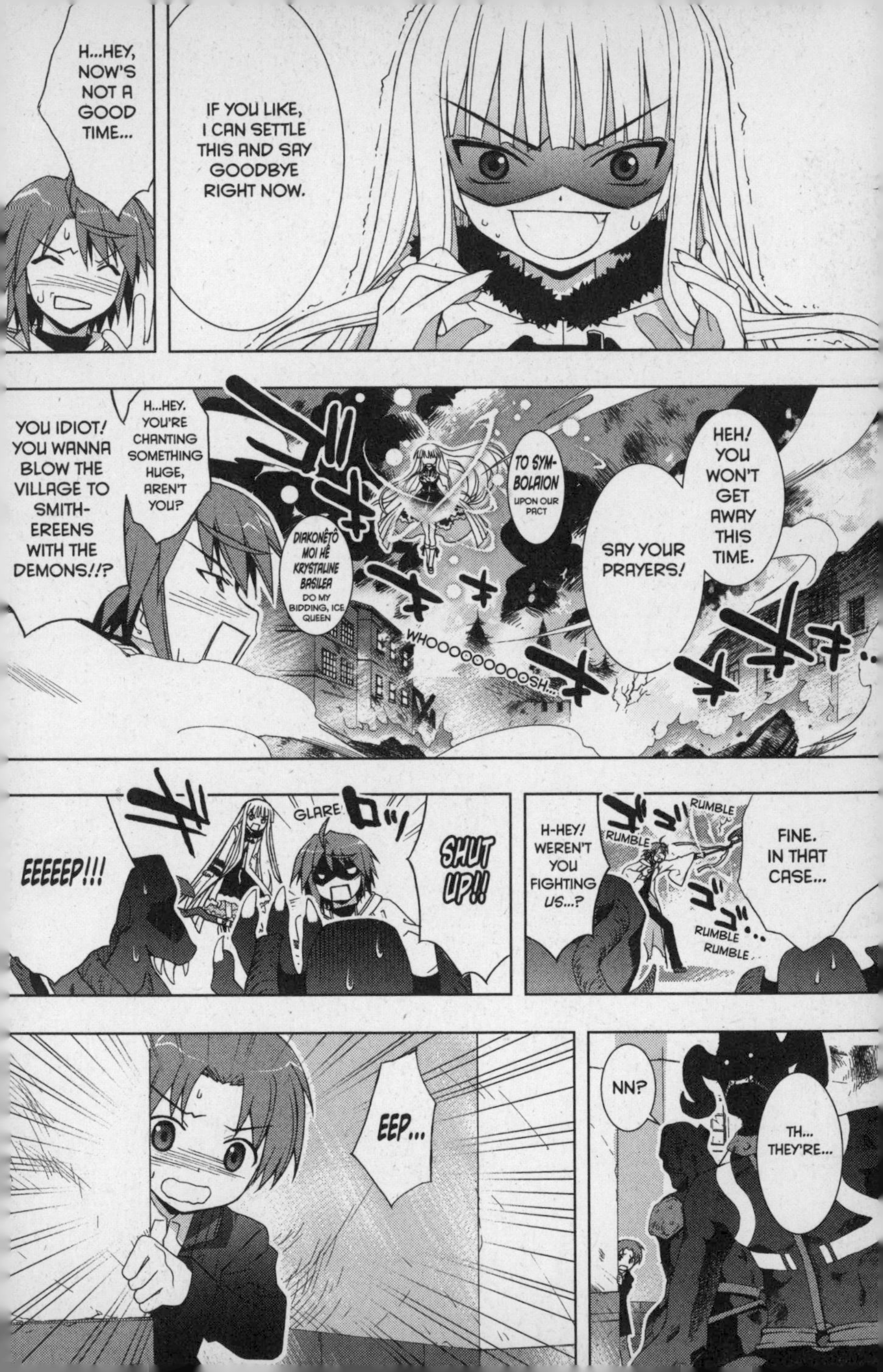
IF YOU LIKE, I CAN SETTLE THIS AND SAY GOODBYE RIGHT NOW.
H...HEY, NOW'S NOT A GOOD TIME...
HEH! YOU WON'T GET AWAY THIS TIME.
SAY YOUR PRAYERS!
TO SYMBOLAION
UPON OUR PACT
DIAKONÊTÔ MOI HÊ KRYSTALINE BASILEA
DO MY BIDDING, ICE QUEEN
WHOOOOOOOOOOSH...
H...HEY. YOU'RE CHANTING SOMETHING HUGE, AREN'T YOU?
YOU IDIOT! YOU WANNA BLOW THE VILLAGE TO SMITHEREENS WITH THE DEMONS!!?
FINE. IN THAT CASE...
RUMBLE
RUMBLE
H-HEY! WEREN'T YOU FIGHTING US...?
RUMBLE
RUMBLE
SHUT UP!!
GLARE
EEEEEP!!!
NN?
TH... THEY'RE...
EEP...

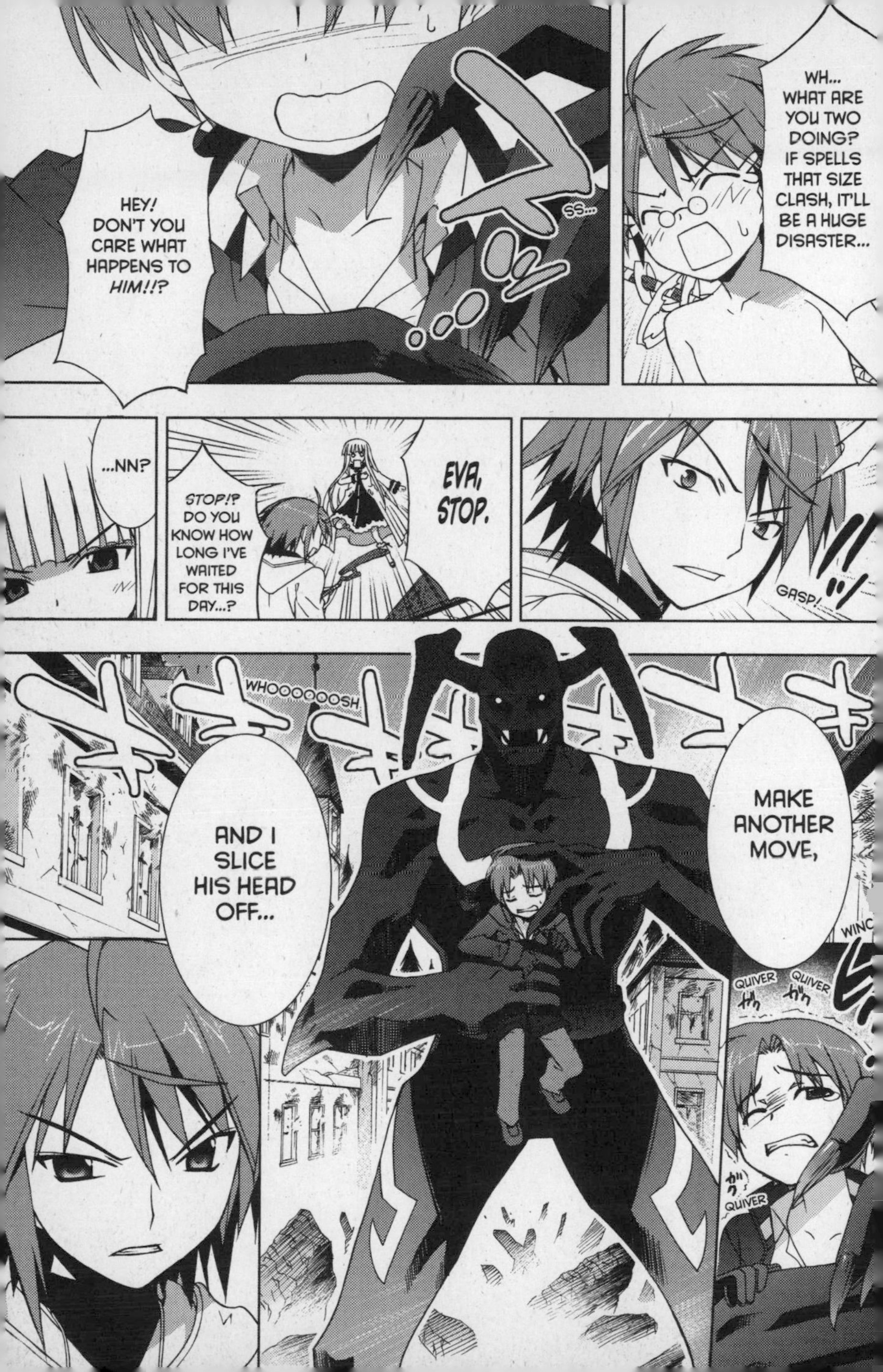
WH... WHAT ARE YOU TWO DOING? IF SPELLS THAT SIZE CLASH, IT'LL BE A HUGE DISASTER...
SS...
HEY! DON'T YOU CARE WHAT HAPPENS TO *HIM!!?*
GASP!
EVA, STOP.
*STOP!?* DO YOU KNOW HOW LONG I'VE WAITED FOR THIS DAY...?
...NN?
WHOOOOOOOSH
MAKE ANOTHER MOVE,
AND I SLICE HIS HEAD OFF...
WINC
QUIVER
QUIVER
QUIVER

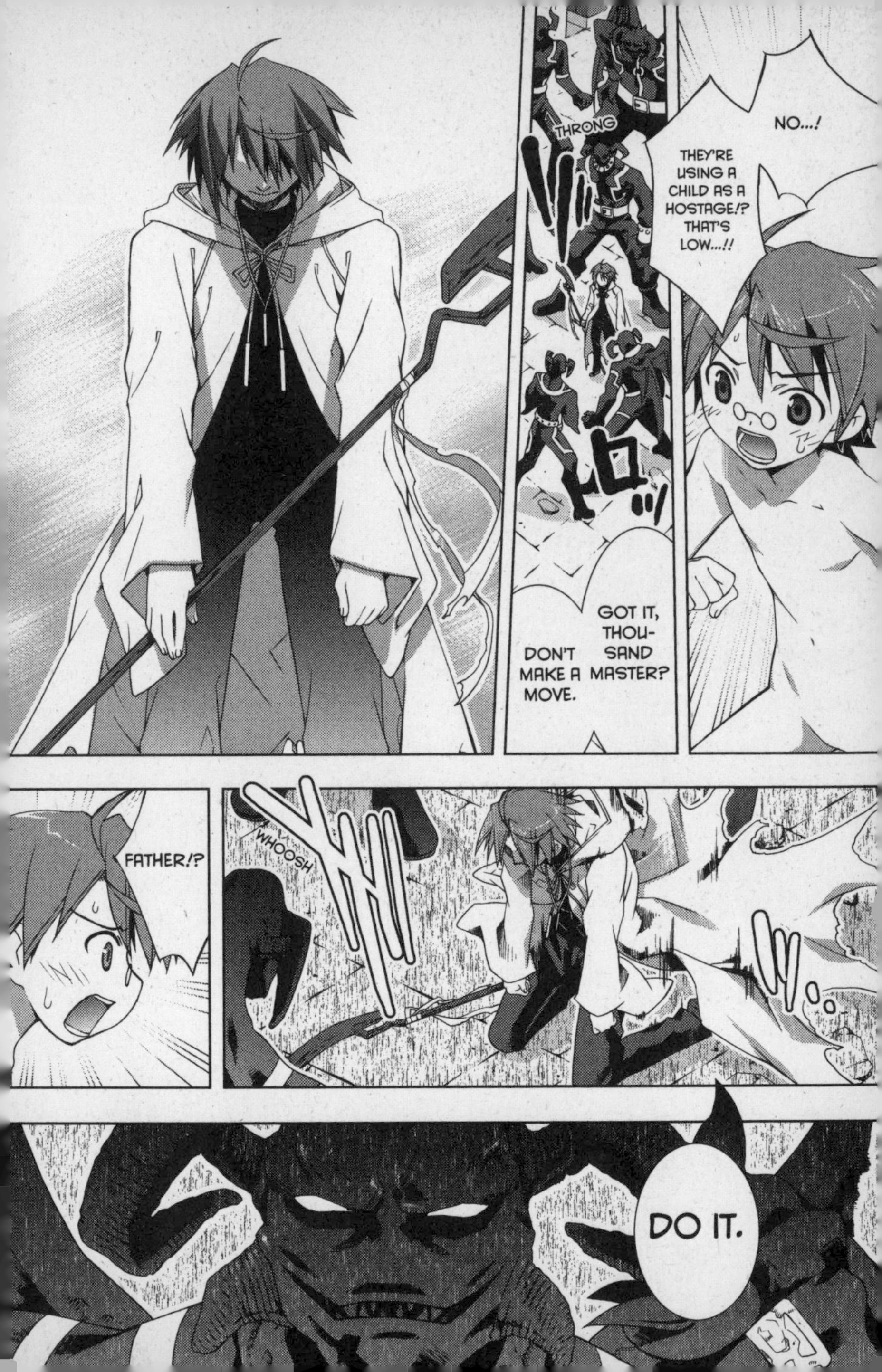
NO...!
THEY'RE USING A CHILD AS A HOSTAGE!? THAT'S LOW...!!
THRONG
GOT IT, THOU- SAND MASTER?
DON'T MAKE A MOVE.
WHOOSH
FATHER!?
DO IT.

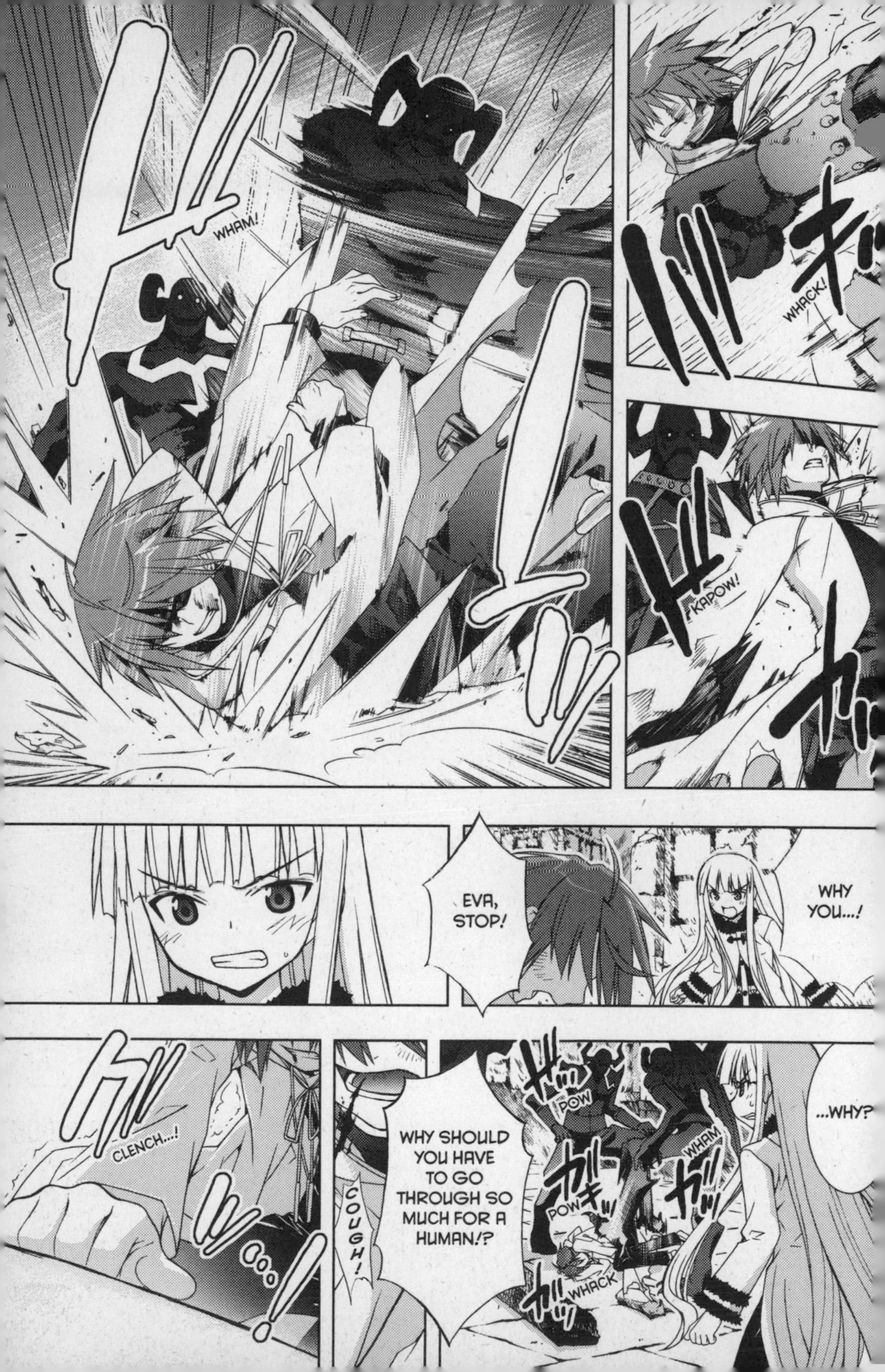
WHACK!
KAPOW!
WHAM!
WHY YOU...!
EVA, STOP!
...WHY?
POW
WHY SHOULD YOU HAVE TO GO THROUGH SO MUCH FOR A HUMAN!?
WHAM
POW
WHACK
COUGH!
CLENCH...!

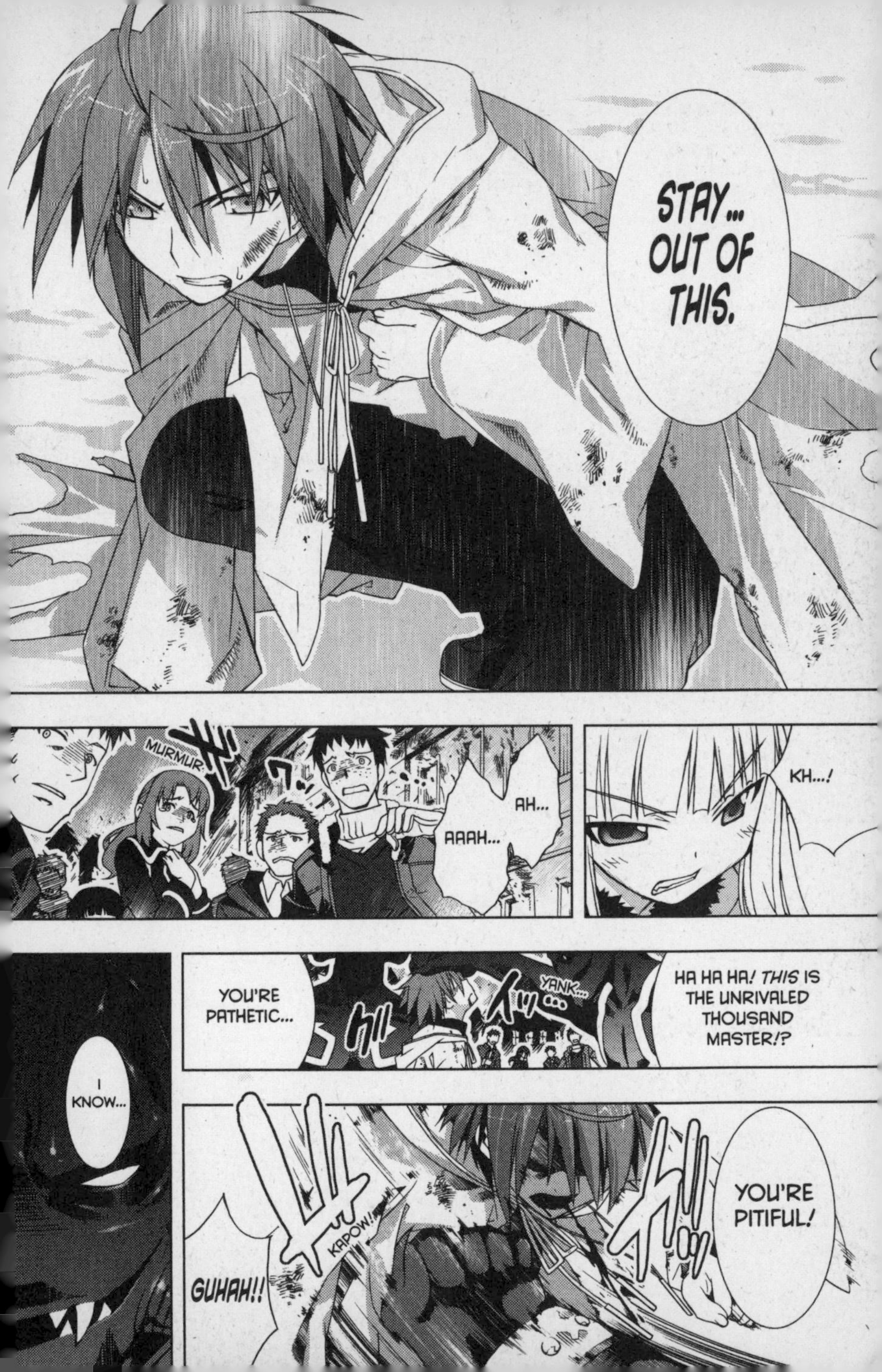
STAY... OUT OF THIS.
KH...!
AH...
AAAH...
MURMUR
HA HA HA! *THIS* IS THE UNRIVALED THOUSAND MASTER!?
YANK...
YOU'RE PATHETIC...
YOU'RE PITIFUL!
KAPOW!!
GUHAH!!
I KNOW...

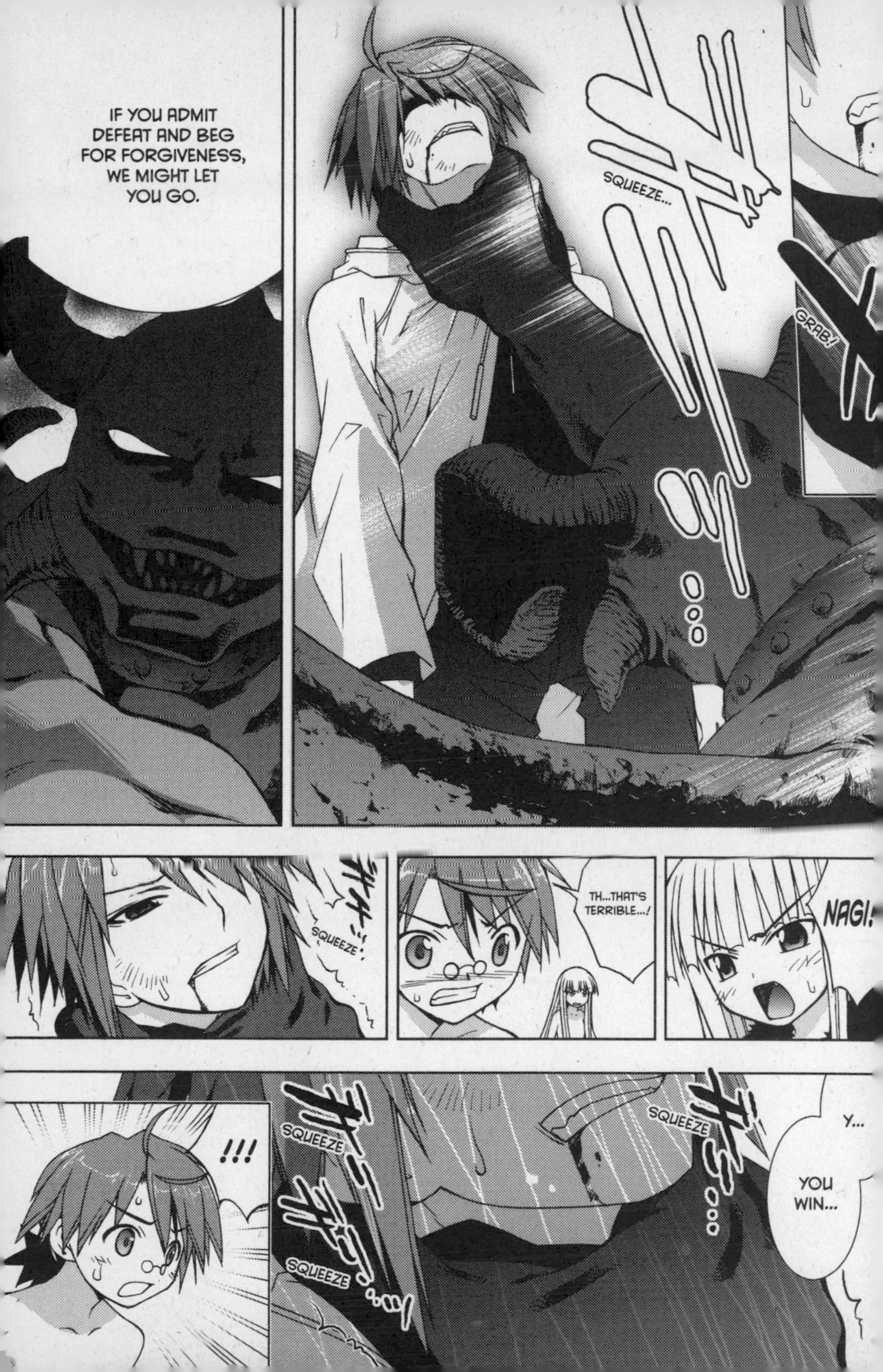
GRAB!
SQUEEZE...
IF YOU ADMIT DEFEAT AND BEG FOR FORGIVENESS, WE MIGHT LET YOU GO.
NAGI!
TH...THAT'S TERRIBLE...!
SQUEEZE
Y...
YOU WIN...
SQUEEZE
SQUEEZE
SQUEEZE
!!!

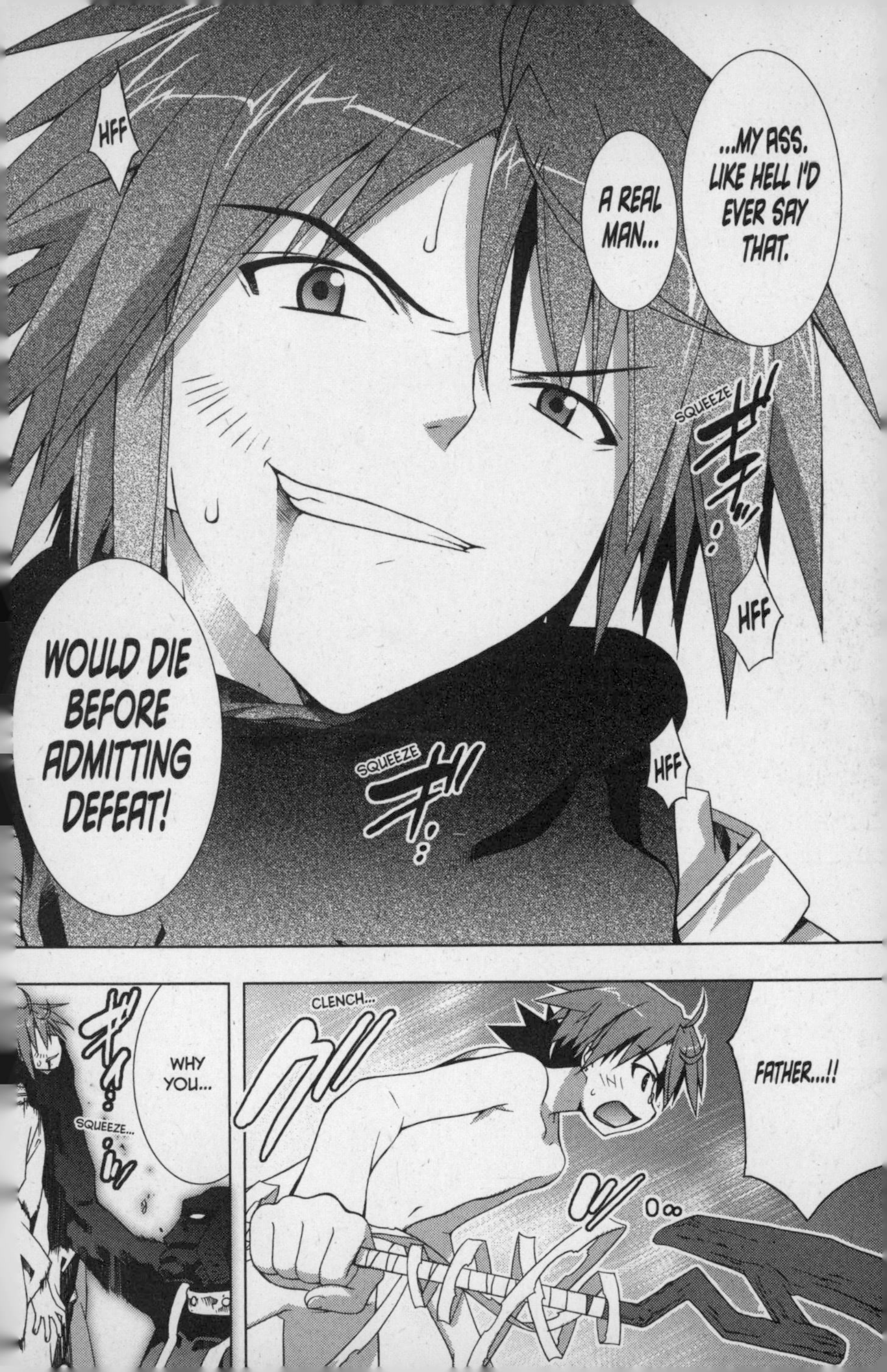
HFF
A REAL MAN...
WOULD DIE BEFORE ADMITTING DEFEAT!
...MY ASS. LIKE HELL I'D EVER SAY THAT.
SQUEEZE
HFF
SQUEEZE
HFF
CLENCH...
FATHER...!!
WHY YOU...
SQUEEZE...

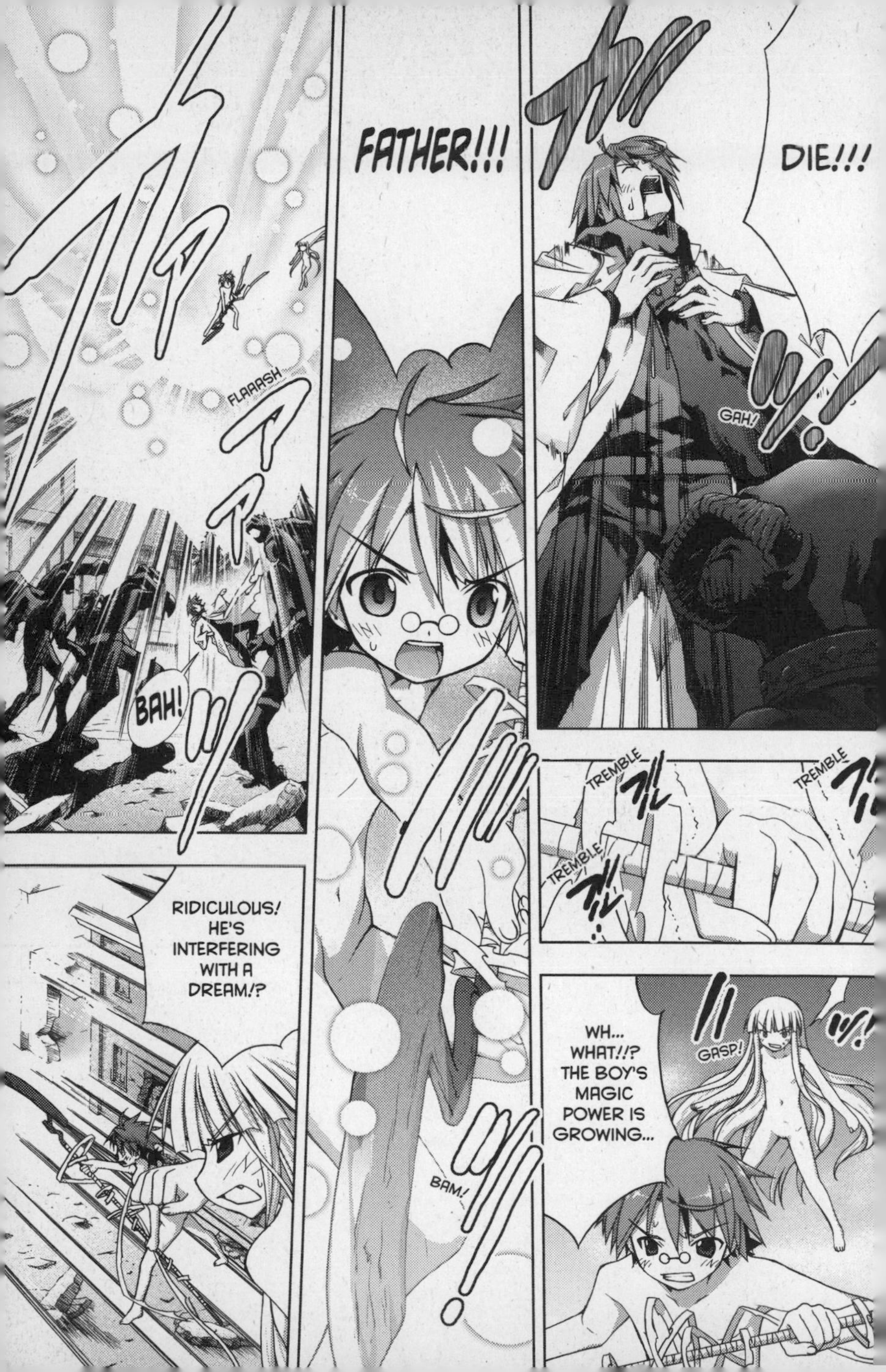
DIE!!!
GAH!
TREMBLE
TREMBLE
TREMBLE
GASP!
WH... WHAT!!? THE BOY'S MAGIC POWER IS GROWING...
FATHER!!!
BAM!
FLAAASH
BAH!
RIDICULOUS! HE'S INTERFERING WITH A DREAM!?

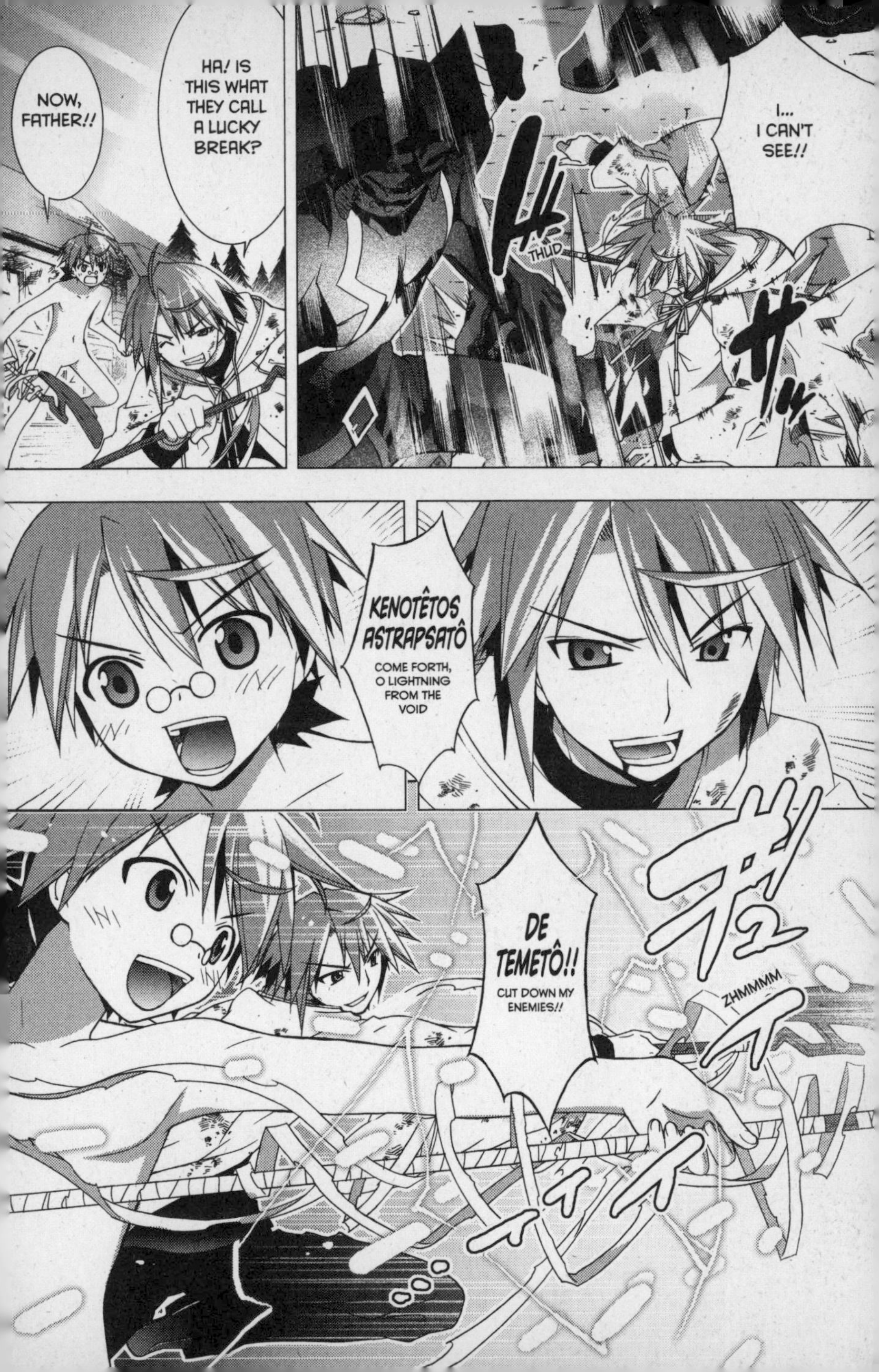
I... I CAN'T SEE!!
THUD
HA! IS THIS WHAT THEY CALL A LUCKY BREAK?
NOW, FATHER!!
KENOTÊTOS ASTRAPSATÔ
COME FORTH, O LIGHTNING FROM THE VOID
DE TEMETÔ!!
CUT DOWN MY ENEMIES!!
ZHMMMM

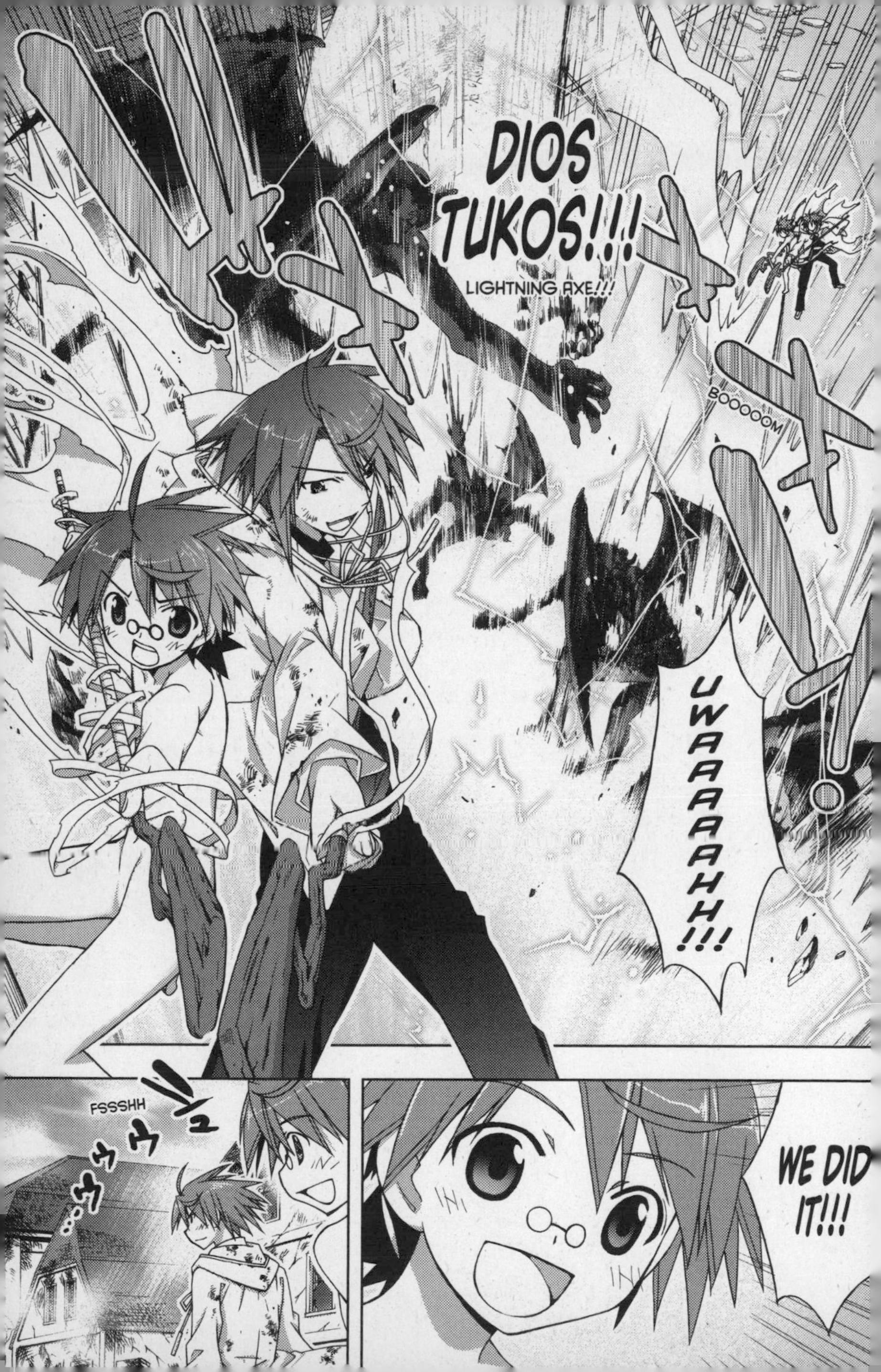
DIOS TUKOS!!!
LIGHTNING AXE!!!
BOOOOOM
UWAAAAAAHH!!!
WE DID IT!!!
FSSSHH

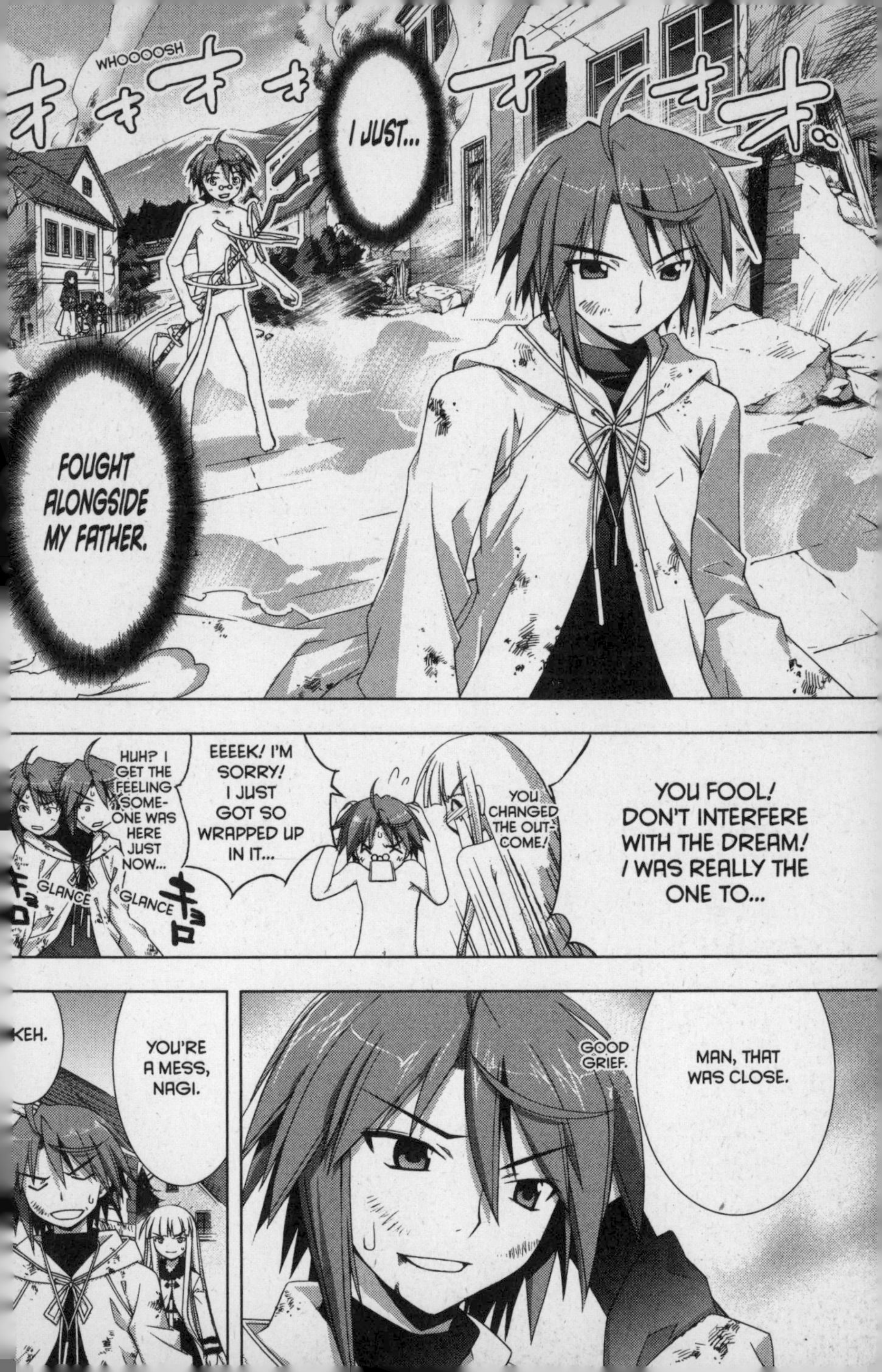
WHOOOOSH
I JUST...
FOUGHT ALONGSIDE MY FATHER.
YOU FOOL! DON'T INTERFERE WITH THE DREAM! I WAS REALLY THE ONE TO...
YOU CHANGED THE OUT-COME!
EEEEK! I'M SORRY! I JUST GOT SO WRAPPED UP IN IT...
HUH? I GET THE FEELING SOME-ONE WAS HERE JUST NOW...
GLANCE
GLANCE
MAN, THAT WAS CLOSE.
GOOD GRIEF.
YOU'RE A MESS, NAGI.
KEH.

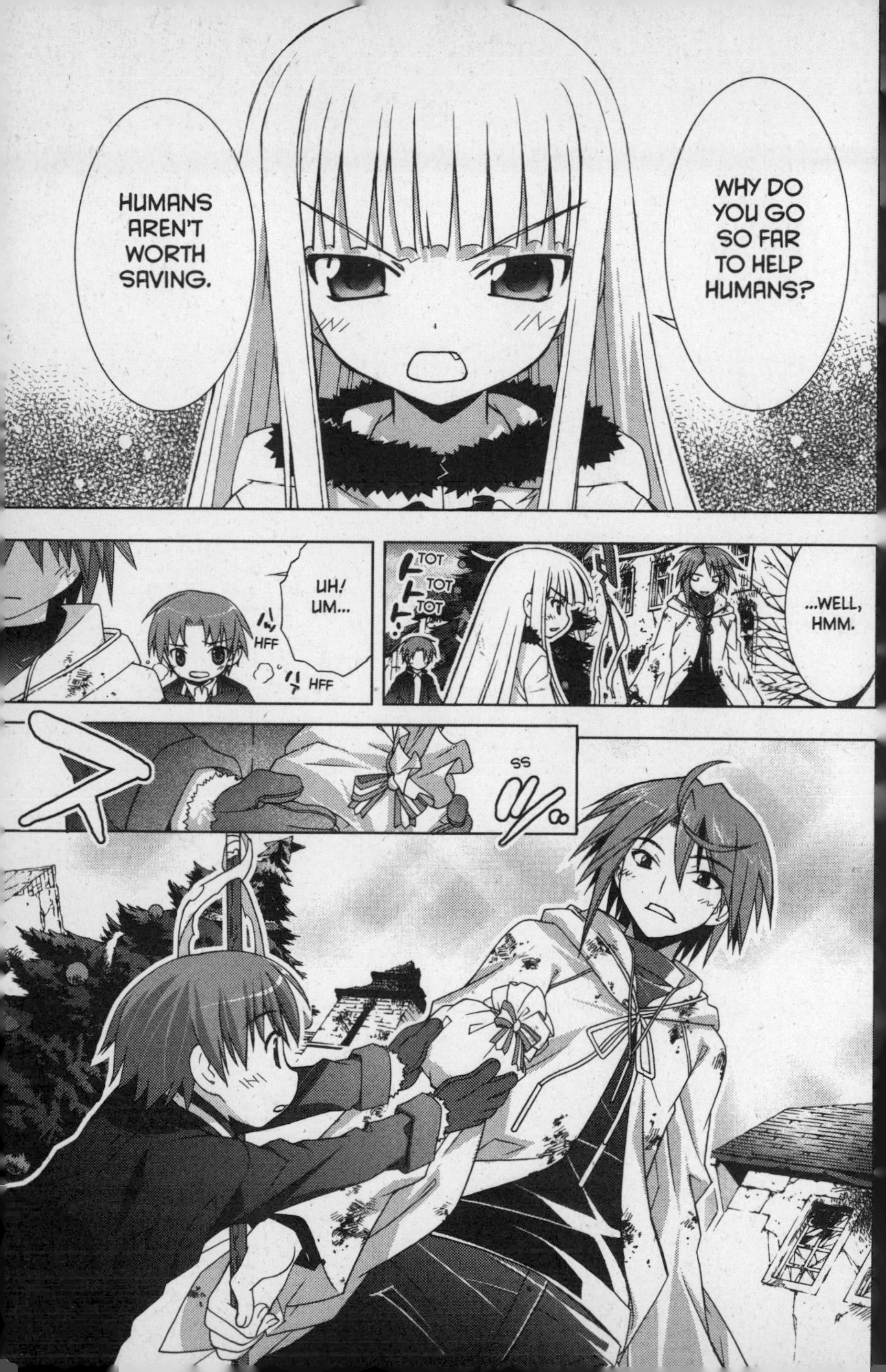
WHY DO YOU GO SO FAR TO HELP HUMANS?
HUMANS AREN'T WORTH SAVING.
...WELL, HMM.
TOT TOT TOT
UH! UM...
HFF
HFF
SS

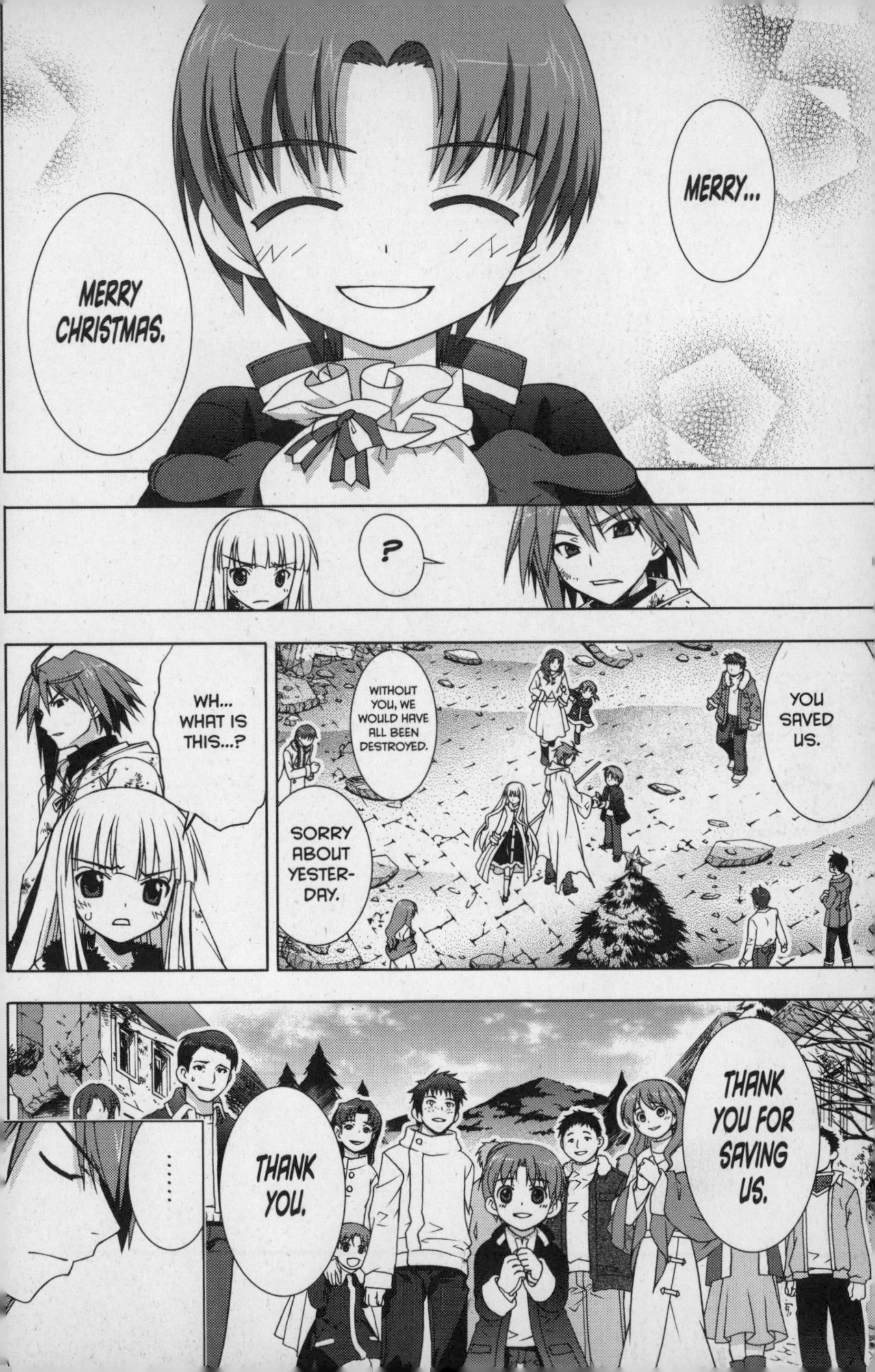

MERRY...
MERRY CHRISTMAS.
?
YOU SAVED US.
WITHOUT YOU, WE WOULD HAVE ALL BEEN DESTROYED.
SORRY ABOUT YESTER-DAY.
WH... WHAT IS THIS...?
THANK YOU FOR SAVING US.
THANK YOU.
......

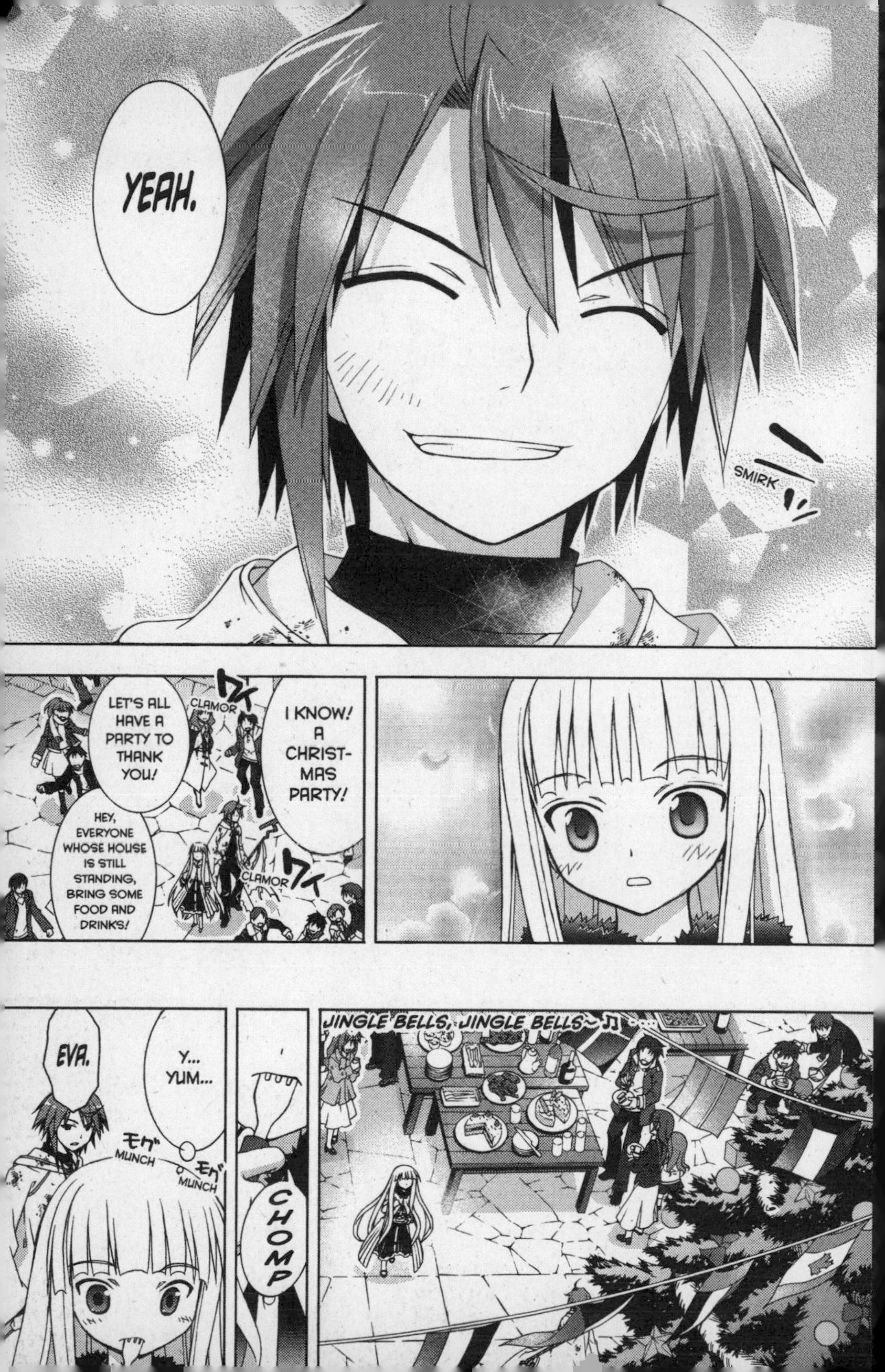
YEAH.
SMIRK
I KNOW! A CHRISTMAS PARTY!
ワイ CLAMOR
LET'S ALL HAVE A PARTY TO THANK YOU!
ワイ CLAMOR
HEY, EVERYONE WHOSE HOUSE IS STILL STANDING, BRING SOME FOOD AND DRINKS!
JINGLE BELLS, JINGLE BELLS~♫ ...
CHOMP
Y... YUM...
EVA.
モグ MUNCH
モグ MUNCH

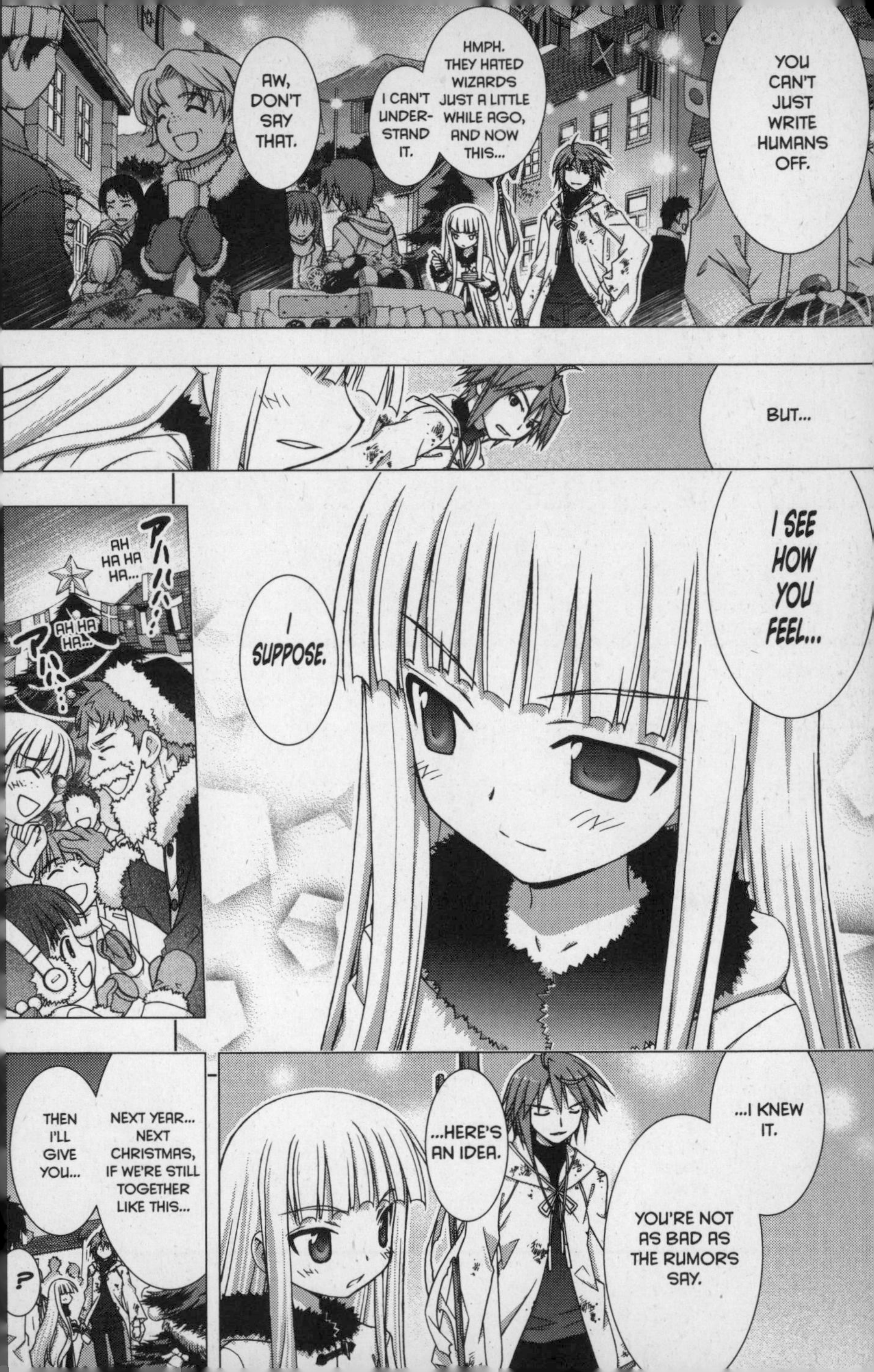
YOU CAN'T JUST WRITE HUMANS OFF.
HMPH. THEY HATED WIZARDS JUST A LITTLE WHILE AGO, AND NOW THIS...
I CAN'T UNDER-STAND IT.
AW, DON'T SAY THAT.
BUT...
I SEE HOW YOU FEEL...
I SUPPOSE.
AH HA HA HA...
AH HA HA...
...I KNEW IT.
YOU'RE NOT AS BAD AS THE RUMORS SAY.
...HERE'S AN IDEA.
NEXT YEAR... NEXT CHRISTMAS, IF WE'RE STILL TOGETHER LIKE THIS...
THEN I'LL GIVE YOU...
?

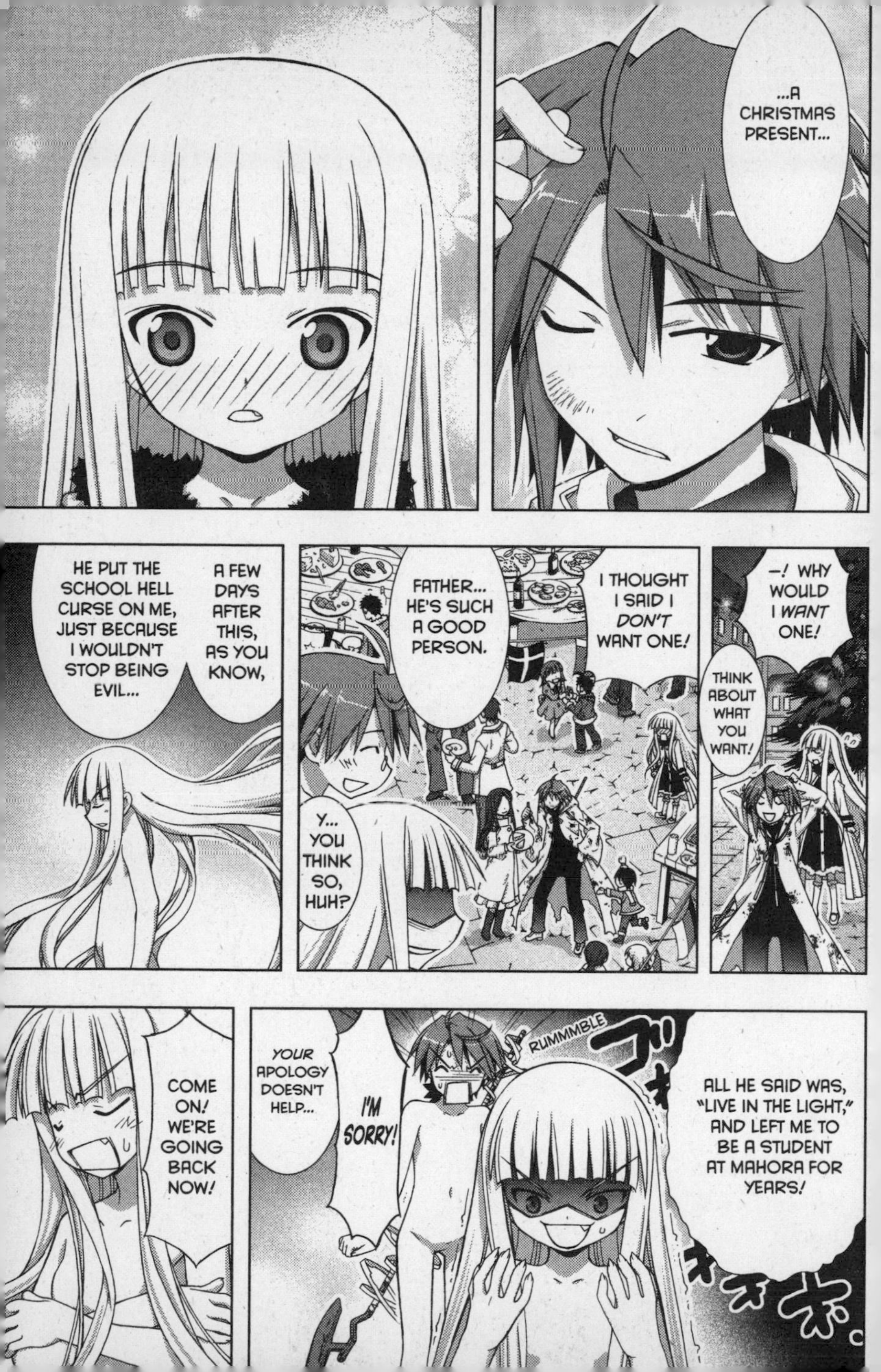
...A CHRISTMAS PRESENT...
—! WHY WOULD I *WANT* ONE!
THINK ABOUT WHAT YOU WANT!
I THOUGHT I SAID I *DON'T* WANT ONE!
FATHER... HE'S SUCH A GOOD PERSON.
Y... YOU THINK SO, HUH?
A FEW DAYS AFTER THIS, AS YOU KNOW,
HE PUT THE SCHOOL HELL CURSE ON ME, JUST BECAUSE I WOULDN'T STOP BEING EVIL...
ALL HE SAID WAS, "LIVE IN THE LIGHT," AND LEFT ME TO BE A STUDENT AT MAHORA FOR YEARS!
RUMMMBLE
I'M SORRY!
*YOUR* APOLOGY DOESN'T HELP...
COME ON! WE'RE GOING BACK NOW!

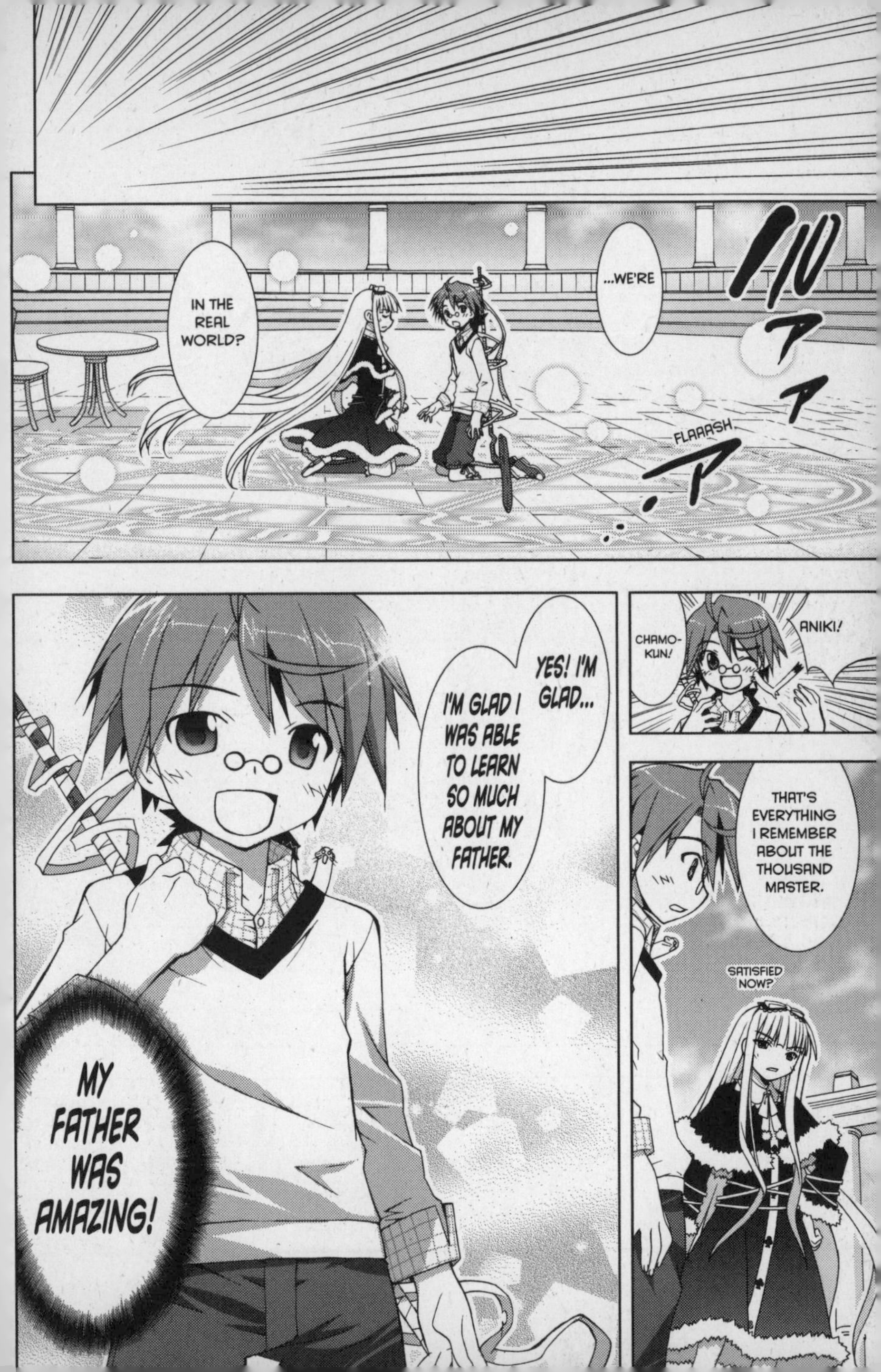
FLAAASH
...WE'RE
IN THE REAL WORLD?
ANIKI!
CHAMO-KUN!
THAT'S EVERYTHING I REMEMBER ABOUT THE THOUSAND MASTER.
SATISFIED NOW?
YES! I'M GLAD...
I'M GLAD I WAS ABLE TO LEARN SO MUCH ABOUT MY FATHER.
MY FATHER WAS AMAZING!

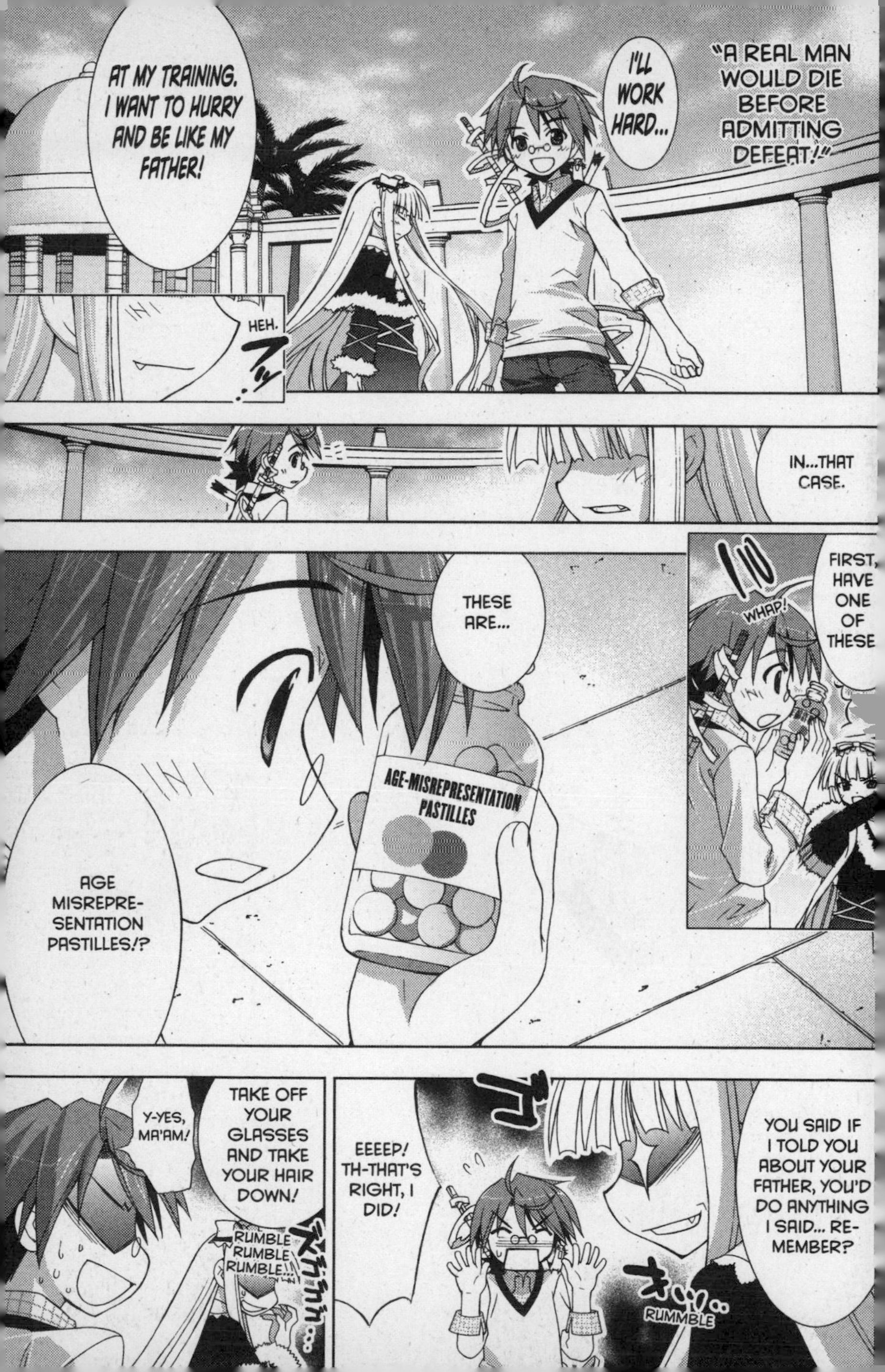
"A REAL MAN WOULD DIE BEFORE ADMITTING DEFEAT!"
I'LL WORK HARD...
AT MY TRAINING. I WANT TO HURRY AND BE LIKE MY FATHER!
HEH.
IN...THAT CASE.
FIRST, HAVE ONE OF THESE
WHAP!
THESE ARE...
AGE-MISREPRESENTATION PASTILLES
AGE MISREPRE-SENTATION PASTILLES!?
YOU SAID IF I TOLD YOU ABOUT YOUR FATHER, YOU'D DO ANYTHING I SAID... RE-MEMBER?
EEEEP! TH-THAT'S RIGHT, I DID!
RUMMBLE
TAKE OFF YOUR GLASSES AND TAKE YOUR HAIR DOWN!
Y-YES, MA'AM!
RUMBLE RUMBLE RUMBLE!

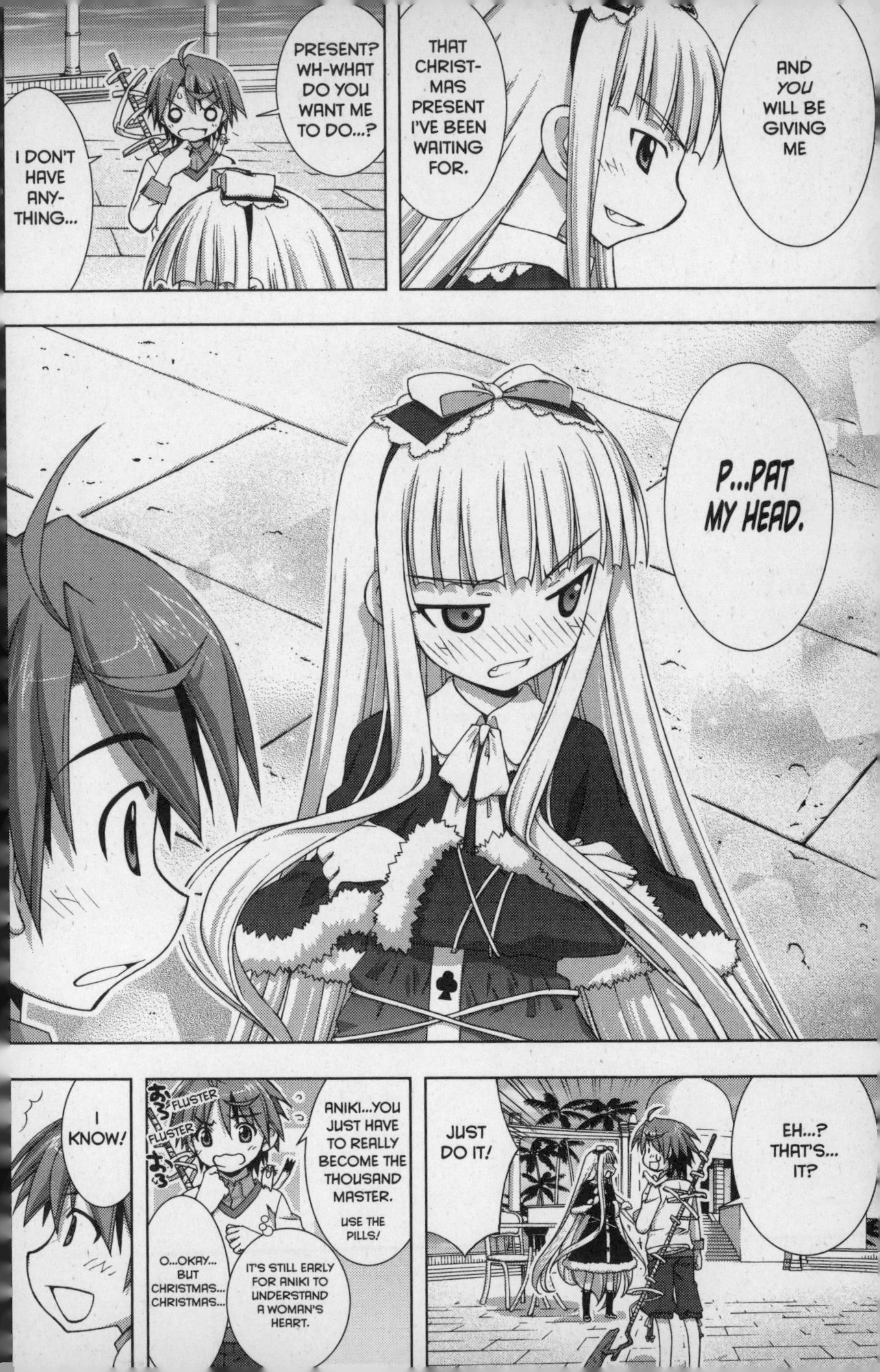
AND *YOU* WILL BE GIVING ME
THAT CHRISTMAS PRESENT I'VE BEEN WAITING FOR.
PRESENT? WH-WHAT DO YOU WANT ME TO DO...?
I DON'T HAVE ANYTHING...
P...PAT MY HEAD.
EH...? THAT'S... IT?
JUST DO IT!
ANIKI...YOU JUST HAVE TO REALLY BECOME THE THOUSAND MASTER.
USE THE PILLS!
FLUSTER
FLUSTER
IT'S STILL EARLY FOR ANIKI TO UNDERSTAND A WOMAN'S HEART.
O...OKAY... BUT CHRISTMAS... CHRISTMAS...
I KNOW!

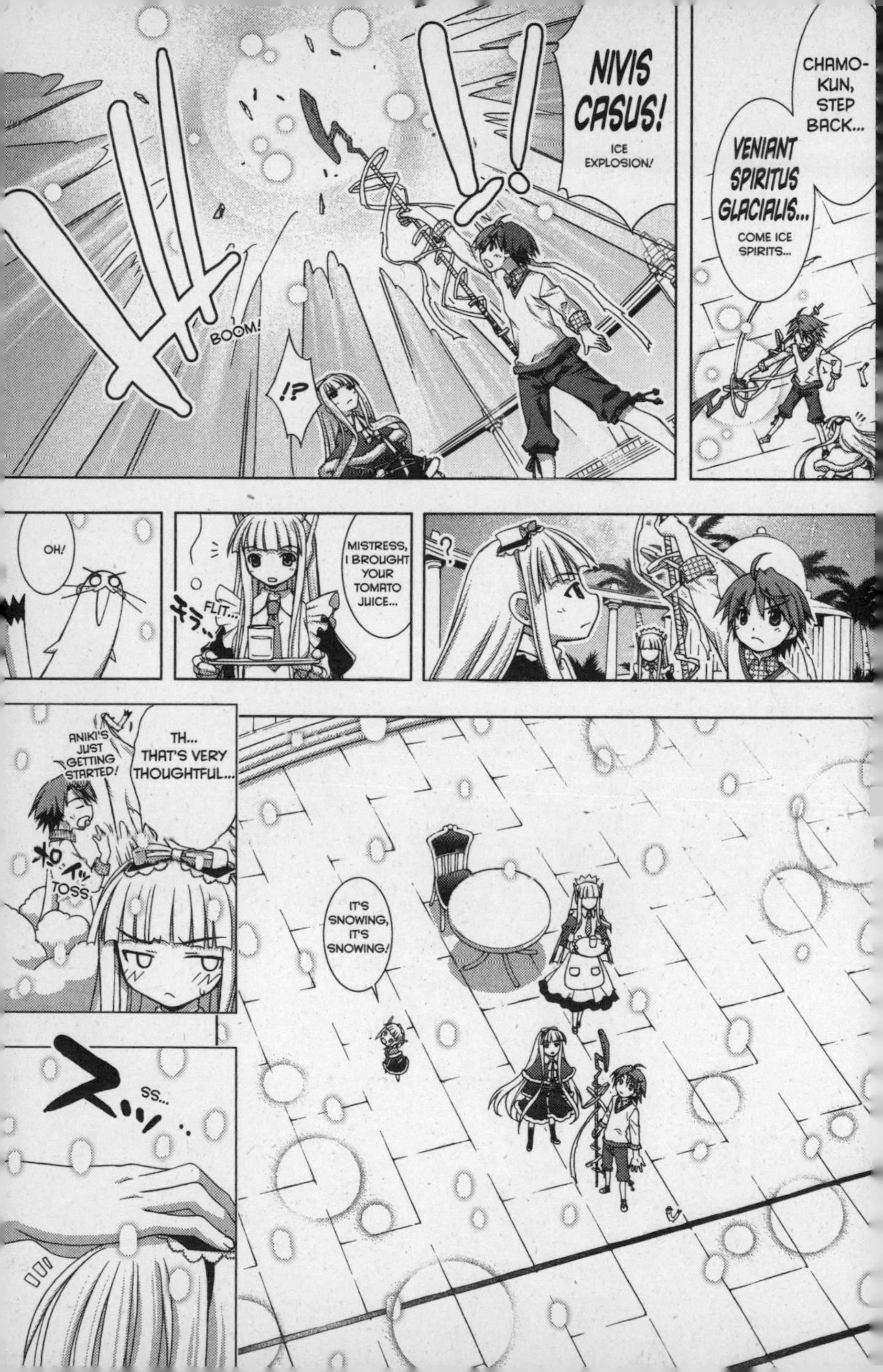
CHAMO-KUN, STEP BACK...
VENIANT SPIRITUS GLACIALIS...
COME ICE SPIRITS...
NIVIS CASUS!
ICE EXPLOSION!
BOOM!
!?
MISTRESS, I BROUGHT YOUR TOMATO JUICE...
FLIT...
OH!
IT'S SNOWING, IT'S SNOWING!
TH... THAT'S VERY THOUGHTFUL...
ANIKI'S JUST GETTING STARTED!
TOSS
SS...

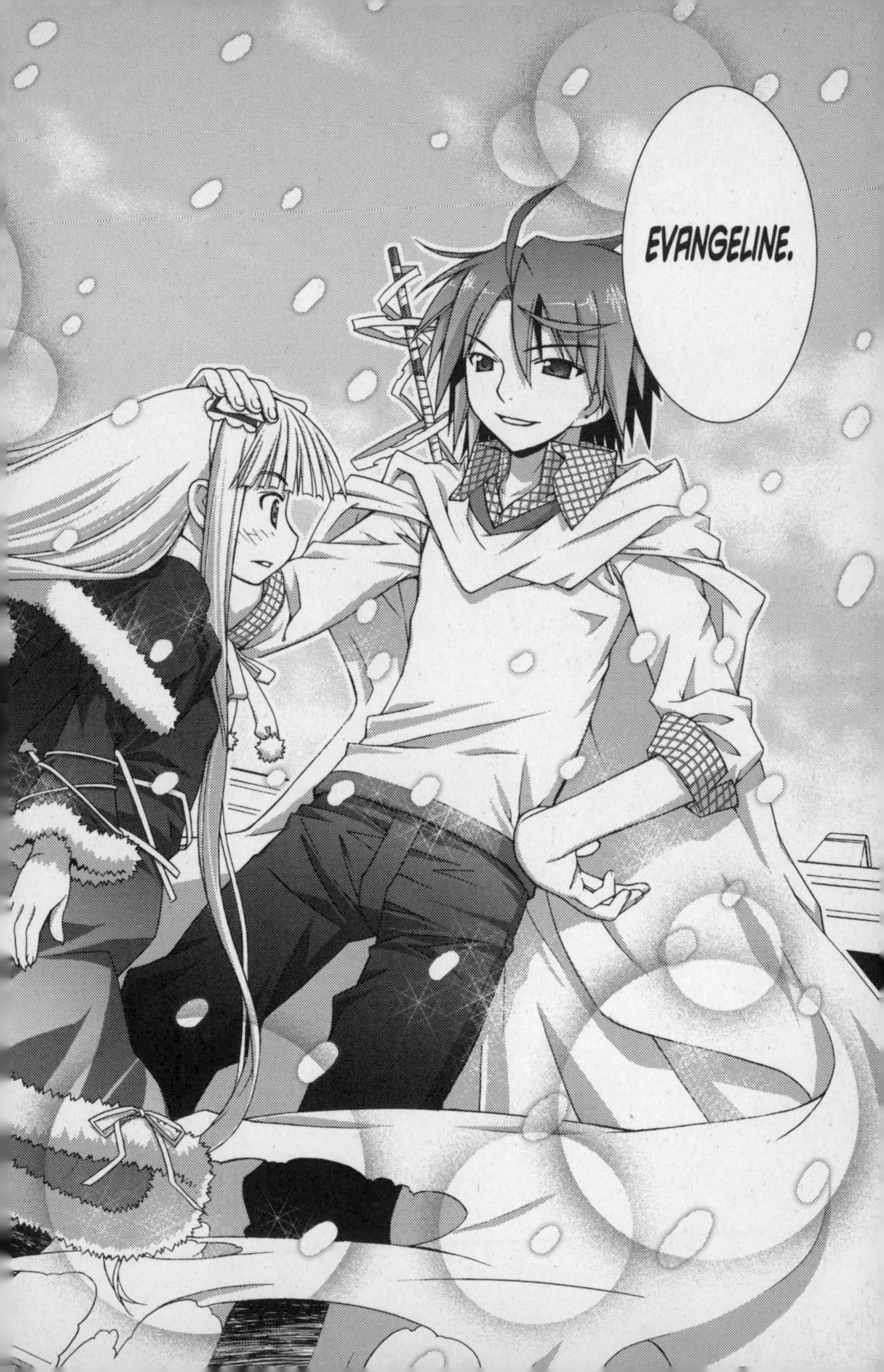
EVANGELINE.

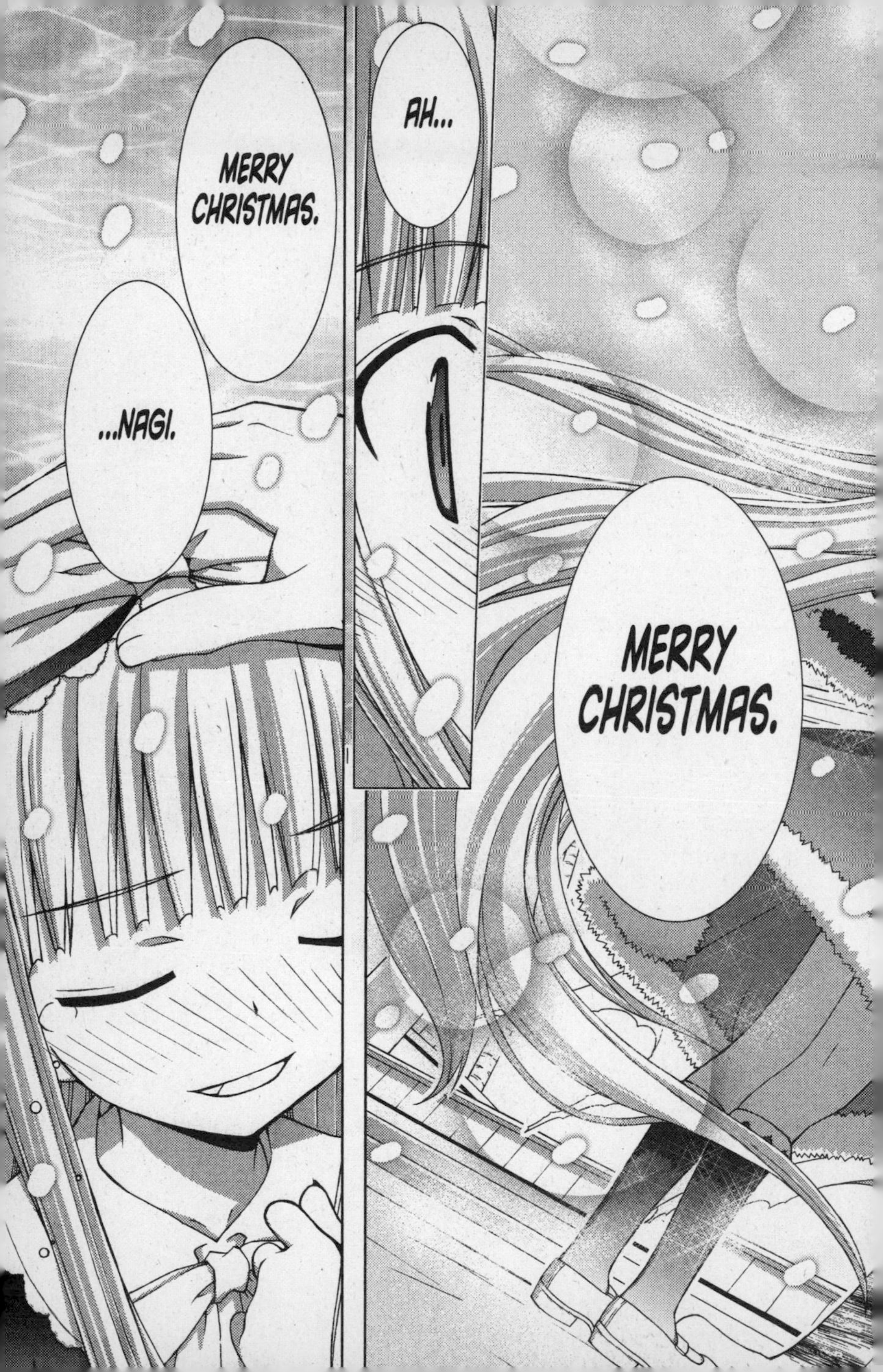
MERRY CHRISTMAS.
AH...
MERRY CHRISTMAS.
...NAGI.

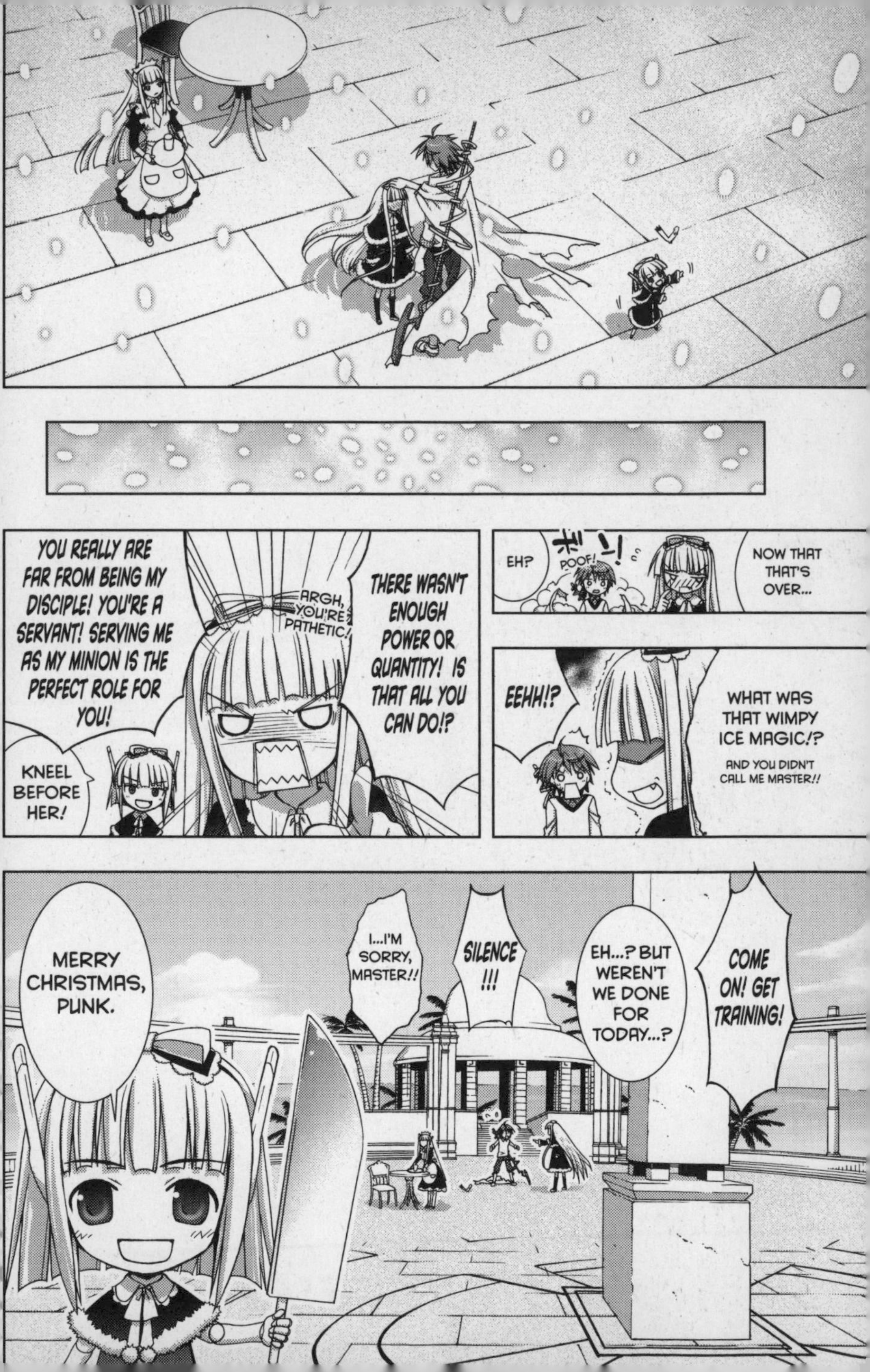
NOW THAT THAT'S OVER...
POOF!
EH?
WHAT WAS THAT WIMPY ICE MAGIC!?
AND YOU DIDN'T CALL ME MASTER!!
EEHH!?
THERE WASN'T ENOUGH POWER OR QUANTITY! IS THAT ALL YOU CAN DO!?
ARGH, YOU'RE PATHETIC!
YOU REALLY ARE FAR FROM BEING MY DISCIPLE! YOU'RE A SERVANT! SERVING ME AS MY MINION IS THE PERFECT ROLE FOR YOU!
KNEEL BEFORE HER!
COME ON! GET TRAINING!
EH...? BUT WEREN'T WE DONE FOR TODAY...?
SILENCE!!!
I...I'M SORRY, MASTER!!
MERRY CHRISTMAS, PUNK.

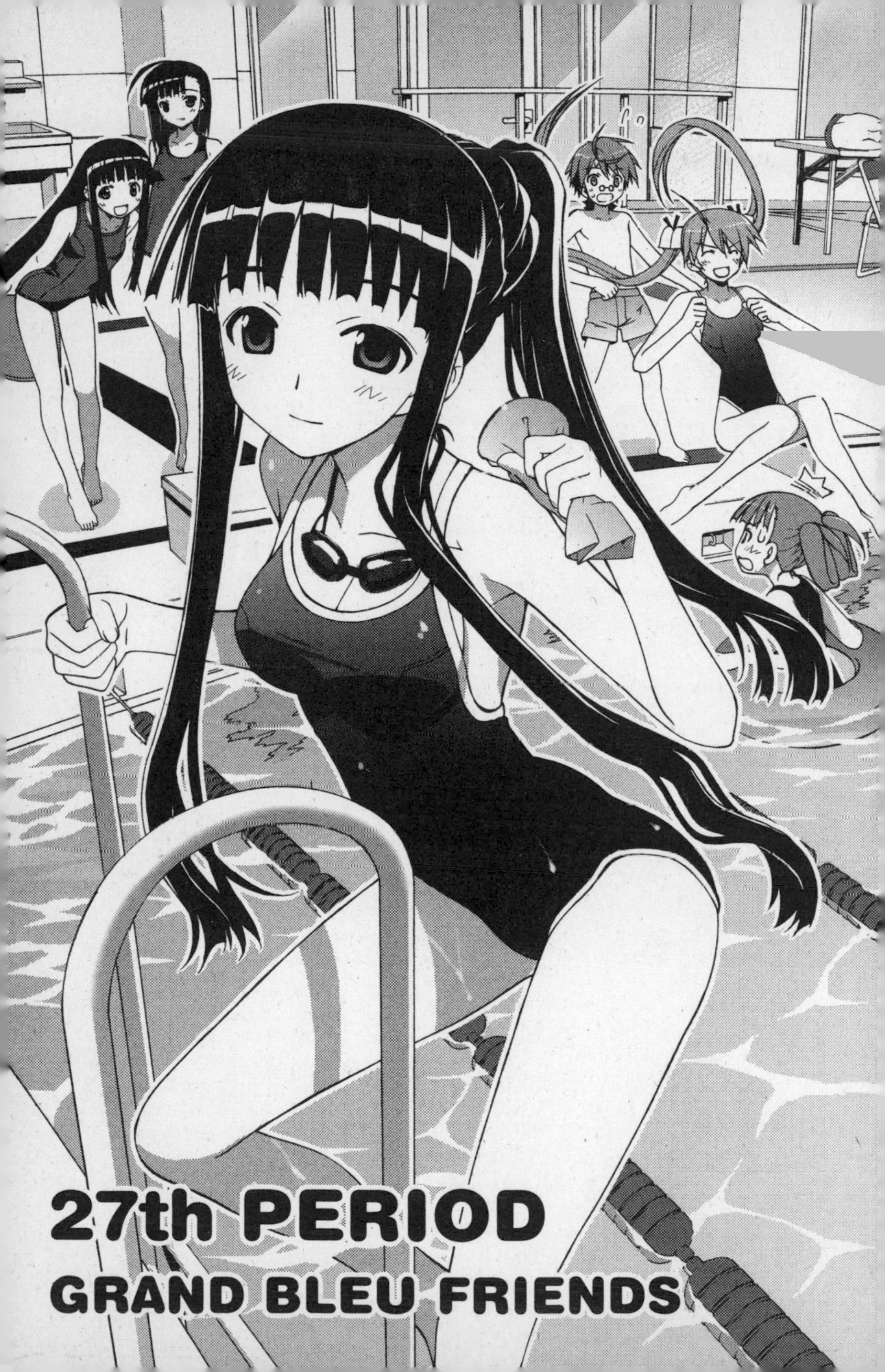
27th PERIOD
GRAND BLEU FRIENDS

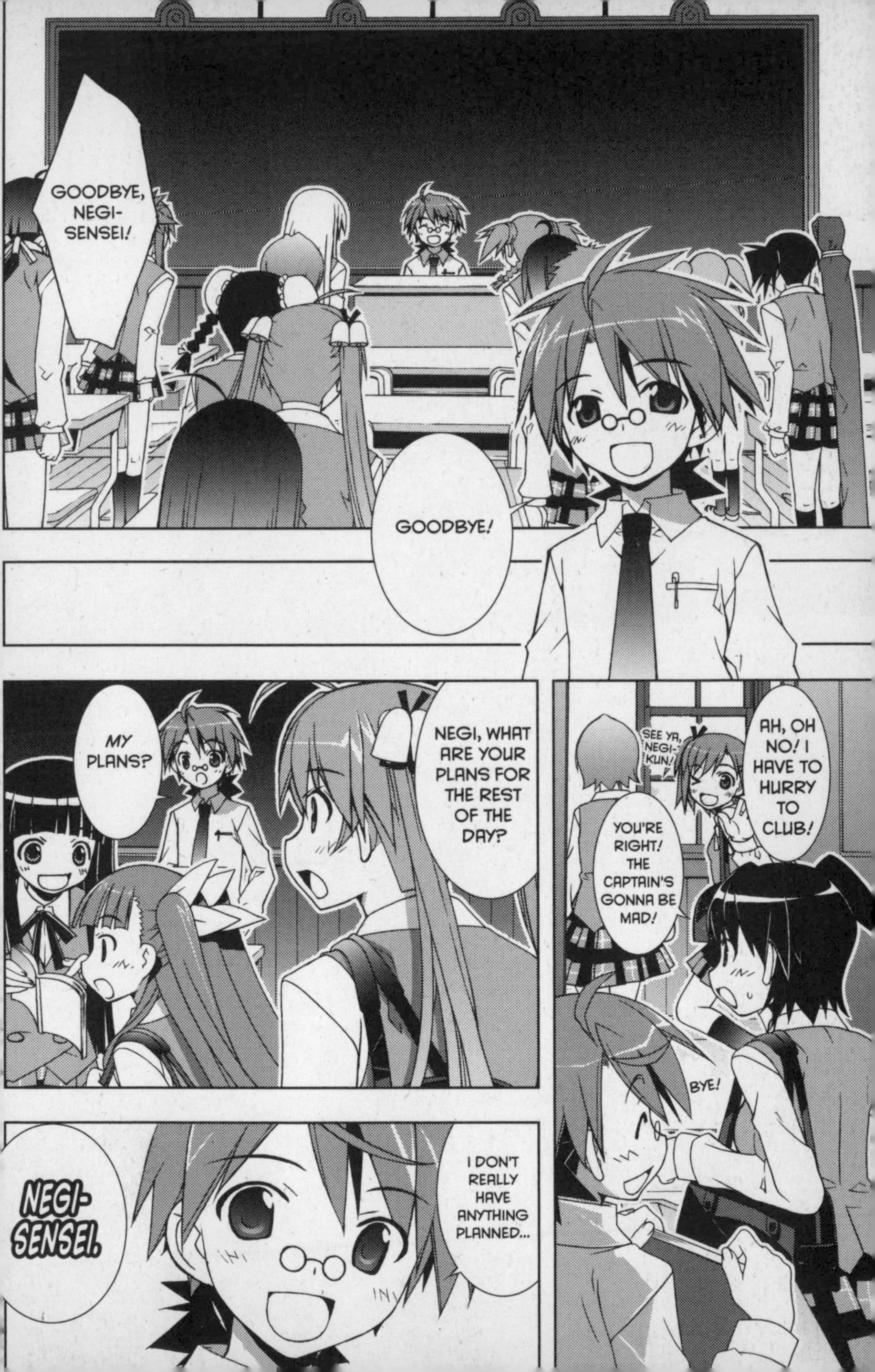
GOODBYE, NEGI-SENSEI!
GOODBYE!
AH, OH NO! I HAVE TO HURRY TO CLUB!
SEE YA, NEGI-KUN!
YOU'RE RIGHT! THE CAPTAIN'S GONNA BE MAD!
BYE!
NEGI, WHAT ARE YOUR PLANS FOR THE REST OF THE DAY?
MY PLANS?
I DON'T REALLY HAVE ANYTHING PLANNED...
NEGI-SENSEI.

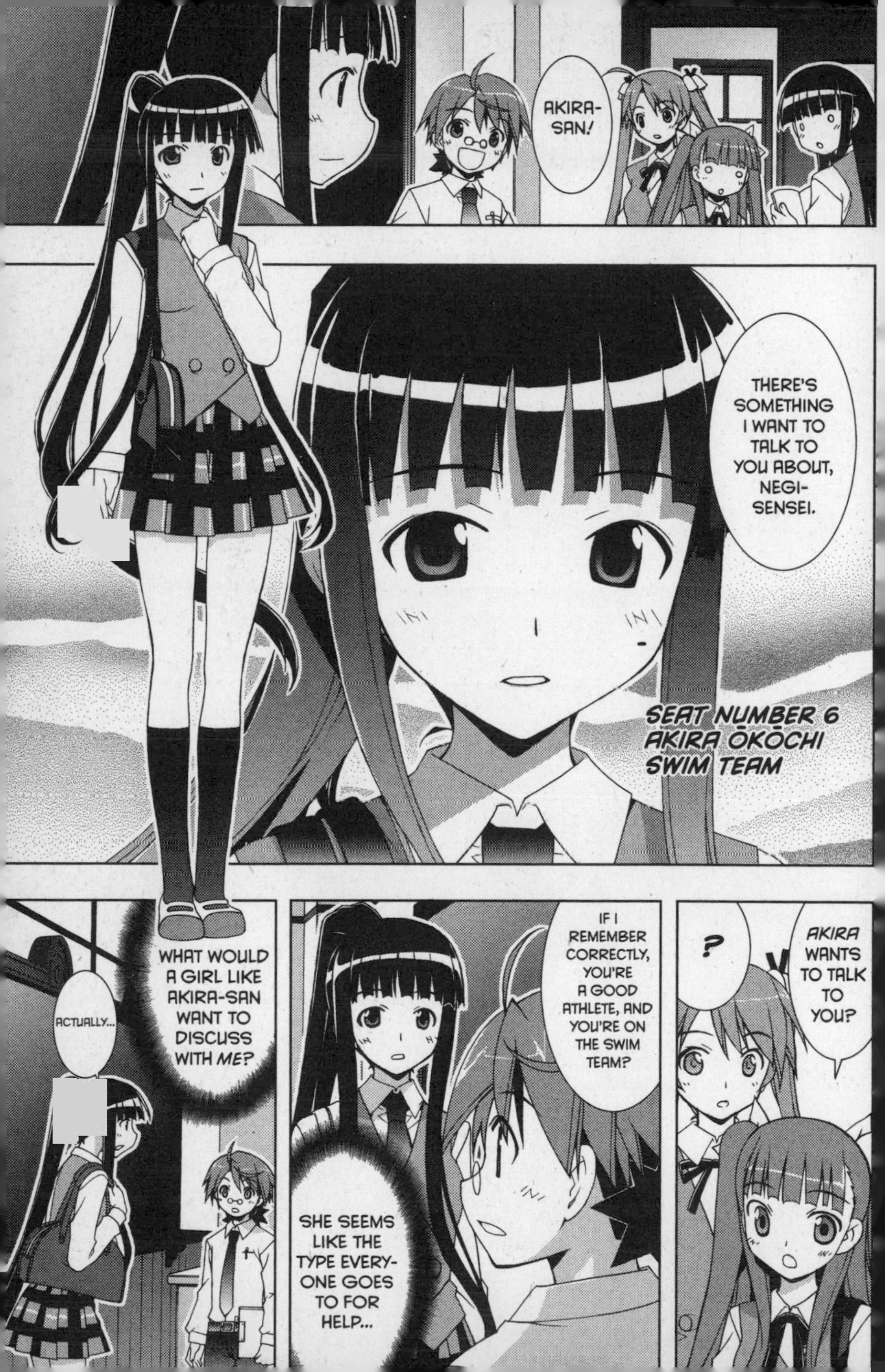
AKIRA-SAN!
THERE'S SOMETHING I WANT TO TALK TO YOU ABOUT, NEGI-SENSEI.
SEAT NUMBER 6 AKIRA ŌKŌCHI SWIM TEAM
?
AKIRA WANTS TO TALK TO YOU?
IF I REMEMBER CORRECTLY, YOU'RE A GOOD ATHLETE, AND YOU'RE ON THE SWIM TEAM?
SHE SEEMS LIKE THE TYPE EVERY-ONE GOES TO FOR HELP...
WHAT WOULD A GIRL LIKE AKIRA-SAN WANT TO DISCUSS WITH *ME*?
ACTUALLY...

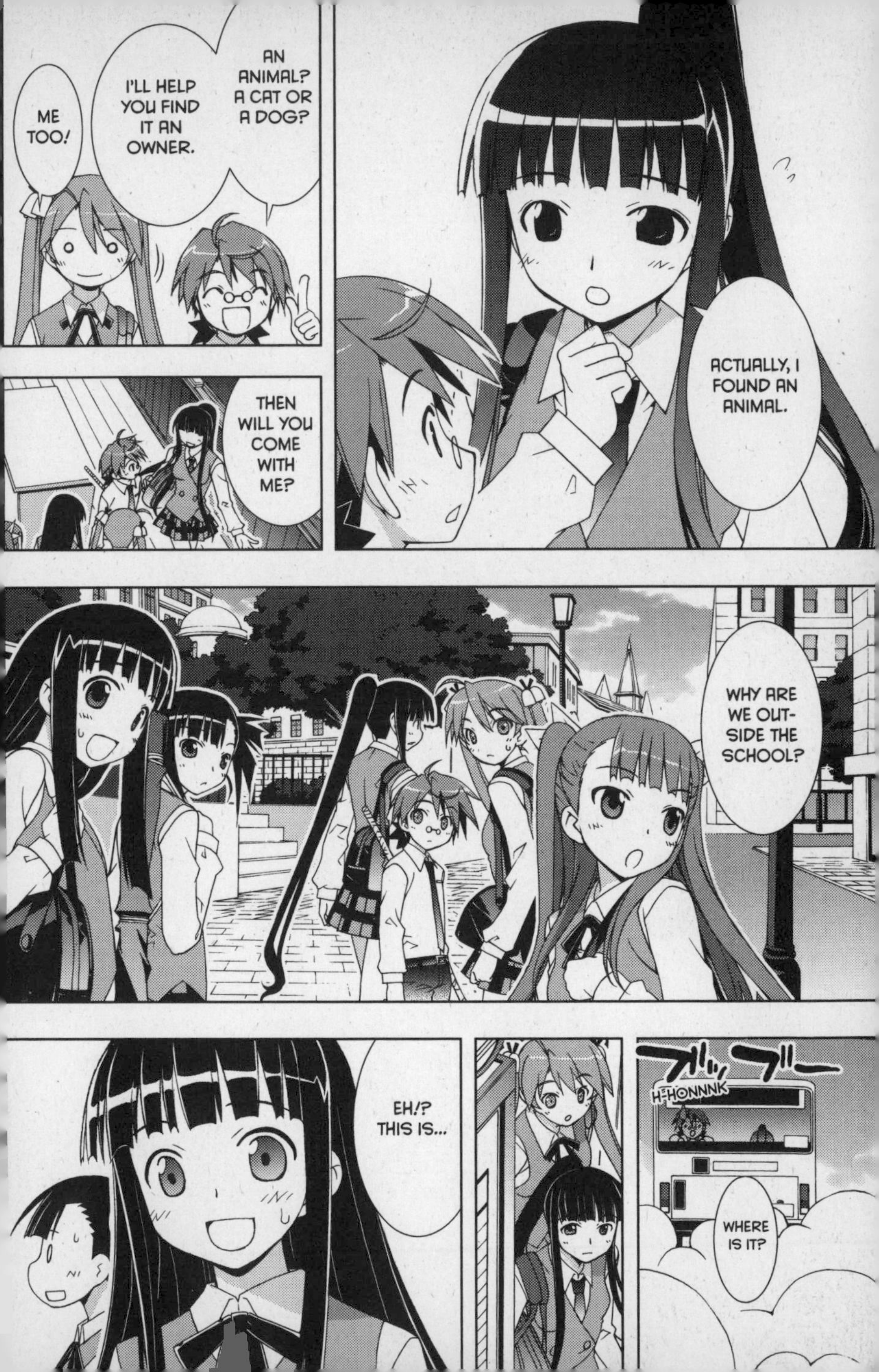
ACTUALLY, I FOUND AN ANIMAL.
AN ANIMAL? A CAT OR A DOG?
I'LL HELP YOU FIND IT AN OWNER.
ME TOO!
THEN WILL YOU COME WITH ME?
WHY ARE WE OUT-SIDE THE SCHOOL?
ブッ ブー
H-HONNNK
WHERE IS IT?
EH!? THIS IS...

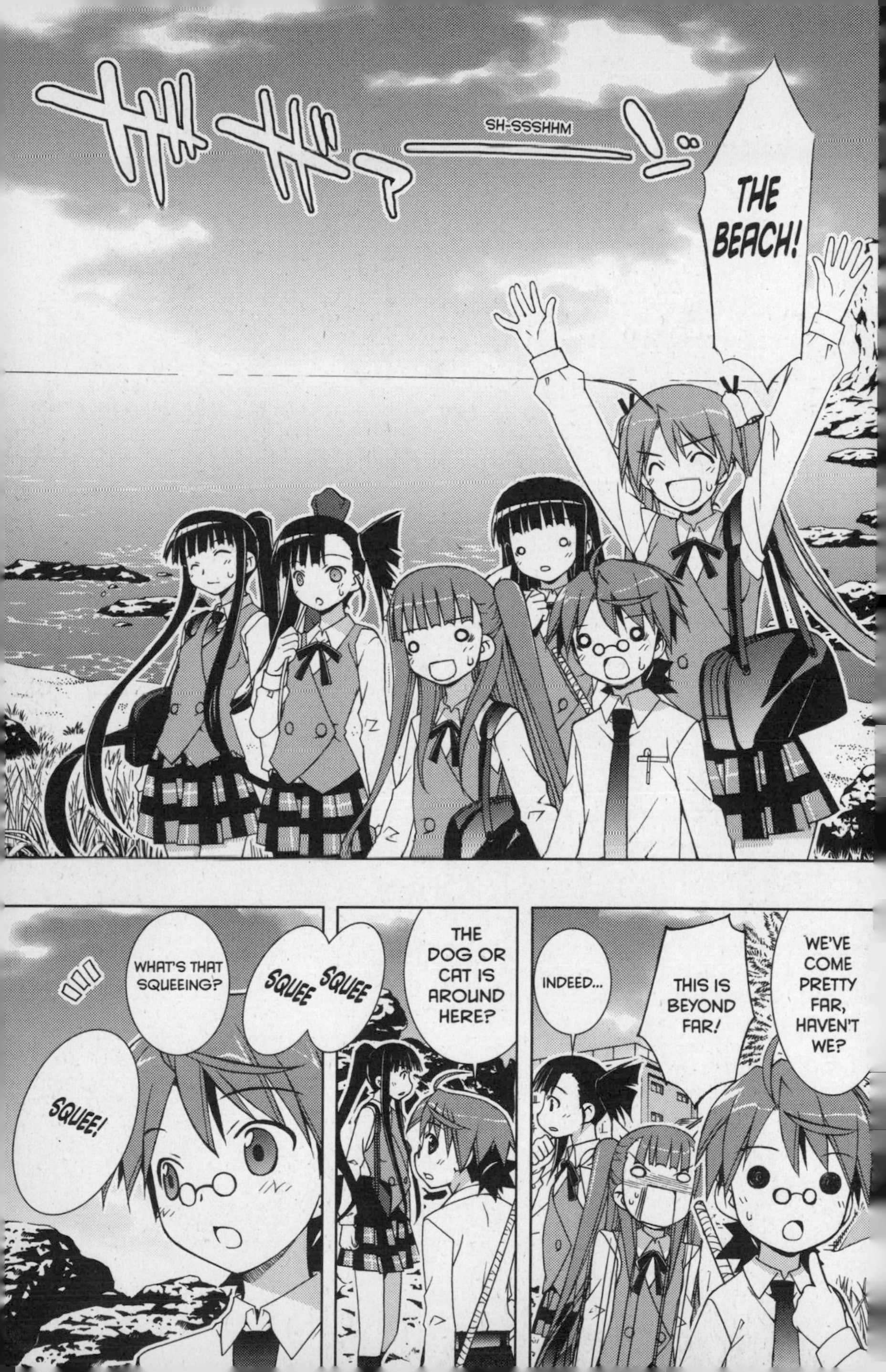
SH-SSSHHM
THE BEACH!
WE'VE COME PRETTY FAR, HAVEN'T WE?
THIS IS BEYOND FAR!
INDEED...
THE DOG OR CAT IS AROUND HERE?
SQUEE SQUEE
WHAT'S THAT SQUEEING?
!!!
SQUEE!

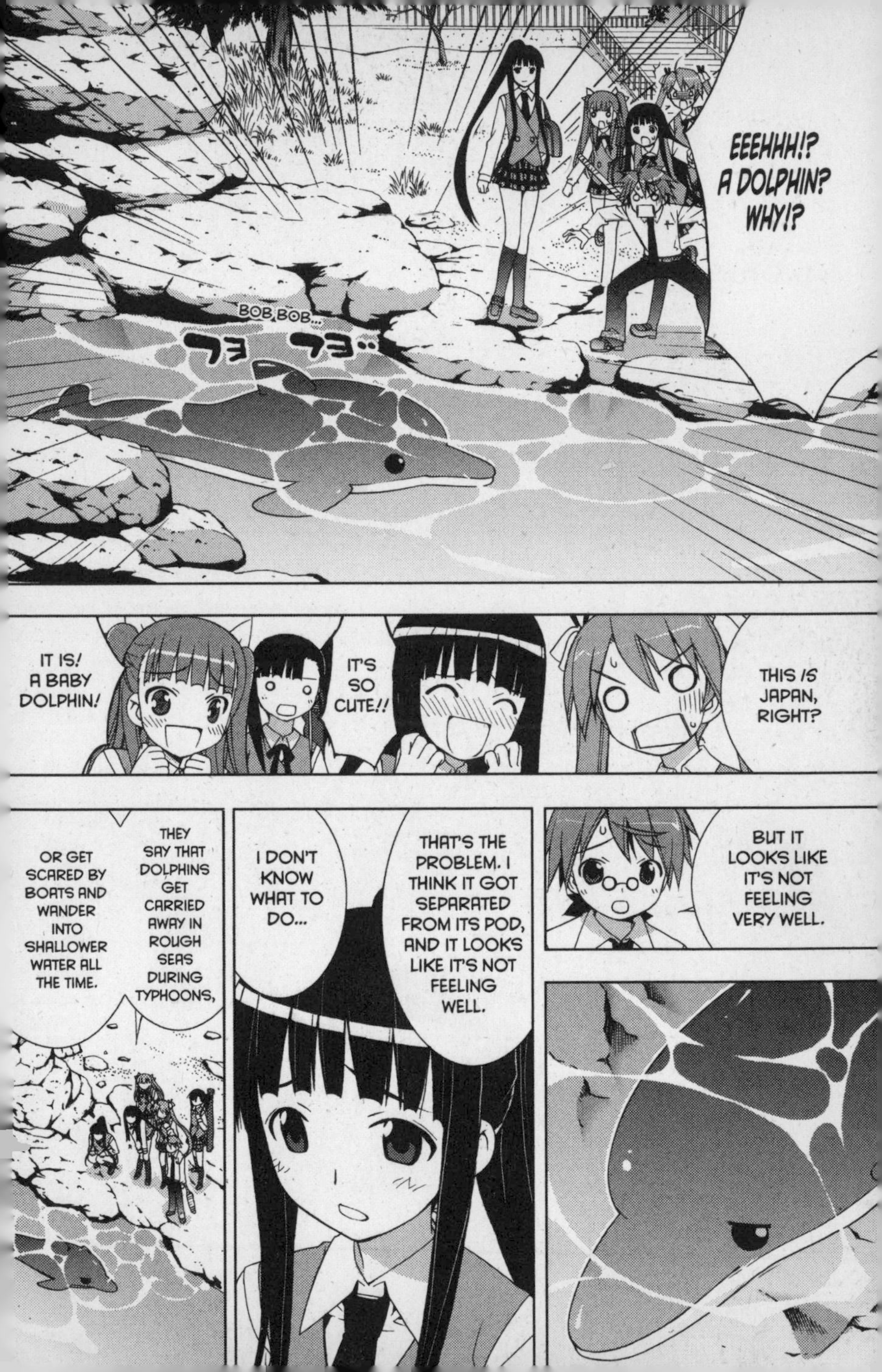
EEEHHH!? A DOLPHIN? WHY!?
BOB, BOB...
フヨ フヨ
THIS *IS* JAPAN, RIGHT?
IT'S SO CUTE!!
IT IS! A BABY DOLPHIN!
BUT IT LOOKS LIKE IT'S NOT FEELING VERY WELL.
THAT'S THE PROBLEM. I THINK IT GOT SEPARATED FROM ITS POD, AND IT LOOKS LIKE IT'S NOT FEELING WELL.
I DON'T KNOW WHAT TO DO...
THEY SAY THAT DOLPHINS GET CARRIED AWAY IN ROUGH SEAS DURING TYPHOONS,
OR GET SCARED BY BOATS AND WANDER INTO SHALLOWER WATER ALL THE TIME.

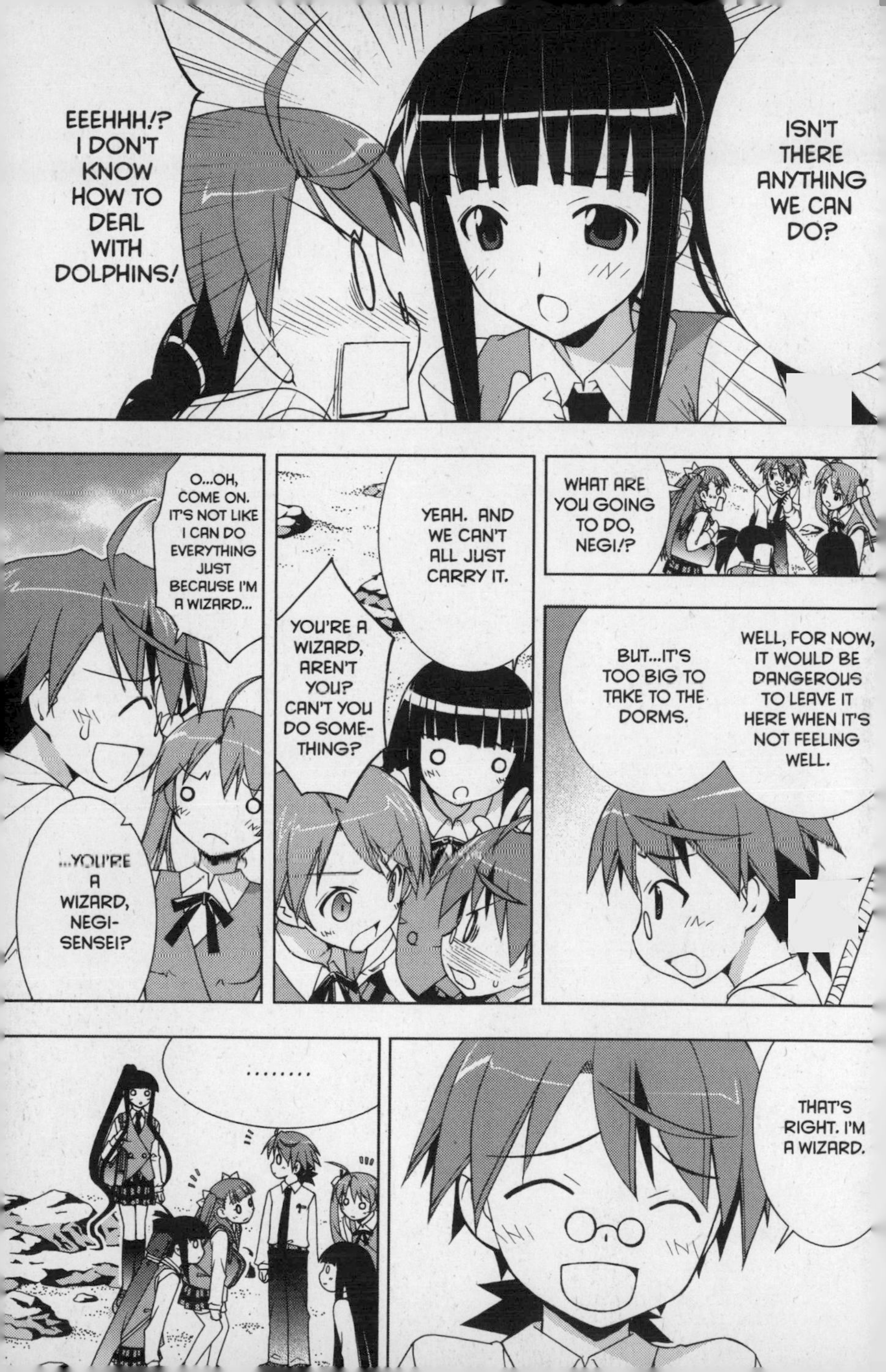
ISN'T THERE ANYTHING WE CAN DO?
EEEHHH!? I DON'T KNOW HOW TO DEAL WITH DOLPHINS!
WHAT ARE YOU GOING TO DO, NEGI!?
WELL, FOR NOW, IT WOULD BE DANGEROUS TO LEAVE IT HERE WHEN IT'S NOT FEELING WELL.
BUT...IT'S TOO BIG TO TAKE TO THE DORMS.
YEAH. AND WE CAN'T ALL JUST CARRY IT.
YOU'RE A WIZARD, AREN'T YOU? CAN'T YOU DO SOME-THING?
O...OH, COME ON. IT'S NOT LIKE I CAN DO EVERYTHING JUST BECAUSE I'M A WIZARD...
...YOU'RE A WIZARD, NEGI-SENSEI?
THAT'S RIGHT. I'M A WIZARD.
.........

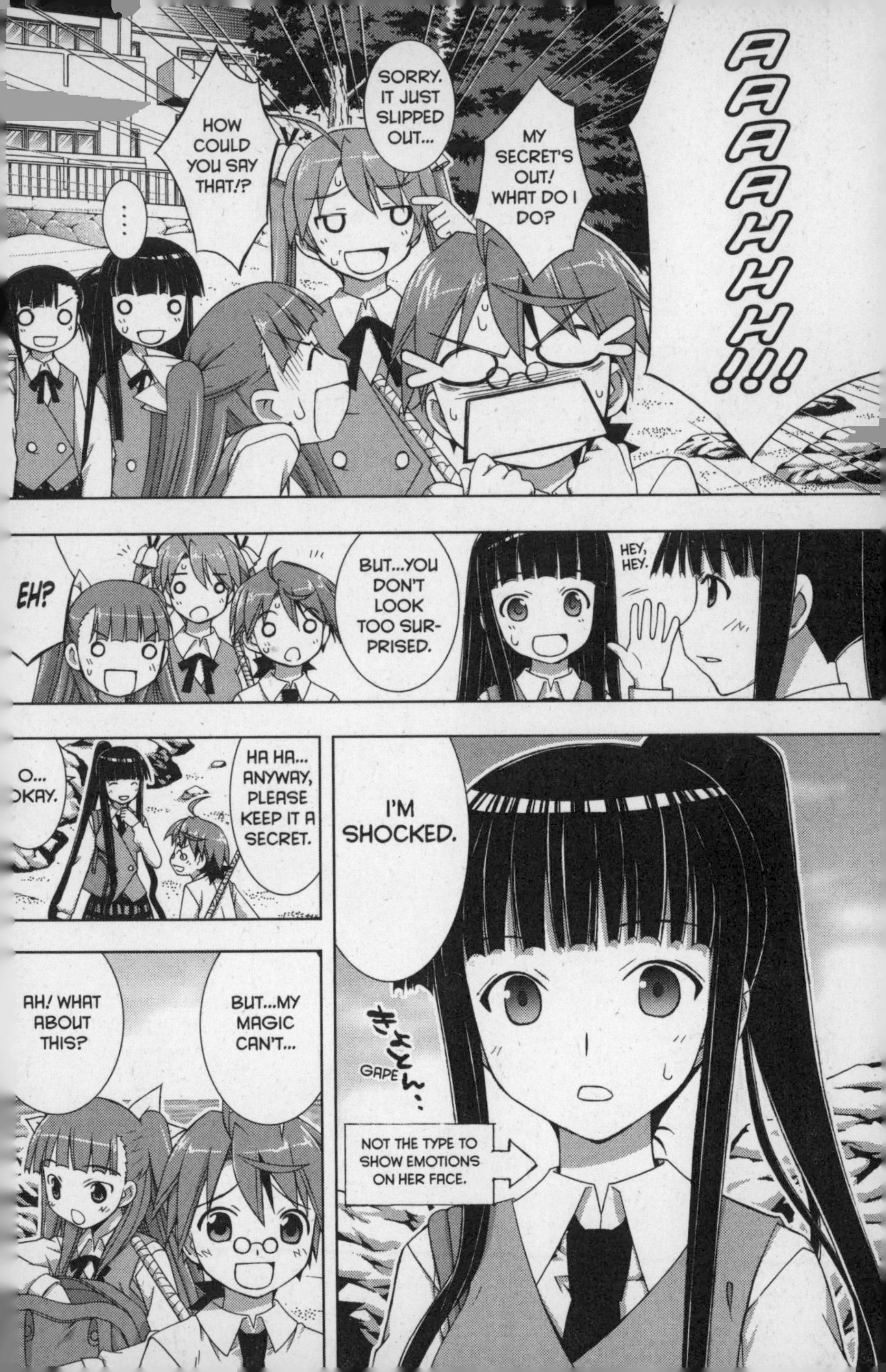
AAAAAHHH!!!
MY SECRET'S OUT! WHAT DO I DO?
SORRY. IT JUST SLIPPED OUT...
HOW COULD YOU SAY THAT!?
....
HEY, HEY.
BUT...YOU DON'T LOOK TOO SURPRISED.
EH?
I'M SHOCKED.
きょとん
GAPE
NOT THE TYPE TO SHOW EMOTIONS ON HER FACE.
HA HA... ANYWAY, PLEASE KEEP IT A SECRET.
O... OKAY.
BUT...MY MAGIC CAN'T...
AH! WHAT ABOUT THIS?

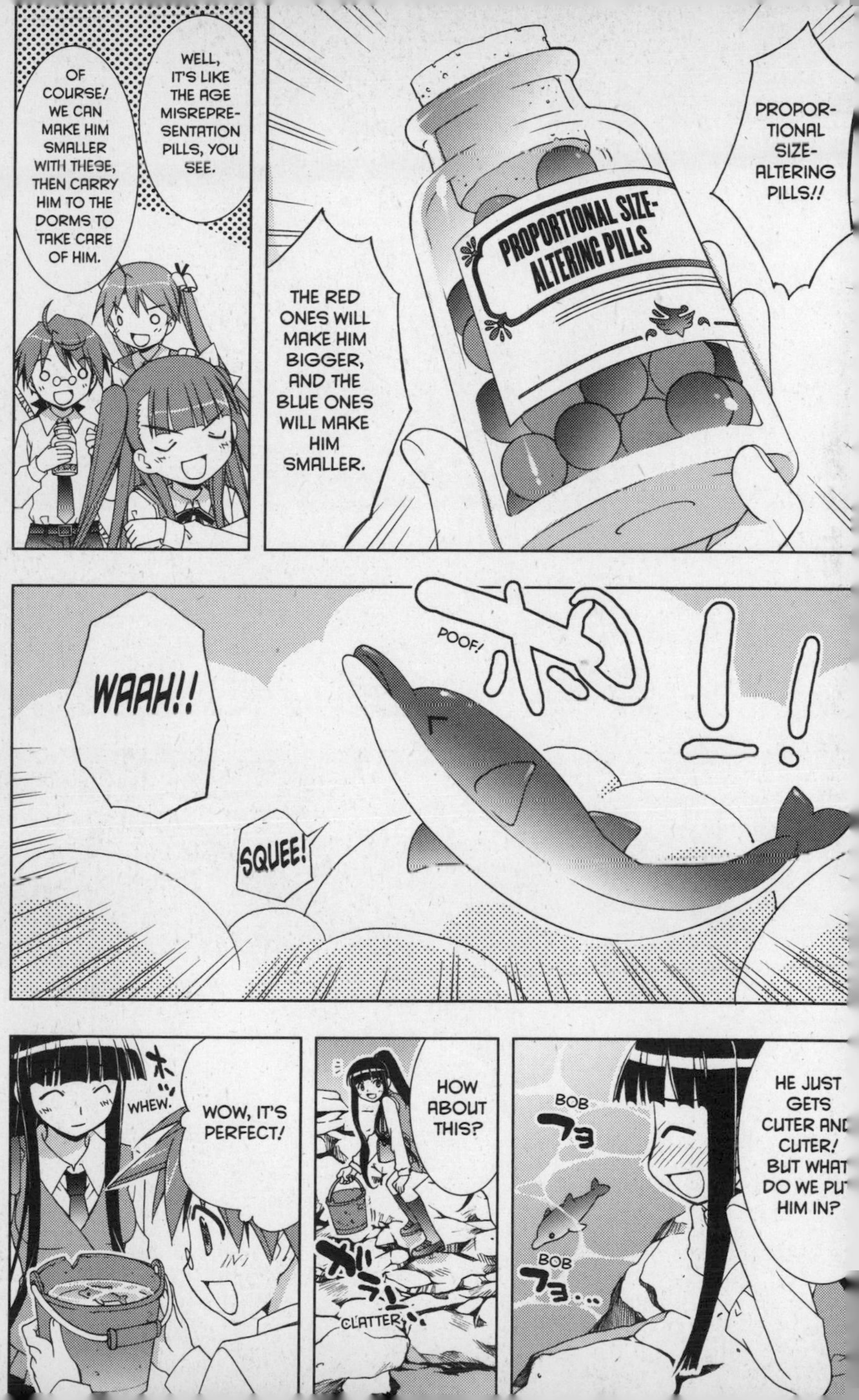
PROPORTIONAL SIZE-ALTERING PILLS!!
PROPORTIONAL SIZE-ALTERING PILLS
THE RED ONES WILL MAKE HIM BIGGER, AND THE BLUE ONES WILL MAKE HIM SMALLER.
WELL, IT'S LIKE THE AGE MISREPRESENTATION PILLS, YOU SEE.
OF COURSE! WE CAN MAKE HIM SMALLER WITH THESE, THEN CARRY HIM TO THE DORMS TO TAKE CARE OF HIM.
POOF!
WAAH!!
SQUEE!
HE JUST GETS CUTER AND CUTER! BUT WHAT DO WE PUT HIM IN?
BOB
BOB
HOW ABOUT THIS?
CLATTER
WHEW.
WOW, IT'S PERFECT!

WE'LL KEEP HIM IN OUR ROOM FOR NOW. IF THE OTHER STUDENTS SEE HIM, IT COULD CAUSE A LOT OF TROUBLE.

WELL, WE'VE GOT HIM IN THE DORMS, BUT WHAT DO WE DO WITH HIM?

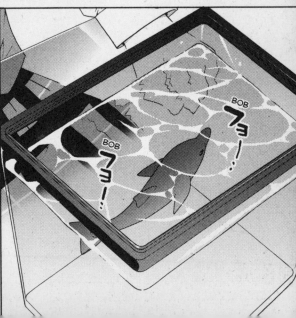

BOB
ブヨ...!

BOB
ブヨ...!

HE REALLY DOESN'T LOOK WELL.

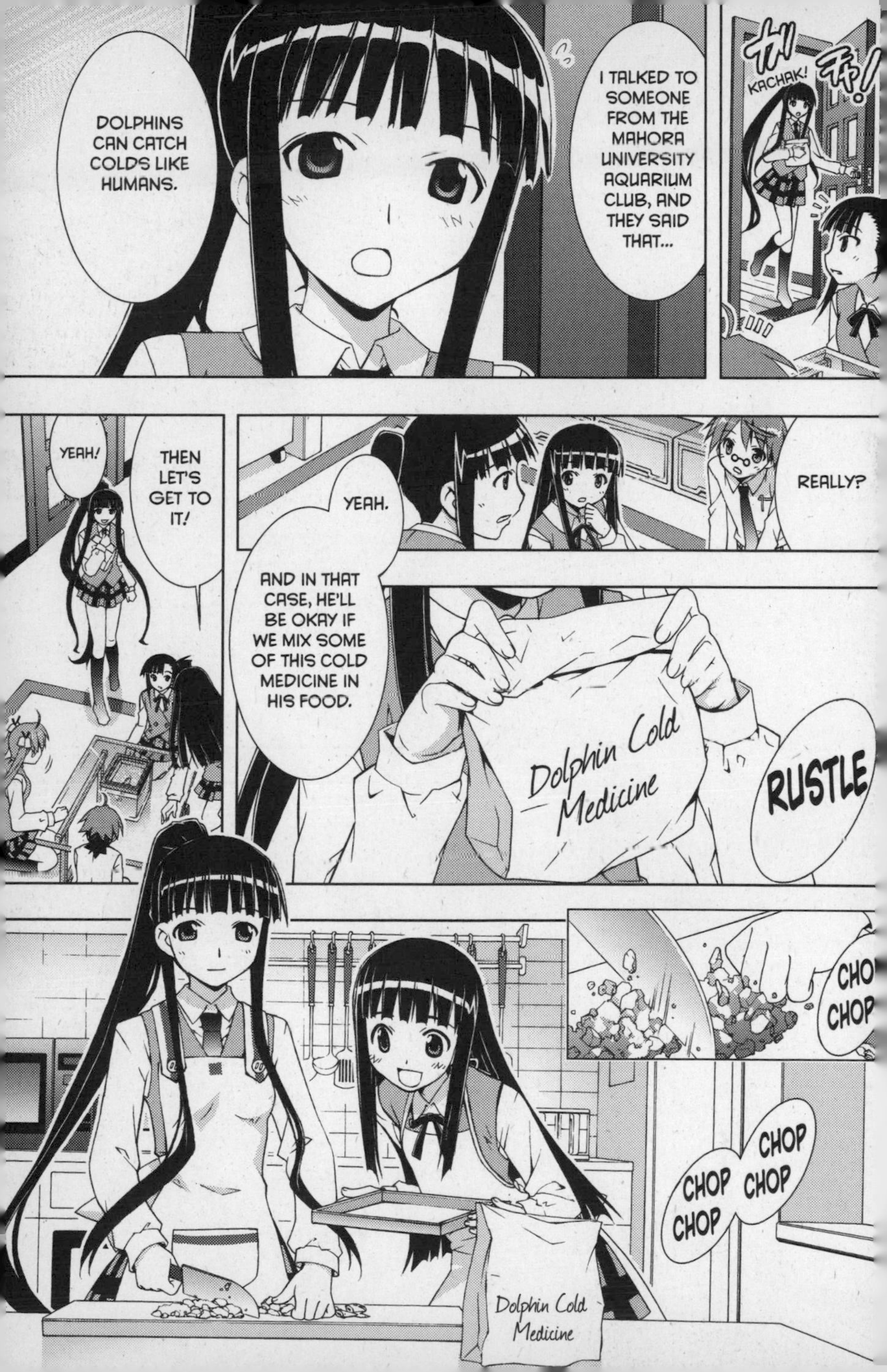
KACHAK!
I TALKED TO SOMEONE FROM THE MAHORA UNIVERSITY AQUARIUM CLUB, AND THEY SAID THAT...
DOLPHINS CAN CATCH COLDS LIKE HUMANS.
REALLY?
YEAH.
AND IN THAT CASE, HE'LL BE OKAY IF WE MIX SOME OF THIS COLD MEDICINE IN HIS FOOD.
RUSTLE
Dolphin Cold Medicine
THEN LET'S GET TO IT!
YEAH!
CHOP CHOP
CHOP CHOP
CHOP CHOP
Dolphin Cold Medicine

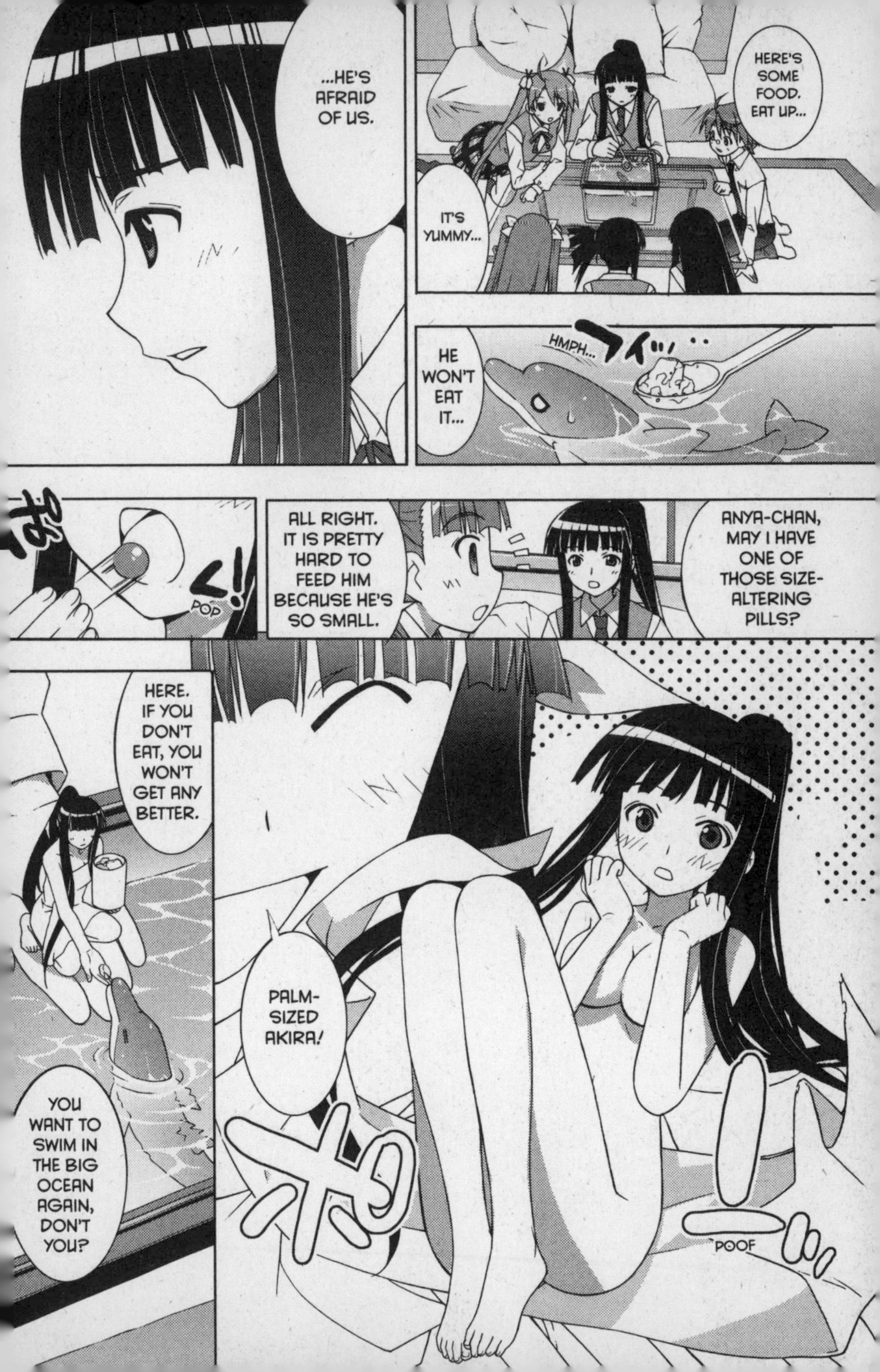
HERE'S SOME FOOD. EAT UP...
IT'S YUMMY...
HMPH...
HE WON'T EAT IT...
...HE'S AFRAID OF US.
ANYA-CHAN, MAY I HAVE ONE OF THOSE SIZE-ALTERING PILLS?
ALL RIGHT. IT IS PRETTY HARD TO FEED HIM BECAUSE HE'S SO SMALL.
POP
POOF
PALM-SIZED AKIRA!
HERE. IF YOU DON'T EAT, YOU WON'T GET ANY BETTER.
YOU WANT TO SWIM IN THE BIG OCEAN AGAIN, DON'T YOU?

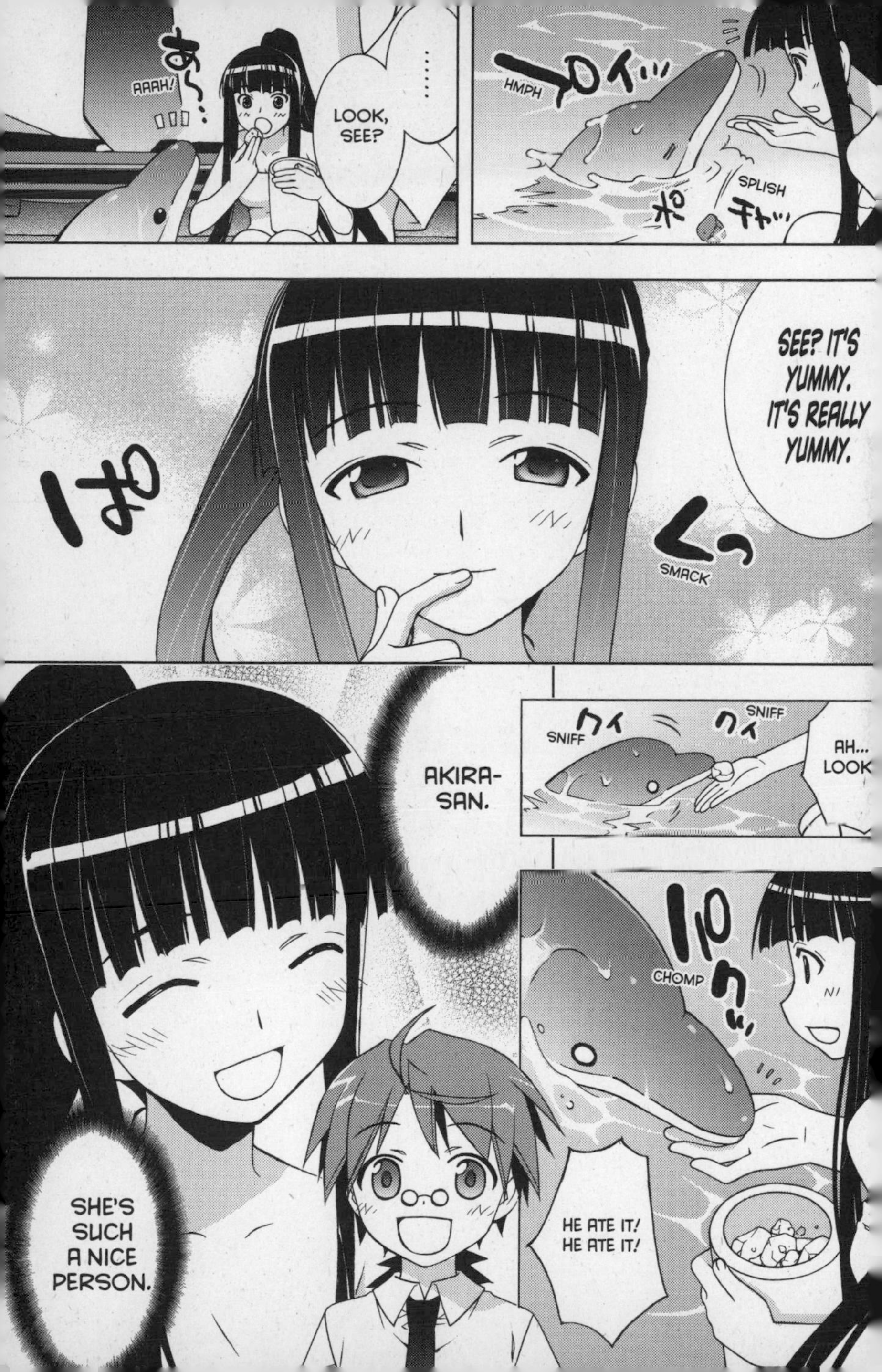
HMPH
SPLISH
......
LOOK, SEE?
AAAH!
SEE? IT'S YUMMY. IT'S REALLY YUMMY.
SMACK
AH... LOOK
SNIFF
SNIFF
CHOMP
HE ATE IT! HE ATE IT!
AKIRA-SAN.
SHE'S SUCH A NICE PERSON.

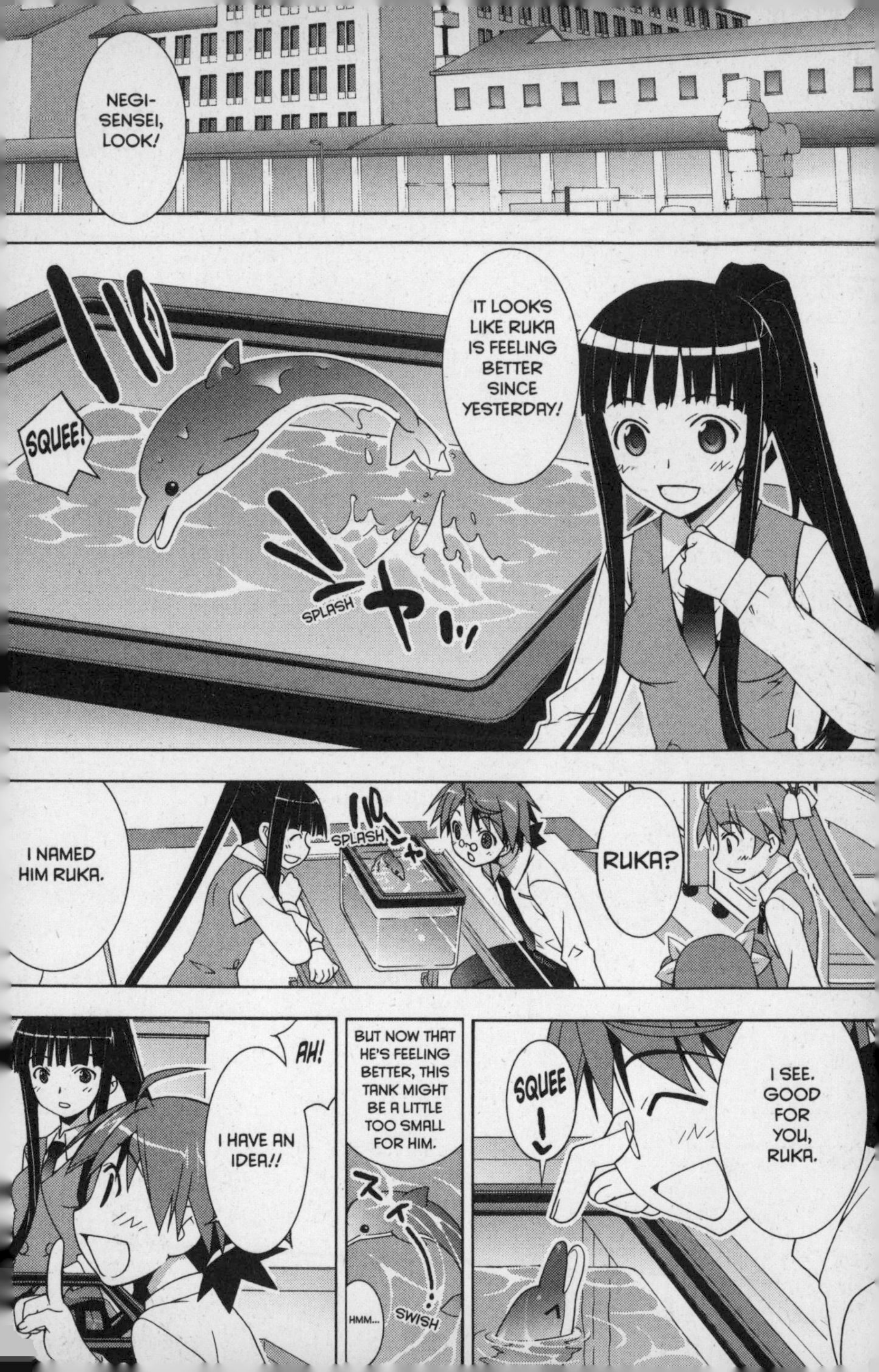

NEGI-SENSEI, LOOK!
IT LOOKS LIKE RUKA IS FEELING BETTER SINCE YESTERDAY!
SQUEE!
SPLASH
RUKA?
SPLASH
I NAMED HIM RUKA.
I SEE. GOOD FOR YOU, RUKA.
SQUEE
BUT NOW THAT HE'S FEELING BETTER, THIS TANK MIGHT BE A LITTLE TOO SMALL FOR HIM.
SWISH
HMM...
AH!
I HAVE AN IDEA!!

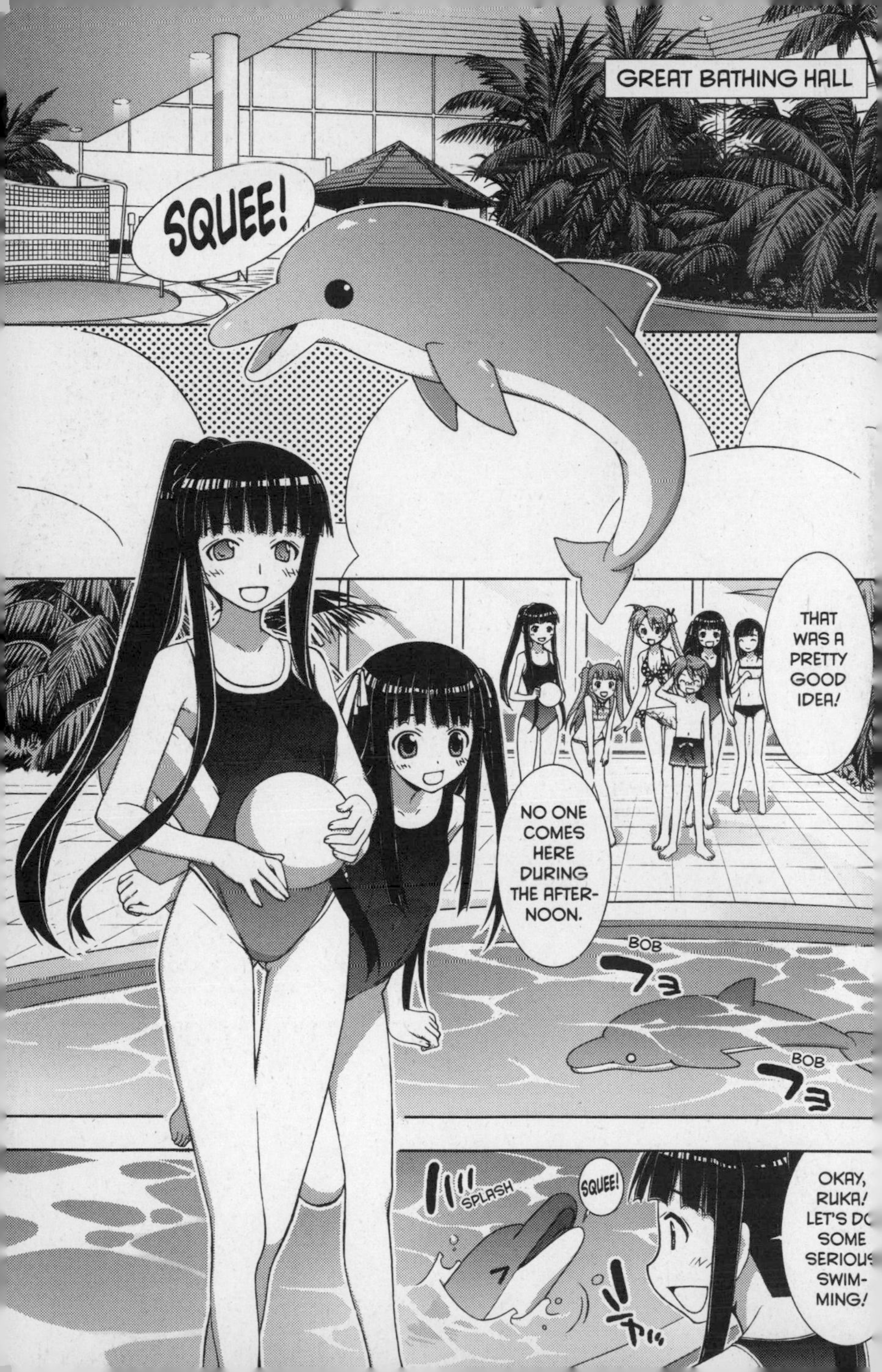

GREAT BATHING HALL
SQUEE!
THAT WAS A PRETTY GOOD IDEA!
NO ONE COMES HERE DURING THE AFTER-NOON.
BOB
BOB
OKAY, RUKA! LET'S DO SOME SERIOUS SWIM-MING!
SQUEE!
SPLASH

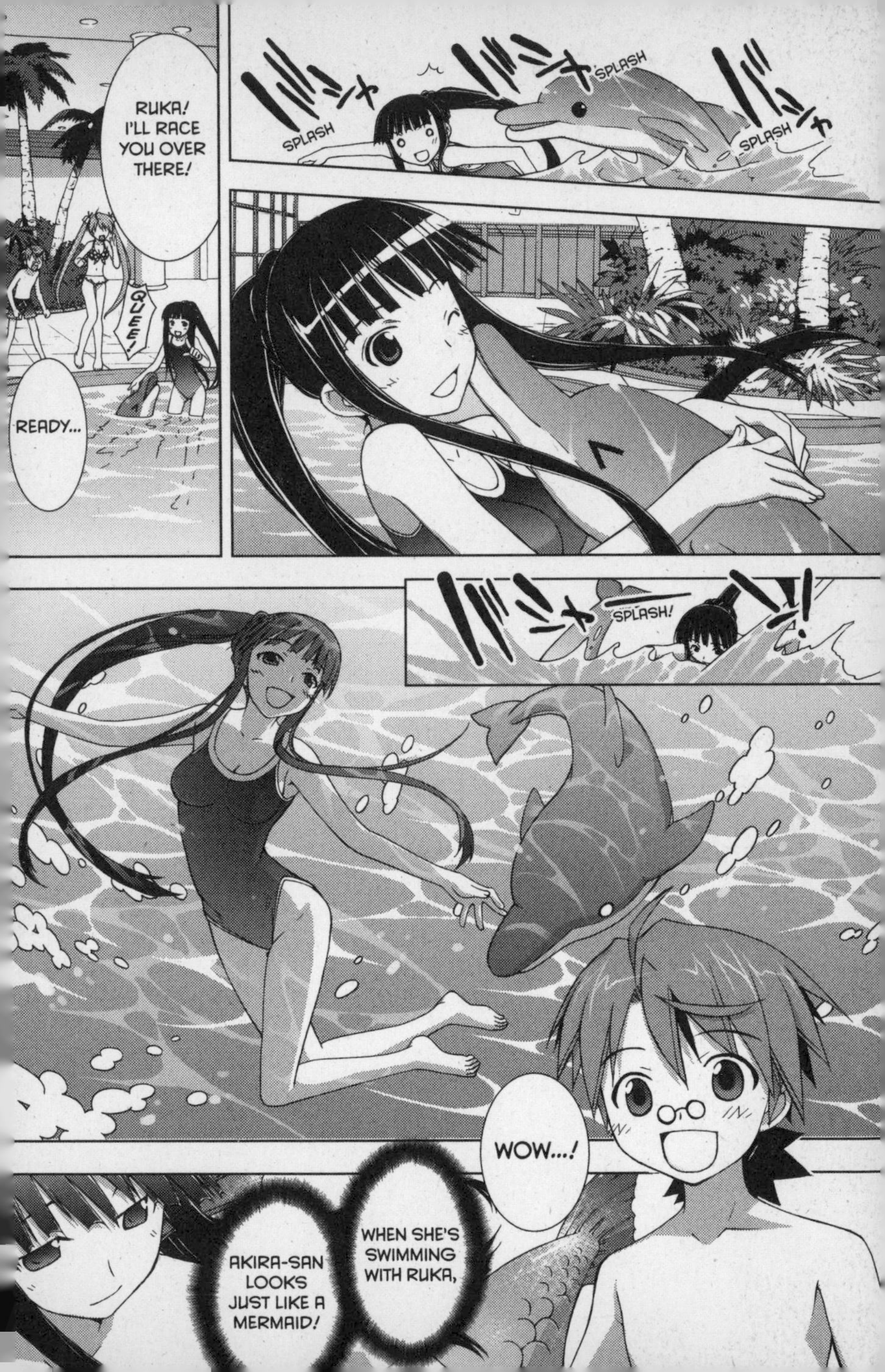
SPLASH
SPLASH
SPLASH
RUKA! I'LL RACE YOU OVER THERE!
QUEEE!
READY...
SPLASH!
WOW...!
WHEN SHE'S SWIMMING WITH RUKA,
AKIRA-SAN LOOKS JUST LIKE A MERMAID!

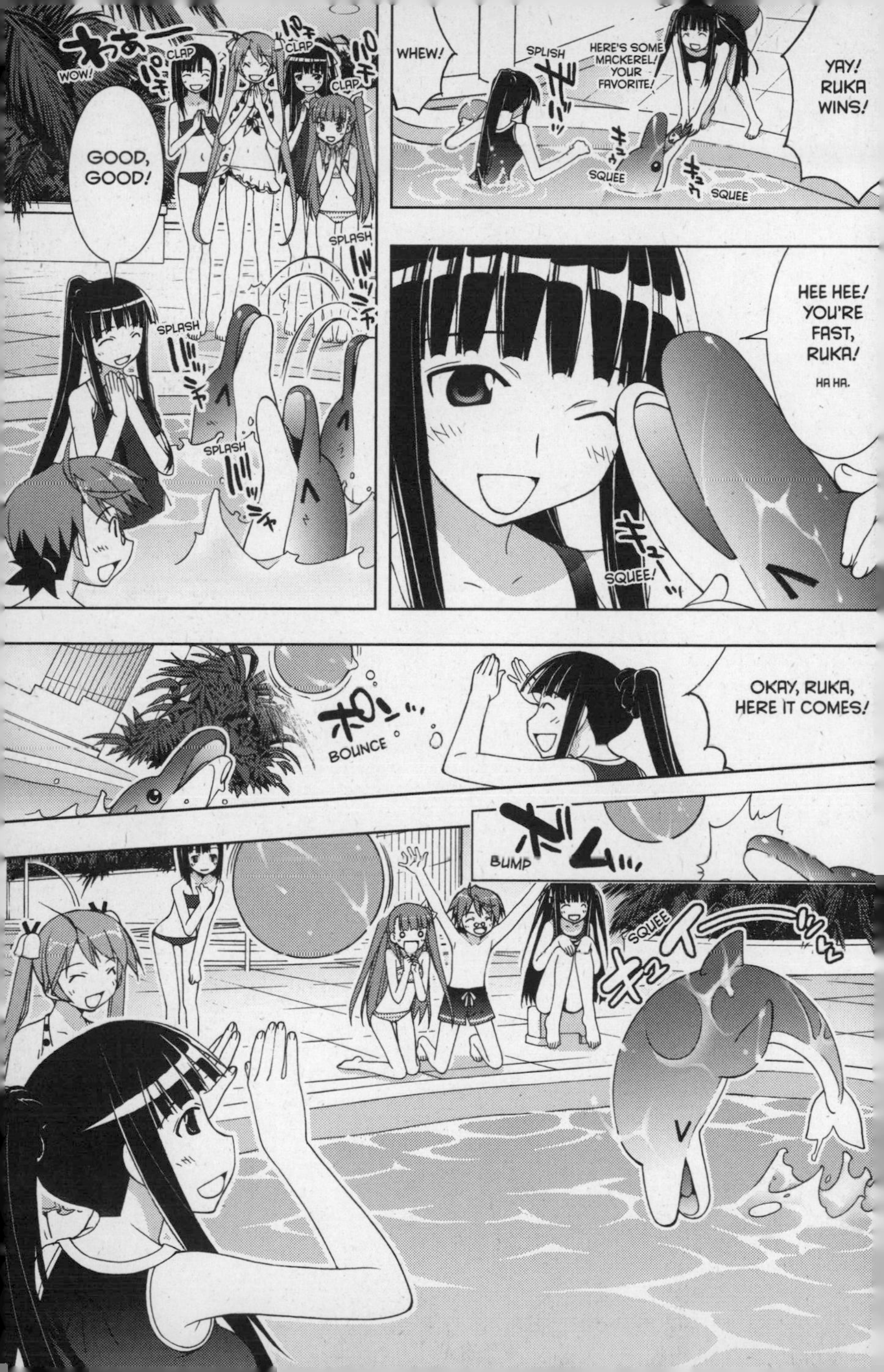
YAY! RUKA WINS!
HERE'S SOME MACKEREL! YOUR FAVORITE!
SPLISH
WHEW!
SQUEE
SQUEE
HEE HEE! YOU'RE FAST, RUKA!
HA HA.
SQUEE!
CLAP
CLAP
CLAP
WOW!
GOOD, GOOD!
SPLASH
SPLASH
SPLASH
OKAY, RUKA, HERE IT COMES!
BOUNCE
BUMP
SQUEE

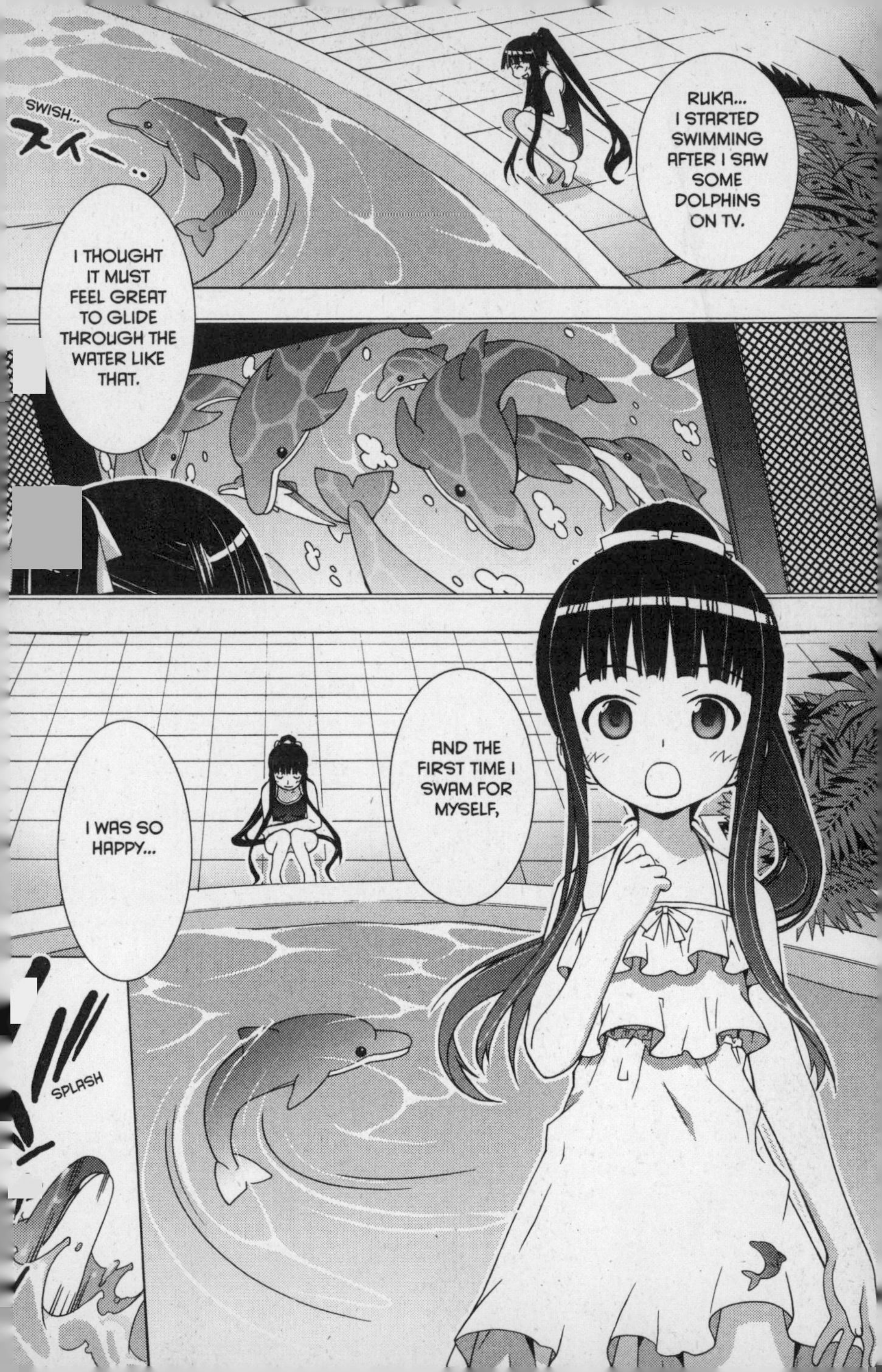
RUKA... I STARTED SWIMMING AFTER I SAW SOME DOLPHINS ON TV.
SWISH...
スイー‥
I THOUGHT IT MUST FEEL GREAT TO GLIDE THROUGH THE WATER LIKE THAT.
AND THE FIRST TIME I SWAM FOR MYSELF,
I WAS SO HAPPY...
SPLASH

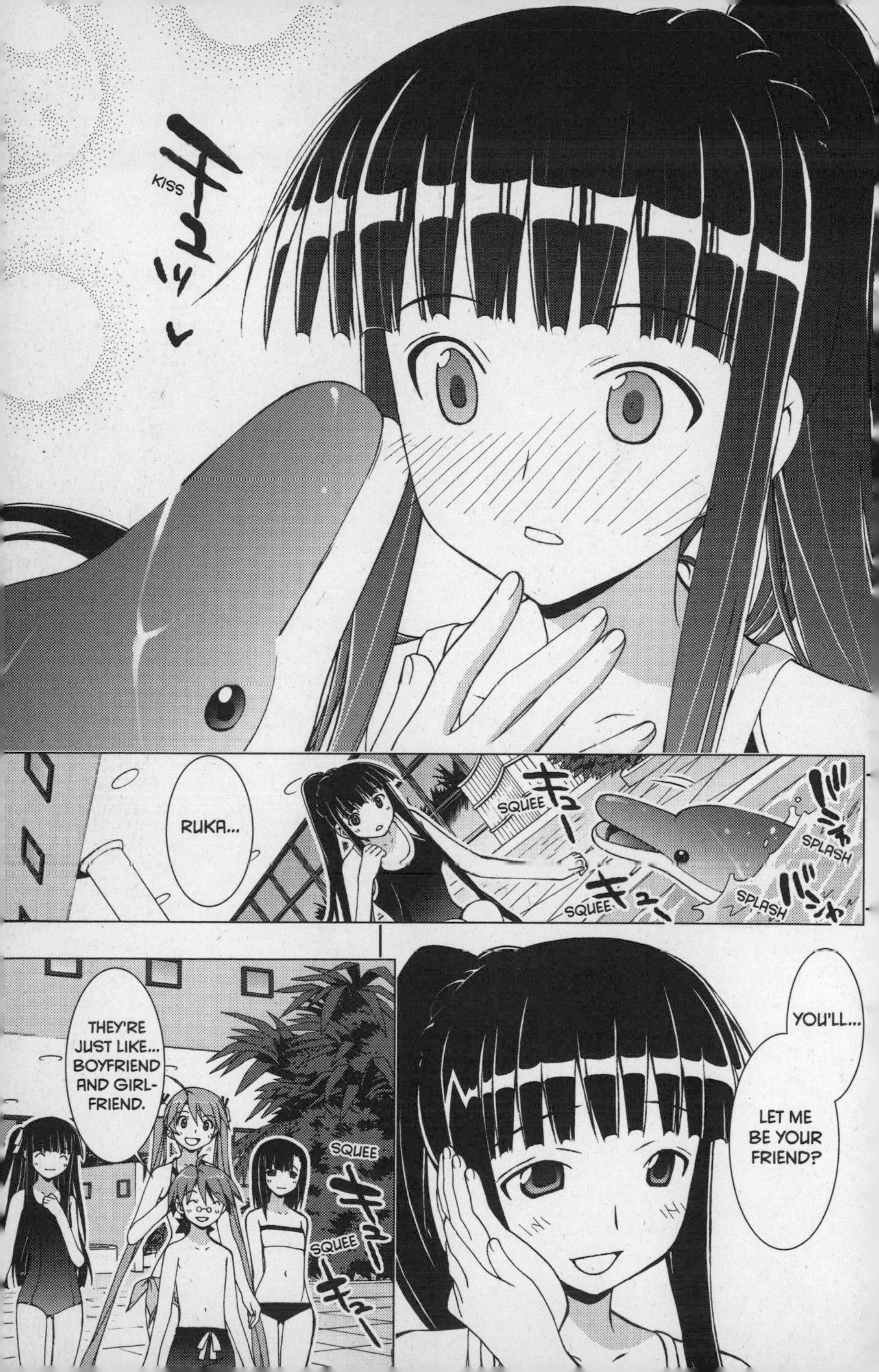
KISS
SPLASH
SQUEE
SPLASH
SQUEE
RUKA...
YOU'LL...
LET ME BE YOUR FRIEND?
THEY'RE JUST LIKE... BOYFRIEND AND GIRL-FRIEND.
SQUEE
SQUEE

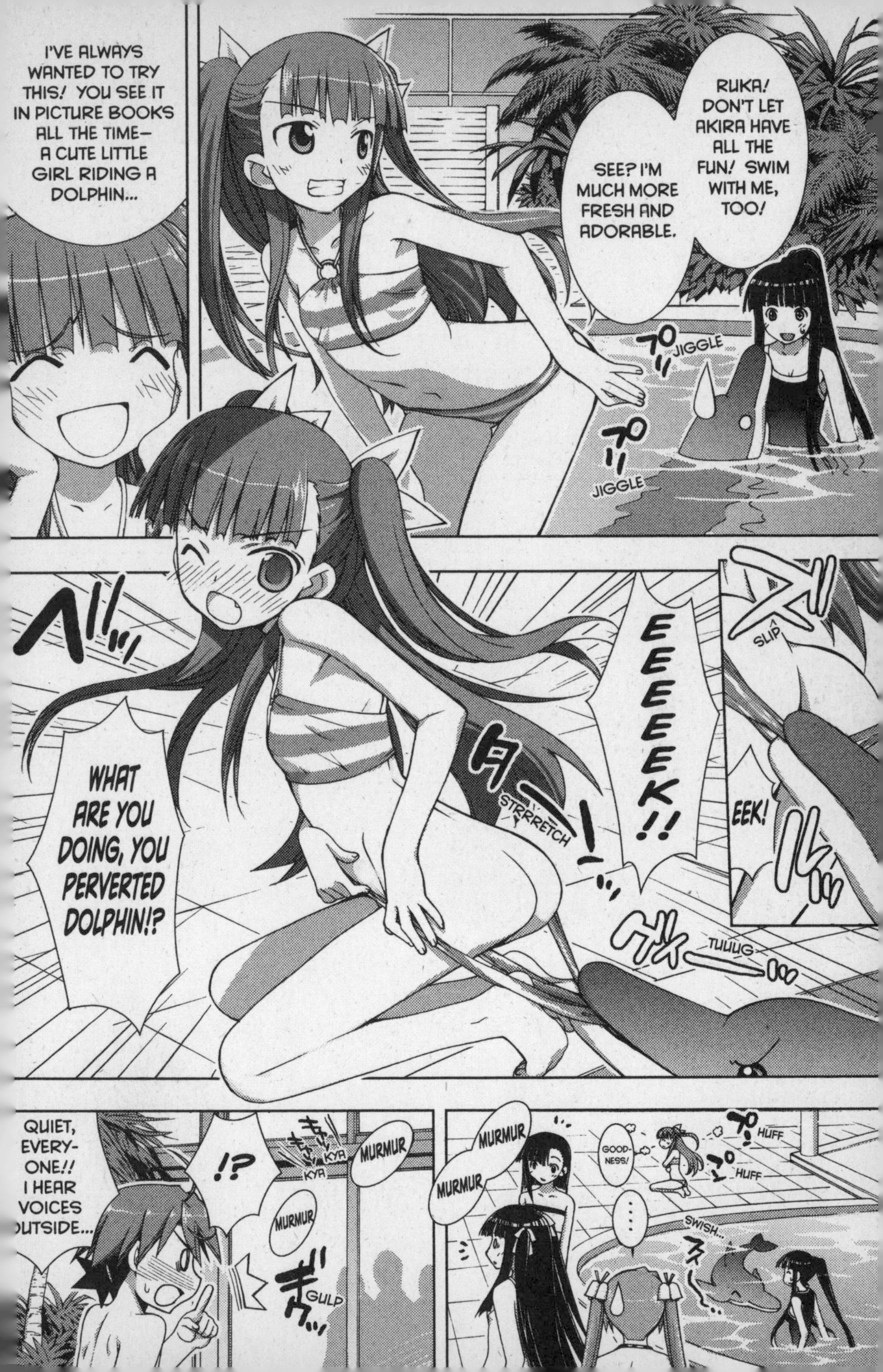
RUKA! DON'T LET AKIRA HAVE ALL THE FUN! SWIM WITH ME, TOO!
SEE? I'M MUCH MORE FRESH AND ADORABLE.
JIGGLE
JIGGLE
I'VE ALWAYS WANTED TO TRY THIS! YOU SEE IT IN PICTURE BOOKS ALL THE TIME— A CUTE LITTLE GIRL RIDING A DOLPHIN...
SLIP
EEK!
EEEEEEK!!
STRRRETCH
TUUUG
WHAT ARE YOU DOING, YOU PERVERTED DOLPHIN!?
GOOD-NESS!
HUFF
HUFF
MURMUR
MURMUR
...
SWISH...
QUIET, EVERY-ONE!! I HEAR VOICES OUTSIDE...
!?
KYA
KYA
MURMUR
MURMUR
GULP

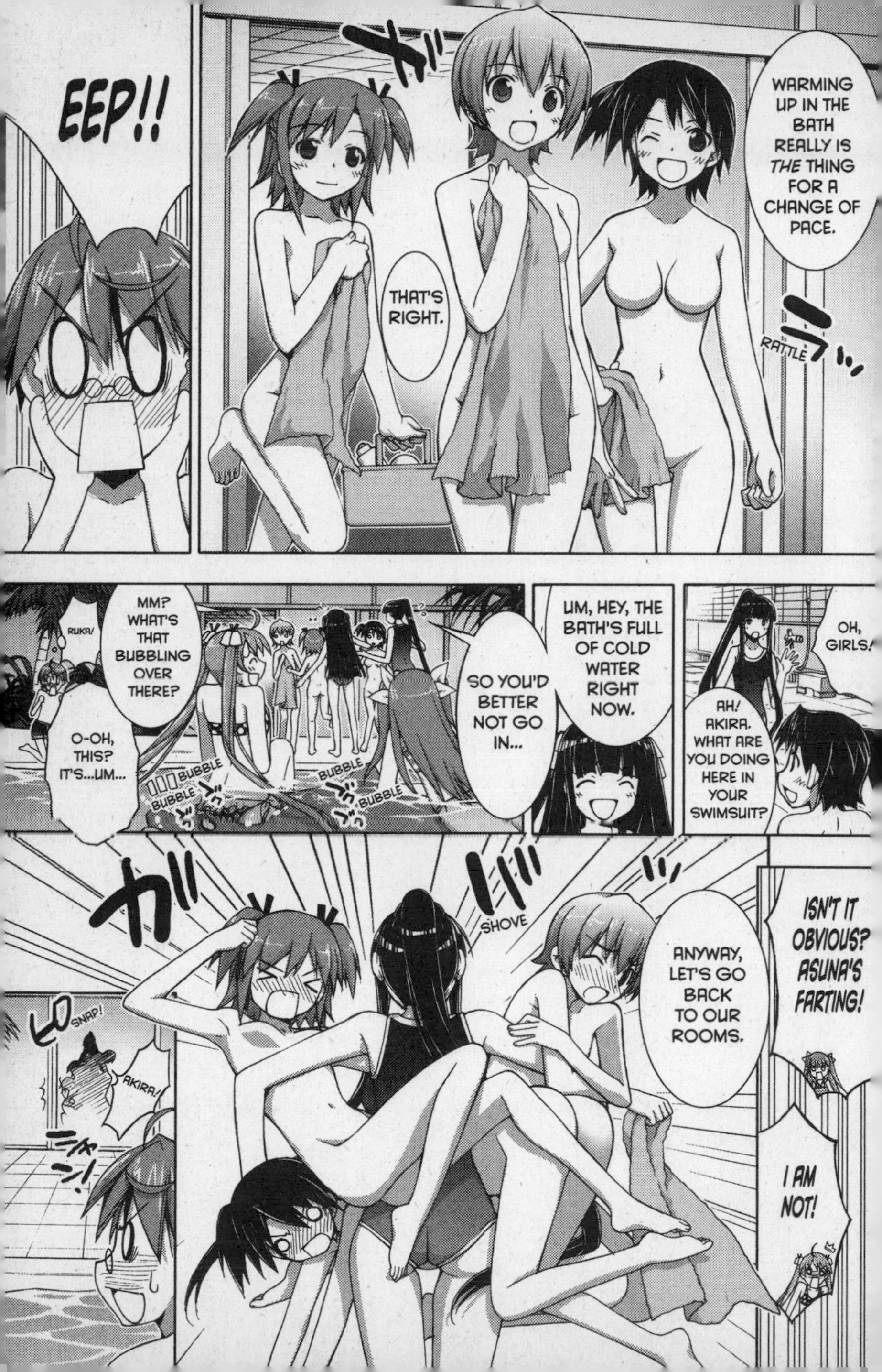
WARMING UP IN THE BATH REALLY IS THE THING FOR A CHANGE OF PACE.
RATTLE
THAT'S RIGHT.
EEP!!
OH, GIRLS!
AH! AKIRA. WHAT ARE YOU DOING HERE IN YOUR SWIMSUIT?
UM, HEY, THE BATH'S FULL OF COLD WATER RIGHT NOW.
SO YOU'D BETTER NOT GO IN...
RUKA!
MM? WHAT'S THAT BUBBLING OVER THERE?
O-OH, THIS? IT'S...UM...
BUBBLE
BUBBLE
BUBBLE
BUBBLE
ISN'T IT OBVIOUS? ASUNA'S FARTING!
I AM NOT!
ANYWAY, LET'S GO BACK TO OUR ROOMS.
SHOVE
AKIRA!
SNAP!

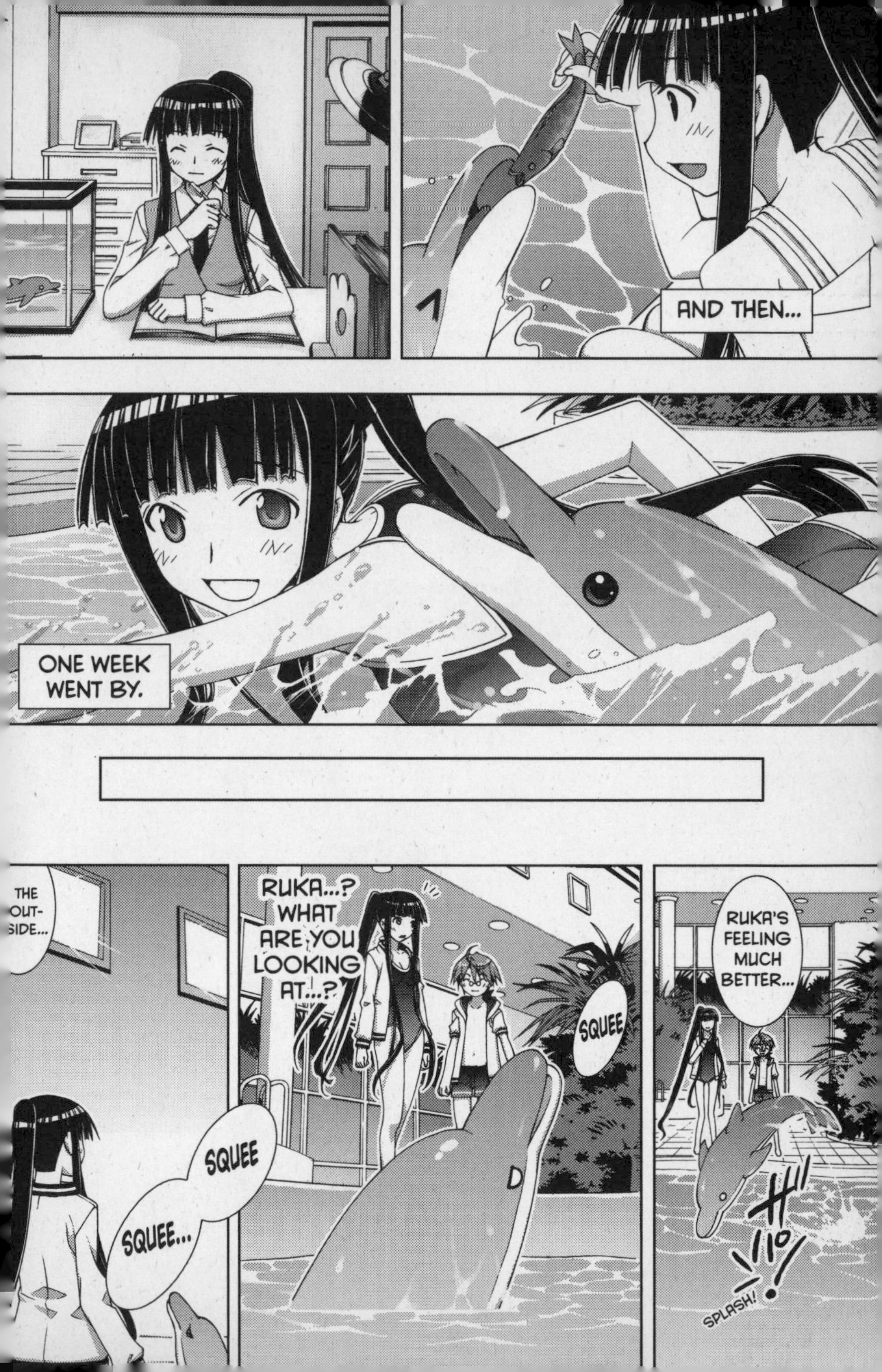
AND THEN...
ONE WEEK WENT BY.
RUKA'S FEELING MUCH BETTER...
SPLASH!
RUKA...? WHAT ARE YOU LOOKING AT...?
SQUEE
THE OUT-SIDE...
SQUEE
SQUEE...

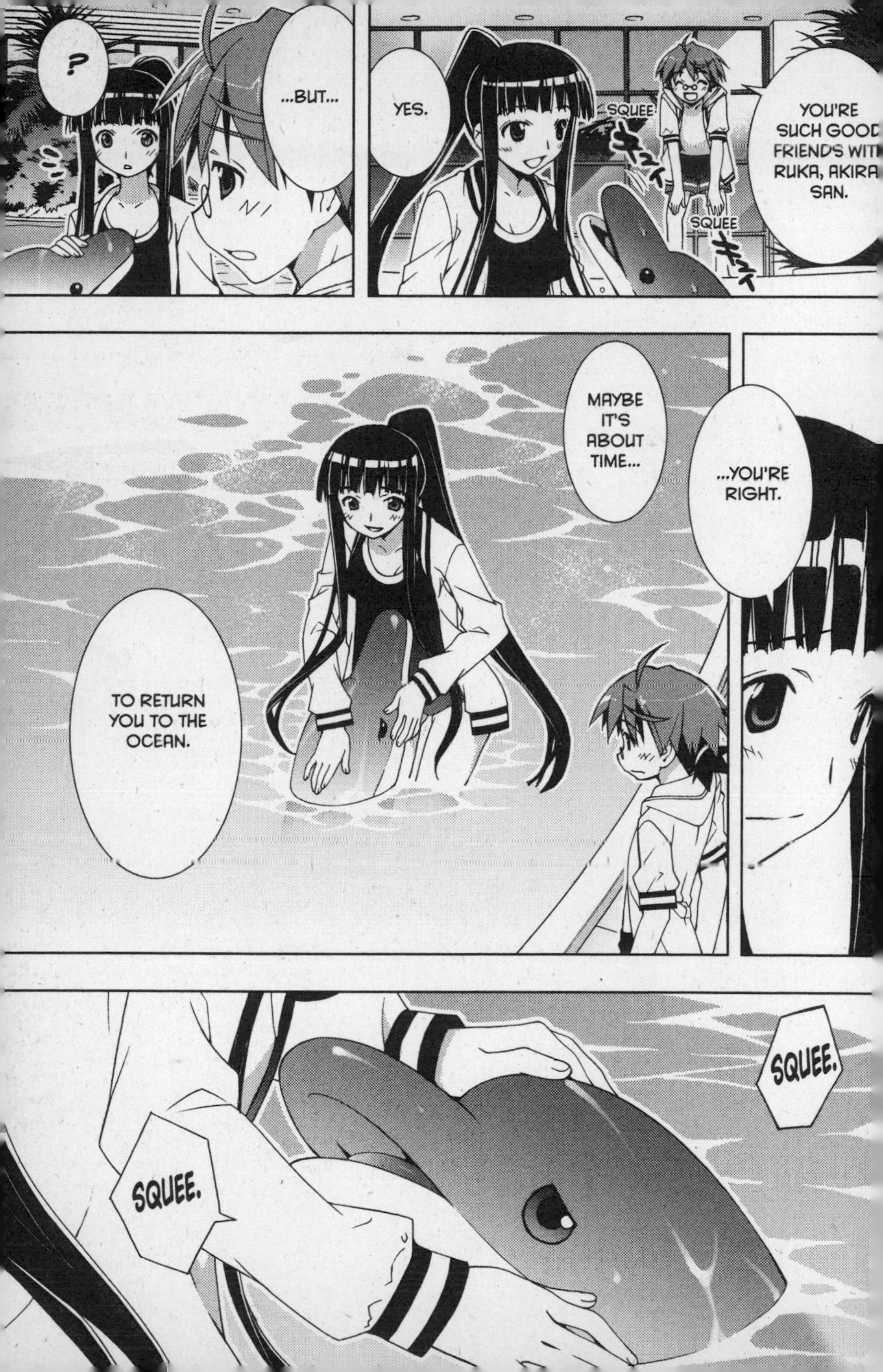
YOU'RE SUCH GOOD FRIENDS WIT RUKA, AKIRA SAN.
SQUEE
SQUEE
YES.
...BUT...
?
...YOU'RE RIGHT.
MAYBE IT'S ABOUT TIME...
TO RETURN YOU TO THE OCEAN.
SQUEE.
SQUEE.

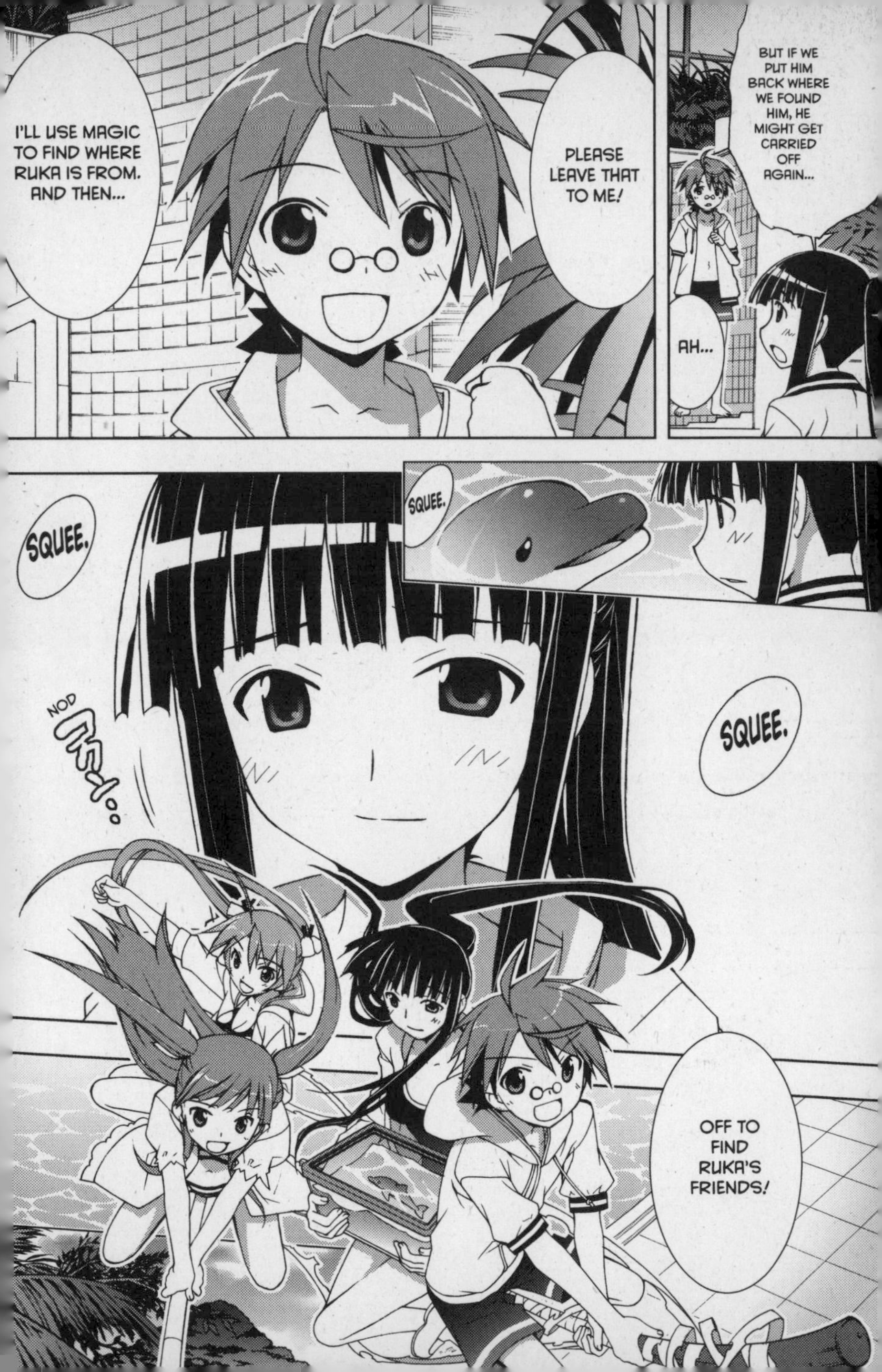
BUT IF WE PUT HIM BACK WHERE WE FOUND HIM, HE MIGHT GET CARRIED OFF AGAIN...
AH...
PLEASE LEAVE THAT TO ME!
I'LL USE MAGIC TO FIND WHERE RUKA IS FROM. AND THEN...
SQUEE.
SQUEE.
NOD
SQUEE.
OFF TO FIND RUKA'S FRIENDS!

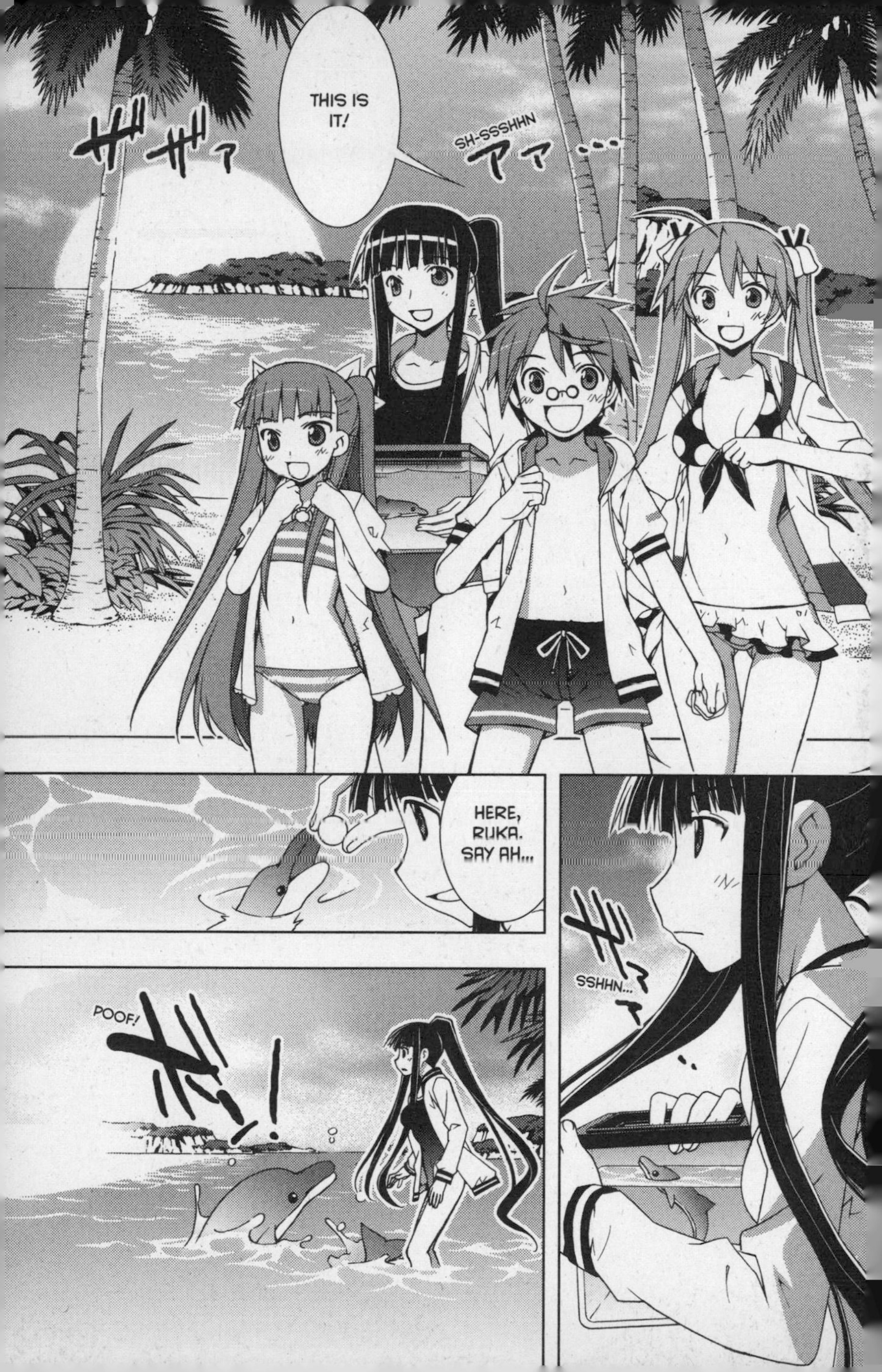
THIS IS IT!
SH-SSSHHN
SSHHN...
HERE, RUKA. SAY AH...
POOF!

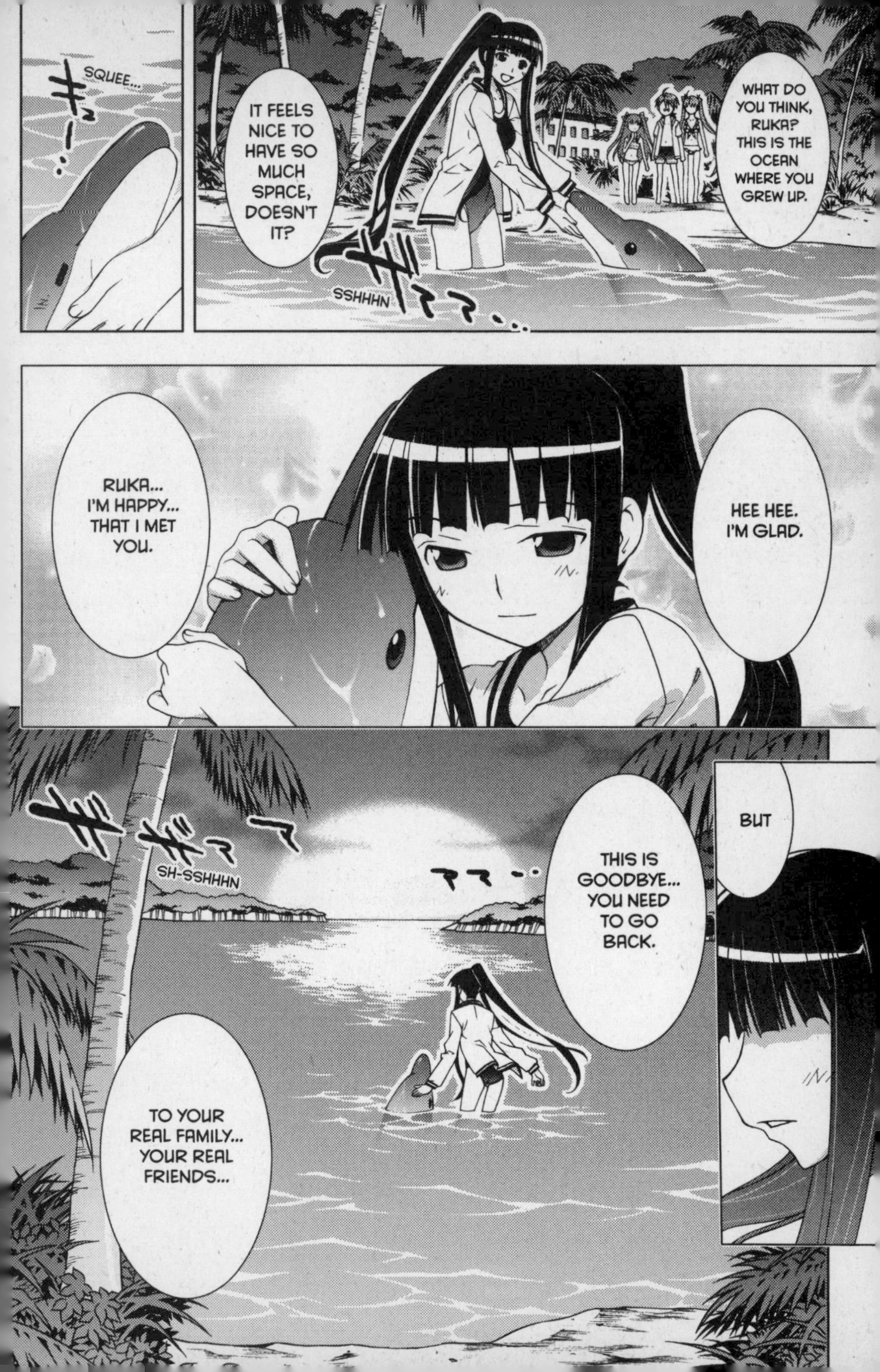
WHAT DO YOU THINK, RUKA? THIS IS THE OCEAN WHERE YOU GREW UP.
IT FEELS NICE TO HAVE SO MUCH SPACE, DOESN'T IT?
SSHHHN
SQUEE...
HEE HEE. I'M GLAD.
RUKA... I'M HAPPY... THAT I MET YOU.
BUT
THIS IS GOODBYE... YOU NEED TO GO BACK.
SH-SSHHHN
TO YOUR REAL FAMILY... YOUR REAL FRIENDS...

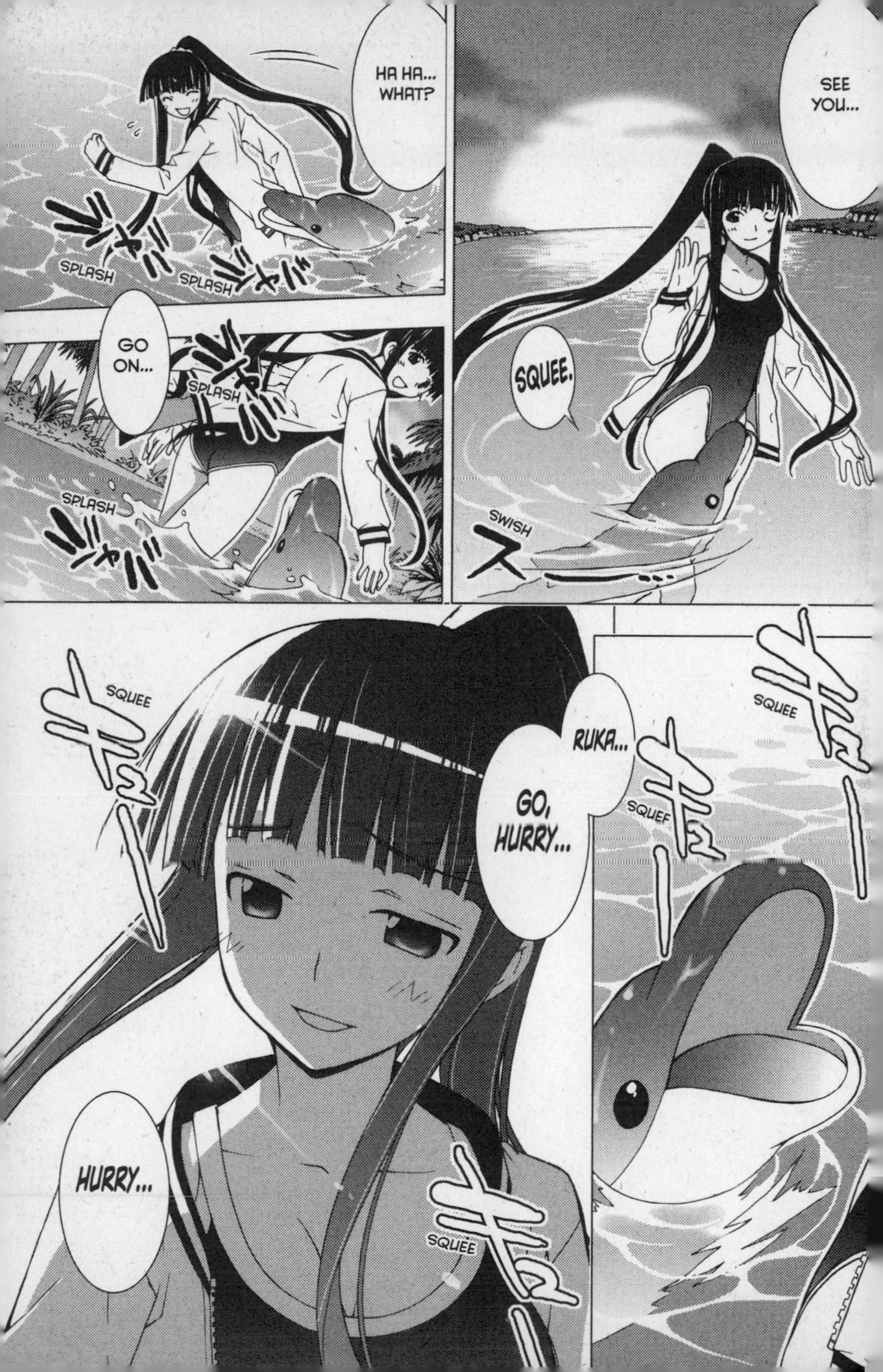
SEE YOU...
SQUEE.
SWISH
HA HA... WHAT?
SPLASH
SPLASH
GO ON...
SPLASH
SPLASH
SQUEE
SQUEE
RUKA...
GO, HURRY...
SQUEE
HURRY...
SQUEE

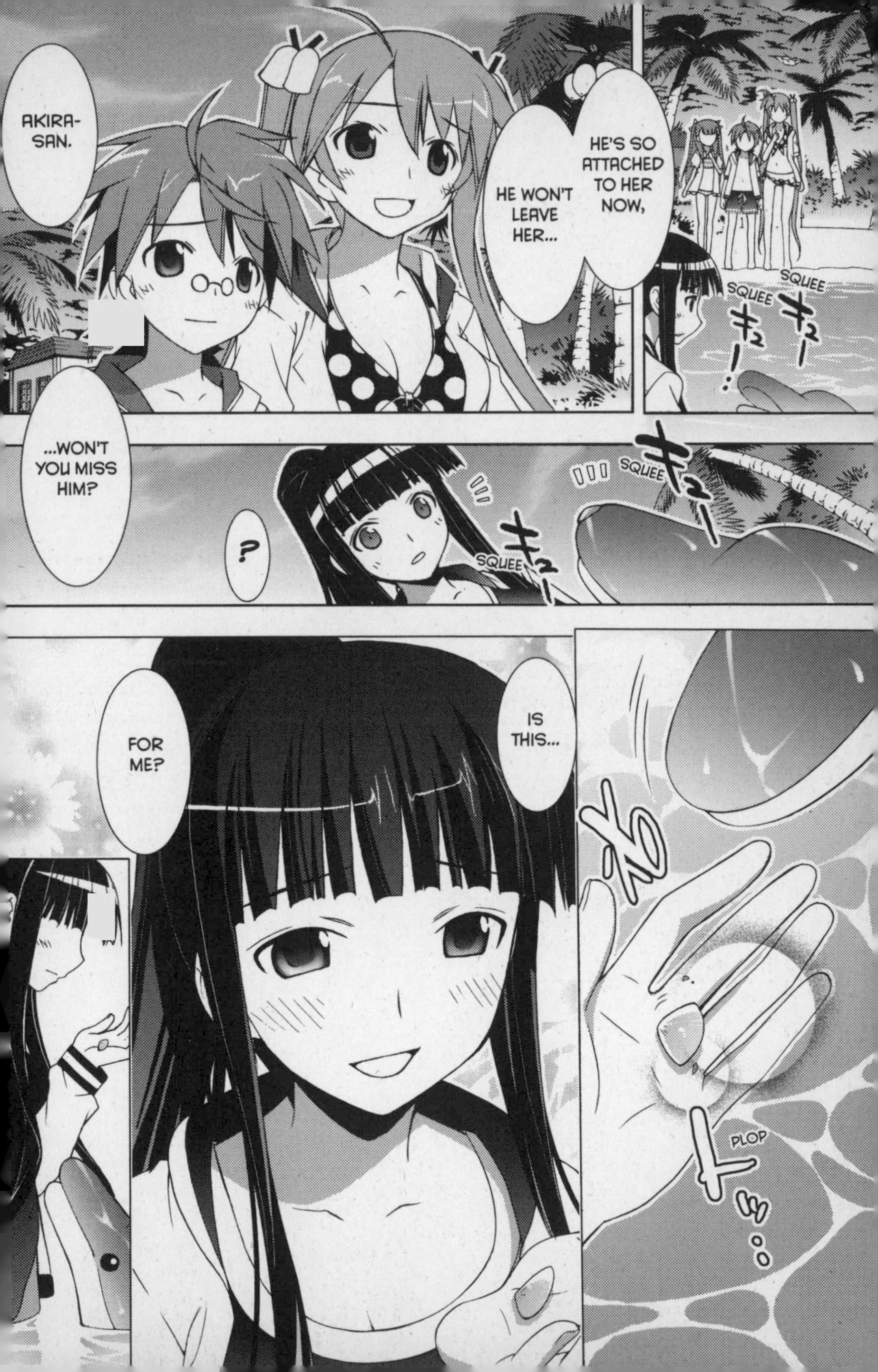
SQUEE
SQUEE
HE'S SO ATTACHED TO HER NOW,
HE WON'T LEAVE HER...
AKIRA-SAN.
SQUEE
...WON'T YOU MISS HIM?
SQUEE
?
PLOP
IS THIS...
FOR ME?

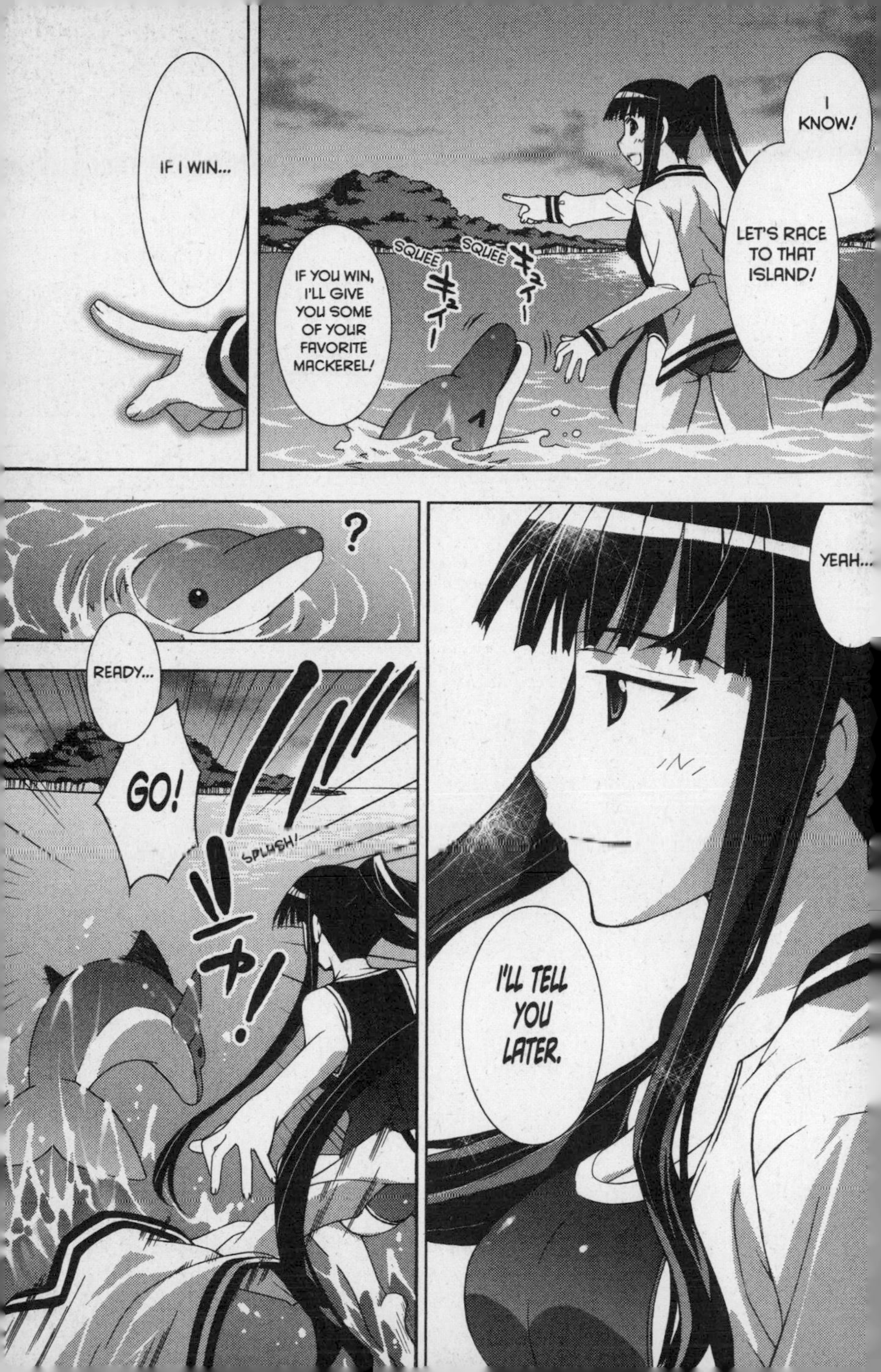
I KNOW!
LET'S RACE TO THAT ISLAND!
SQUEE
SQUEE
IF YOU WIN, I'LL GIVE YOU SOME OF YOUR FAVORITE MACKEREL!
IF I WIN...
YEAH...
I'LL TELL YOU LATER.
?
READY...
GO!
SPLASH!

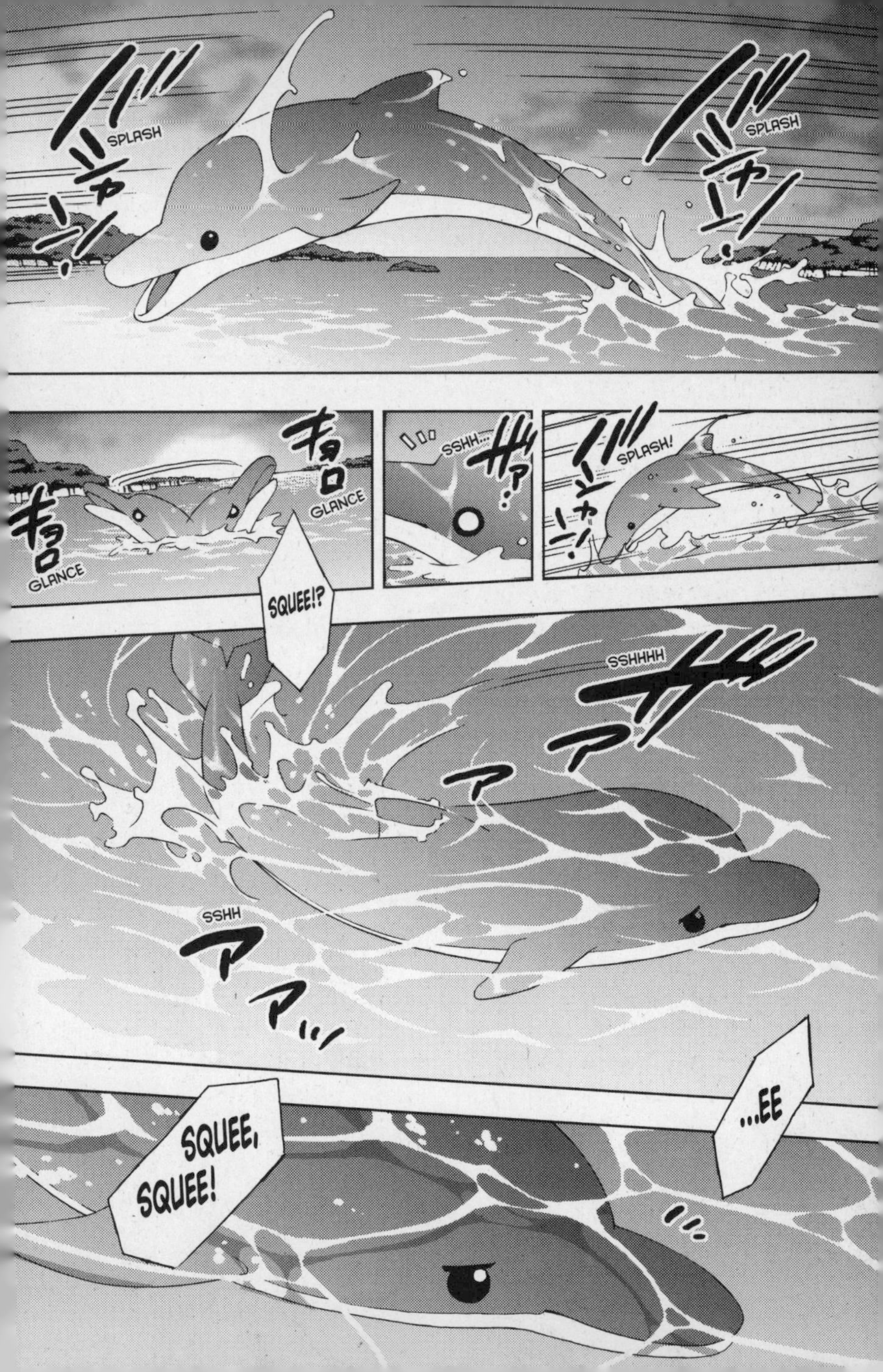
SPLASH
SPLASH
SPLASH!
SSHH...
GLANCE
GLANCE
SQUEE!?
SSHHHH
SSHH
...EE
SQUEE, SQUEE!

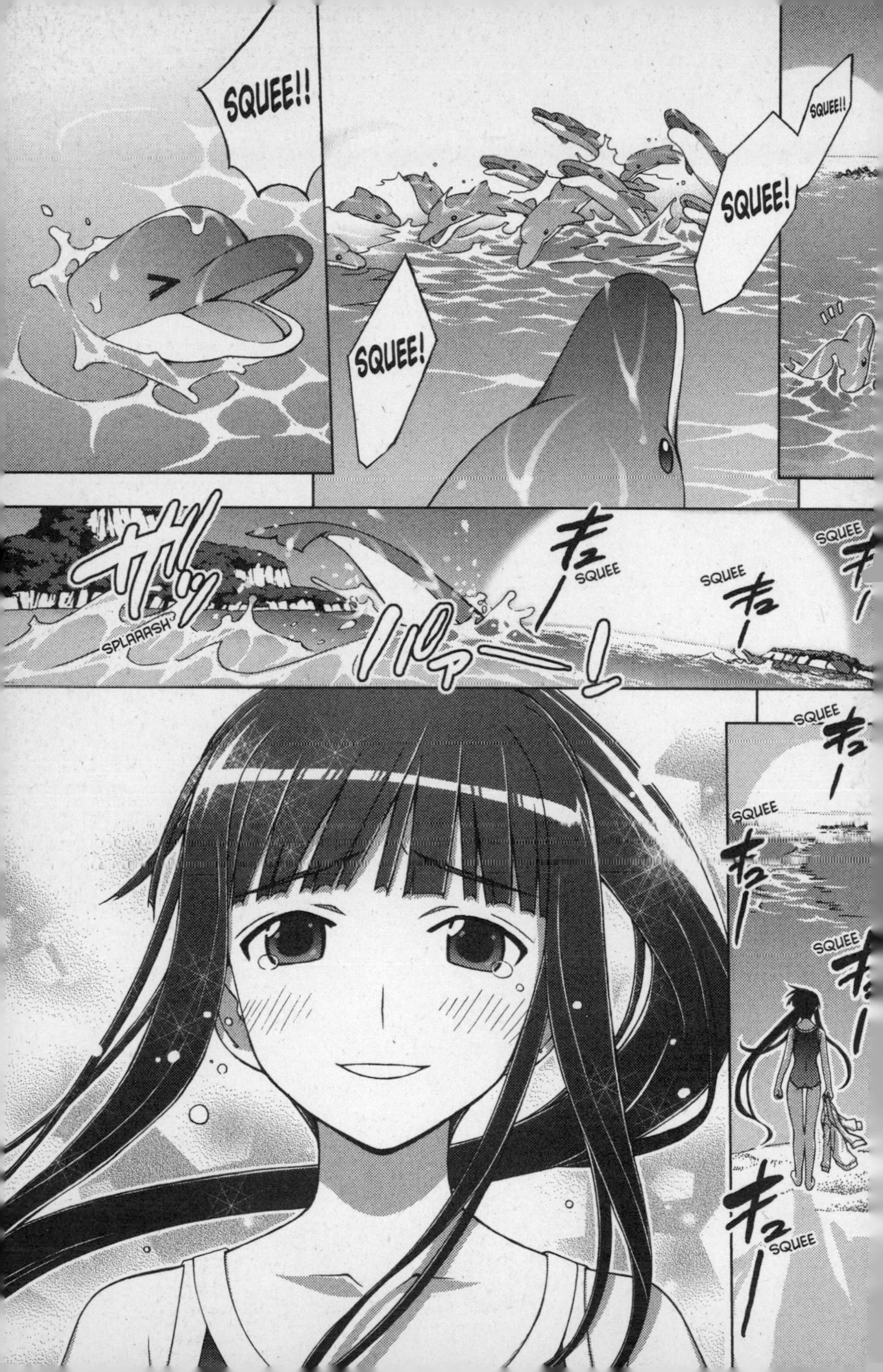
SQUEE!!
SQUEE!
SQUEE!
SQUEE!!
SQUEE
SQUEE
SQUEE
SPLAAASH
SQUEE
SQUEE
SQUEE
SQUEE

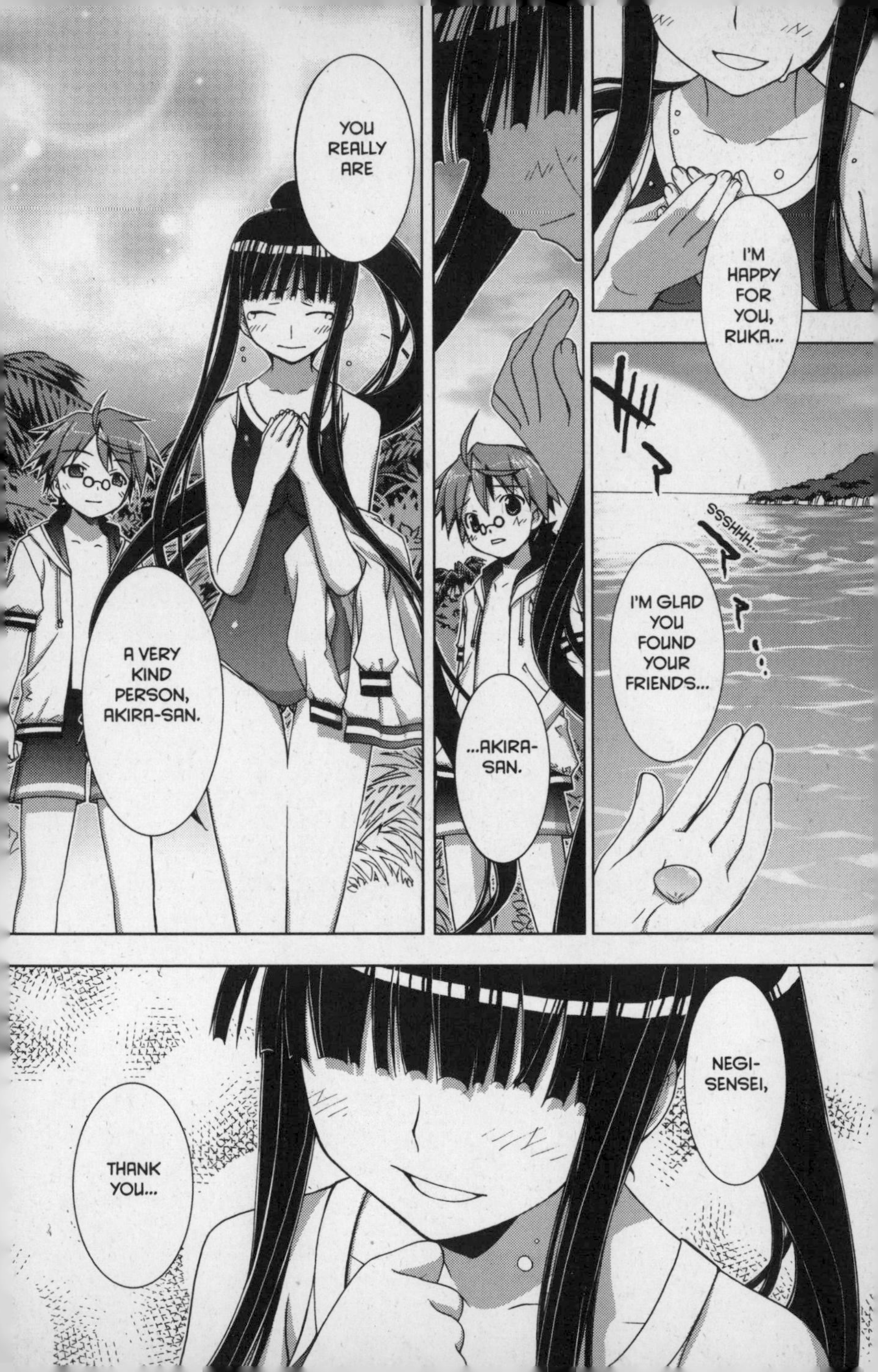
I'M HAPPY FOR YOU, RUKA...
SSSHHH...
I'M GLAD YOU FOUND YOUR FRIENDS...
...AKIRA-SAN.
YOU REALLY ARE
A VERY KIND PERSON, AKIRA-SAN.
NEGI-SENSEI,
THANK YOU...

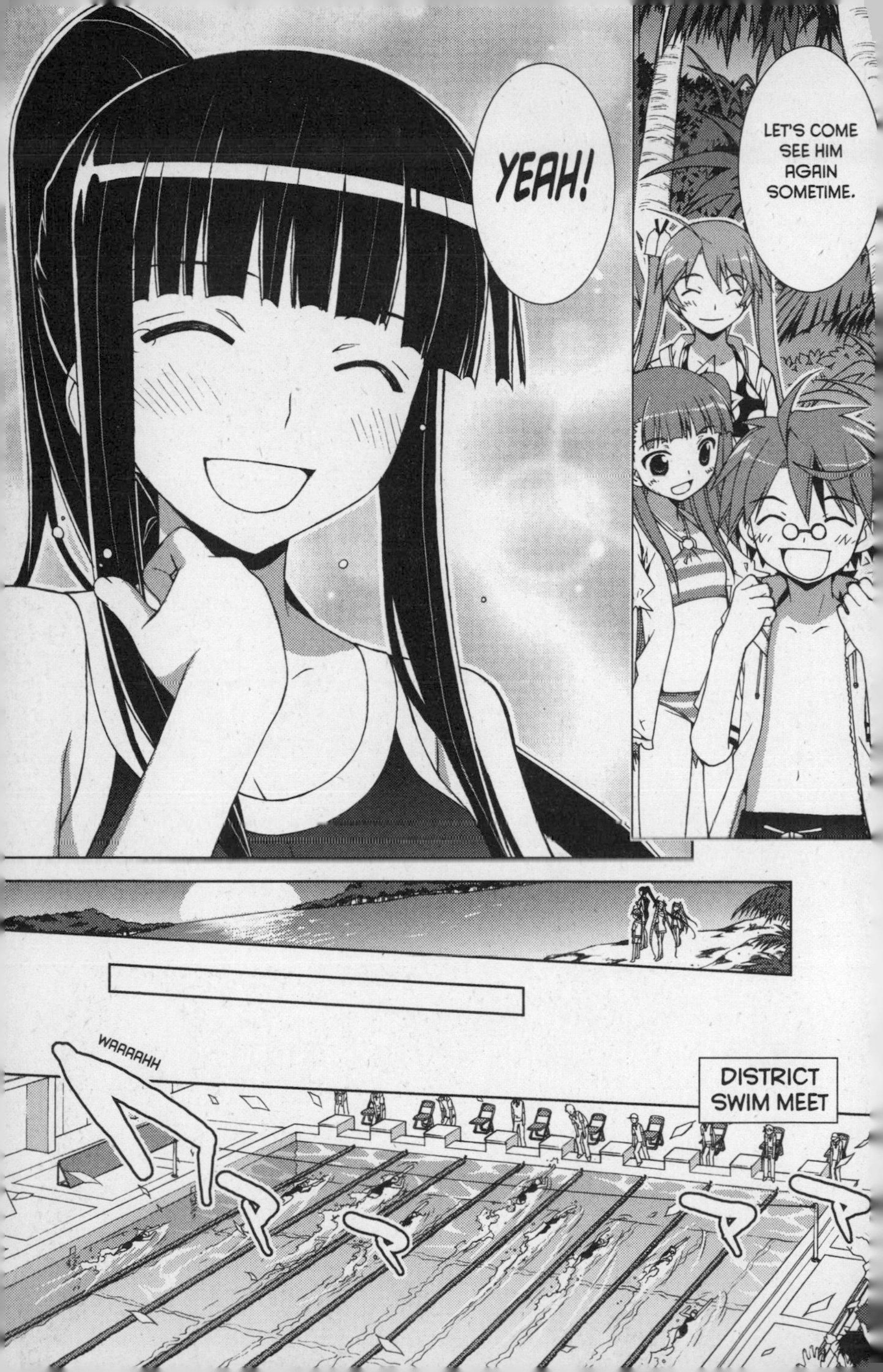
LET'S COME SEE HIM AGAIN SOMETIME.
YEAH!
DISTRICT SWIM MEET
WAAAAAHH

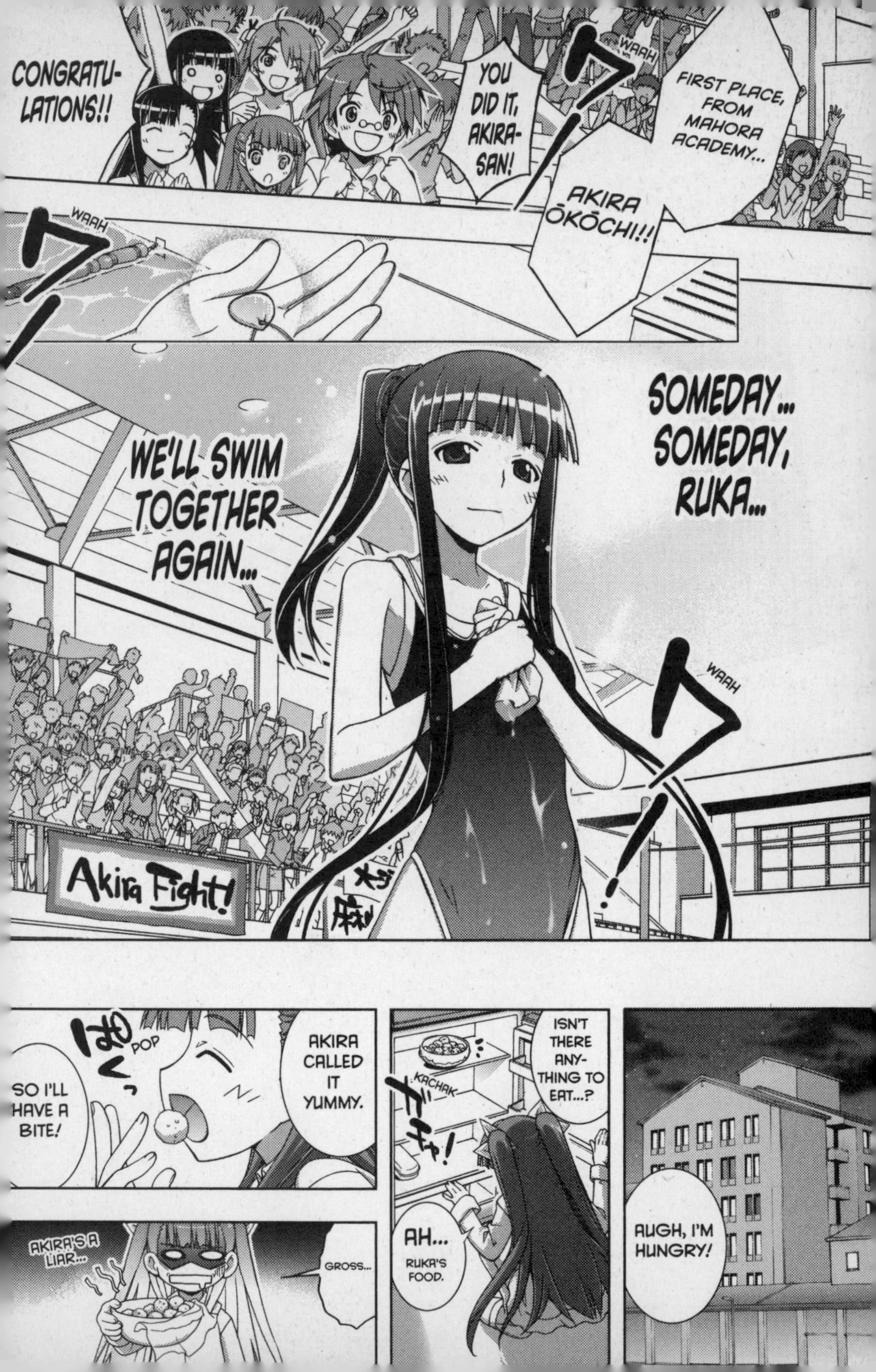
FIRST PLACE, FROM MAHORA ACADEMY...
AKIRA ŌKŌCHI!!
WAAH
YOU DID IT, AKIRA-SAN!
CONGRATU-LATIONS!!
WAAH
SOMEDAY... SOMEDAY, RUKA...
WE'LL SWIM TOGETHER AGAIN...
WAAH
Akira Fight!
AUGH, I'M HUNGRY!
ISN'T THERE ANY-THING TO EAT...?
KACHAK
AH...
RUKA'S FOOD.
AKIRA CALLED IT YUMMY.
POP
SO I'LL HAVE A BITE!
GROSS...
AKIRA'S A LIAR...

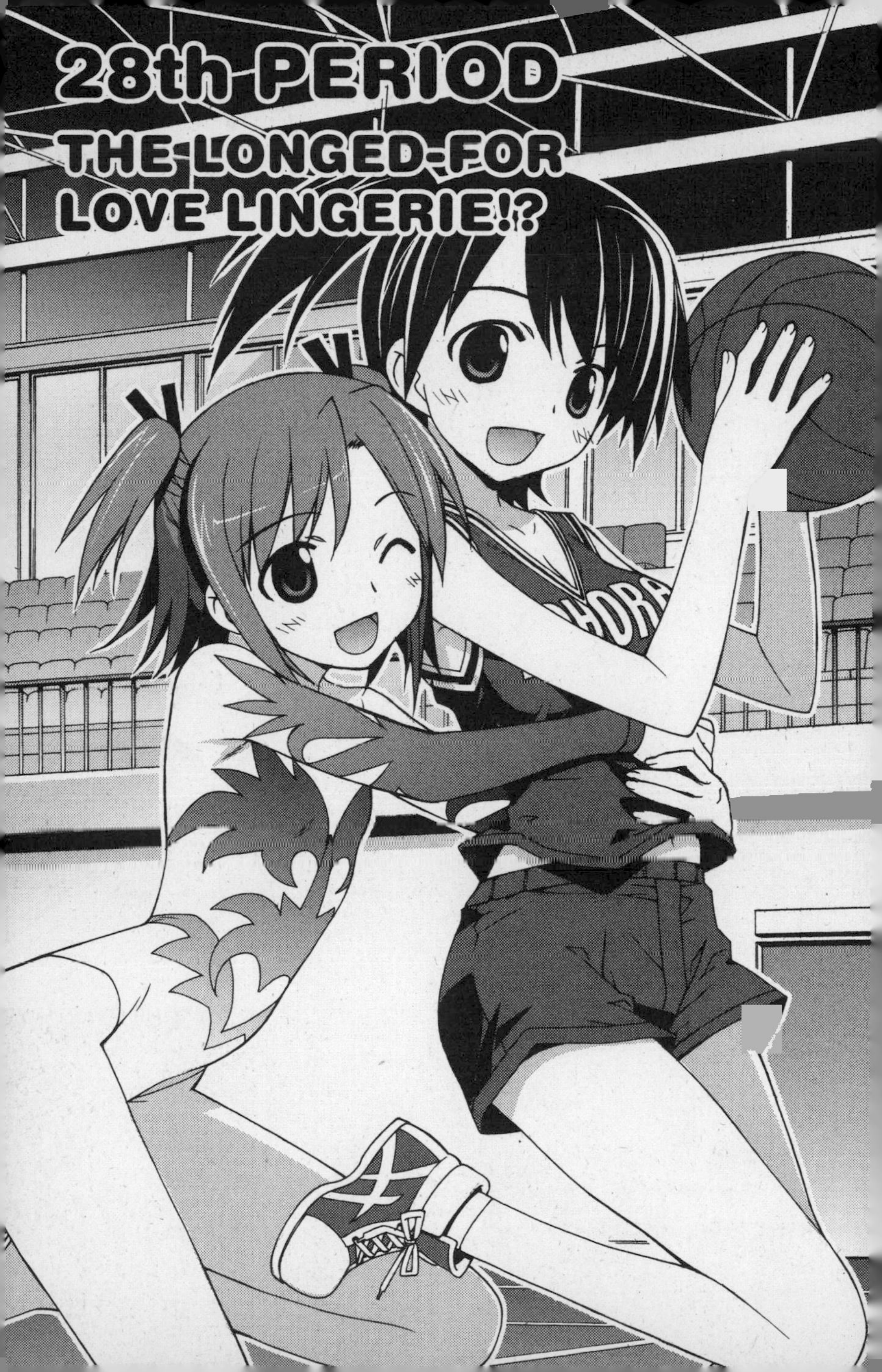
28th PERIOD
THE LONGED-FOR LOVE LINGERIE!?

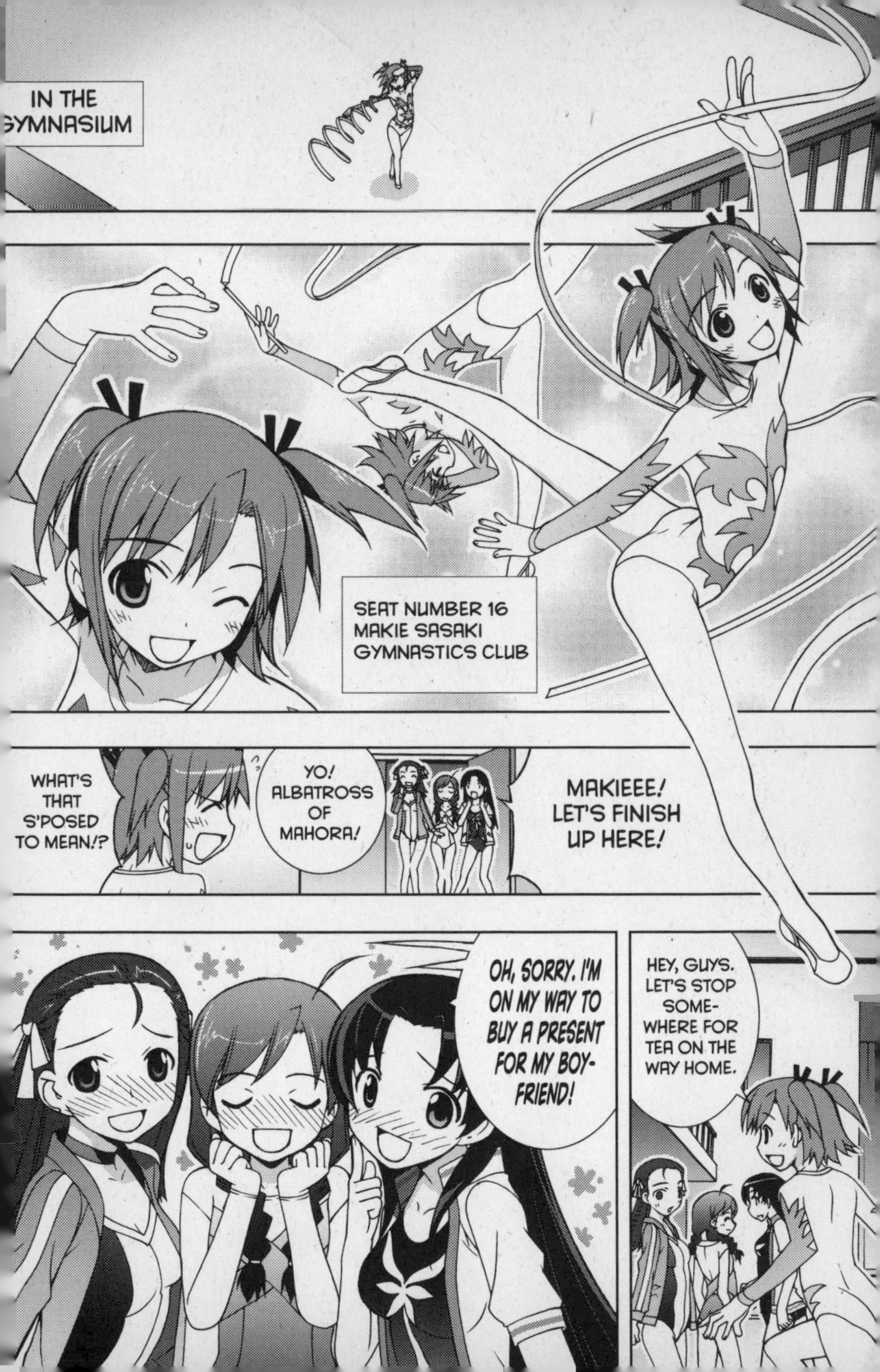
IN THE GYMNASIUM
SEAT NUMBER 16
MAKIE SASAKI
GYMNASTICS CLUB
MAKIEEE! LET'S FINISH UP HERE!
YO! ALBATROSS OF MAHORA!
WHAT'S THAT S'POSED TO MEAN!?
HEY, GUYS. LET'S STOP SOME-WHERE FOR TEA ON THE WAY HOME.
OH, SORRY. I'M ON MY WAY TO BUY A PRESENT FOR MY BOY-FRIEND!

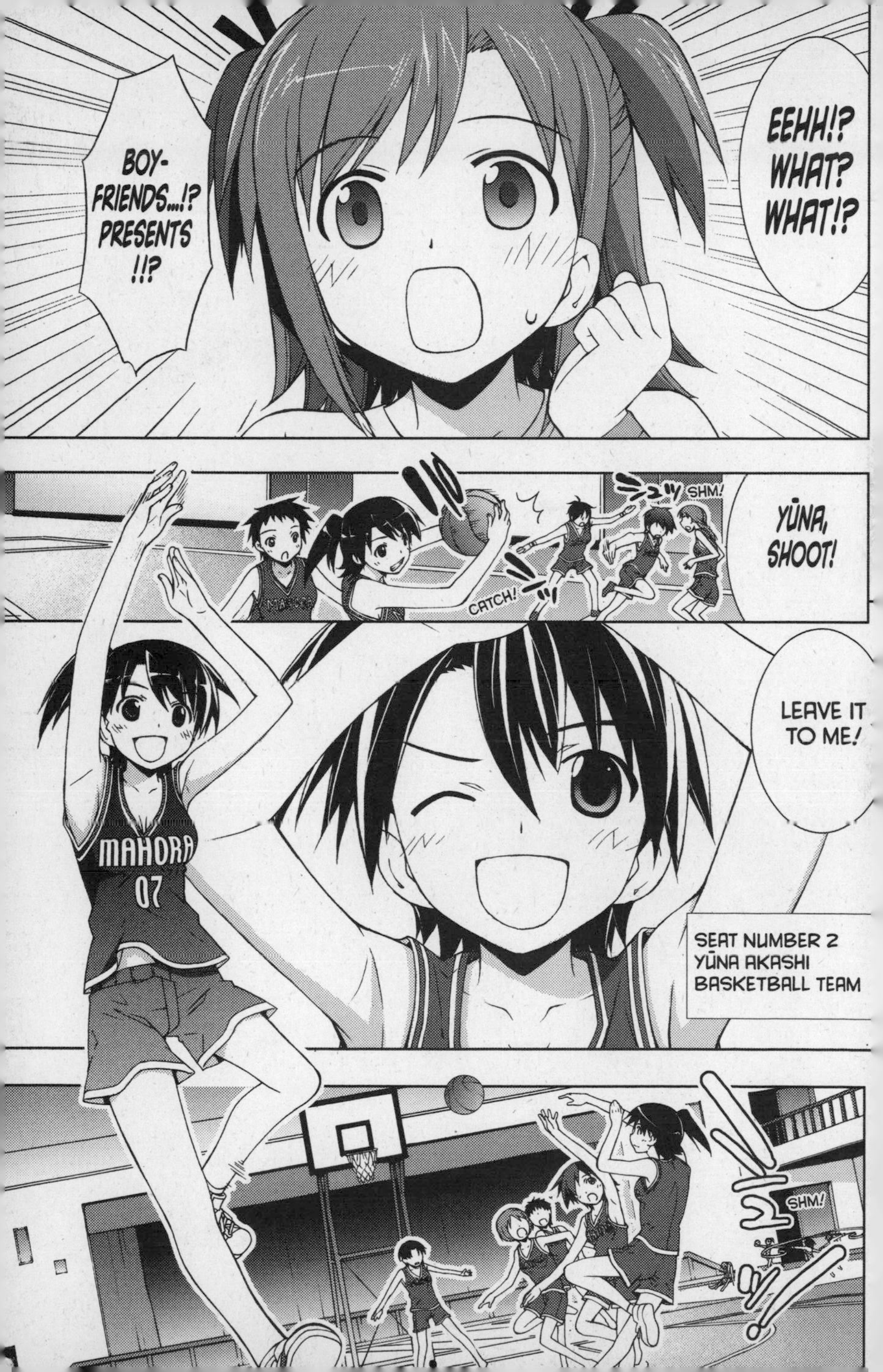
EEHH!? WHAT? WHAT!?
BOY-FRIENDS...!? PRESENTS !!?
YŪNA, SHOOT!
SHM!
CATCH!
MAHORA
LEAVE IT TO ME!
SEAT NUMBER 2
YŪNA AKASHI
BASKETBALL TEAM
MAHORA
07
SHM!

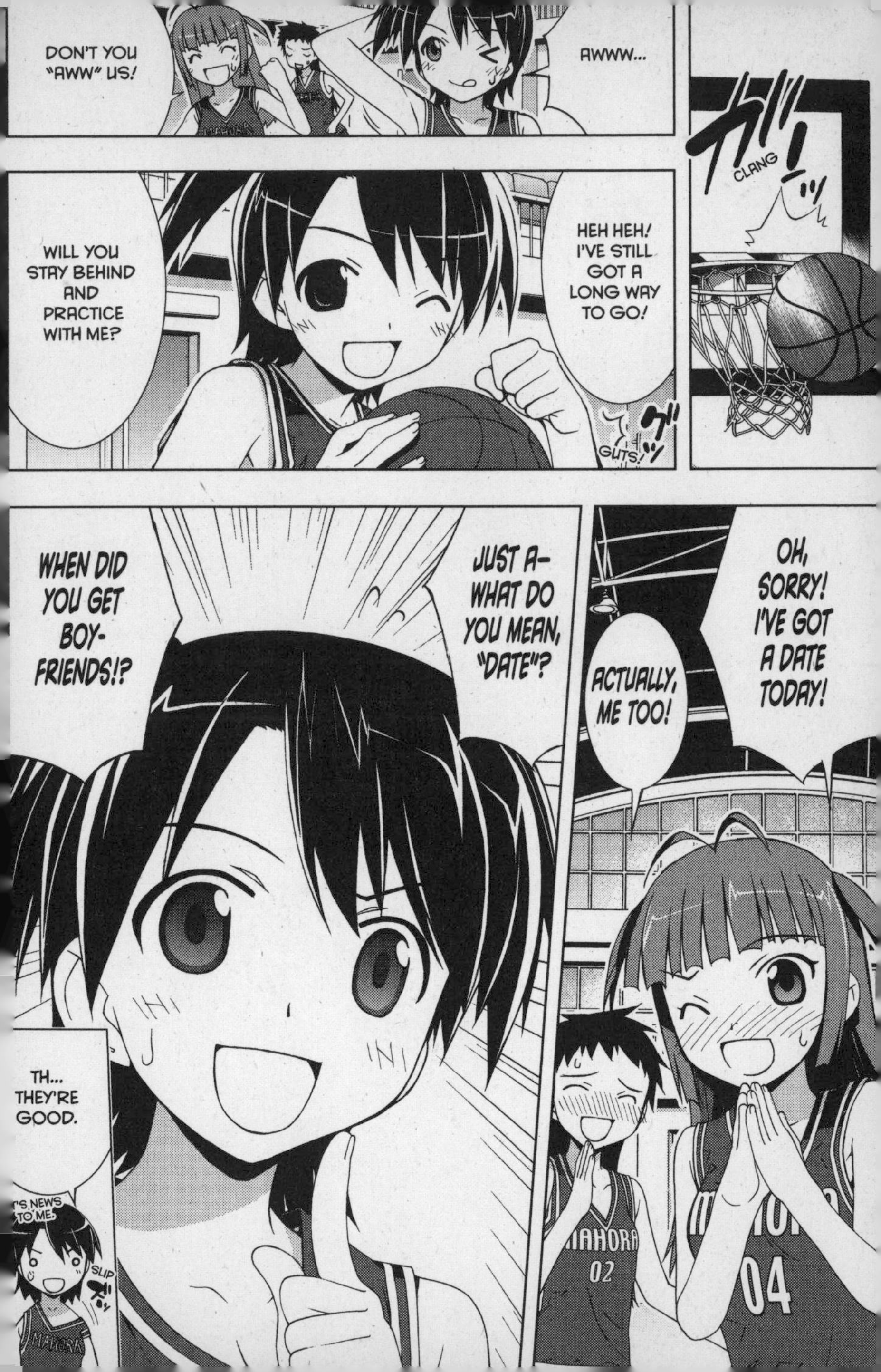
CLANG
AWWW...
DON'T YOU "AWW" US!
HEH HEH! I'VE STILL GOT A LONG WAY TO GO!
GUTS!
WILL YOU STAY BEHIND AND PRACTICE WITH ME?
OH, SORRY! I'VE GOT A DATE TODAY!
ACTUALLY, ME TOO!
JUST A— WHAT DO YOU MEAN, "DATE"?
WHEN DID YOU GET BOY-FRIENDS!?
TH... THEY'RE GOOD.
'S NEWS TO ME.
SLIP

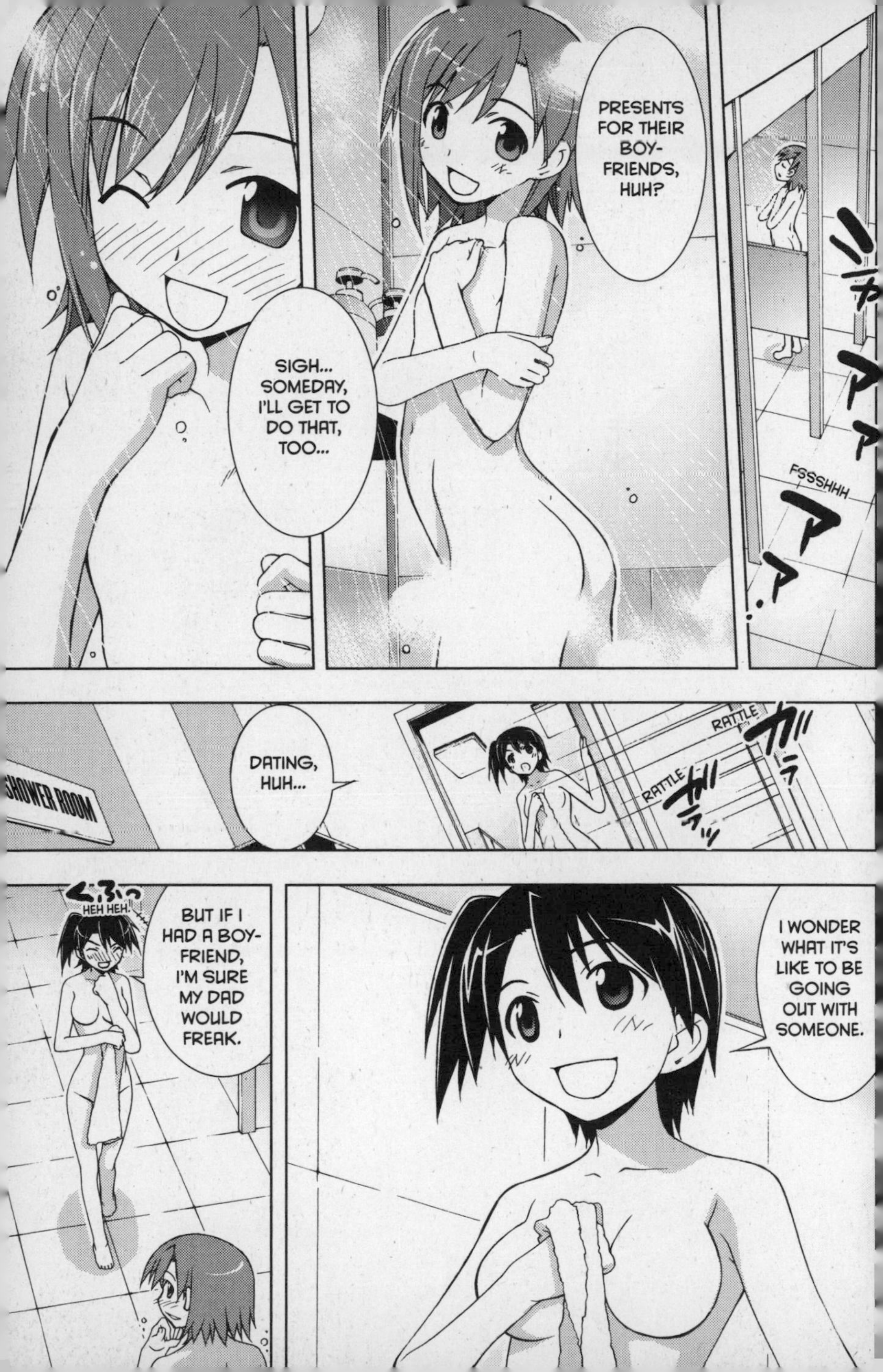
シャアアアア
FSSSHHH
PRESENTS FOR THEIR BOY-FRIENDS, HUH?
SIGH... SOMEDAY, I'LL GET TO DO THAT, TOO...
ガラ
RATTLE
ガラッ
RATTLE
DATING, HUH...
SHOWER ROOM
I WONDER WHAT IT'S LIKE TO BE GOING OUT WITH SOMEONE.
BUT IF I HAD A BOY-FRIEND, I'M SURE MY DAD WOULD FREAK.
くふっ
HEH HEH

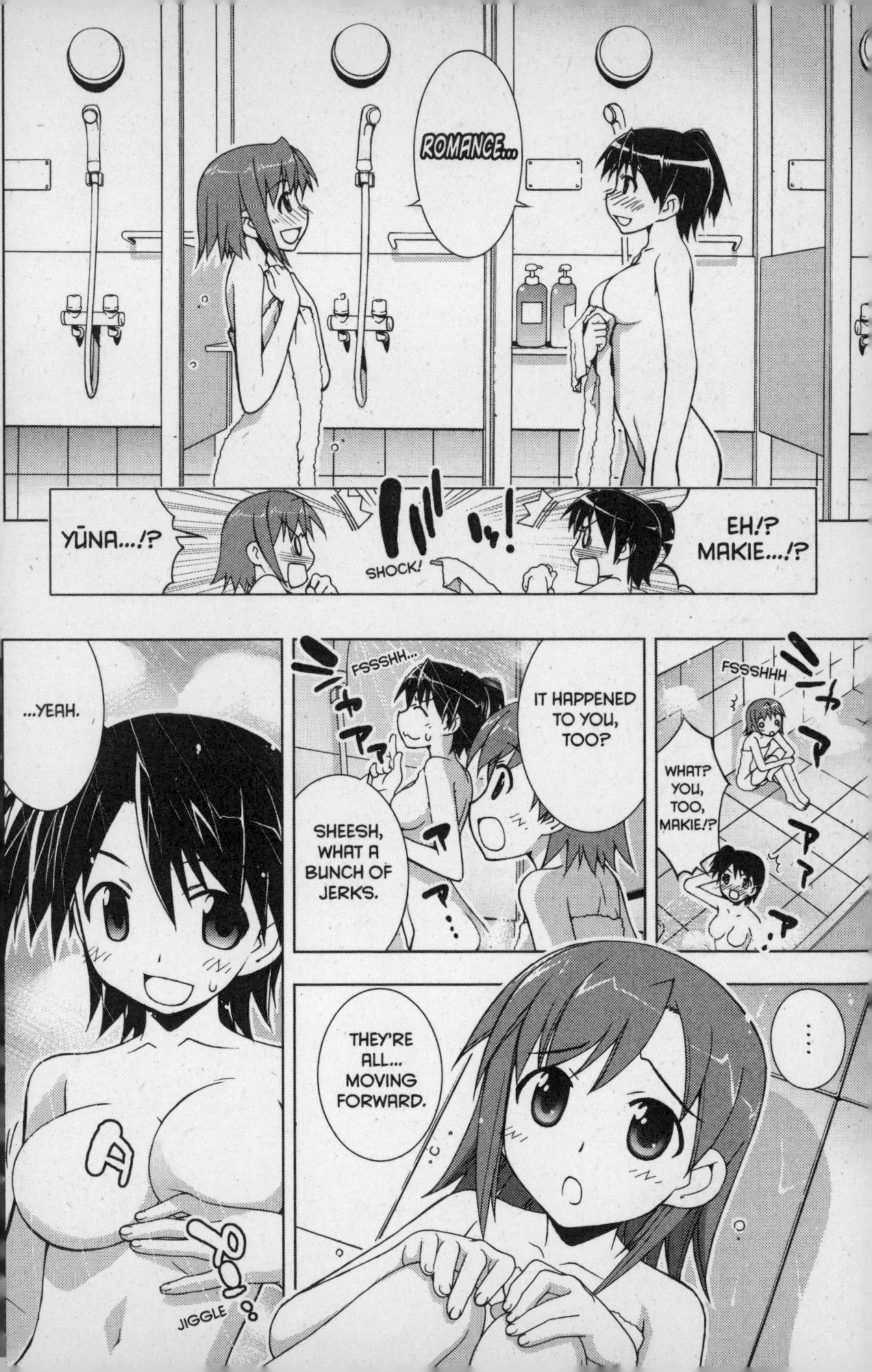
ROMANCE...
EH!? MAKIE...!?
SHOCK!
YŪNA...!?
FSSSHHH
WHAT? YOU, TOO, MAKIE!?
IT HAPPENED TO YOU, TOO?
FSSSHH...
SHEESH, WHAT A BUNCH OF JERKS.
....
THEY'RE ALL... MOVING FORWARD.
...YEAH.
JIGGLE

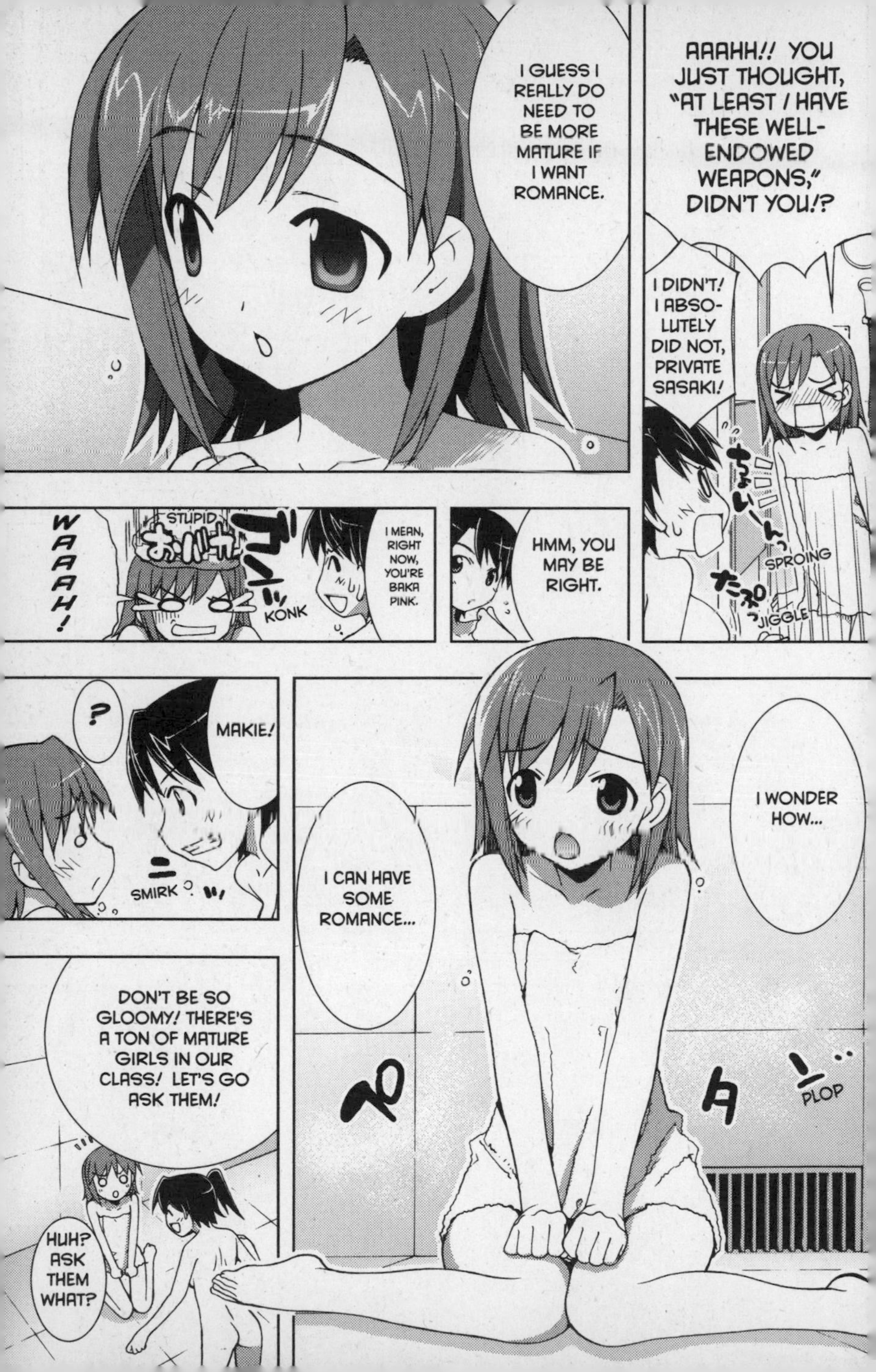
AAAHH!! YOU JUST THOUGHT, "AT LEAST I HAVE THESE WELL-ENDOWED WEAPONS," DIDN'T YOU!?
I DIDN'T! I ABSOLUTELY DID NOT, PRIVATE SASAKI!
SPROING
JIGGLE
I GUESS I REALLY DO NEED TO BE MORE MATURE IF I WANT ROMANCE.
HMM, YOU MAY BE RIGHT.
I MEAN, RIGHT NOW, YOU'RE BAKA PINK.
STUPID
KONK
WAAAAH!
I WONDER HOW...
I CAN HAVE SOME ROMANCE...
PLOP
MAKIE!
?
SMIRK
DON'T BE SO GLOOMY! THERE'S A TON OF MATURE GIRLS IN OUR CLASS! LET'S GO ASK THEM!
HUH? ASK THEM WHAT?

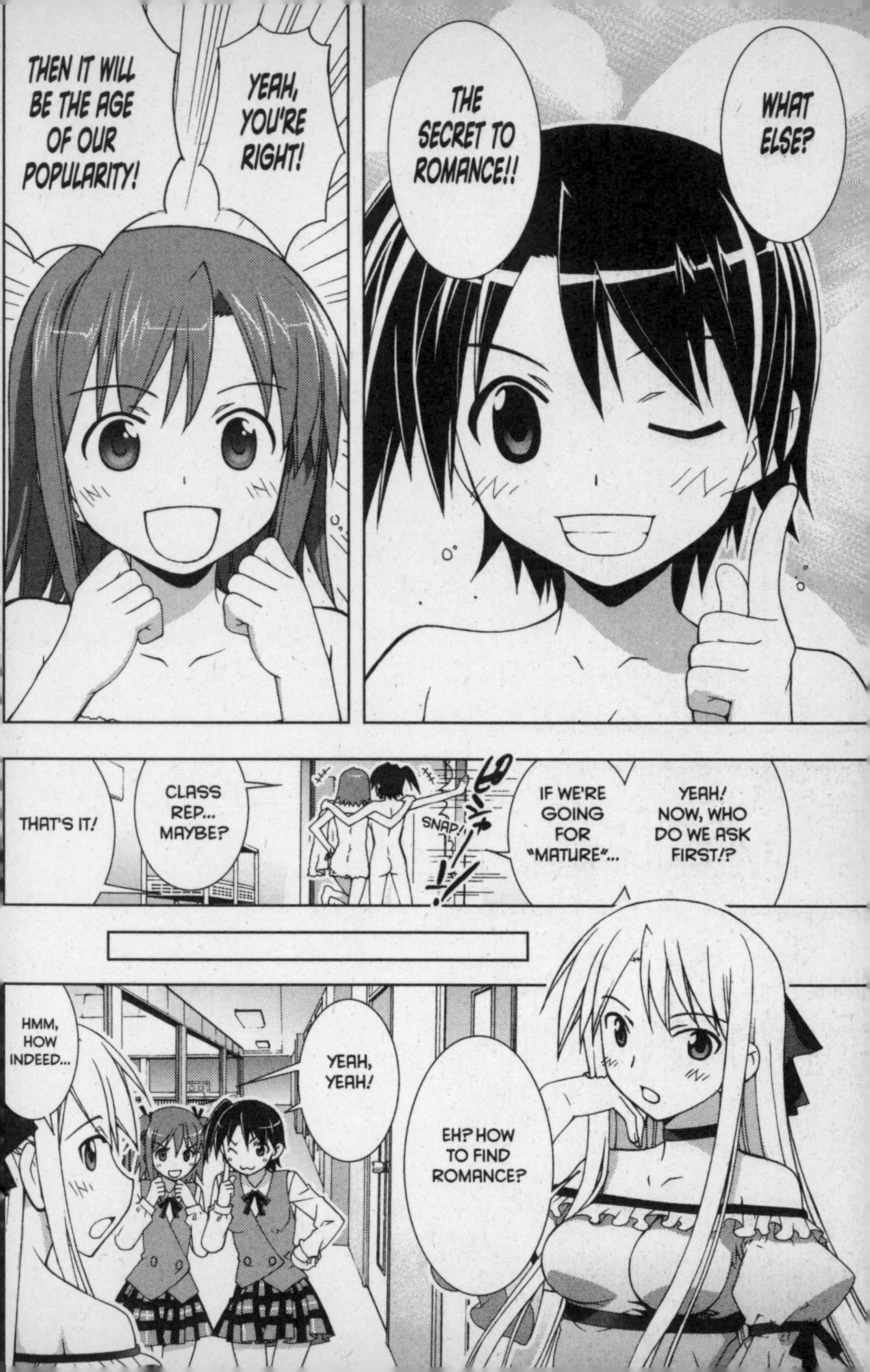
WHAT ELSE?
THE SECRET TO ROMANCE!!
YEAH, YOU'RE RIGHT!
THEN IT WILL BE THE AGE OF OUR POPULARITY!
YEAH! NOW, WHO DO WE ASK FIRST!?
IF WE'RE GOING FOR "MATURE"...
SNAP!
CLASS REP... MAYBE?
THAT'S IT!
EH? HOW TO FIND ROMANCE?
YEAH, YEAH!
HMM, HOW INDEED...

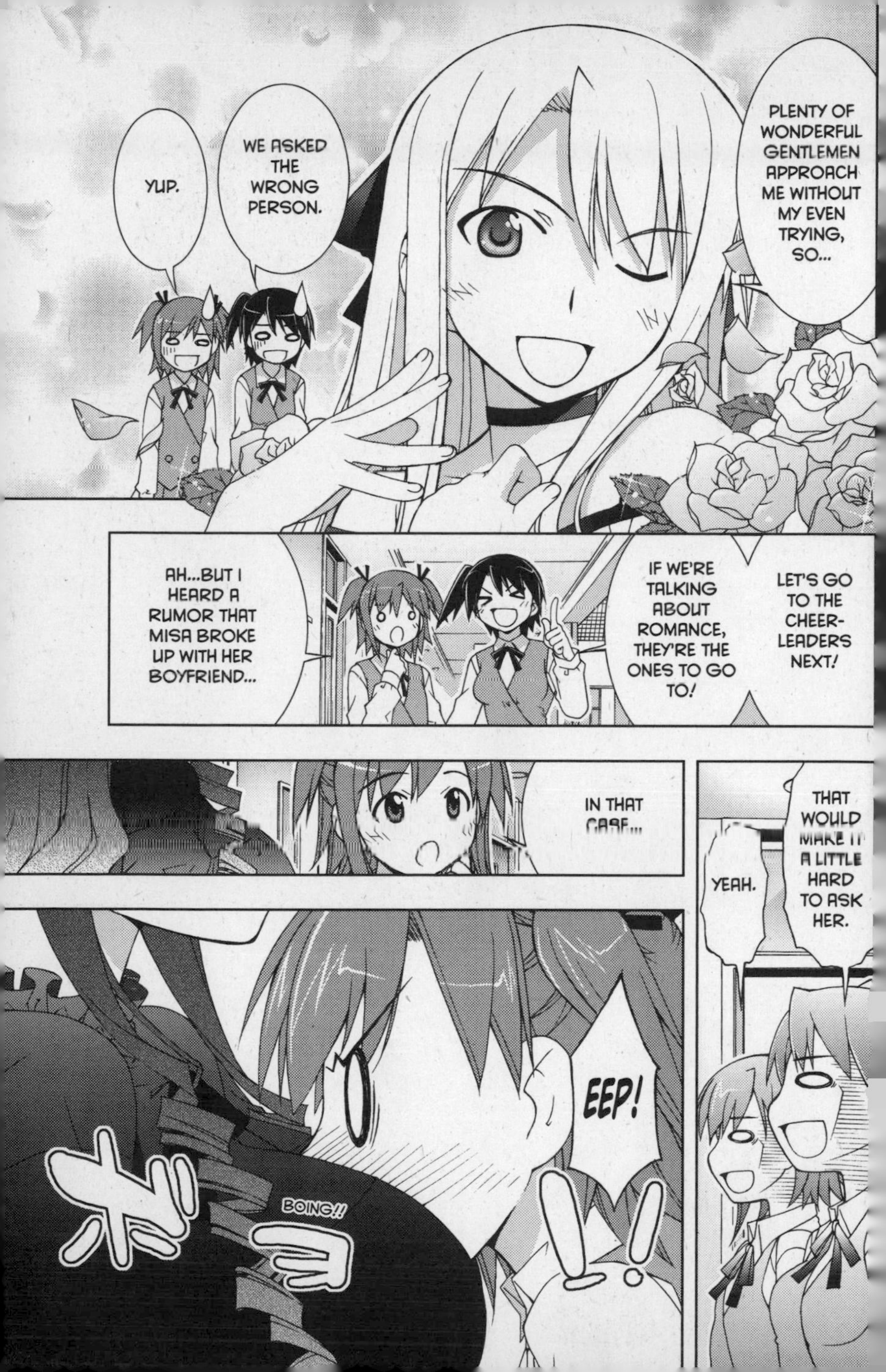
PLENTY OF WONDERFUL GENTLEMEN APPROACH ME WITHOUT MY EVEN TRYING, SO...
WE ASKED THE WRONG PERSON.
YUP.
LET'S GO TO THE CHEER-LEADERS NEXT!
IF WE'RE TALKING ABOUT ROMANCE, THEY'RE THE ONES TO GO TO!
AH...BUT I HEARD A RUMOR THAT MISA BROKE UP WITH HER BOYFRIEND...
THAT WOULD MAKE IT A LITTLE HARD TO ASK HER.
YEAH.
IN THAT CASE...
EEP!
BOING!!

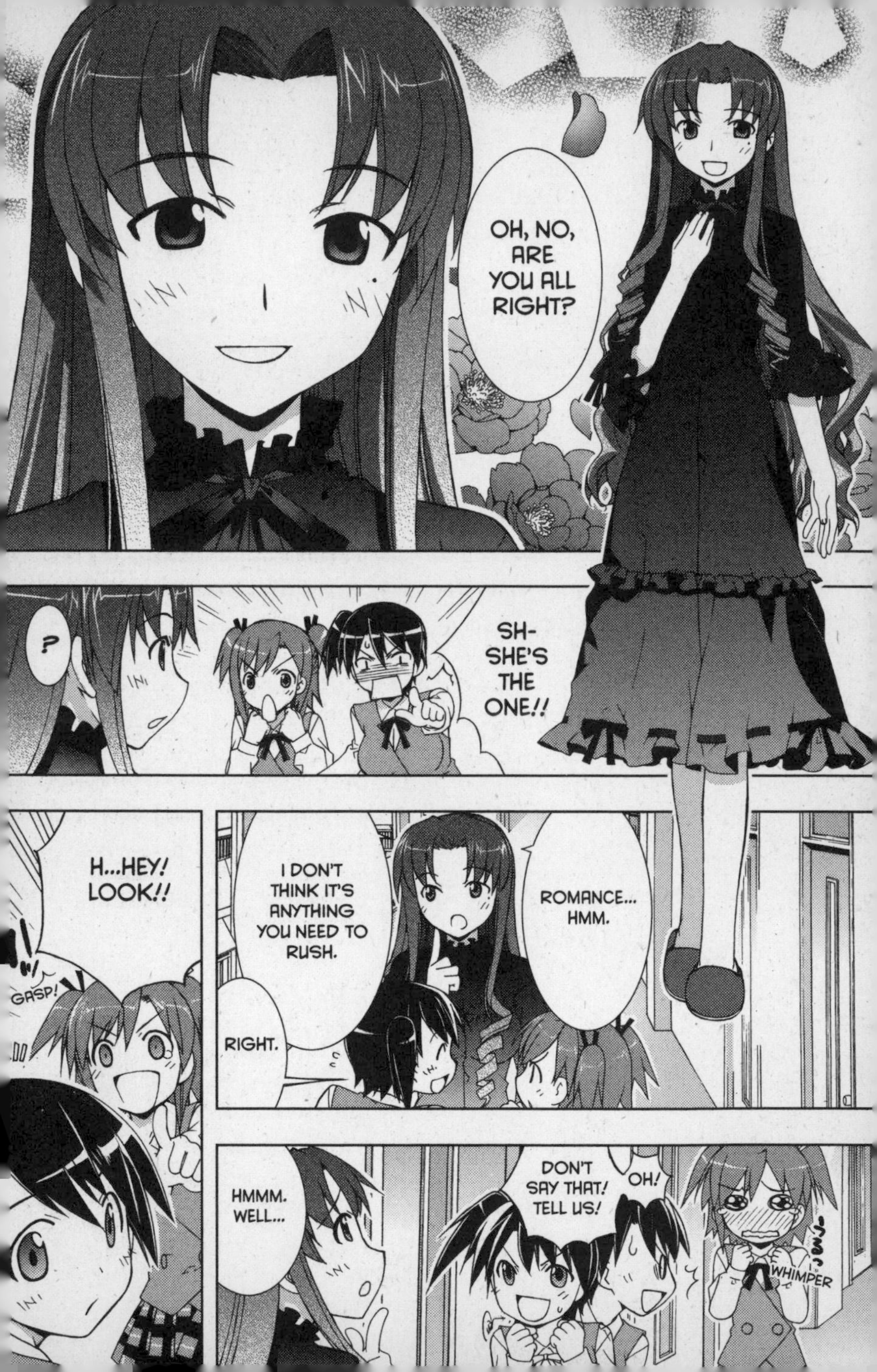
OH, NO, ARE YOU ALL RIGHT?
SH- SHE'S THE ONE!!
?
ROMANCE... HMM.
I DON'T THINK IT'S ANYTHING YOU NEED TO RUSH.
RIGHT.
WHIMPER
OH!
DON'T SAY THAT! TELL US!
HMMM. WELL...
H...HEY! LOOK!!
GASP!

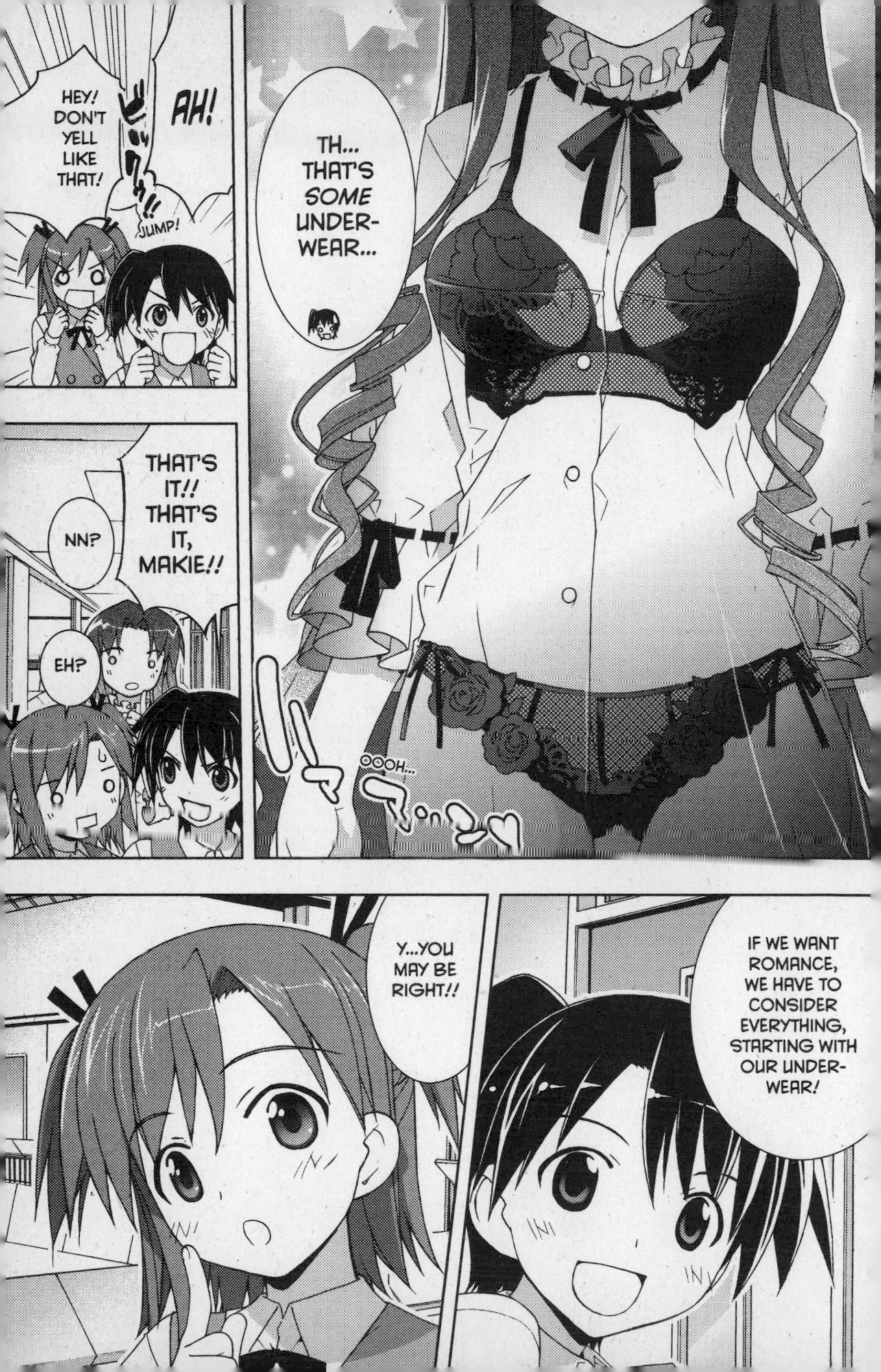
TH... THAT'S SOME UNDER-WEAR...
OOOH...
AH!
HEY! DON'T YELL LIKE THAT!
JUMP!
THAT'S IT!! THAT'S IT, MAKIE!!
NN?
EH?
IF WE WANT ROMANCE, WE HAVE TO CONSIDER EVERYTHING, STARTING WITH OUR UNDER-WEAR!
Y...YOU MAY BE RIGHT!!

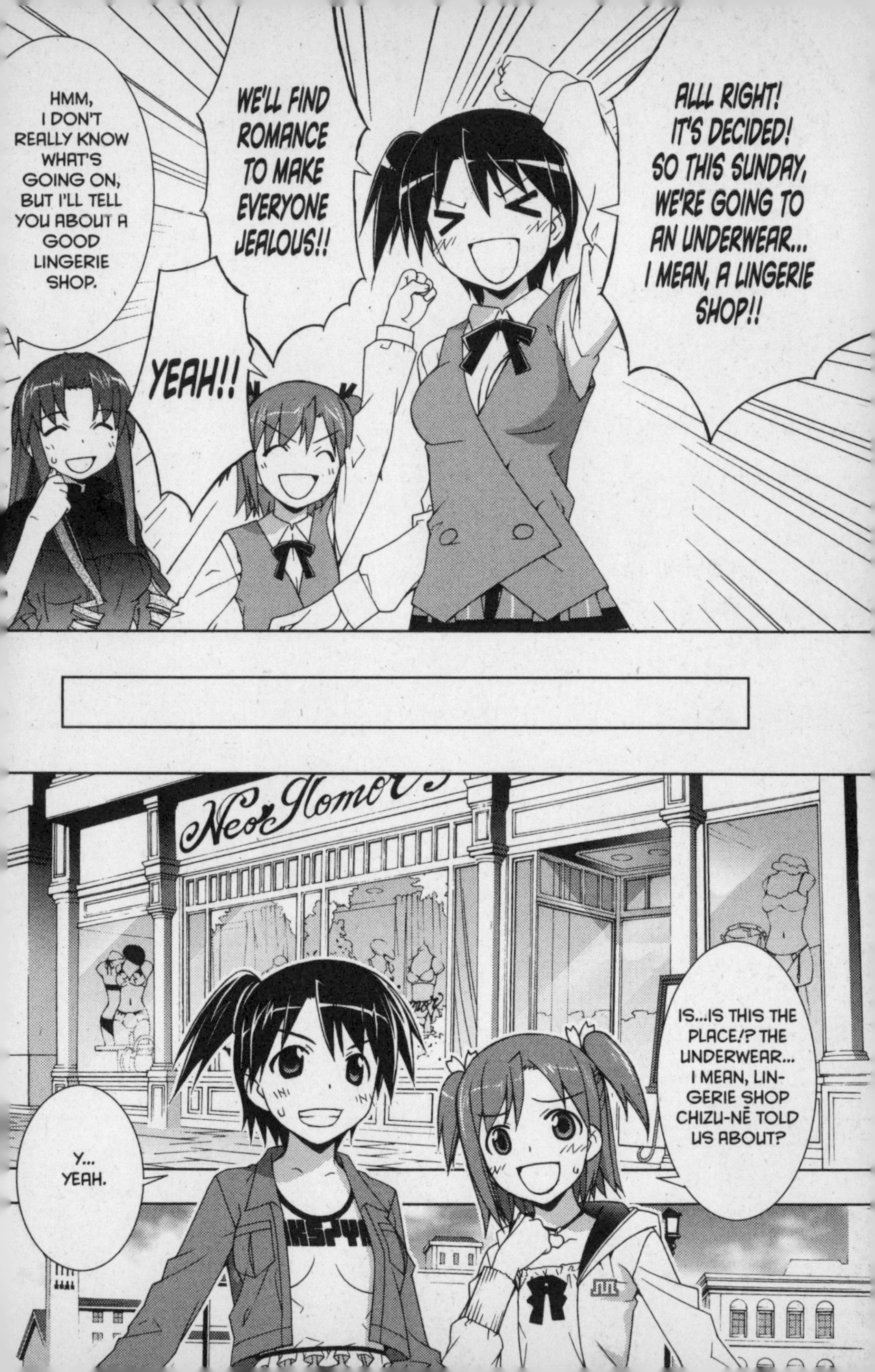
ALL RIGHT! IT'S DECIDED! SO THIS SUNDAY, WE'RE GOING TO AN UNDERWEAR... I MEAN, A LINGERIE SHOP!!
WE'LL FIND ROMANCE TO MAKE EVERYONE JEALOUS!!
YEAH!!
HMM, I DON'T REALLY KNOW WHAT'S GOING ON, BUT I'LL TELL YOU ABOUT A GOOD LINGERIE SHOP.
IS...IS THIS THE PLACE!? THE UNDERWEAR... I MEAN, LIN-GERIE SHOP CHIZU-NĒ TOLD US ABOUT?
Y... YEAH.

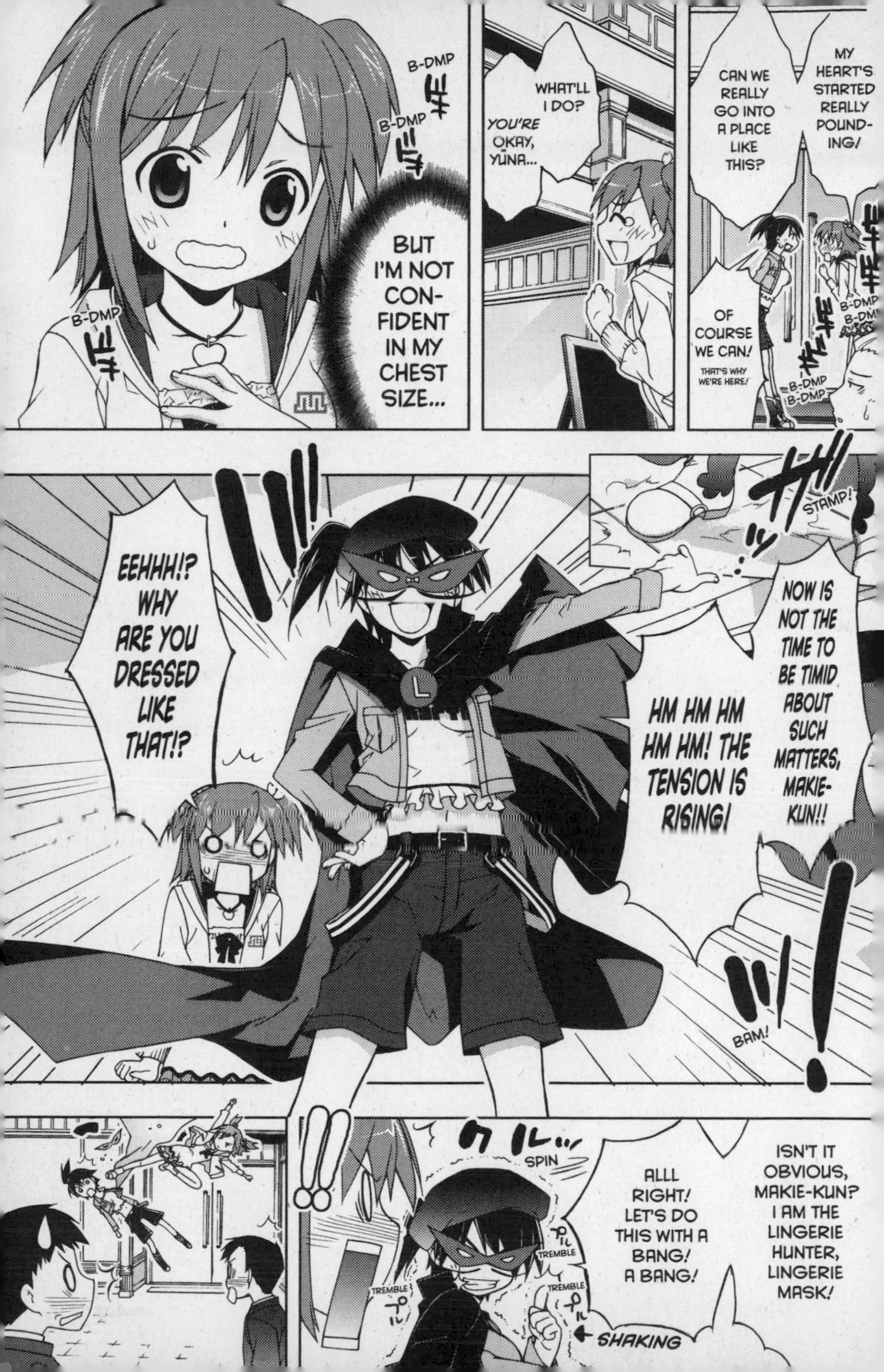
MY HEART'S STARTED REALLY POUNDING!
CAN WE REALLY GO INTO A PLACE LIKE THIS?
B-DMP B-DMP
OF COURSE WE CAN!
THAT'S WHY WE'RE HERE!
B-DMP B-DMP
WHAT'LL I DO?
YOU'RE OKAY, YUNA...
B-DMP
B-DMP
BUT I'M NOT CONFIDENT IN MY CHEST SIZE...
B-DMP
STAMP!
NOW IS NOT THE TIME TO BE TIMID ABOUT SUCH MATTERS, MAKIE-KUN!!
HM HM HM HM HM! THE TENSION IS RISING!
BAM!
EEHHH!? WHY ARE YOU DRESSED LIKE THAT!?
ISN'T IT OBVIOUS, MAKIE-KUN? I AM THE LINGERIE HUNTER, LINGERIE MASK!
ALLL RIGHT! LET'S DO THIS WITH A BANG! A BANG!
SPIN
TREMBLE
TREMBLE
TREMBLE
SHAKING

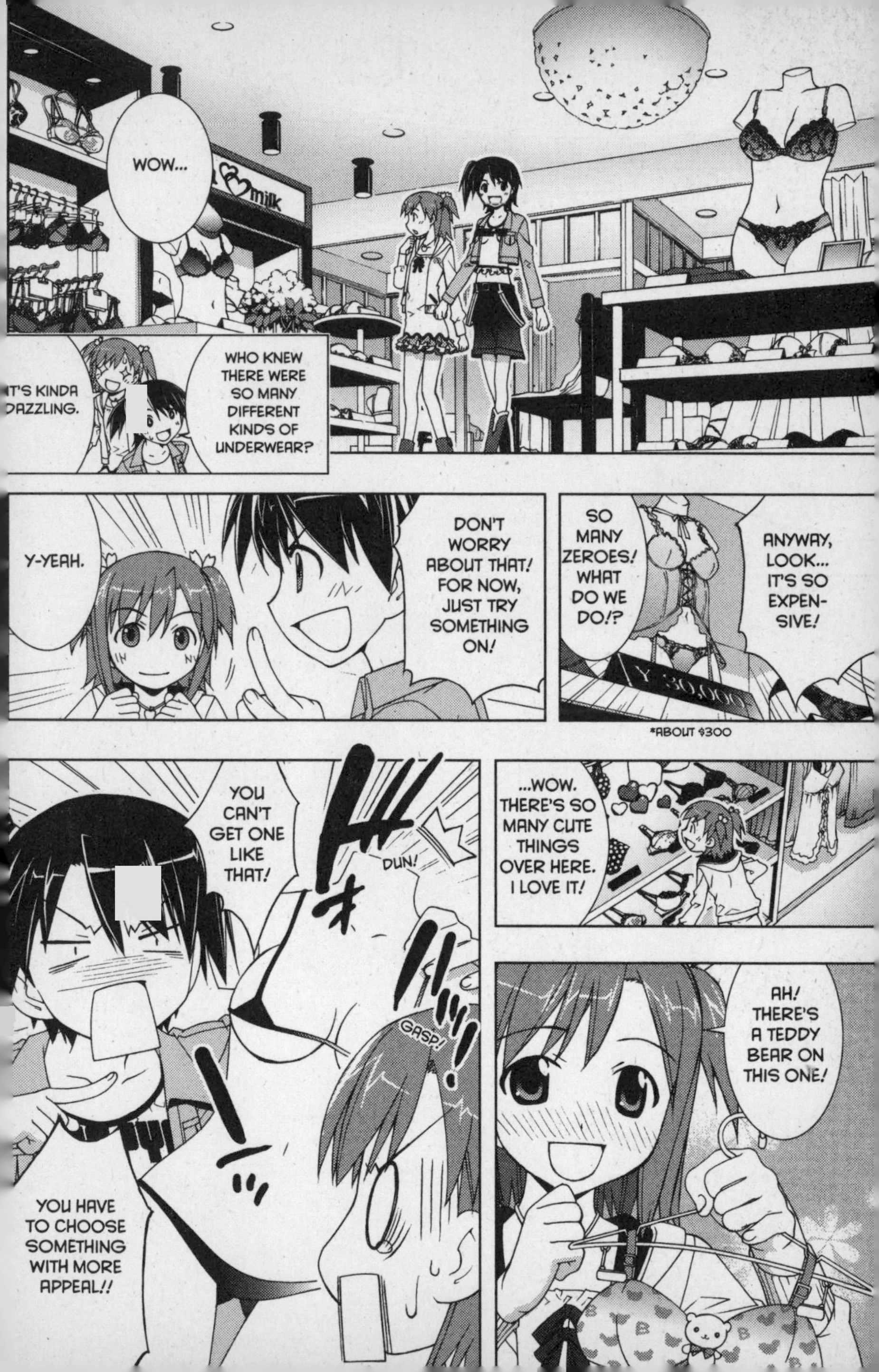
WOW...
milk
WHO KNEW THERE WERE SO MANY DIFFERENT KINDS OF UNDERWEAR?
IT'S KINDA DAZZLING.
ANYWAY, LOOK... IT'S SO EXPEN-SIVE!
SO MANY ZEROES! WHAT DO WE DO!?
¥ 30,000
DON'T WORRY ABOUT THAT! FOR NOW, JUST TRY SOMETHING ON!
Y-YEAH.
*ABOUT $300
...WOW. THERE'S SO MANY CUTE THINGS OVER HERE. I LOVE IT!
AH! THERE'S A TEDDY BEAR ON THIS ONE!
DUN!
GASP!
YOU CAN'T GET ONE LIKE THAT!
YOU HAVE TO CHOOSE SOMETHING WITH MORE APPEAL!!

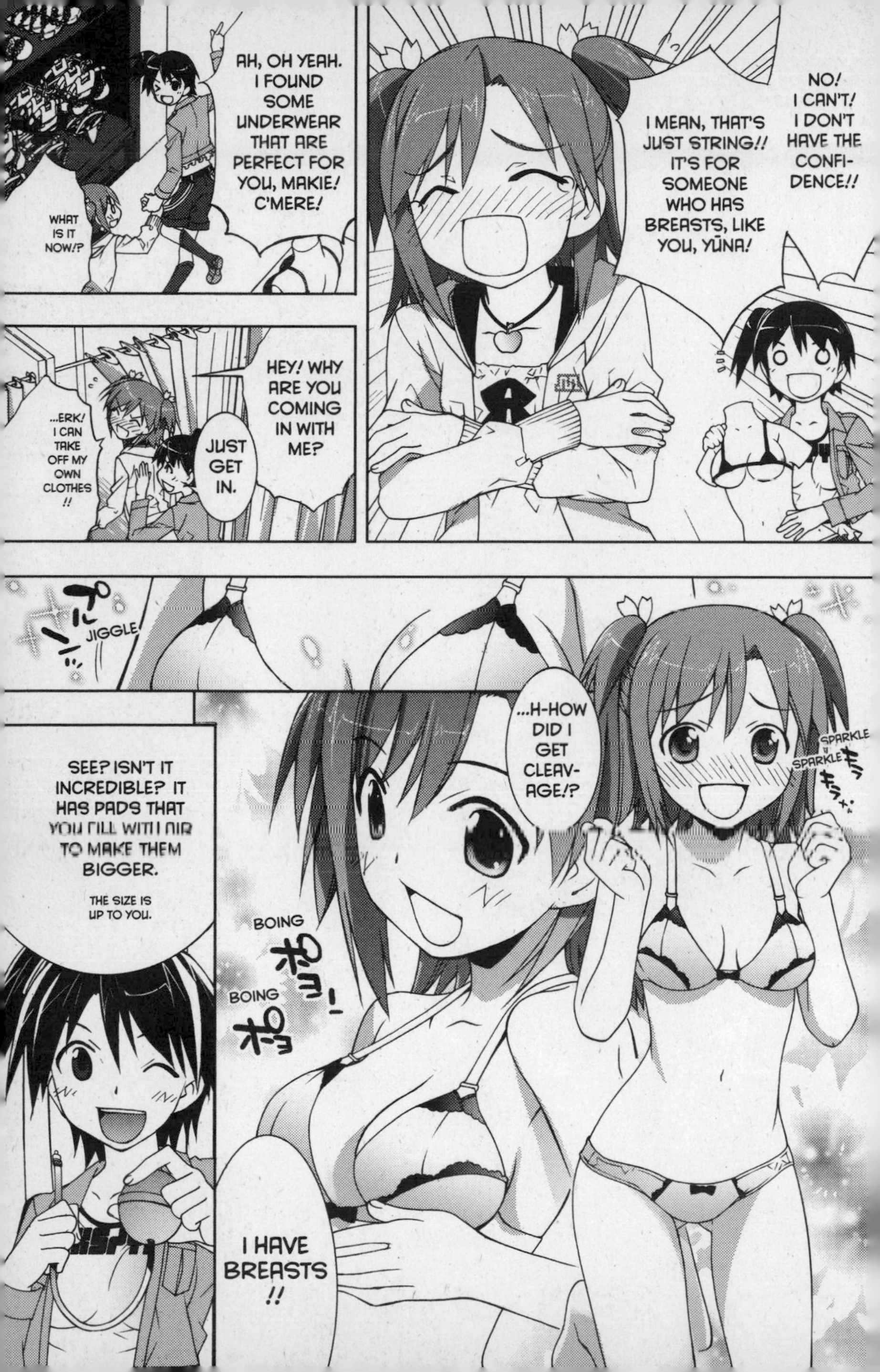
NO! I CAN'T! I DON'T HAVE THE CONFIDENCE!!
I MEAN, THAT'S JUST STRING!! IT'S FOR SOMEONE WHO HAS BREASTS, LIKE YOU, YŪNA!
AH, OH YEAH. I FOUND SOME UNDERWEAR THAT ARE PERFECT FOR YOU, MAKIE! C'MERE!
WHAT IS IT NOW!?
HEY! WHY ARE YOU COMING IN WITH ME?
JUST GET IN.
...ERK! I CAN TAKE OFF MY OWN CLOTHES!!
JIGGLE
...H-HOW DID I GET CLEAVAGE!?
SPARKLE SPARKLE
BOING
BOING
I HAVE BREASTS!!
SEE? ISN'T IT INCREDIBLE? IT HAS PADS THAT YOU FILL WITH AIR TO MAKE THEM BIGGER.
THE SIZE IS UP TO YOU.

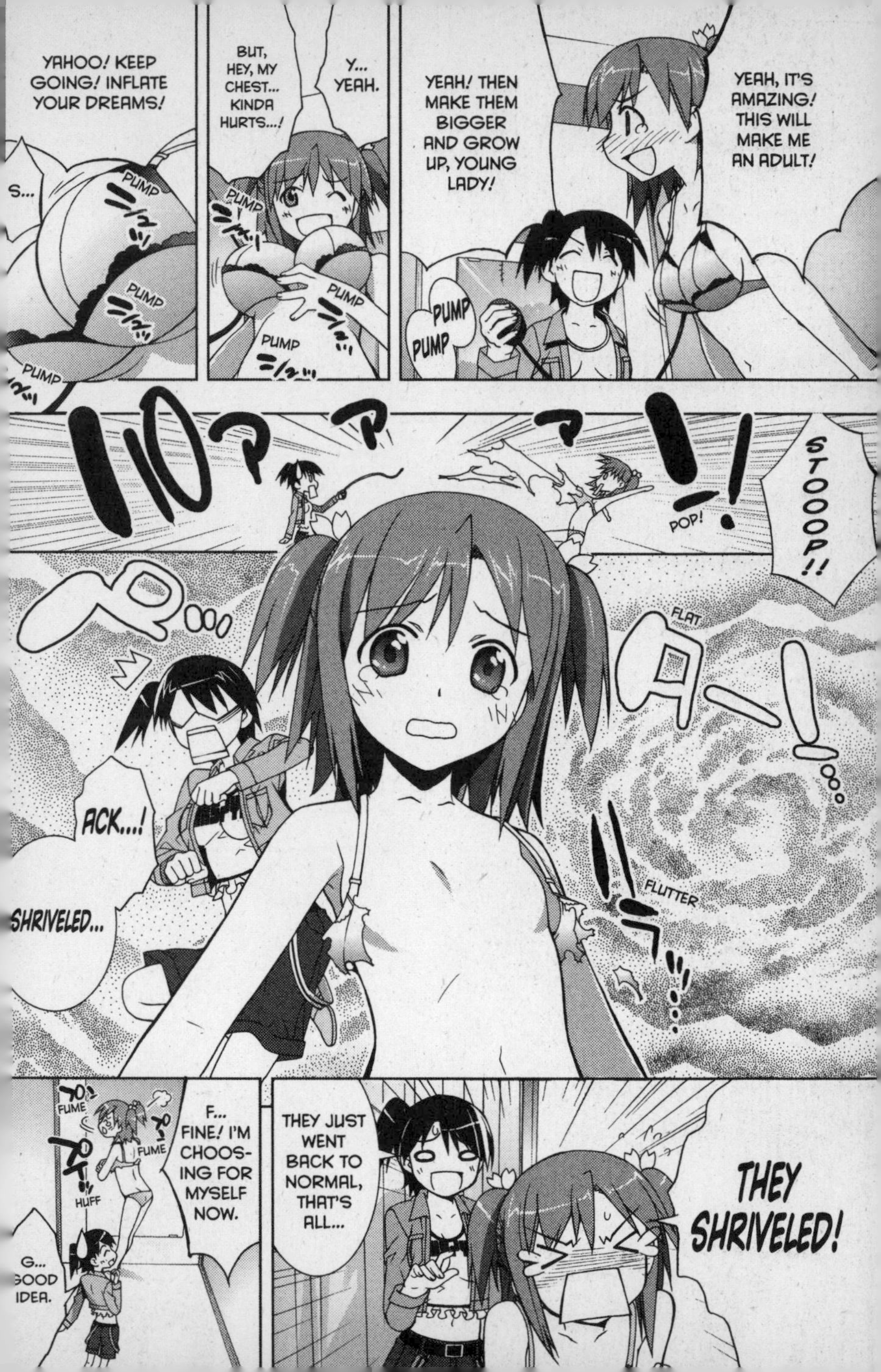
YEAH, IT'S AMAZING! THIS WILL MAKE ME AN ADULT!
YEAH! THEN MAKE THEM BIGGER AND GROW UP, YOUNG LADY!
PUMP PUMP
Y... YEAH.
BUT, HEY, MY CHEST... KINDA HURTS...!
PUMP
PUMP
PUMP
YAHOO! KEEP GOING! INFLATE YOUR DREAMS!
S...
PUMP
PUMP
PUMP
STOOOP!!
POP!
FLAT
FLUTTER
ACK...!
SHRIVELED...
THEY SHRIVELED!
THEY JUST WENT BACK TO NORMAL, THAT'S ALL...
F... FINE! I'M CHOOSING FOR MYSELF NOW.
FUME
FUME
HUFF
G... GOOD IDEA.

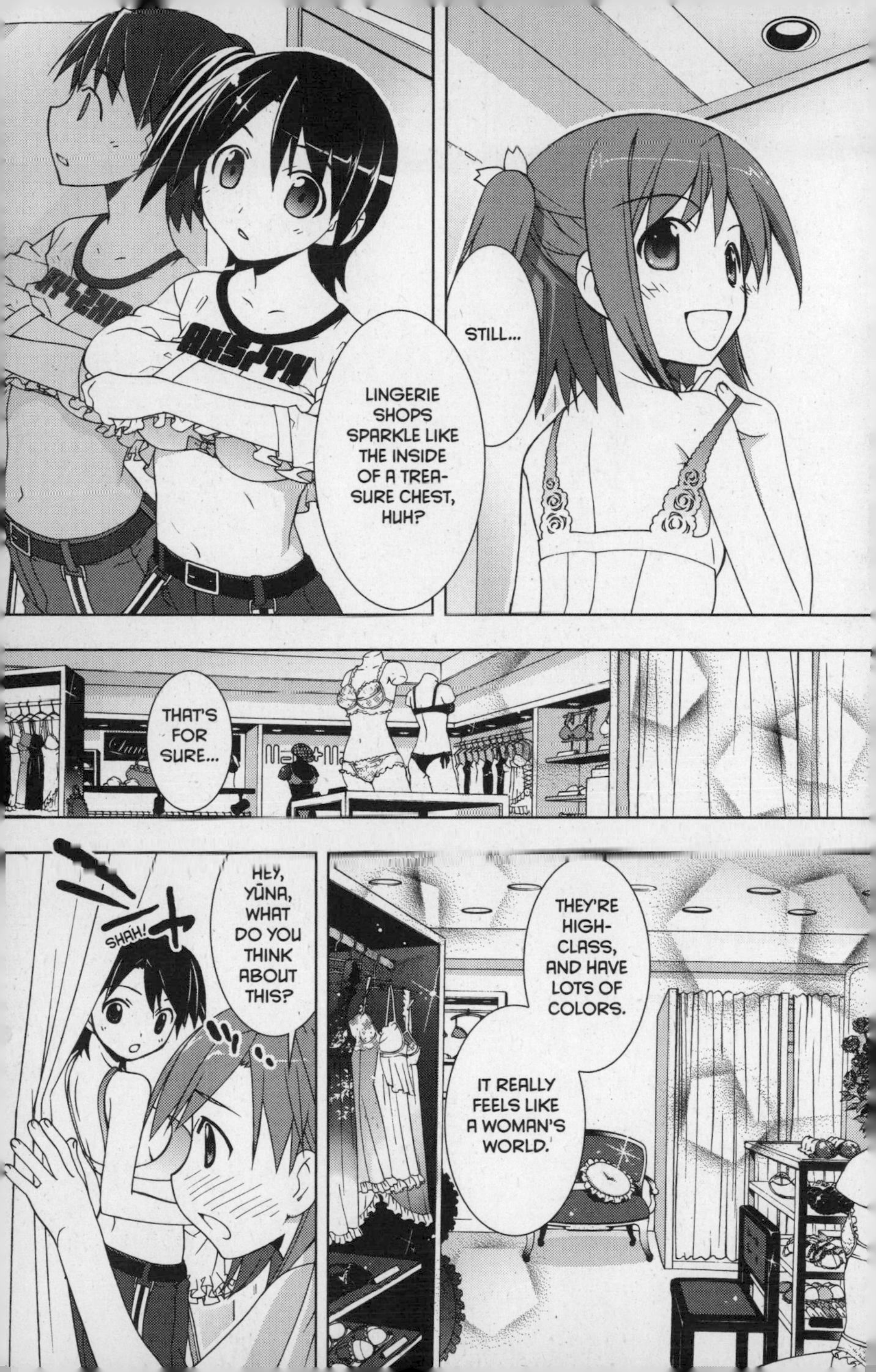
STILL...
LINGERIE SHOPS SPARKLE LIKE THE INSIDE OF A TREA-SURE CHEST, HUH?
THAT'S FOR SURE...
THEY'RE HIGH-CLASS, AND HAVE LOTS OF COLORS.
IT REALLY FEELS LIKE A WOMAN'S WORLD.
SHAH!
HEY, YŪNA, WHAT DO YOU THINK ABOUT THIS?

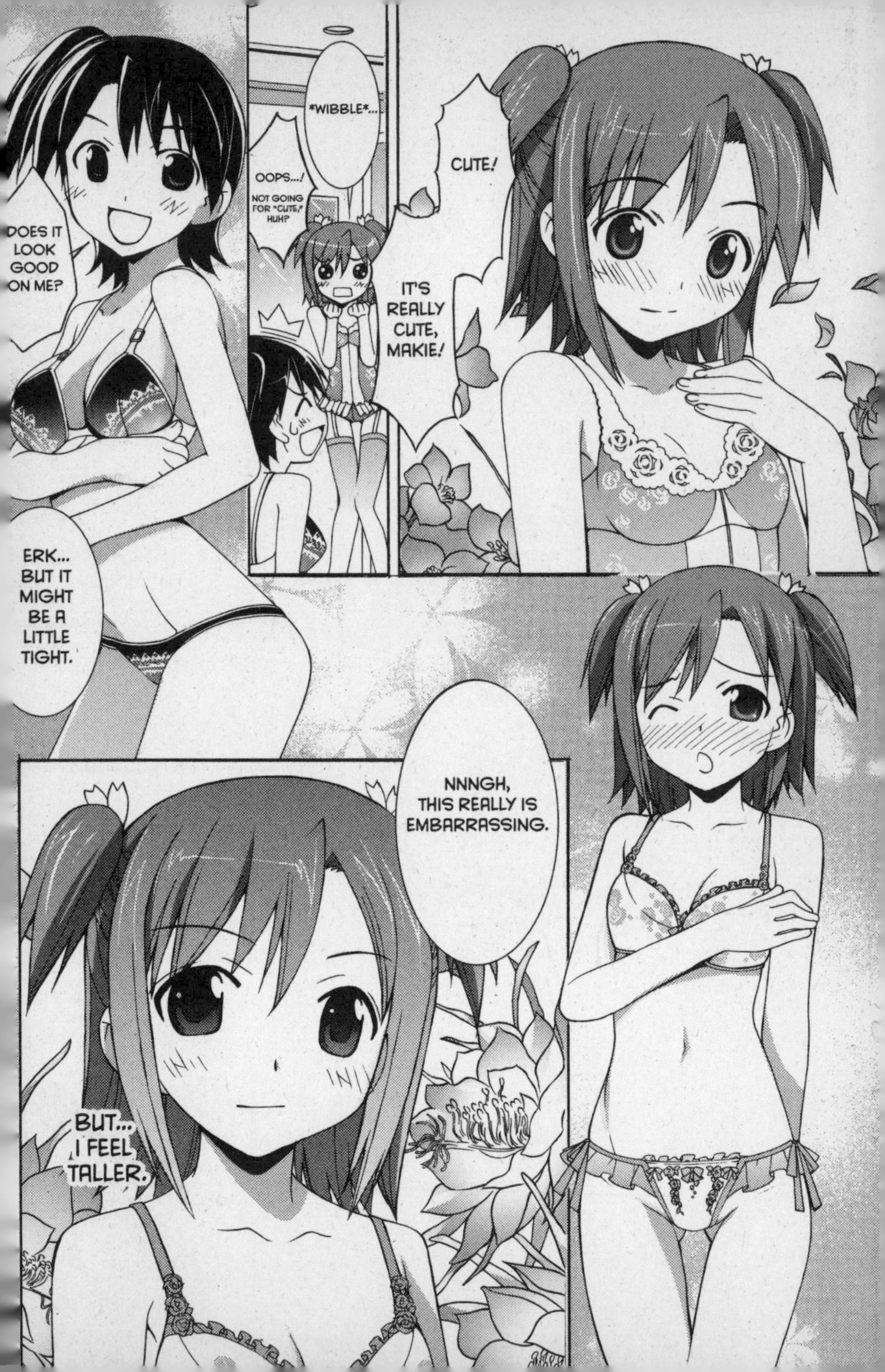
CUTE!
IT'S REALLY CUTE, MAKIE!
*WIBBLE*...
OOPS...!
NOT GOING FOR "CUTE," HUH?
DOES IT LOOK GOOD ON ME?
ERK... BUT IT MIGHT BE A LITTLE TIGHT.
NNNGH, THIS REALLY IS EMBARRASSING.
BUT... I FEEL TALLER.

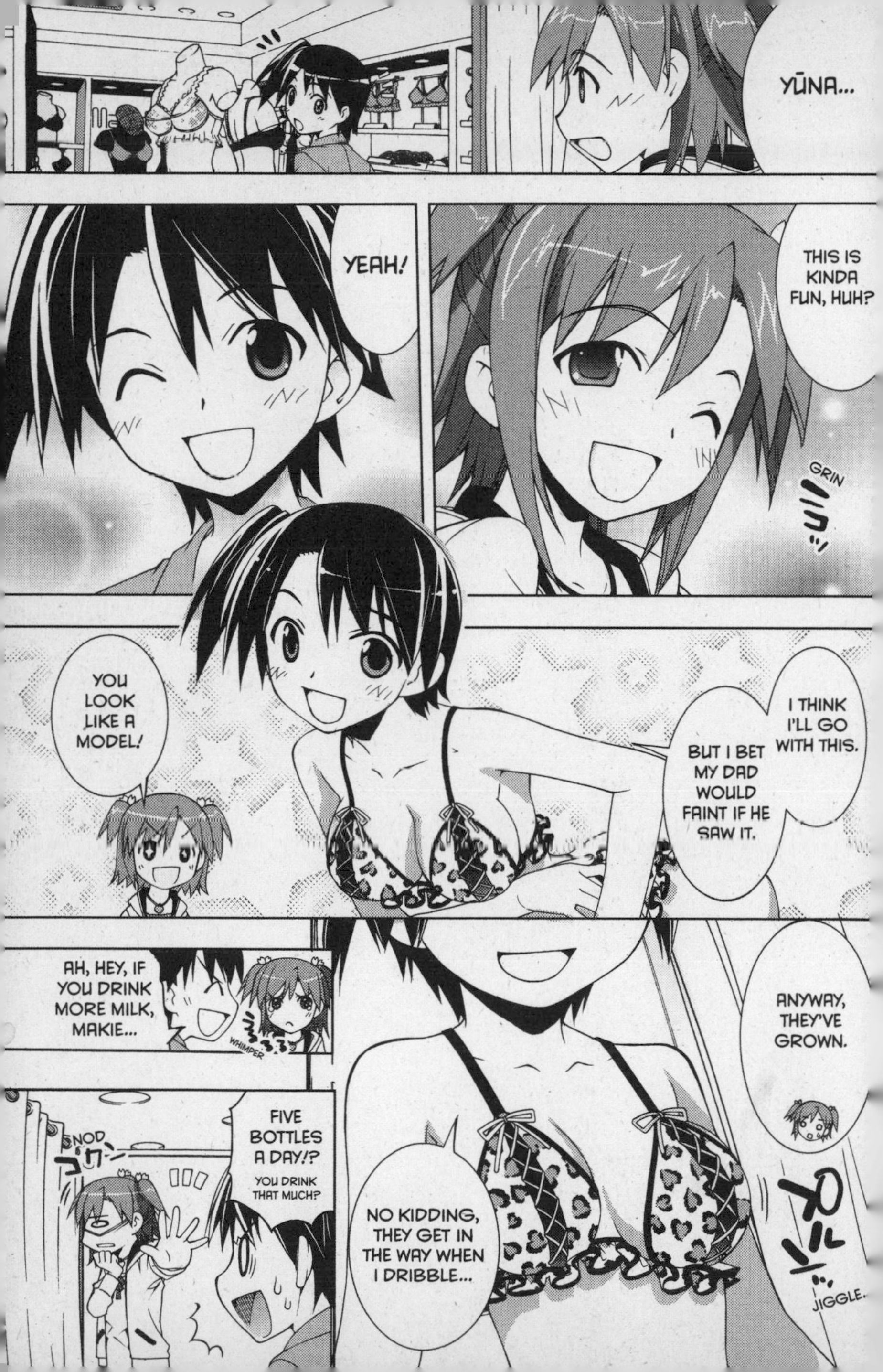
YŪNA...
THIS IS KINDA FUN, HUH?
GRIN
YEAH!
I THINK I'LL GO WITH THIS.
BUT I BET MY DAD WOULD FAINT IF HE SAW IT.
YOU LOOK LIKE A MODEL!
ANYWAY, THEY'VE GROWN.
JIGGLE.
NO KIDDING, THEY GET IN THE WAY WHEN I DRIBBLE...
AH, HEY, IF YOU DRINK MORE MILK, MAKIE...
WHIMPER
FIVE BOTTLES A DAY!?
YOU DRINK THAT MUCH?
NOD

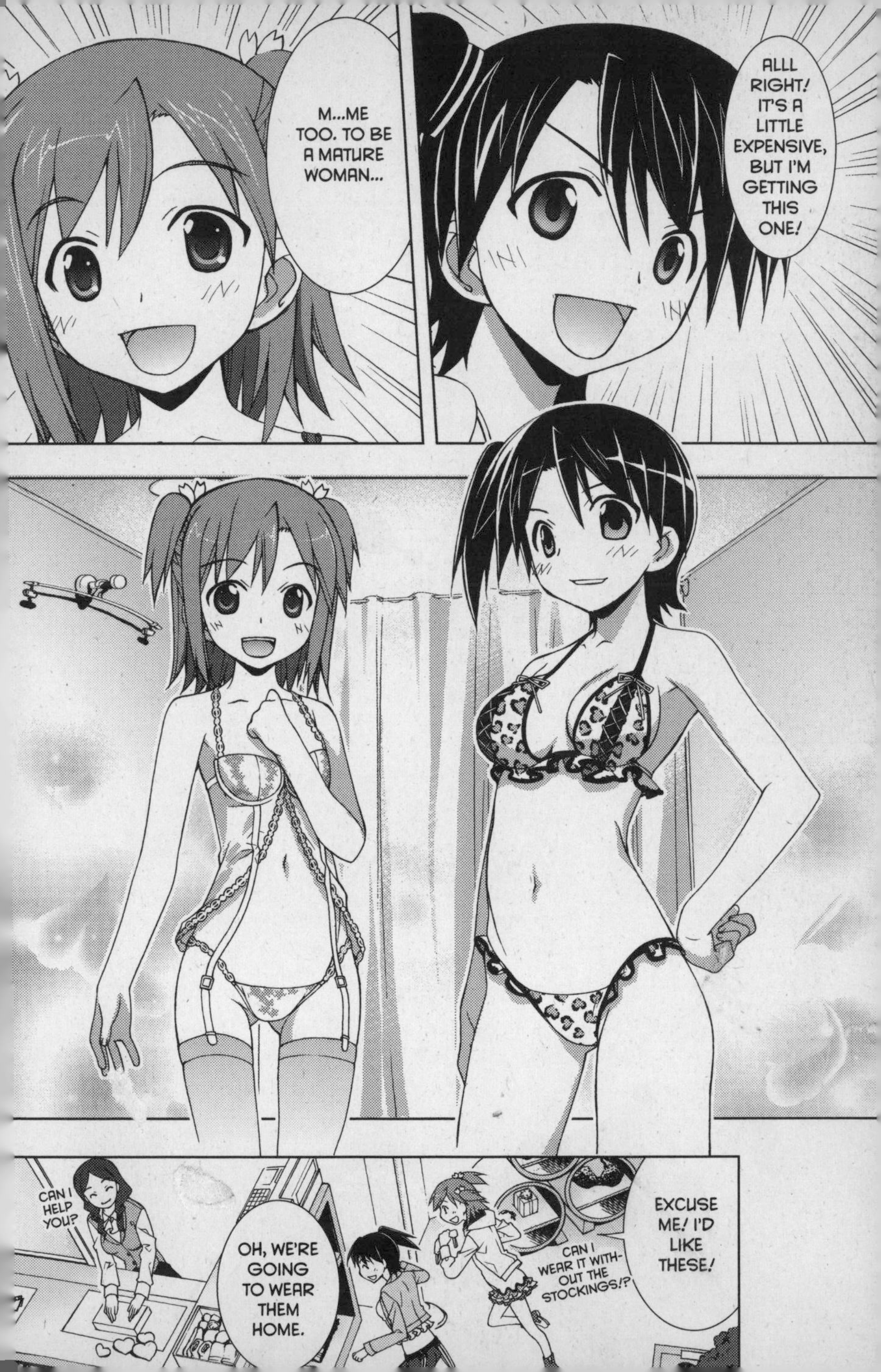
ALLL RIGHT! IT'S A LITTLE EXPENSIVE, BUT I'M GETTING THIS ONE!
M...ME TOO. TO BE A MATURE WOMAN...
EXCUSE ME! I'D LIKE THESE!
CAN I HELP YOU?
OH, WE'RE GOING TO WEAR THEM HOME.
CAN I WEAR IT WITH-OUT THE STOCKINGS!?

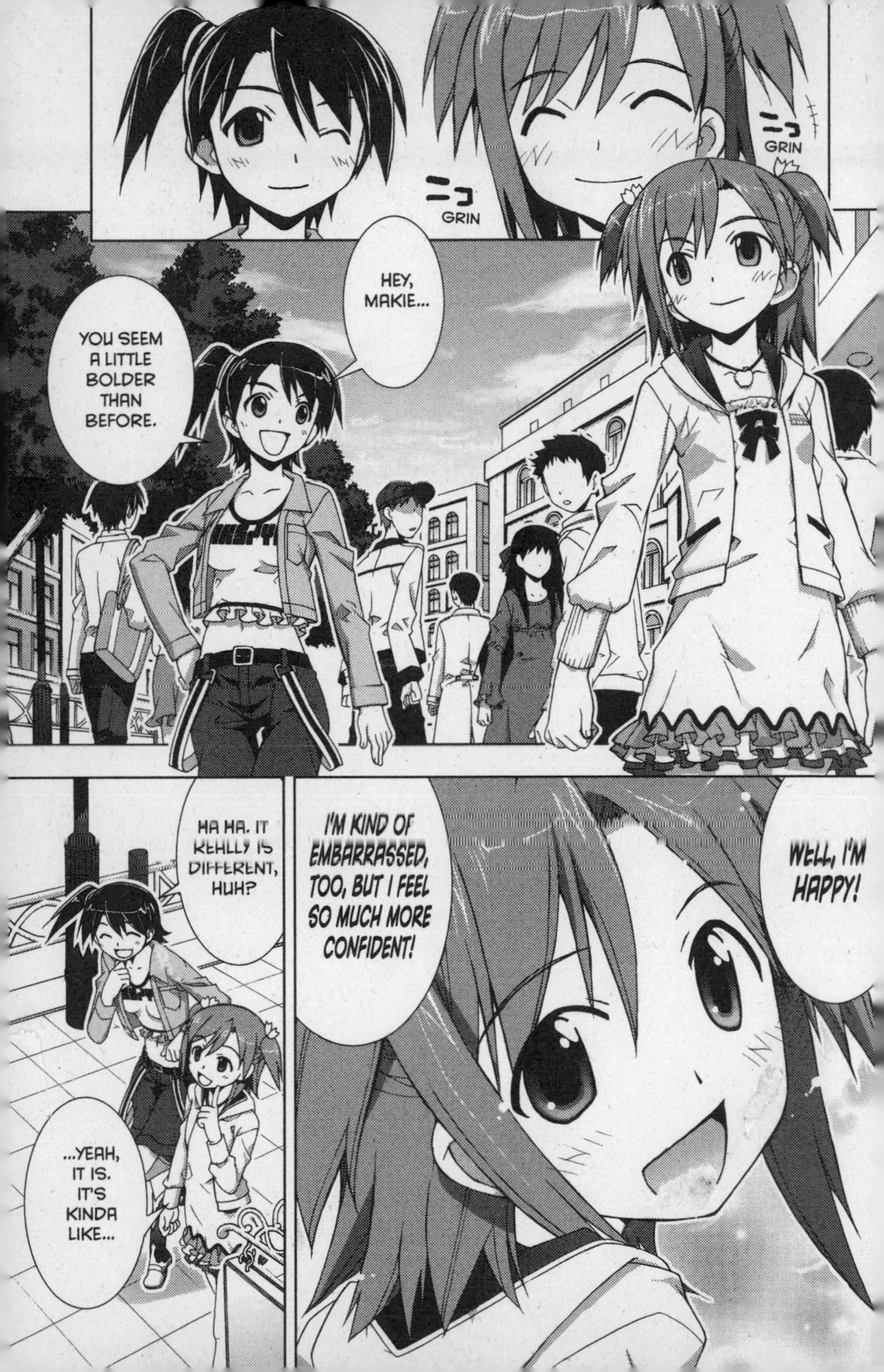
ニコ
GRIN
ニコ
GRIN
HEY, MAKIE...
YOU SEEM A LITTLE BOLDER THAN BEFORE.
WELL, I'M HAPPY!
I'M KIND OF EMBARRASSED, TOO, BUT I FEEL SO MUCH MORE CONFIDENT!
HA HA. IT REALLY IS DIFFERENT, HUH?
...YEAH, IT IS. IT'S KINDA LIKE...

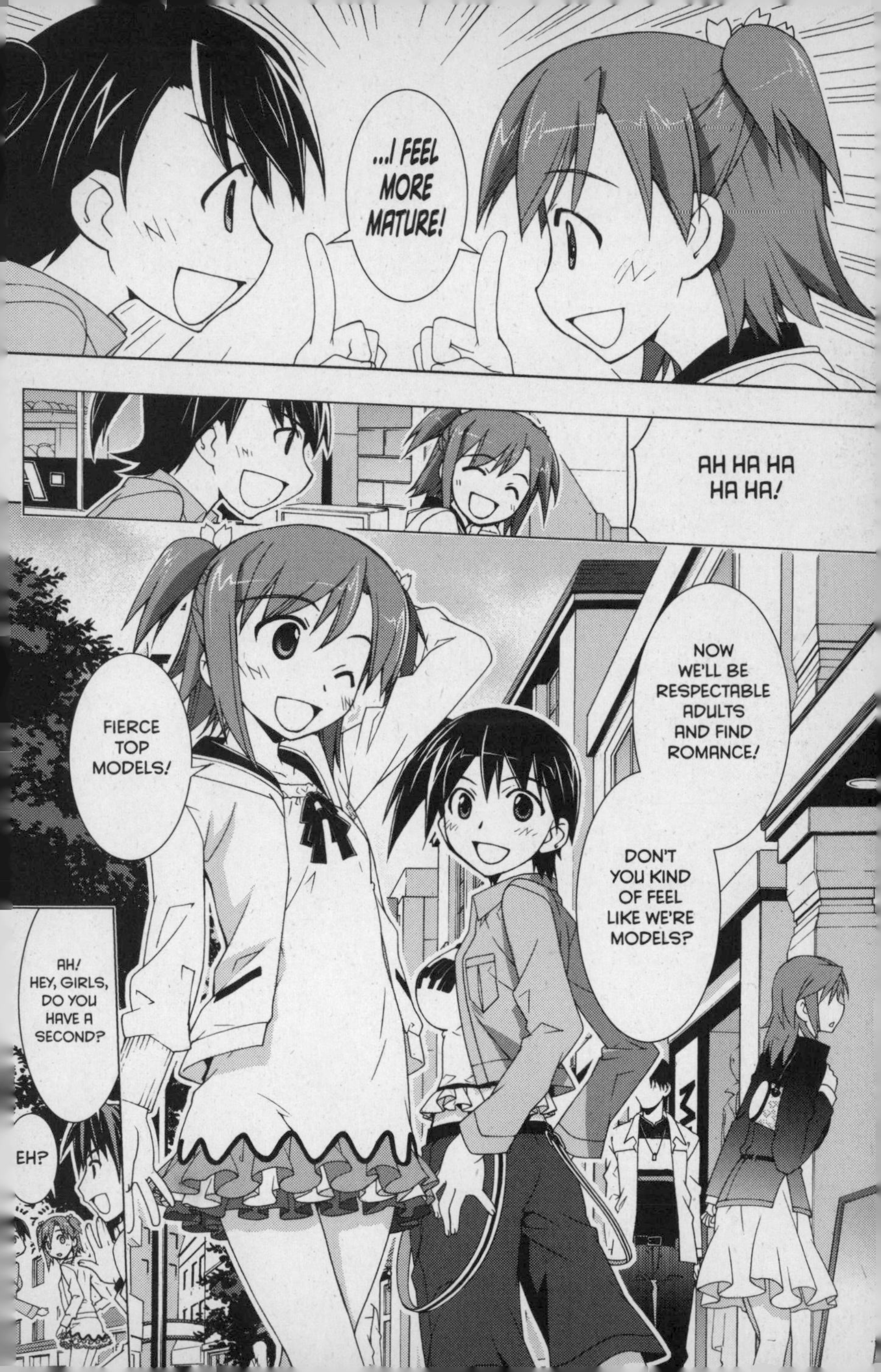
...I FEEL MORE MATURE!
AH HA HA HA HA!
NOW WE'LL BE RESPECTABLE ADULTS AND FIND ROMANCE!
DON'T YOU KIND OF FEEL LIKE WE'RE MODELS?
FIERCE TOP MODELS!
AH! HEY, GIRLS, DO YOU HAVE A SECOND?
EH?

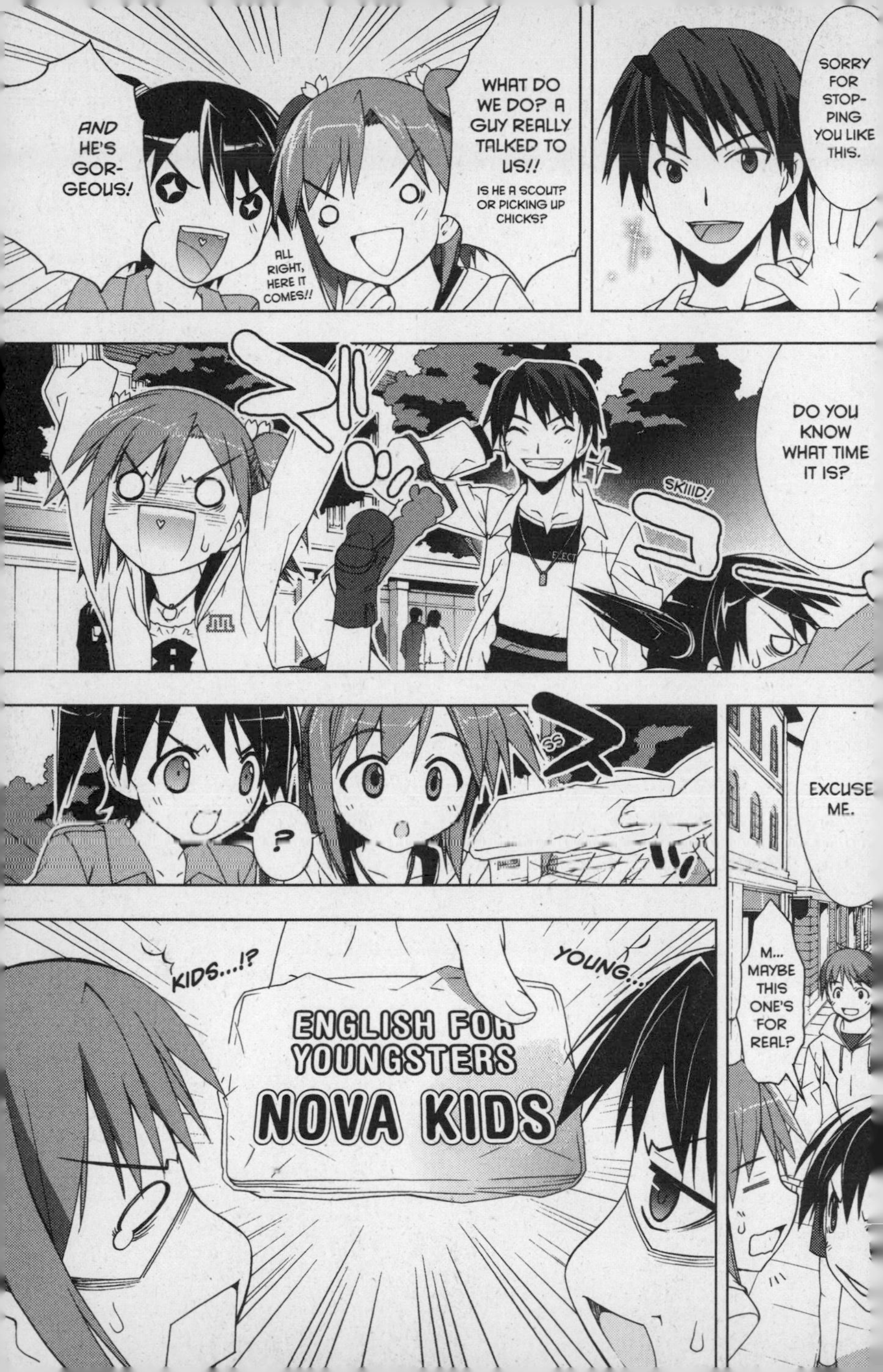
SORRY FOR STOP-PING YOU LIKE THIS.
WHAT DO WE DO? A GUY REALLY TALKED TO US!!
IS HE A SCOUT? OR PICKING UP CHICKS?
AND HE'S GOR-GEOUS!
ALL RIGHT, HERE IT COMES!!
DO YOU KNOW WHAT TIME IT IS?
SKIIID!
EXCUSE ME.
SS
?
M... MAYBE THIS ONE'S FOR REAL?
YOUNG...
ENGLISH FOR YOUNGSTERS
NOVA KIDS
KIDS...!?

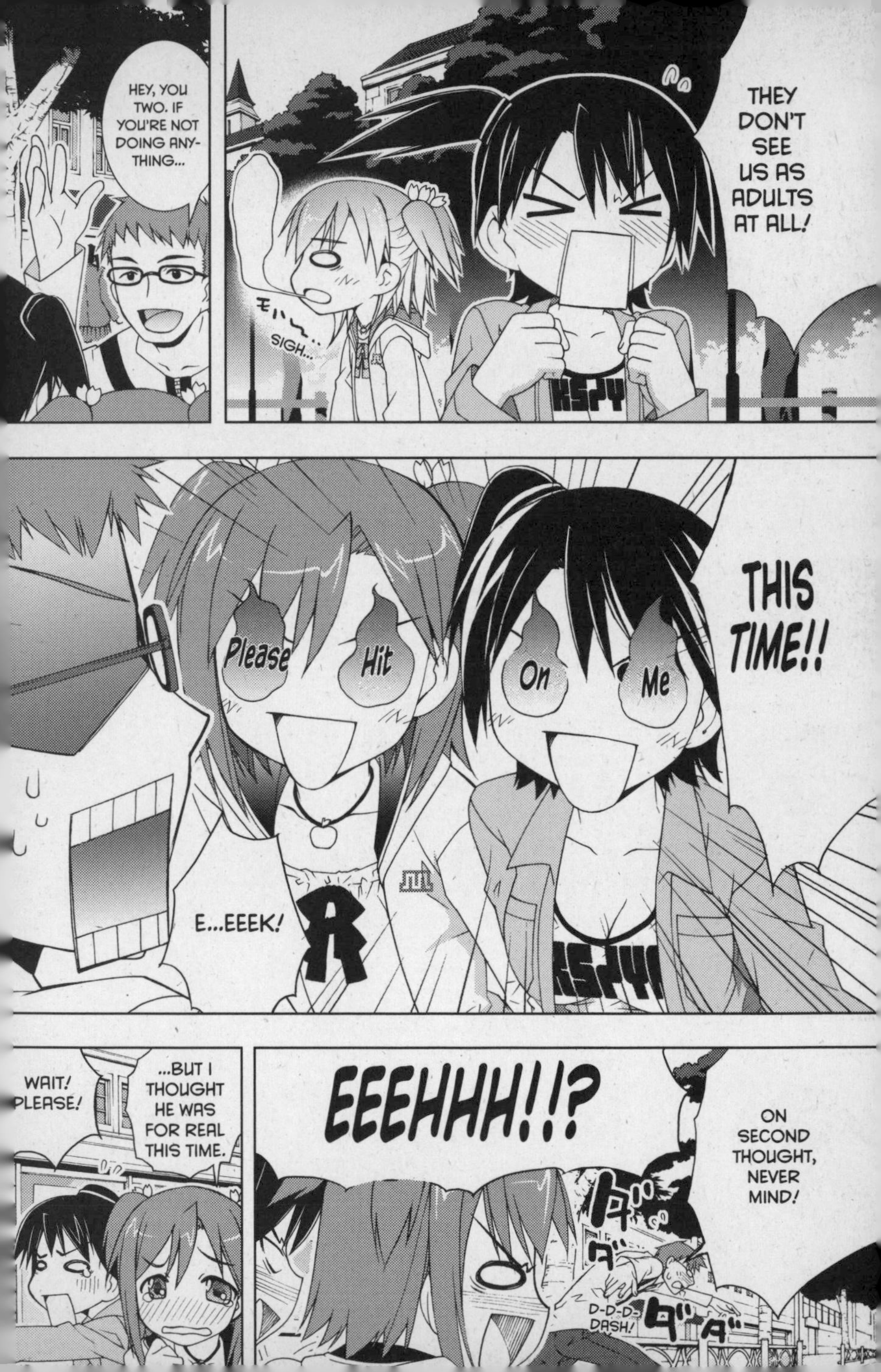
THEY DON'T SEE US AS ADULTS AT ALL!
SIGH...
HEY, YOU TWO. IF YOU'RE NOT DOING ANY-THING...
THIS TIME!!
Please Hit On Me
E...EEEK!
ON SECOND THOUGHT, NEVER MIND!
EEEHHH!!?
D-D-D-DASH!
...BUT I THOUGHT HE WAS FOR REAL THIS TIME.
WAIT! PLEASE!

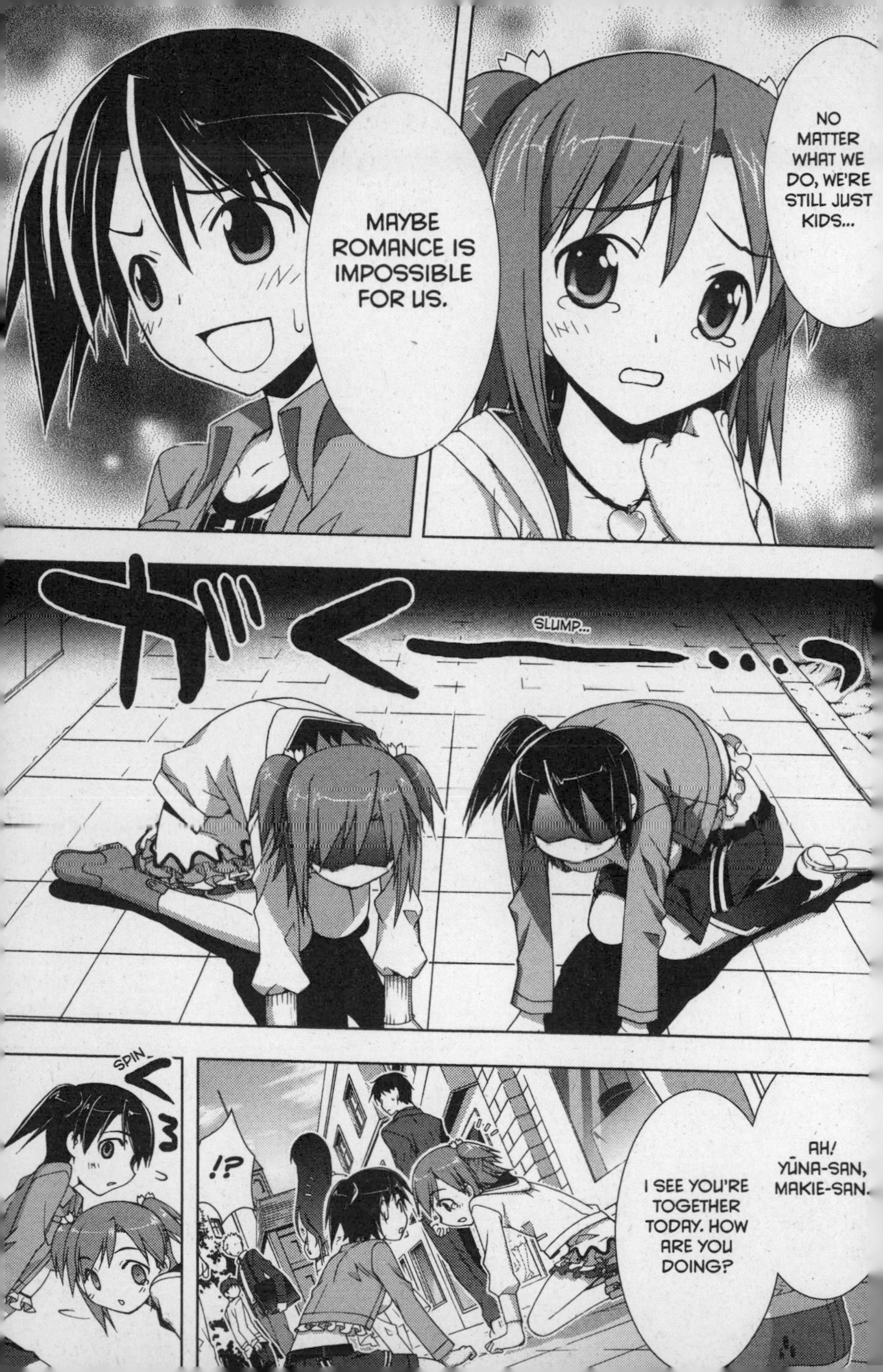
NO MATTER WHAT WE DO, WE'RE STILL JUST KIDS...
MAYBE ROMANCE IS IMPOSSIBLE FOR US.
SLUMP...
AH! YŪNA-SAN, MAKIE-SAN.
I SEE YOU'RE TOGETHER TODAY. HOW ARE YOU DOING?
!?
SPIN

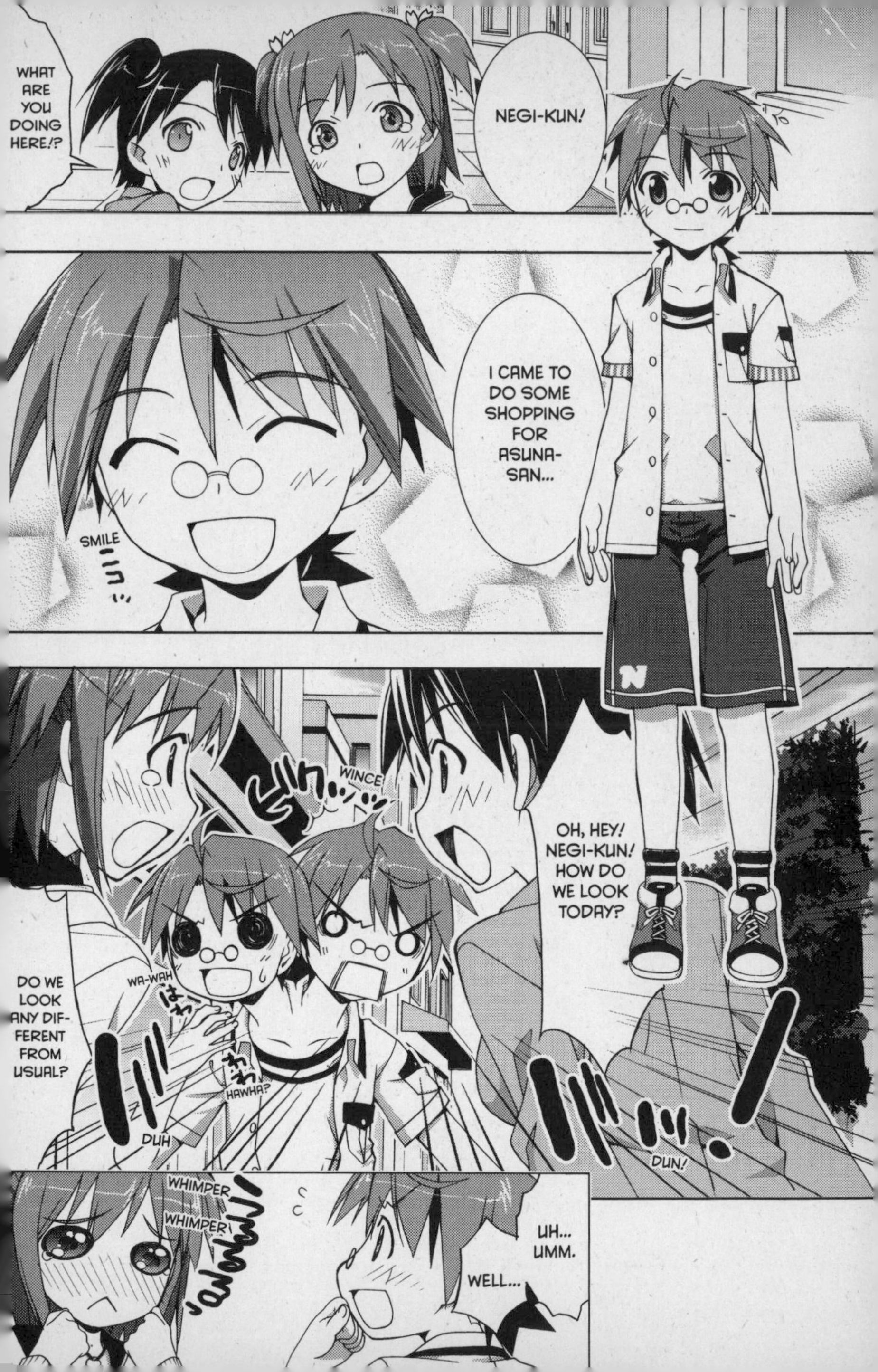
NEGI-KUN!
WHAT ARE YOU DOING HERE!?
I CAME TO DO SOME SHOPPING FOR ASUNA-SAN...
SMILE
OH, HEY! NEGI-KUN! HOW DO WE LOOK TODAY?
WINCE!
DO WE LOOK ANY DIF-FERENT FROM USUAL?
WA-WAH
HAWHA?
DUH
DUN!
UH... UMM.
WELL...
WHIMPER
WHIMPER

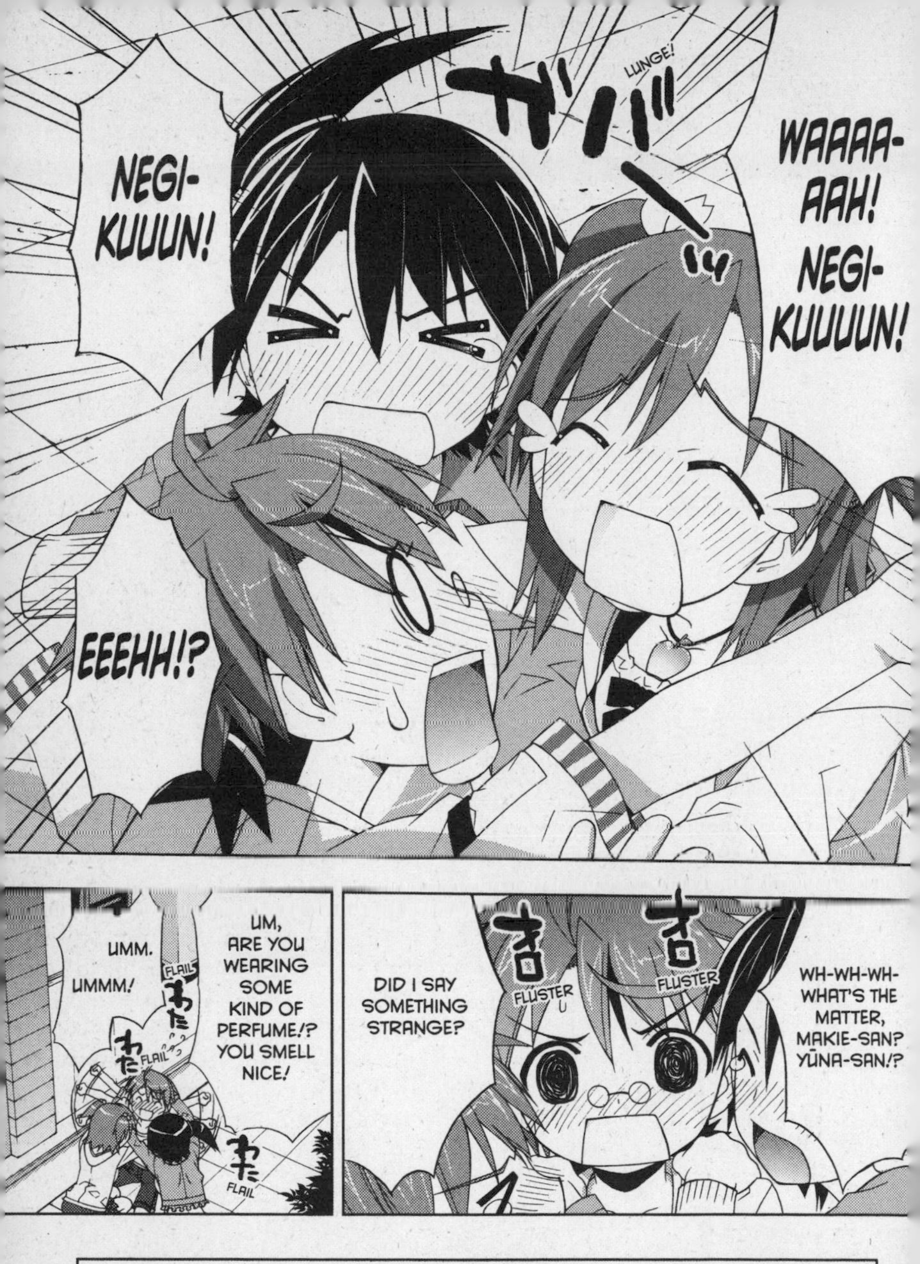
LUNGE!
WAAAA-AAH! NEGI-KUUUUN!
NEGI-KUUUN!
EEEHH!?
WH-WH-WH-WHAT'S THE MATTER, MAKIE-SAN? YŪNA-SAN!?
FLUSTER
FLUSTER
DID I SAY SOMETHING STRANGE?
UM, ARE YOU WEARING SOME KIND OF PERFUME!? YOU SMELL NICE!
FLAIL
FLAIL
UMM.
UMMM!
FLAIL

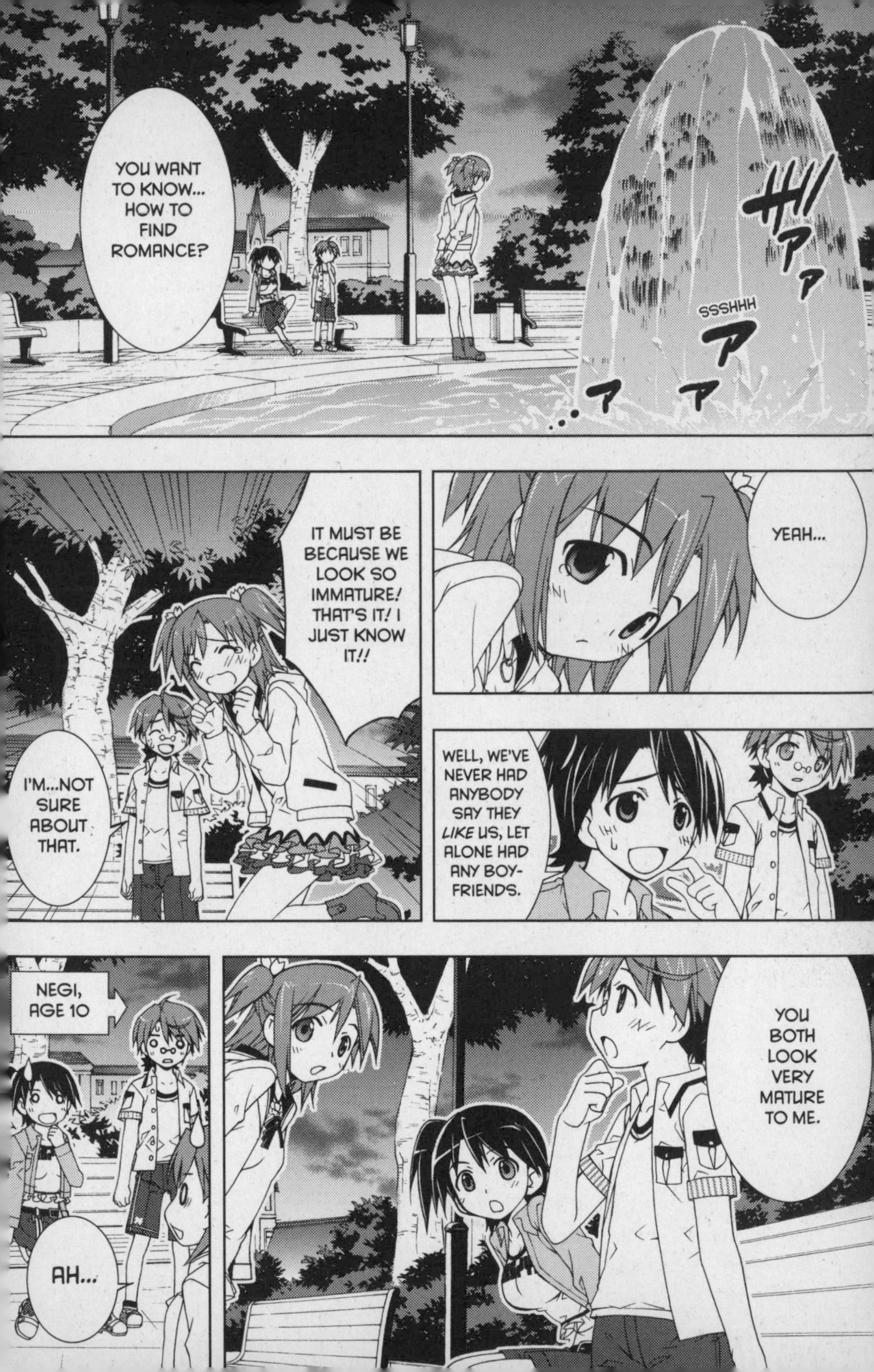
SSSHHH
YOU WANT TO KNOW... HOW TO FIND ROMANCE?
YEAH...
WELL, WE'VE NEVER HAD ANYBODY SAY THEY *LIKE* US, LET ALONE HAD ANY BOY-FRIENDS.
IT MUST BE BECAUSE WE LOOK SO IMMATURE! THAT'S IT! I JUST KNOW IT!!
I'M...NOT SURE ABOUT THAT.
YOU BOTH LOOK VERY MATURE TO ME.
NEGI, AGE 10
AH...

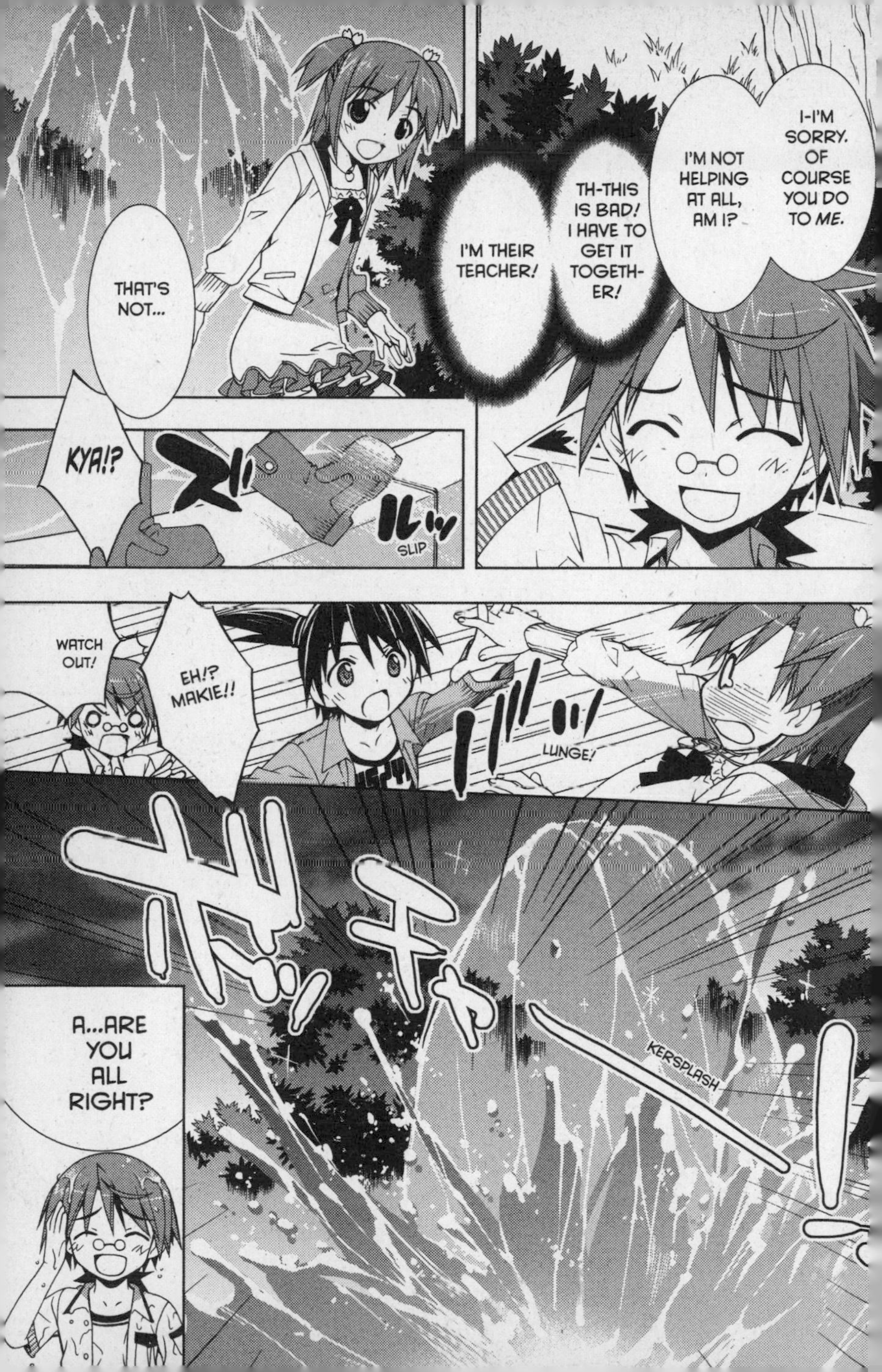
I-I'M SORRY. OF COURSE YOU DO TO *ME*.
I'M NOT HELPING AT ALL, AM I?
TH-THIS IS BAD! I HAVE TO GET IT TOGETHER!
I'M THEIR TEACHER!
THAT'S NOT...
KYA!?
SLIP
LUNGE!
EH!? MAKIE!!
WATCH OUT!
KERSPLASH
A...ARE YOU ALL RIGHT?

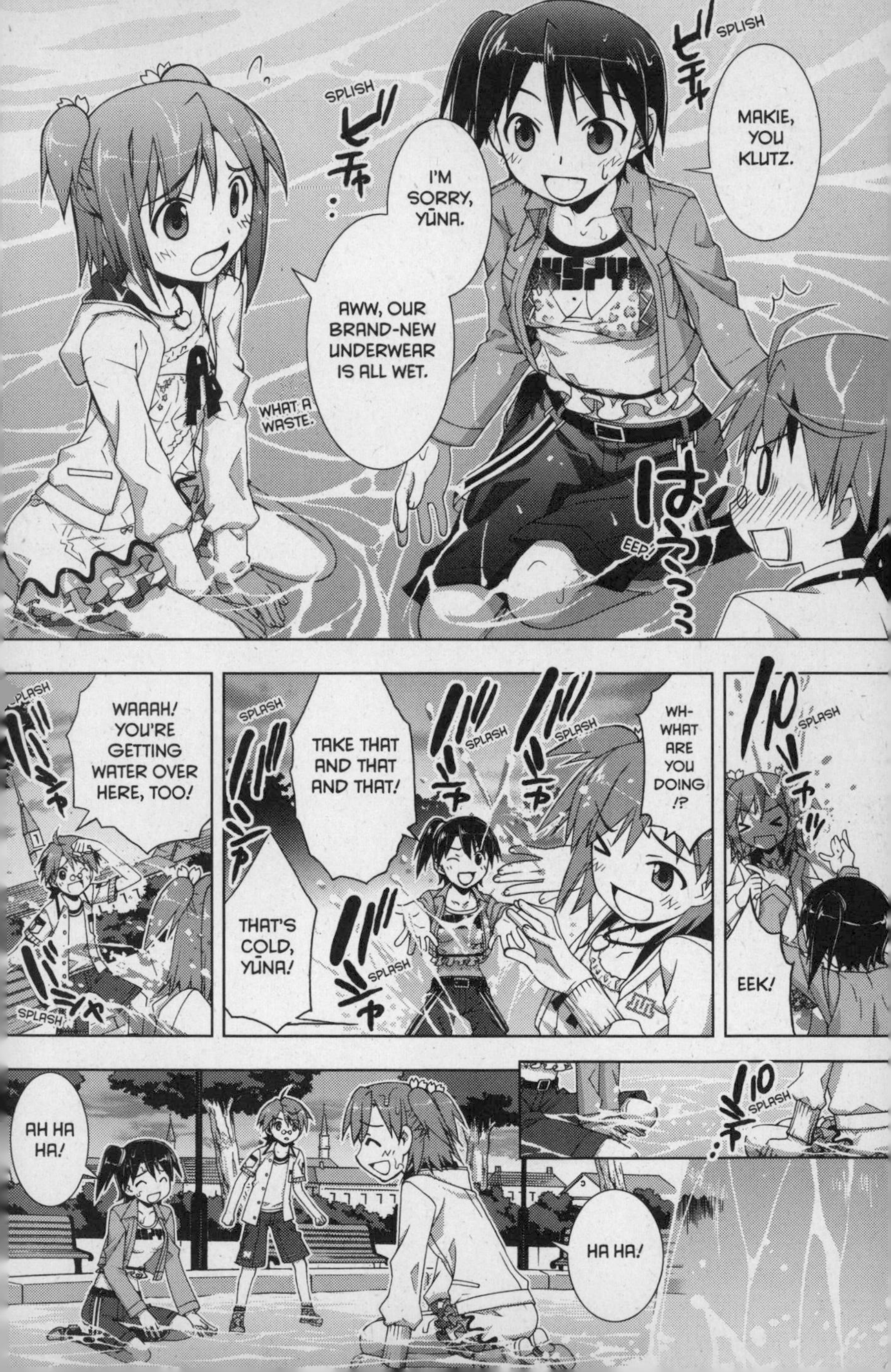
SPLISH
MAKIE, YOU KLUTZ.
SPLISH
I'M SORRY, YŪNA.
AWW, OUR BRAND-NEW UNDERWEAR IS ALL WET.
WHAT A WASTE.
EEP!
SPLASH
WH-WHAT ARE YOU DOING!?
EEK!
SPLASH
TAKE THAT AND THAT AND THAT!
SPLASH
SPLASH
THAT'S COLD, YŪNA!
SPLASH
SPLASH
WAAAH! YOU'RE GETTING WATER OVER HERE, TOO!
SPLASH
SPLASH
HA HA!
AH HA HA!

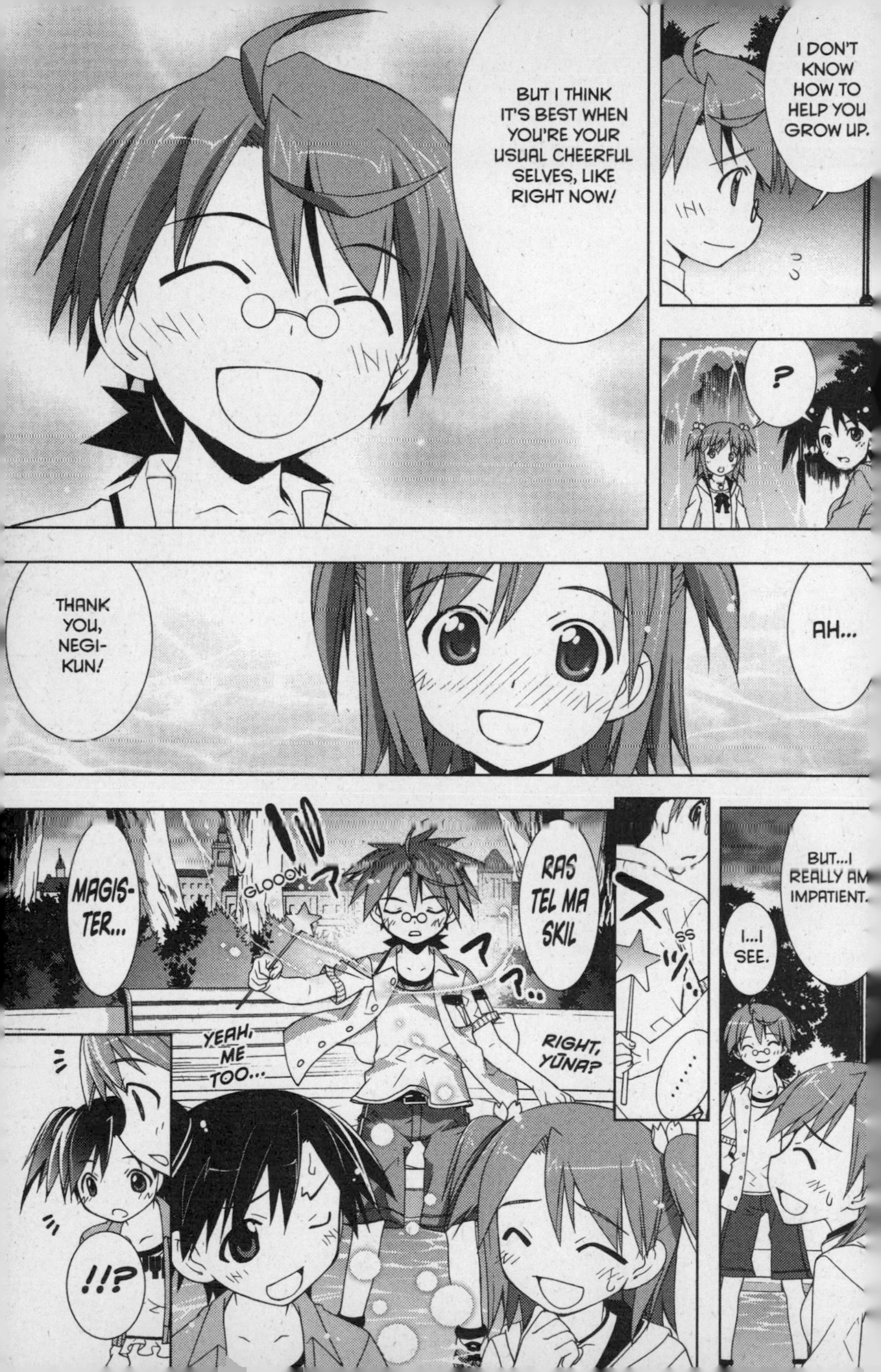
I DON'T KNOW HOW TO HELP YOU GROW UP.
?
BUT I THINK IT'S BEST WHEN YOU'RE YOUR USUAL CHEERFUL SELVES, LIKE RIGHT NOW!
AH...
THANK YOU, NEGI-KUN!
BUT...I REALLY AM IMPATIENT.
I...I SEE.
......
SS
RAS TEL MA SKIL
MAGISTER...
GLOOOW
RIGHT, YŪNA?
YEAH, ME TOO...
!!?

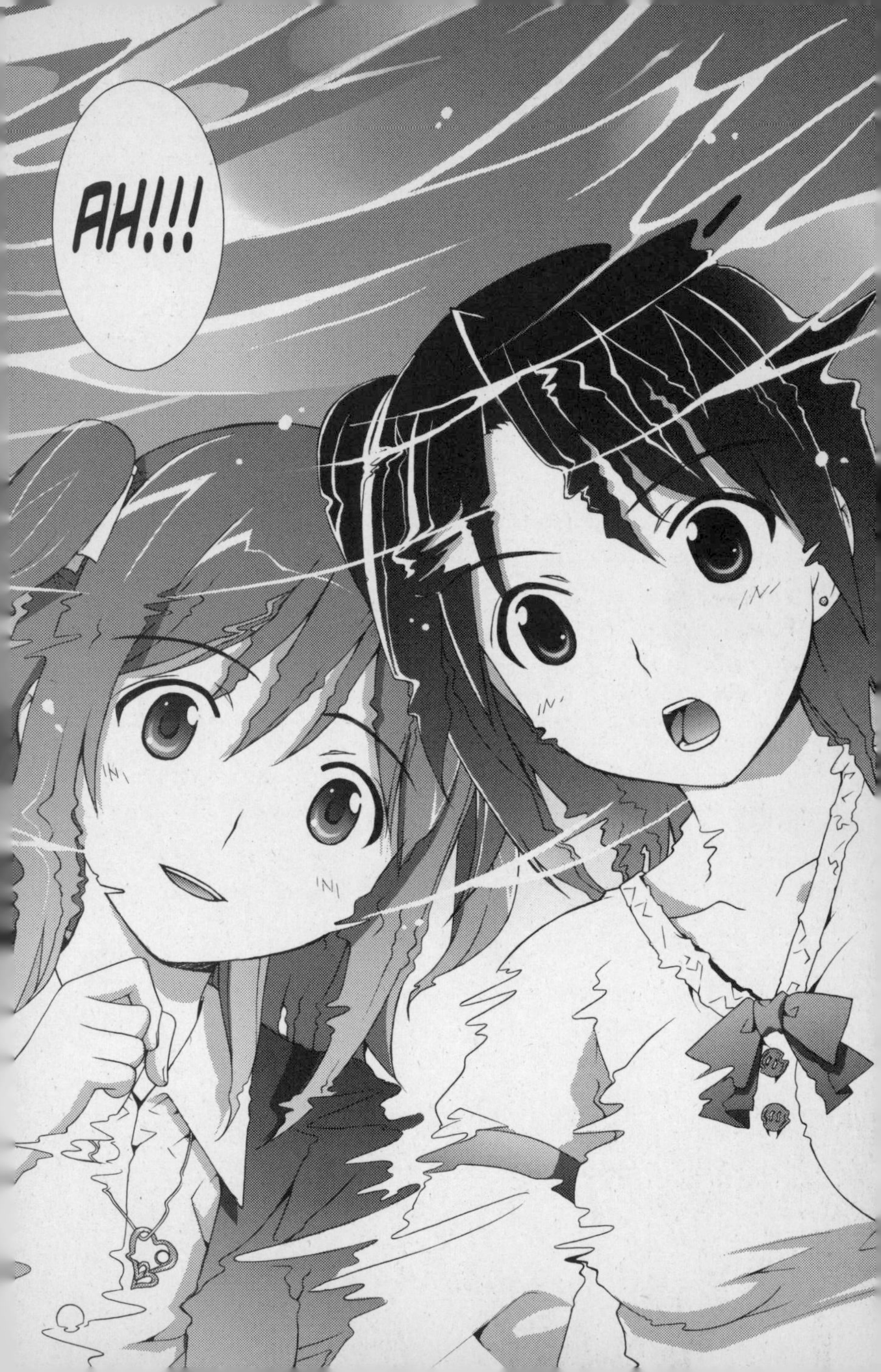
AH!!!

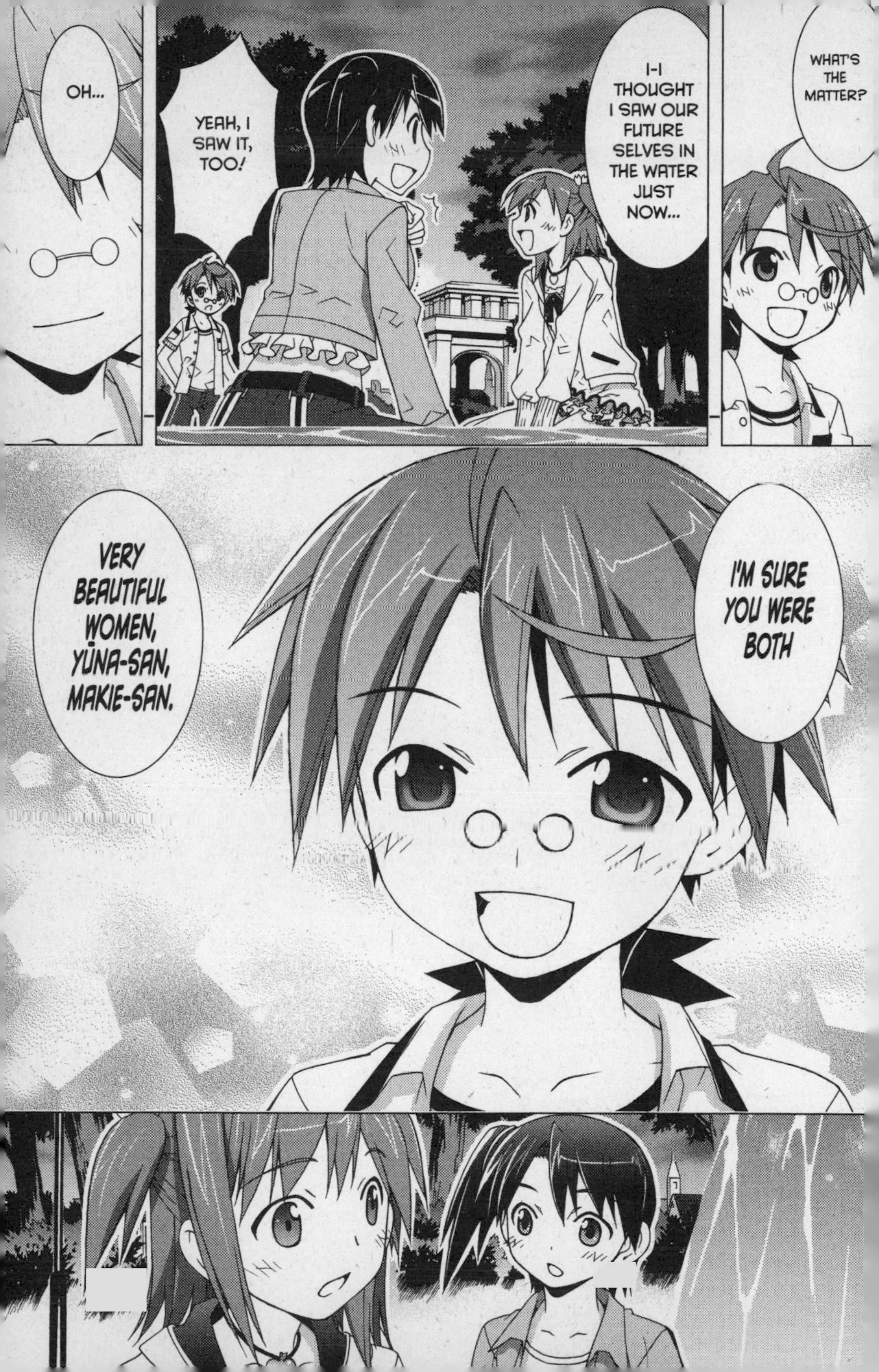
WHAT'S THE MATTER?
I-I THOUGHT I SAW OUR FUTURE SELVES IN THE WATER JUST NOW...
YEAH, I SAW IT, TOO!
OH...
I'M SURE YOU WERE BOTH
VERY BEAUTIFUL WOMEN, YŪNA-SAN, MAKIE-SAN.

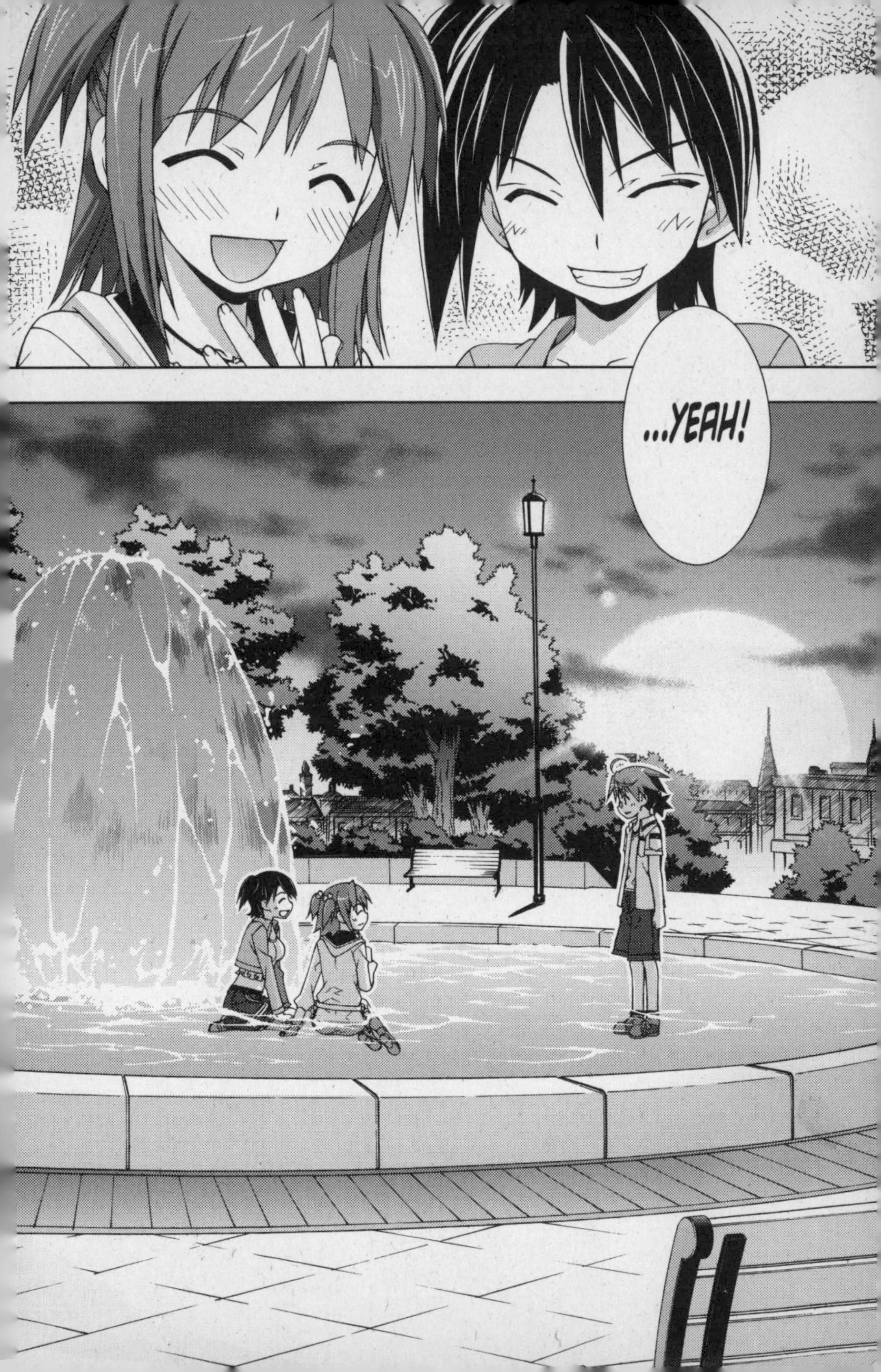
...YEAH!

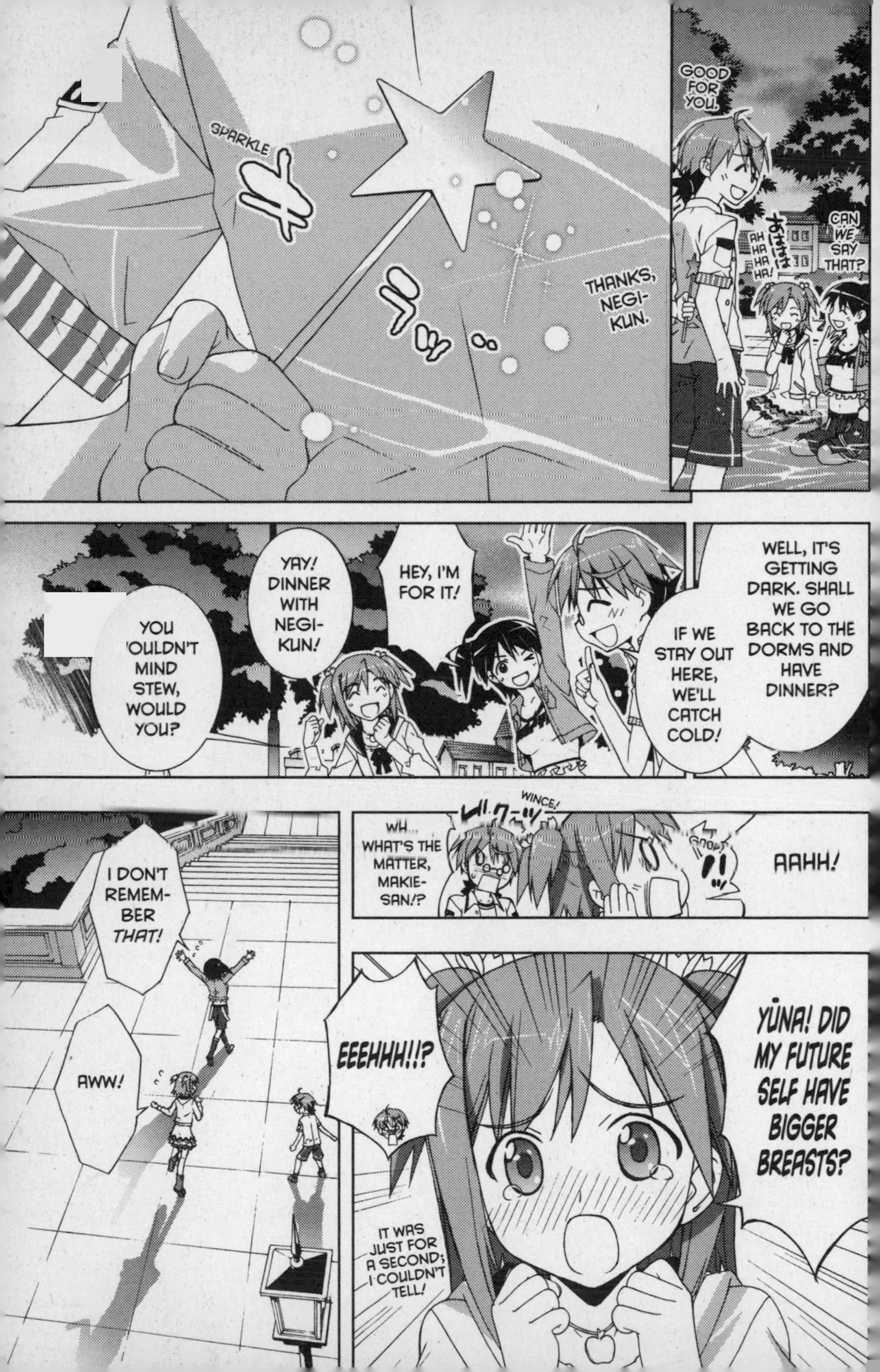
GOOD FOR YOU.
CAN WE SAY THAT?
AH HA HA HA!
SPARKLE
THANKS, NEGI-KUN.
WELL, IT'S GETTING DARK. SHALL WE GO BACK TO THE DORMS AND HAVE DINNER?
IF WE STAY OUT HERE, WE'LL CATCH COLD!
HEY, I'M FOR IT!
YAY! DINNER WITH NEGI-KUN!
YOU WOULDN'T MIND STEW, WOULD YOU?
WINCE!
AAHH!
WH... WHAT'S THE MATTER, MAKIE-SAN!?
YŪNA! DID MY FUTURE SELF HAVE BIGGER BREASTS?
EEEHHH!!?
IT WAS JUST FOR A SECOND; I COULDN'T TELL!
I DON'T REMEM-BER THAT!
AWW!

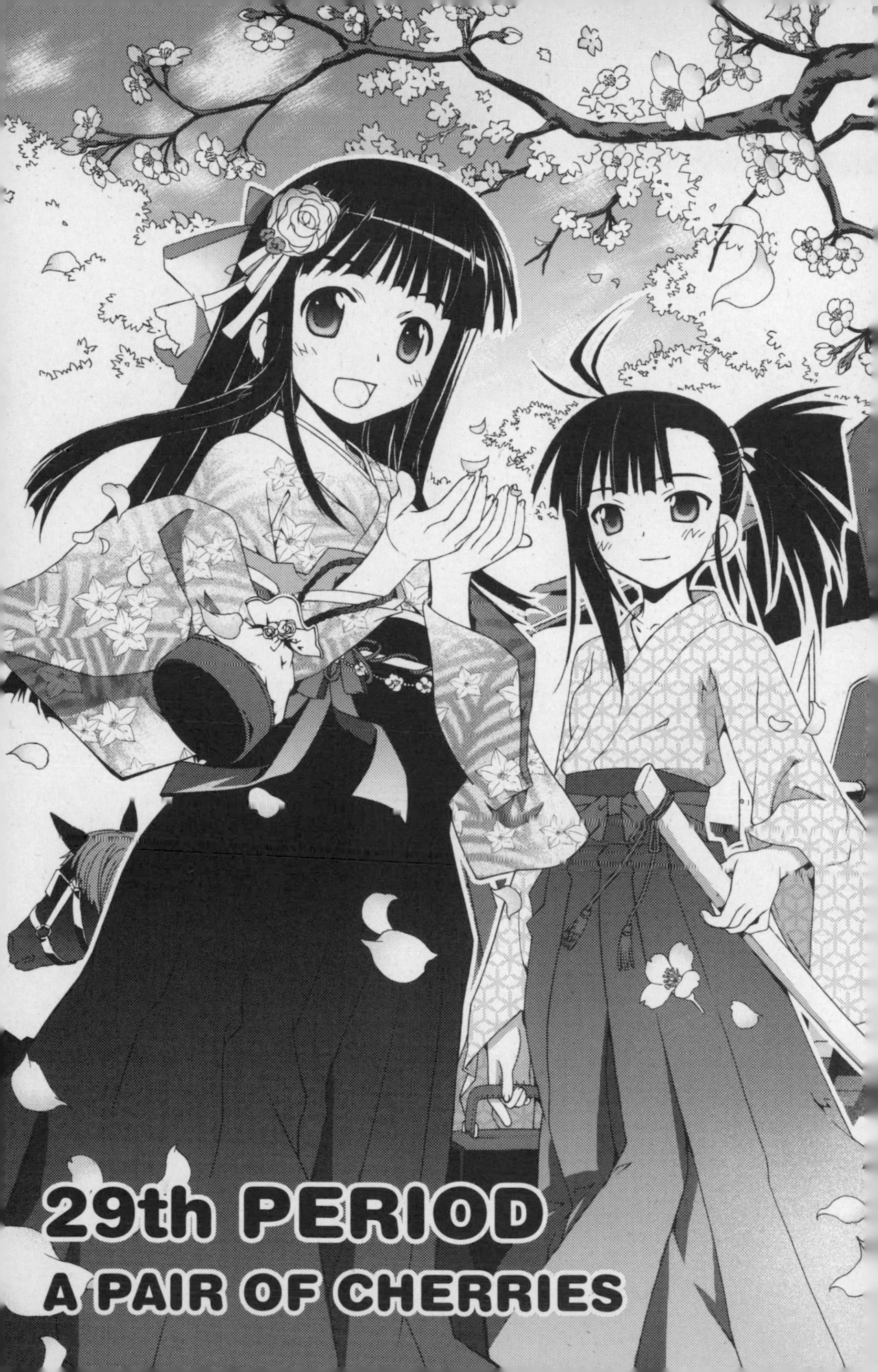
29th PERIOD
A PAIR OF CHERRIES

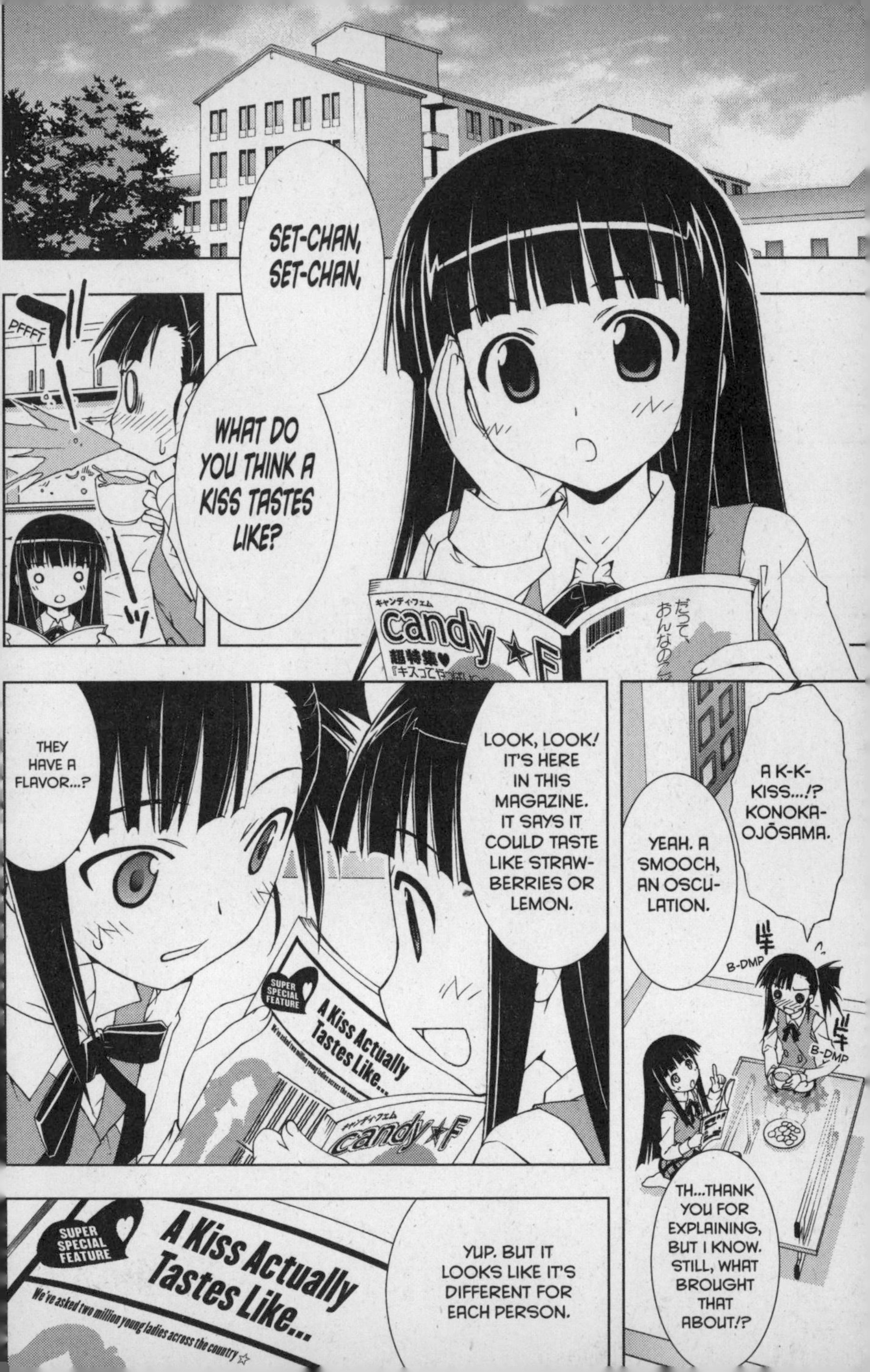
SET-CHAN, SET-CHAN,
WHAT DO YOU THINK A KISS TASTES LIKE?
キャンディ・フェム
candy★F
超特集♥
だって、おんなの
PFFFT
ッ
A K-K-KISS...!? KONOKA-OJŌSAMA.
YEAH. A SMOOCH, AN OSCULATION.
B-DMP
B-DMP
TH...THANK YOU FOR EXPLAINING, BUT I KNOW. STILL, WHAT BROUGHT THAT ABOUT!?
LOOK, LOOK! IT'S HERE IN THIS MAGAZINE. IT SAYS IT COULD TASTE LIKE STRAWBERRIES OR LEMON.
THEY HAVE A FLAVOR...?
SUPER SPECIAL FEATURE
A Kiss Actually Tastes Like...
candy★F
YUP. BUT IT LOOKS LIKE IT'S DIFFERENT FOR EACH PERSON.
SUPER SPECIAL FEATURE
A Kiss Actually Tastes Like...
We've asked two million young ladies across the country☆

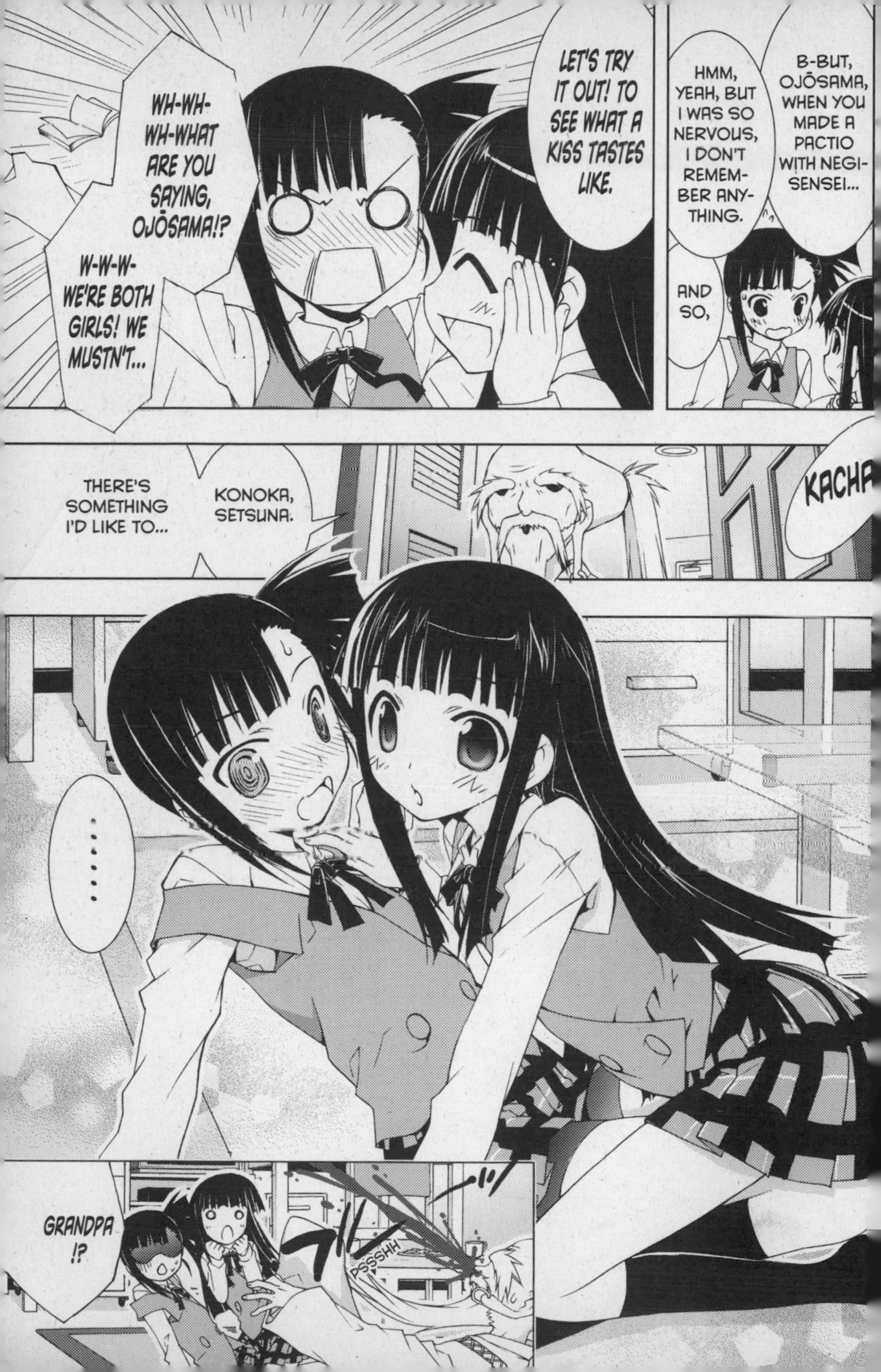
B-BUT, OJŌSAMA, WHEN YOU MADE A PACTIO WITH NEGI-SENSEI...
HMM, YEAH, BUT I WAS SO NERVOUS, I DON'T REMEMBER ANYTHING.
AND SO,
LET'S TRY IT OUT! TO SEE WHAT A KISS TASTES LIKE.
WH-WH-WH-WHAT ARE YOU SAYING, OJŌSAMA!?
W-W-W-WE'RE BOTH GIRLS! WE MUSTN'T...
KACHA
KONOKA, SETSUNA.
THERE'S SOMETHING I'D LIKE TO...
......
PSSSHH
GRANDPA!?

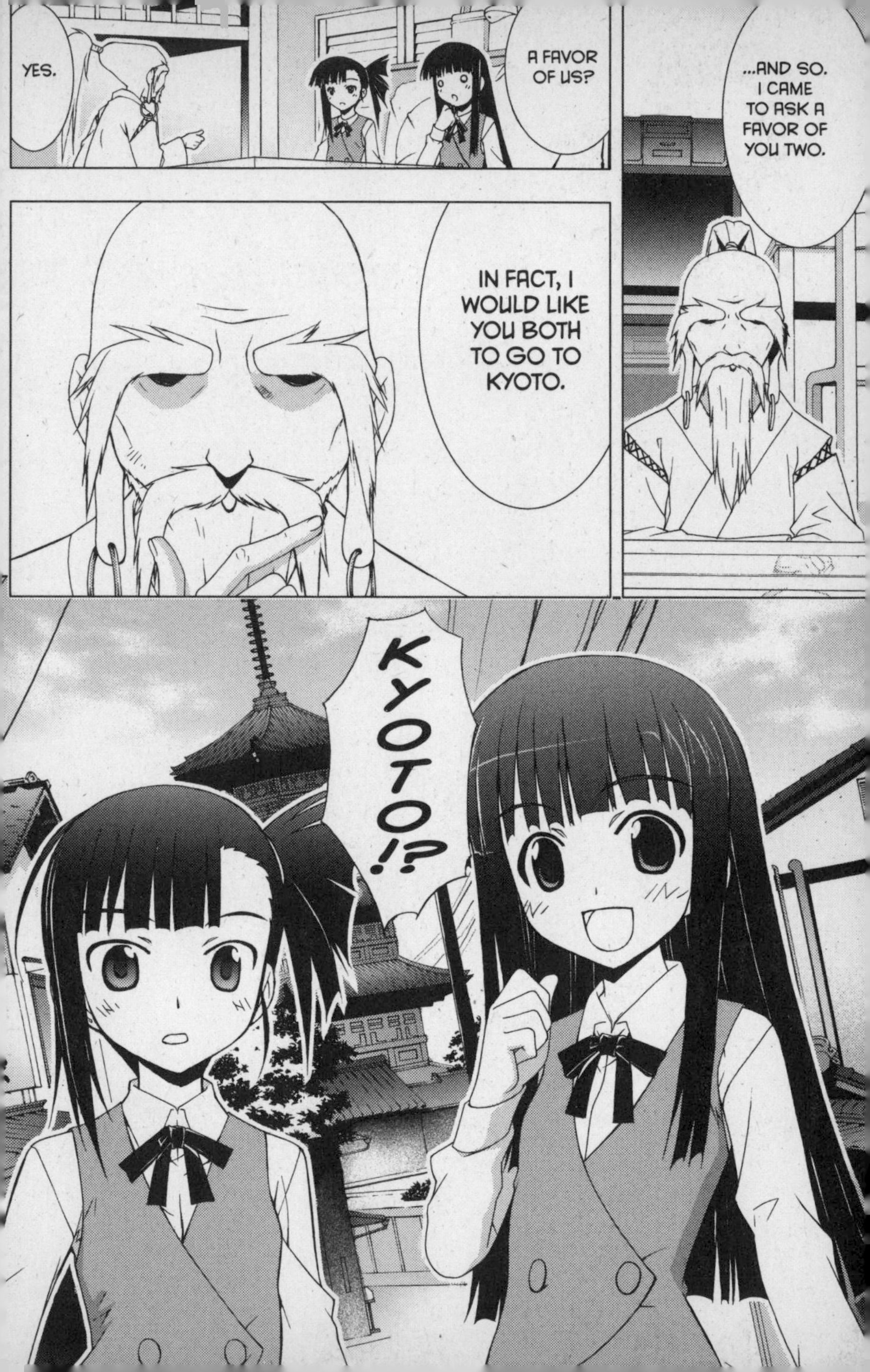
...AND SO. I CAME TO ASK A FAVOR OF YOU TWO.
A FAVOR OF US?
YES.
IN FACT, I WOULD LIKE YOU BOTH TO GO TO KYOTO.
KYOTO!?

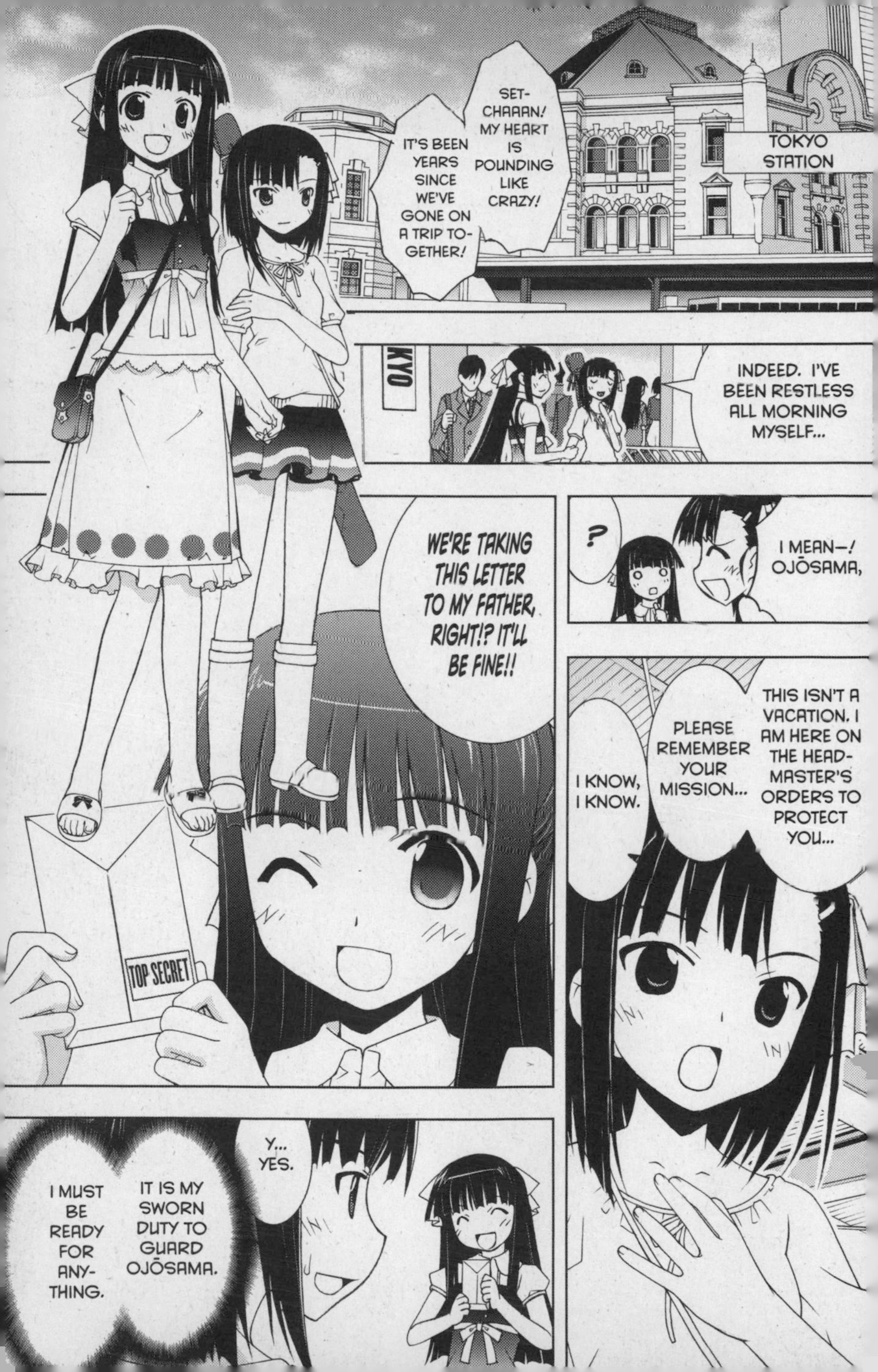
TOKYO STATION
SET-CHAAAN! MY HEART IS POUNDING LIKE CRAZY!
IT'S BEEN YEARS SINCE WE'VE GONE ON A TRIP TO-GETHER!
KYO
INDEED. I'VE BEEN RESTLESS ALL MORNING MYSELF...
I MEAN—! OJŌSAMA,
?
THIS ISN'T A VACATION. I AM HERE ON THE HEAD-MASTER'S ORDERS TO PROTECT YOU...
PLEASE REMEMBER YOUR MISSION...
I KNOW, I KNOW.
WE'RE TAKING THIS LETTER TO MY FATHER, RIGHT!? IT'LL BE FINE!!
TOP SECRET
Y... YES.
IT IS MY SWORN DUTY TO GUARD OJŌSAMA.
I MUST BE READY FOR ANY-THING.

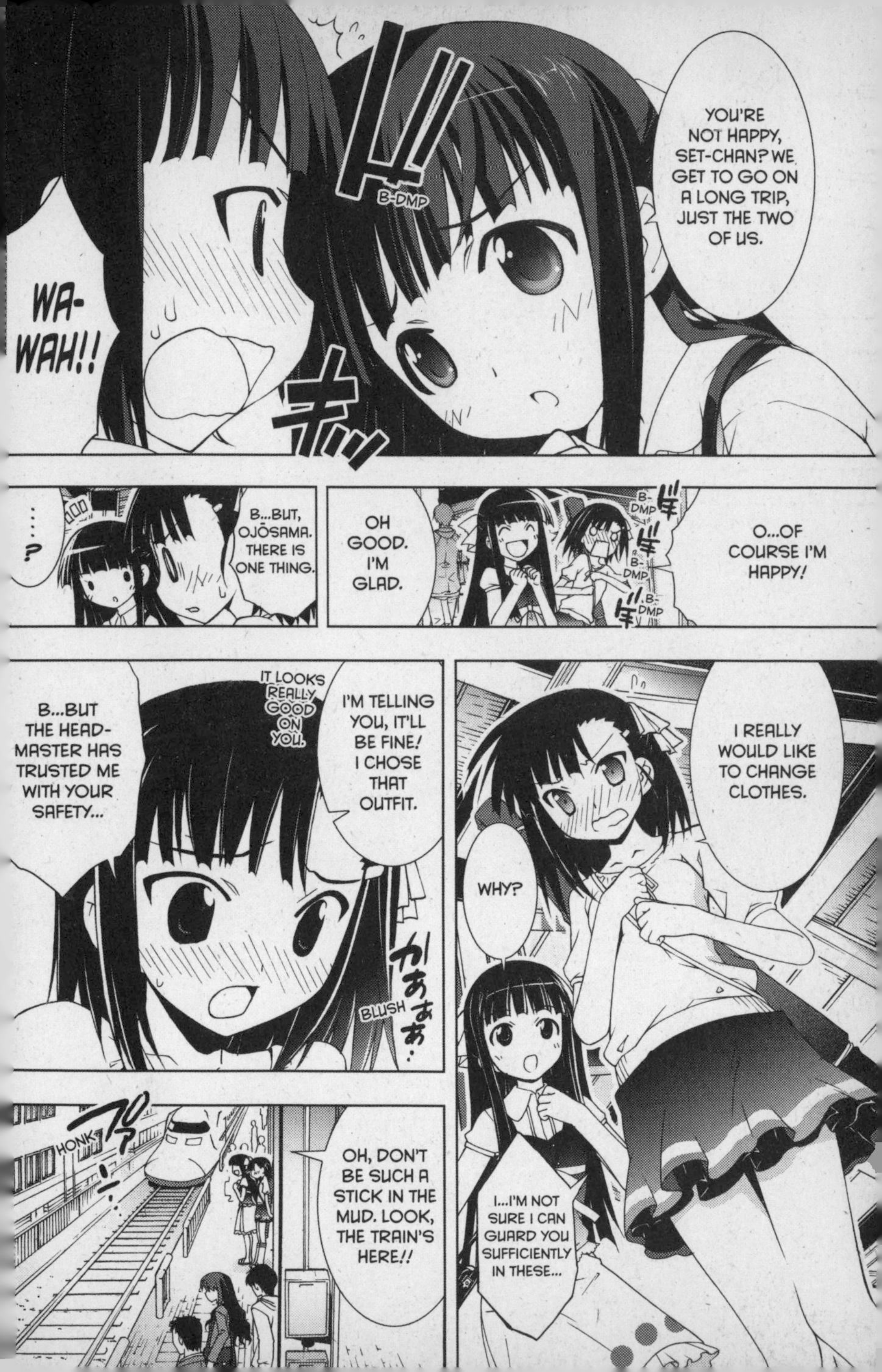
YOU'RE NOT HAPPY, SET-CHAN? WE GET TO GO ON A LONG TRIP, JUST THE TWO OF US.
B-DMP
WA-WAH!!
O...OF COURSE I'M HAPPY!
B-DMP
B-DMP
B-DMP
OH GOOD. I'M GLAD.
B...BUT, OJŌSAMA. THERE IS ONE THING.
...?
I REALLY WOULD LIKE TO CHANGE CLOTHES.
WHY?
I...I'M NOT SURE I CAN GUARD YOU SUFFICIENTLY IN THESE...
I'M TELLING YOU, IT'LL BE FINE! I CHOSE THAT OUTFIT.
IT LOOKS REALLY GOOD ON YOU.
B...BUT THE HEAD-MASTER HAS TRUSTED ME WITH YOUR SAFETY...
BLUSH
OH, DON'T BE SUCH A STICK IN THE MUD. LOOK, THE TRAIN'S HERE!!
HONK

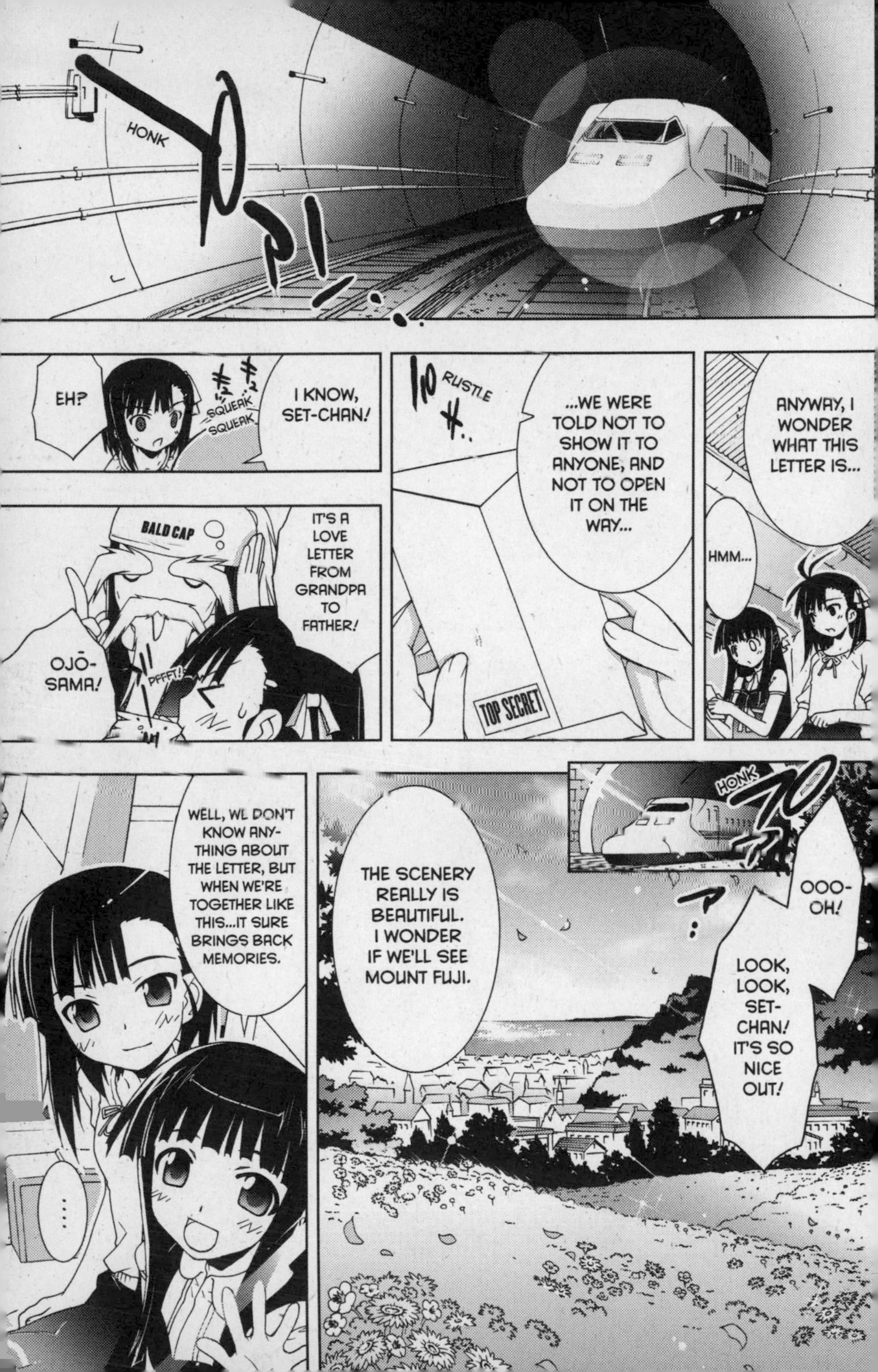
HONK
ANYWAY, I WONDER WHAT THIS LETTER IS...
HMM...
RUSTLE
...WE WERE TOLD NOT TO SHOW IT TO ANYONE, AND NOT TO OPEN IT ON THE WAY...
TOP SECRET
I KNOW, SET-CHAN!
SQUEAK
SQUEAK
EH?
IT'S A LOVE LETTER FROM GRANDPA TO FATHER!
BALD CAP
OJŌ-SAMA!
PFFFT!
HONK
OOO-OH!
LOOK, LOOK, SET-CHAN! IT'S SO NICE OUT!
THE SCENERY REALLY IS BEAUTIFUL. I WONDER IF WE'LL SEE MOUNT FUJI.
WELL, WL DON'T KNOW ANY-THING ABOUT THE LETTER, BUT WHEN WE'RE TOGETHER LIKE THIS...IT SURE BRINGS BACK MEMORIES.
....

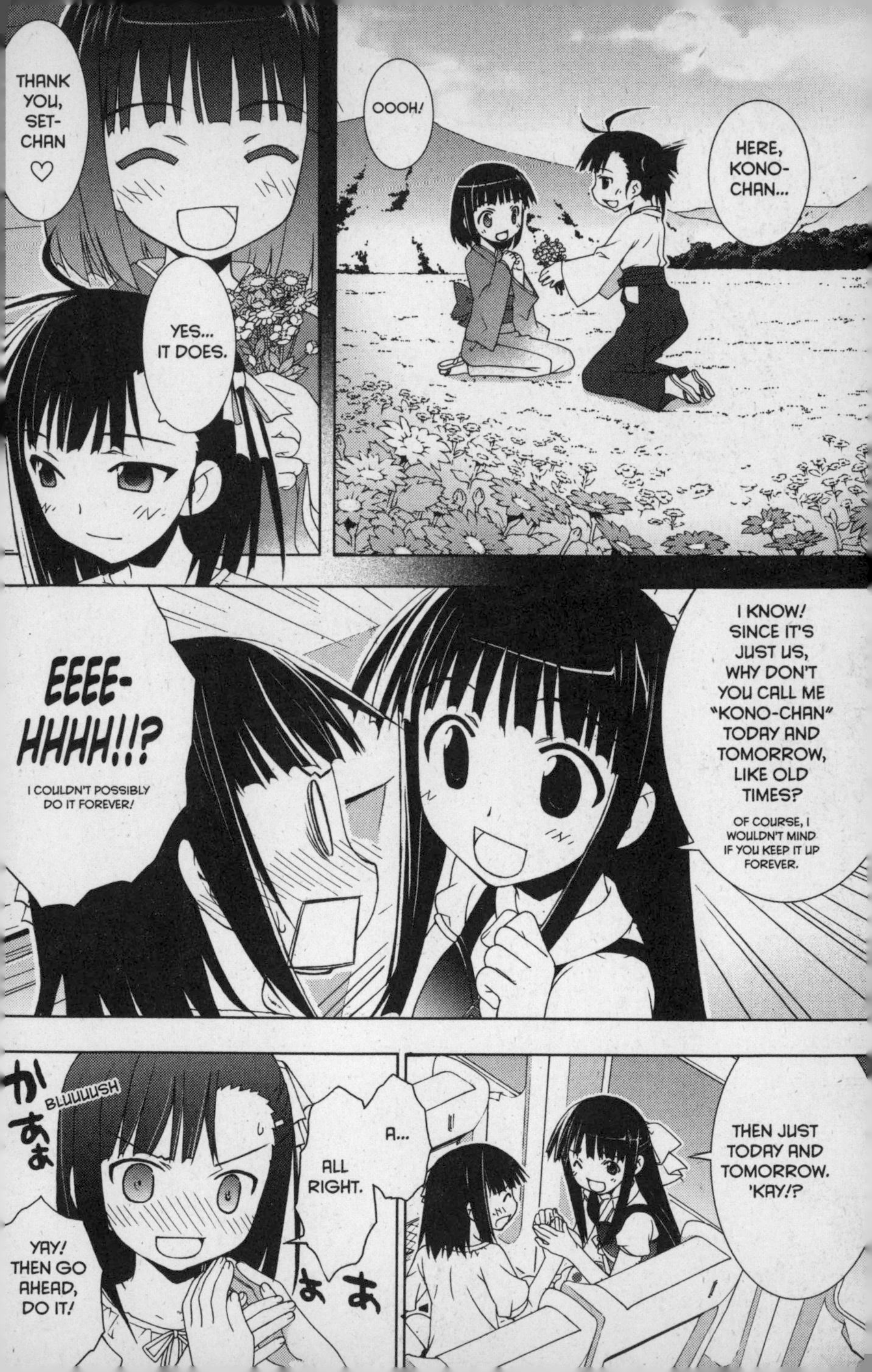
HERE, KONO-CHAN...
OOOH!
THANK YOU, SET-CHAN ♡
YES... IT DOES.
I KNOW! SINCE IT'S JUST US, WHY DON'T YOU CALL ME "KONO-CHAN" TODAY AND TOMORROW, LIKE OLD TIMES?
OF COURSE, I WOULDN'T MIND IF YOU KEEP IT UP FOREVER.
EEEE-HHHH!!!?
I COULDN'T POSSIBLY DO IT FOREVER!
THEN JUST TODAY AND TOMORROW. 'KAY!?
A... ALL RIGHT.
かぁ
BLUUUUSH
YAY! THEN GO AHEAD, DO IT!
ぁあ

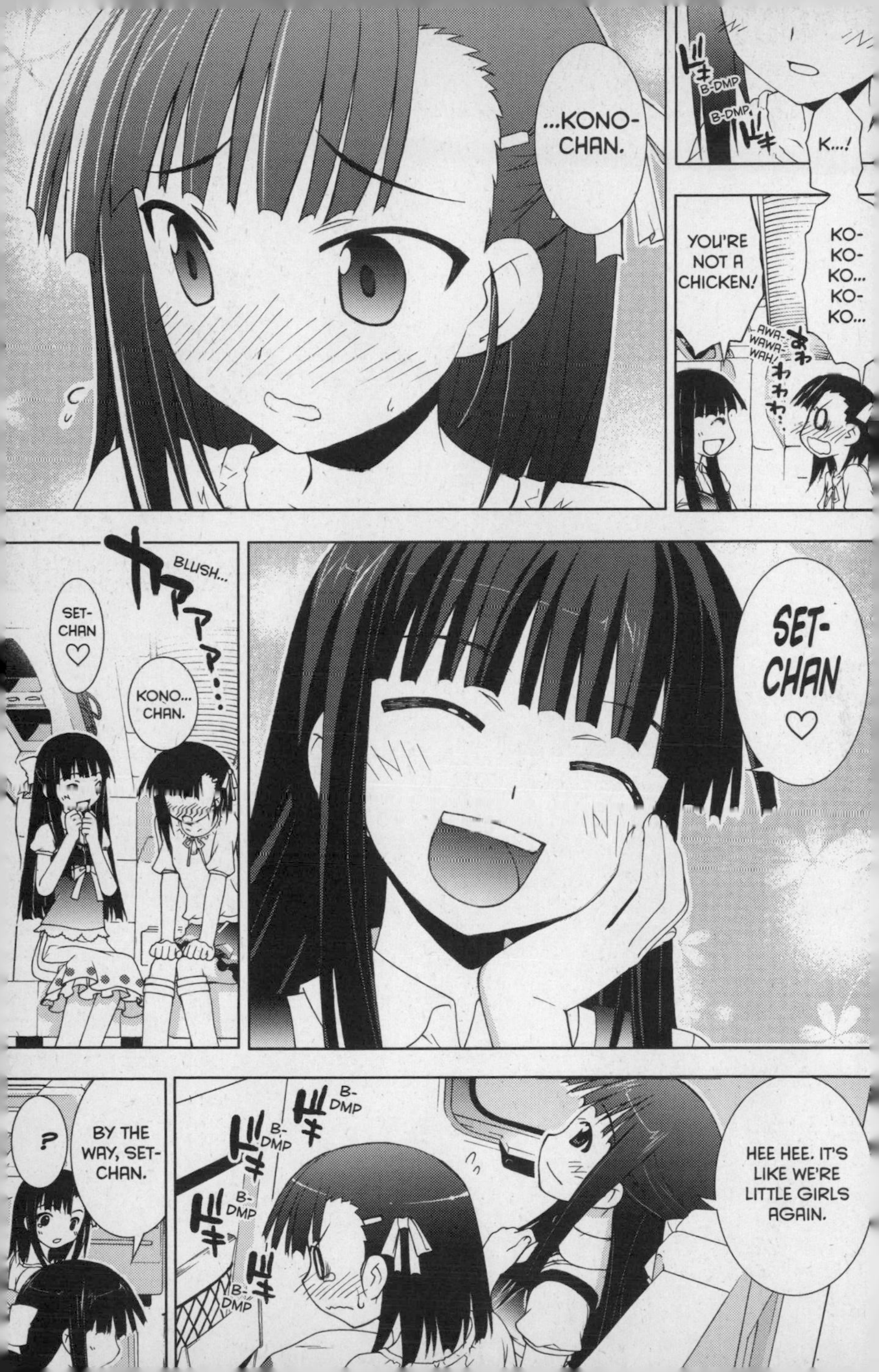
B-DMP
B-DMP
K...!
KO-KO-KO... KO-KO...
YOU'RE NOT A CHICKEN!
AWA-WAWA-WAH!
...KONO-CHAN.
SET-CHAN ♡
BLUSH...
SET-CHAN ♡
KONO... CHAN.
HEE HEE. IT'S LIKE WE'RE LITTLE GIRLS AGAIN.
B-DMP
B-DMP
B-DMP
B-DMP
BY THE WAY, SET-CHAN.
?

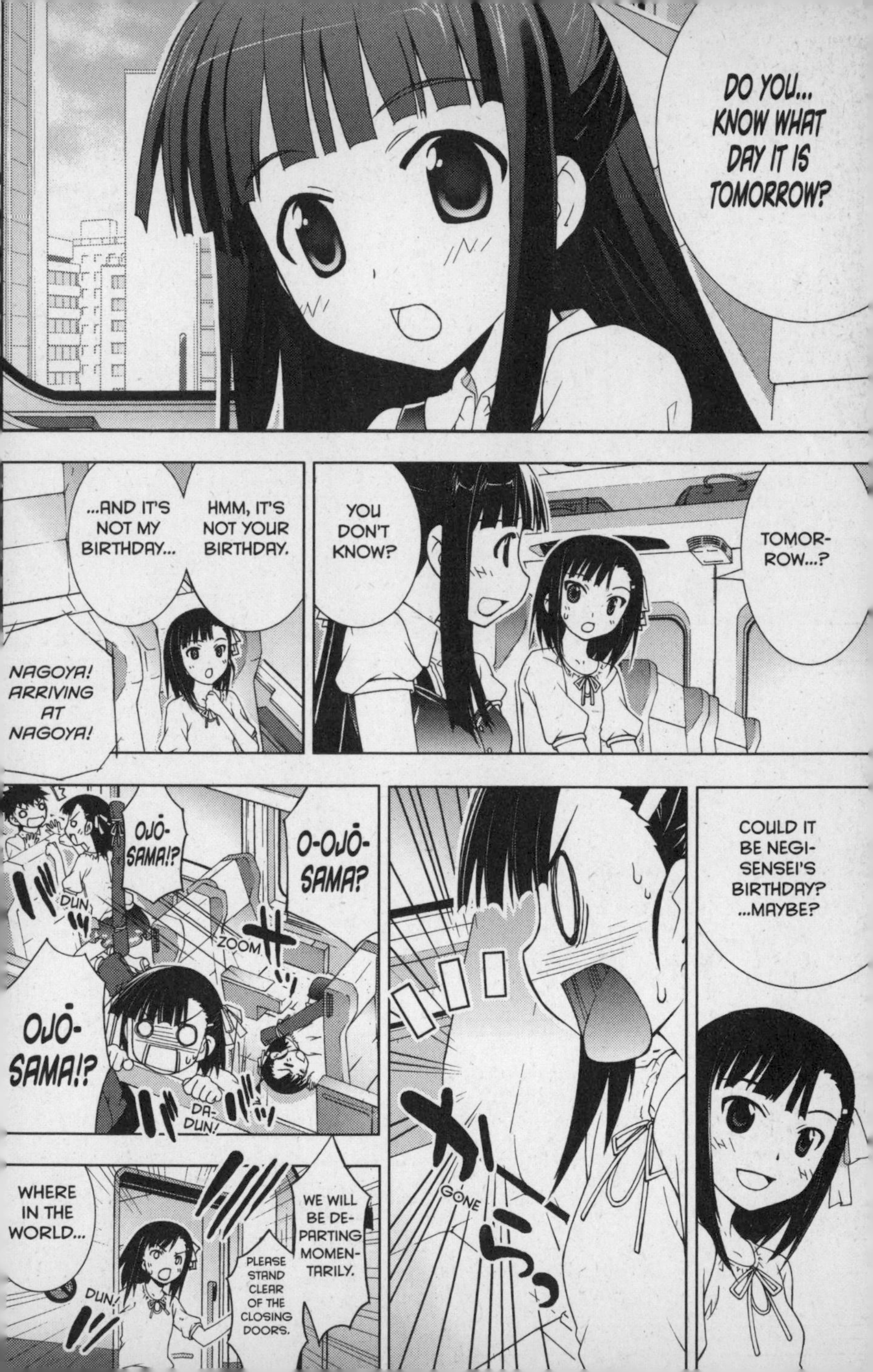
DO YOU... KNOW WHAT DAY IT IS TOMORROW?
TOMORROW...?
YOU DON'T KNOW?
HMM, IT'S NOT YOUR BIRTHDAY.
...AND IT'S NOT MY BIRTHDAY...
NAGOYA! ARRIVING AT NAGOYA!
COULD IT BE NEGI-SENSEI'S BIRTHDAY? ...MAYBE?
GONE
O-OJŌ-SAMA?
OJŌ-SAMA!?
DUN
ZOOM
OJŌ-SAMA!?
DA-DUN!
WE WILL BE DEPARTING MOMENTARILY.
PLEASE STAND CLEAR OF THE CLOSING DOORS.
WHERE IN THE WORLD...
DUN!

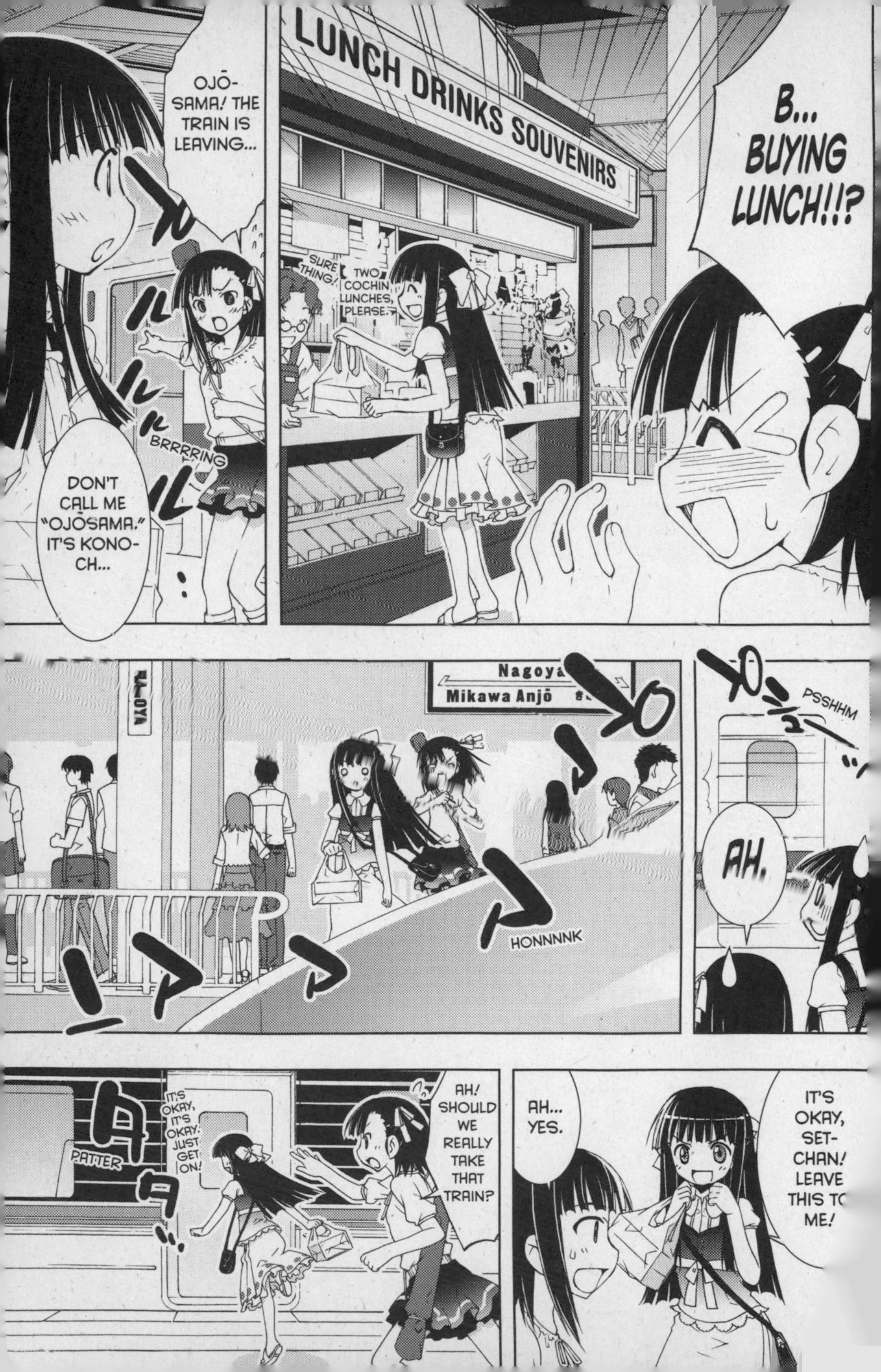
B... BUYING LUNCH!!?
LUNCH DRINKS SOUVENIRS
TWO COCHIN LUNCHES, PLEASE.
SURE THING!
OJŌ-SAMA! THE TRAIN IS LEAVING...
BRRRRING
DON'T CALL ME "OJŌSAMA." IT'S KONOCH...
PSSHHM
AH.
Nagoya
Mikawa Anjō
HONNNNK
IT'S OKAY, SET-CHAN! LEAVE THIS TO ME!
AH... YES.
AH! SHOULD WE REALLY TAKE THAT TRAIN?
IT'S OKAY, IT'S OKAY! JUST GET ON!
PATTER

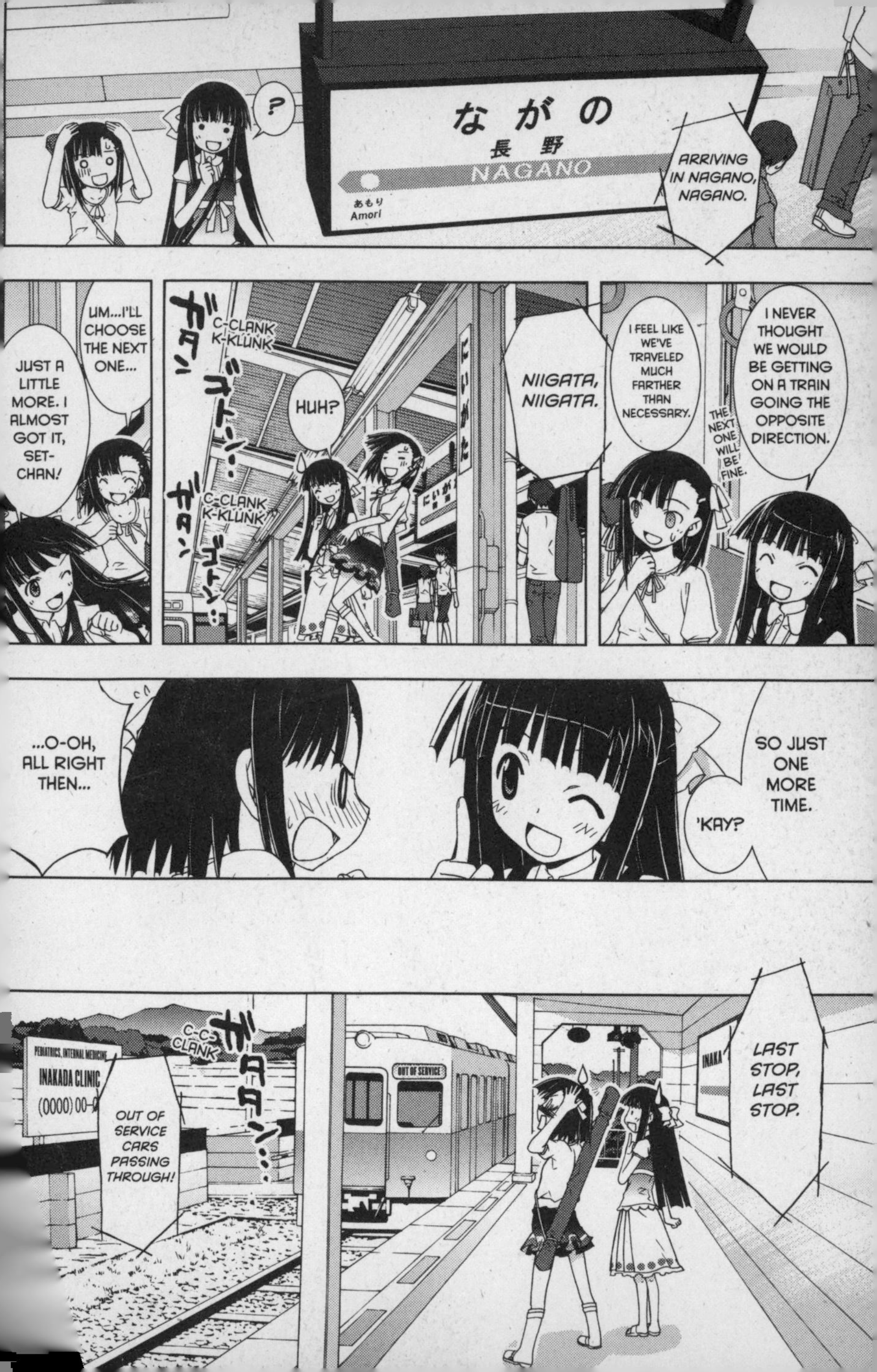
ARRIVING IN NAGANO, NAGANO.
ながの
長野
NAGANO
あもり
Amori
?
I NEVER THOUGHT WE WOULD BE GETTING ON A TRAIN GOING THE OPPOSITE DIRECTION.
THE NEXT ONE WILL BE FINE.
I FEEL LIKE WE'VE TRAVELED MUCH FARTHER THAN NECESSARY.
NIIGATA, NIIGATA.
HUH?
C-CLANK K-KLUNK
C-CLANK K-KLUNK
UM...I'LL CHOOSE THE NEXT ONE...
JUST A LITTLE MORE. I ALMOST GOT IT, SET-CHAN!
SO JUST ONE MORE TIME.
'KAY?
...O-OH, ALL RIGHT THEN...
LAST STOP, LAST STOP.
INAKA
OUT OF SERVICE
C-C-CLANK
OUT OF SERVICE CARS PASSING THROUGH!
PEDIATRICS, INTERNAL MEDICINE
INAKADA CLINIC
(0000) 00-

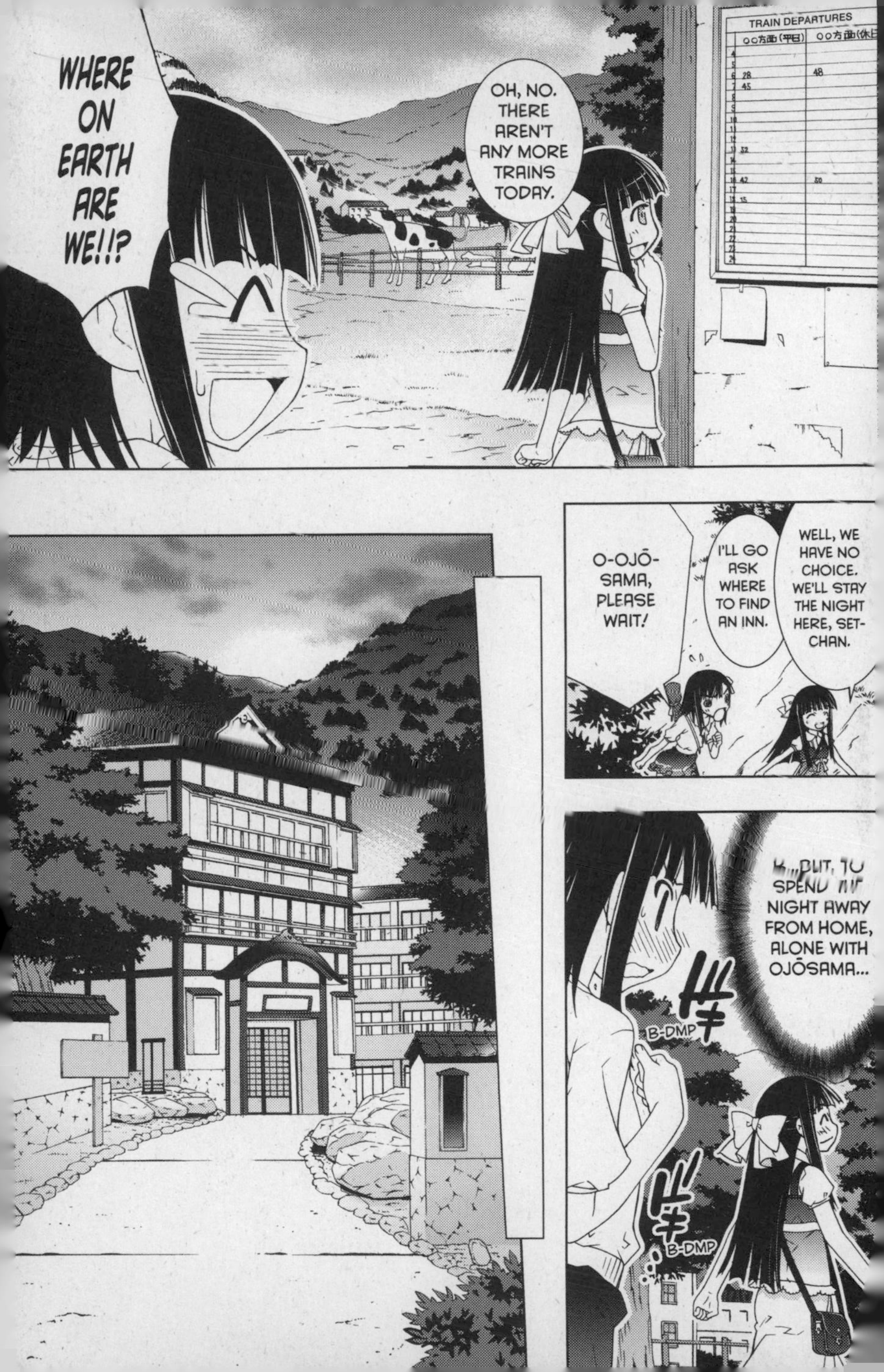
TRAIN DEPARTURES
OH, NO. THERE AREN'T ANY MORE TRAINS TODAY.
WHERE ON EARTH ARE WE!!?
WELL, WE HAVE NO CHOICE. WE'LL STAY THE NIGHT HERE, SET-CHAN.
I'LL GO ASK WHERE TO FIND AN INN.
O-OJŌ-SAMA, PLEASE WAIT!
...BUT, TO SPEND NIGHT AWAY FROM HOME, ALONE WITH OJŌSAMA...
B-DMP
B-DMP

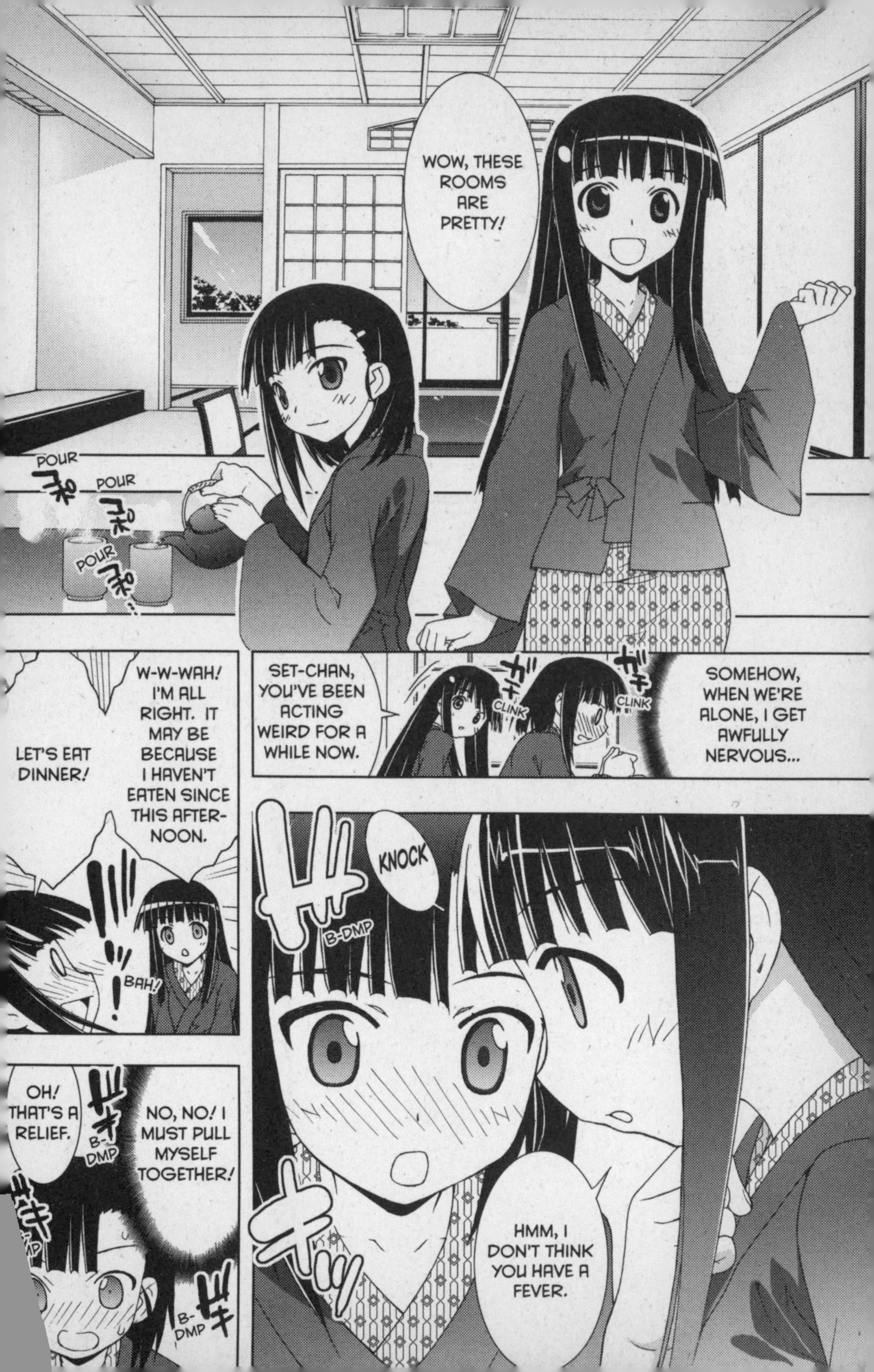

WOW, THESE ROOMS ARE PRETTY!
POUR
POUR
POUR
SOMEHOW, WHEN WE'RE ALONE, I GET AWFULLY NERVOUS...
CLINK
CLINK
SET-CHAN, YOU'VE BEEN ACTING WEIRD FOR A WHILE NOW.
KNOCK
B-DMP
HMM, I DON'T THINK YOU HAVE A FEVER.
W-W-WAH! I'M ALL RIGHT. IT MAY BE BECAUSE I HAVEN'T EATEN SINCE THIS AFTERNOON.
LET'S EAT DINNER!
BAH!
NO, NO! I MUST PULL MYSELF TOGETHER!
B-DMP
OH! THAT'S A RELIEF.
B-DMP

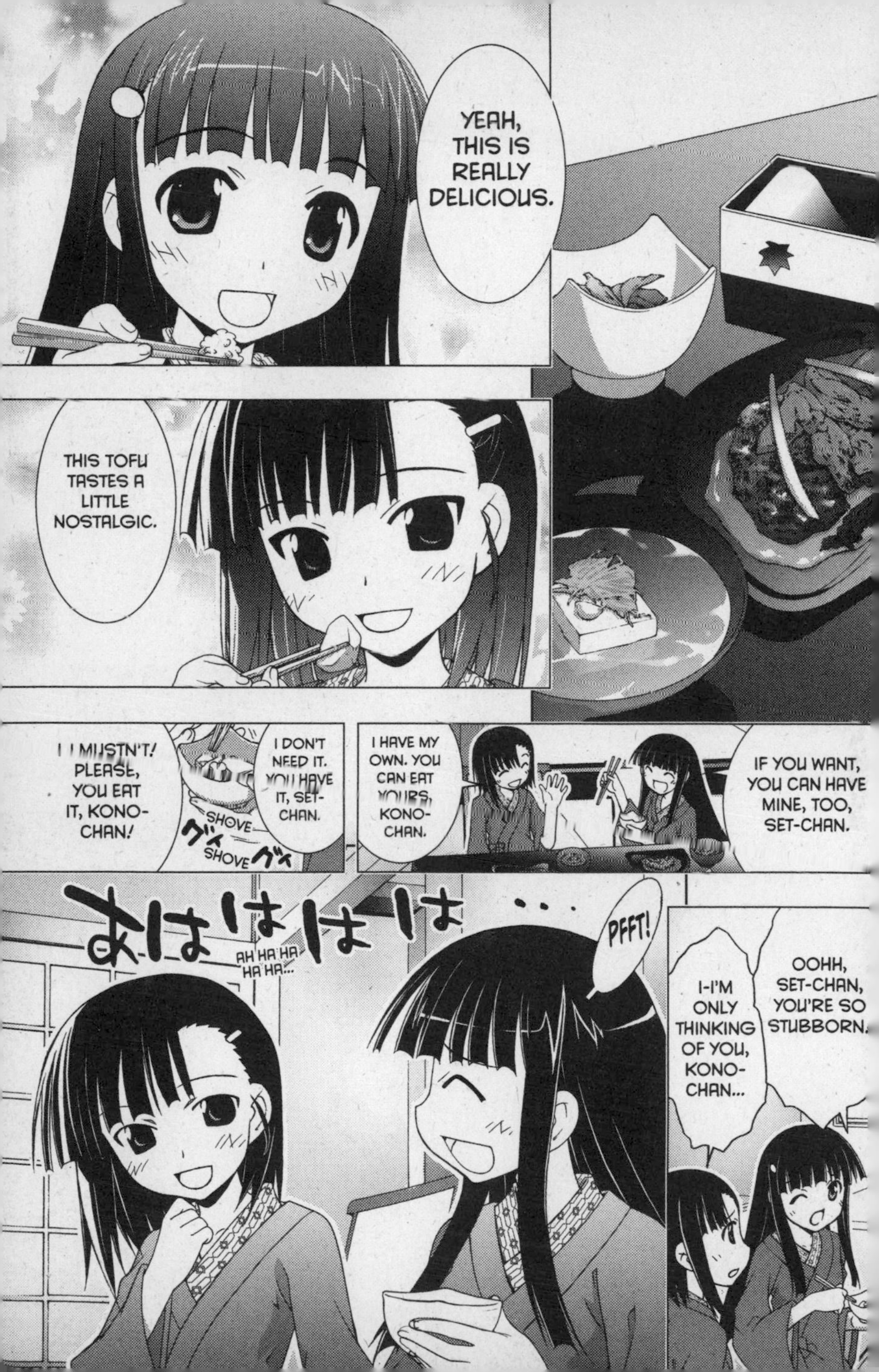
YEAH, THIS IS REALLY DELICIOUS.
THIS TOFU TASTES A LITTLE NOSTALGIC.
IF YOU WANT, YOU CAN HAVE MINE, TOO, SET-CHAN.
I HAVE MY OWN. YOU CAN EAT YOURS, KONO-CHAN.
I DON'T NEED IT. YOU HAVE IT, SET-CHAN.
SHOVE グイ SHOVE グイ
I-I MUSTN'T! PLEASE, YOU EAT IT, KONO-CHAN!
OOHH, SET-CHAN, YOU'RE SO STUBBORN.
I-I'M ONLY THINKING OF YOU, KONO-CHAN...
PFFT!
あはははは...
AH HA HA HA HA...

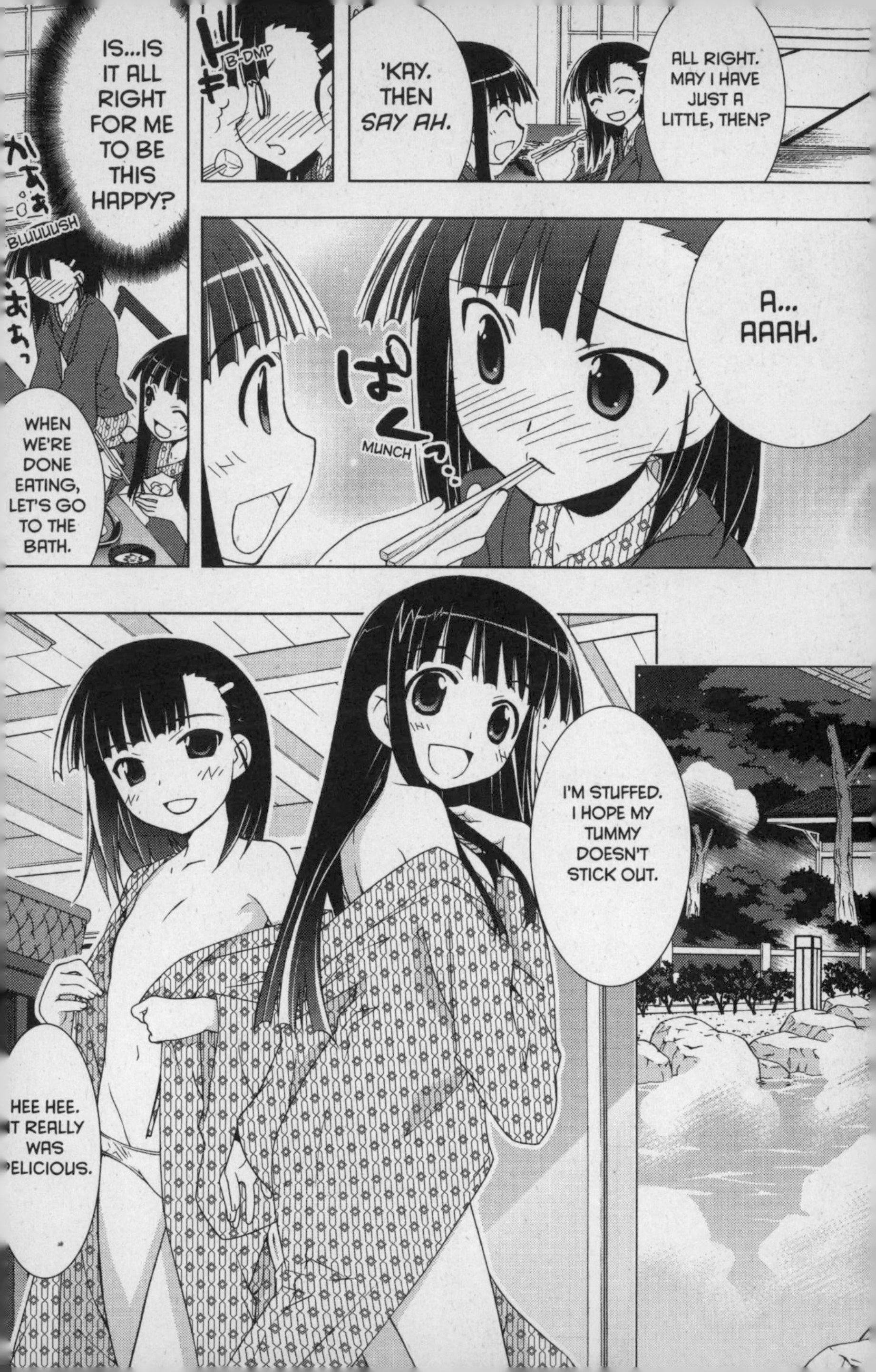
ALL RIGHT. MAY I HAVE JUST A LITTLE, THEN?
'KAY. THEN SAY AH.
B-DMP
A... AAAH.
MUNCH
IS...IS IT ALL RIGHT FOR ME TO BE THIS HAPPY?
BLUUUUSH
WHEN WE'RE DONE EATING, LET'S GO TO THE BATH.
I'M STUFFED. I HOPE MY TUMMY DOESN'T STICK OUT.
HEE HEE. IT REALLY WAS DELICIOUS.

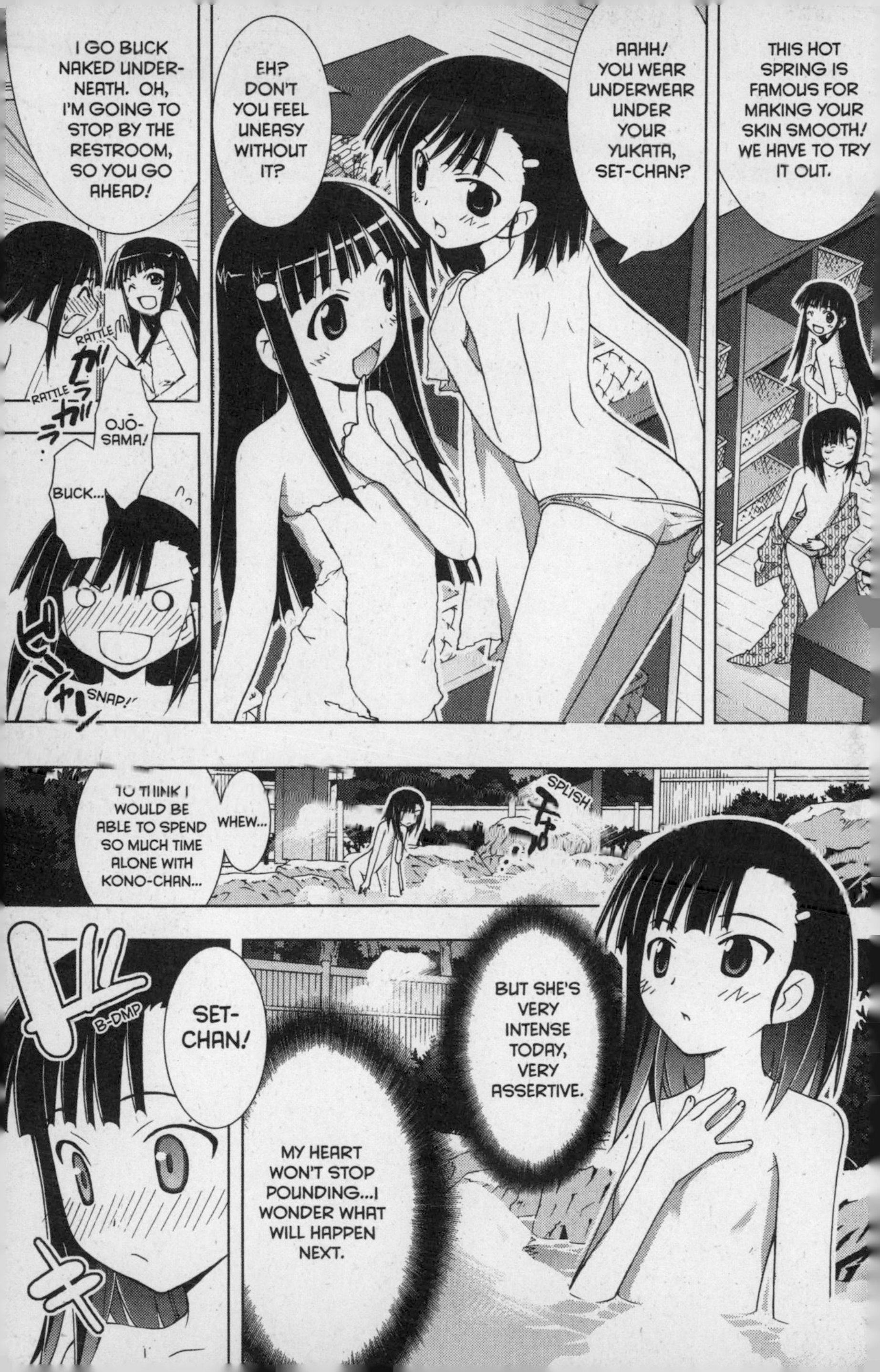
THIS HOT SPRING IS FAMOUS FOR MAKING YOUR SKIN SMOOTH! WE HAVE TO TRY IT OUT.
AAHH! YOU WEAR UNDERWEAR UNDER YOUR YUKATA, SET-CHAN?
EH? DON'T YOU FEEL UNEASY WITHOUT IT?
I GO BUCK NAKED UNDERNEATH. OH, I'M GOING TO STOP BY THE RESTROOM, SO YOU GO AHEAD!
RATTLE
RATTLE
OJŌ-SAMA!
BUCK...
SNAP!
SPLISH
WHEW...
TO THINK I WOULD BE ABLE TO SPEND SO MUCH TIME ALONE WITH KONO-CHAN...
BUT SHE'S VERY INTENSE TODAY, VERY ASSERTIVE.
MY HEART WON'T STOP POUNDING...I WONDER WHAT WILL HAPPEN NEXT.
SET-CHAN!
B-DMP

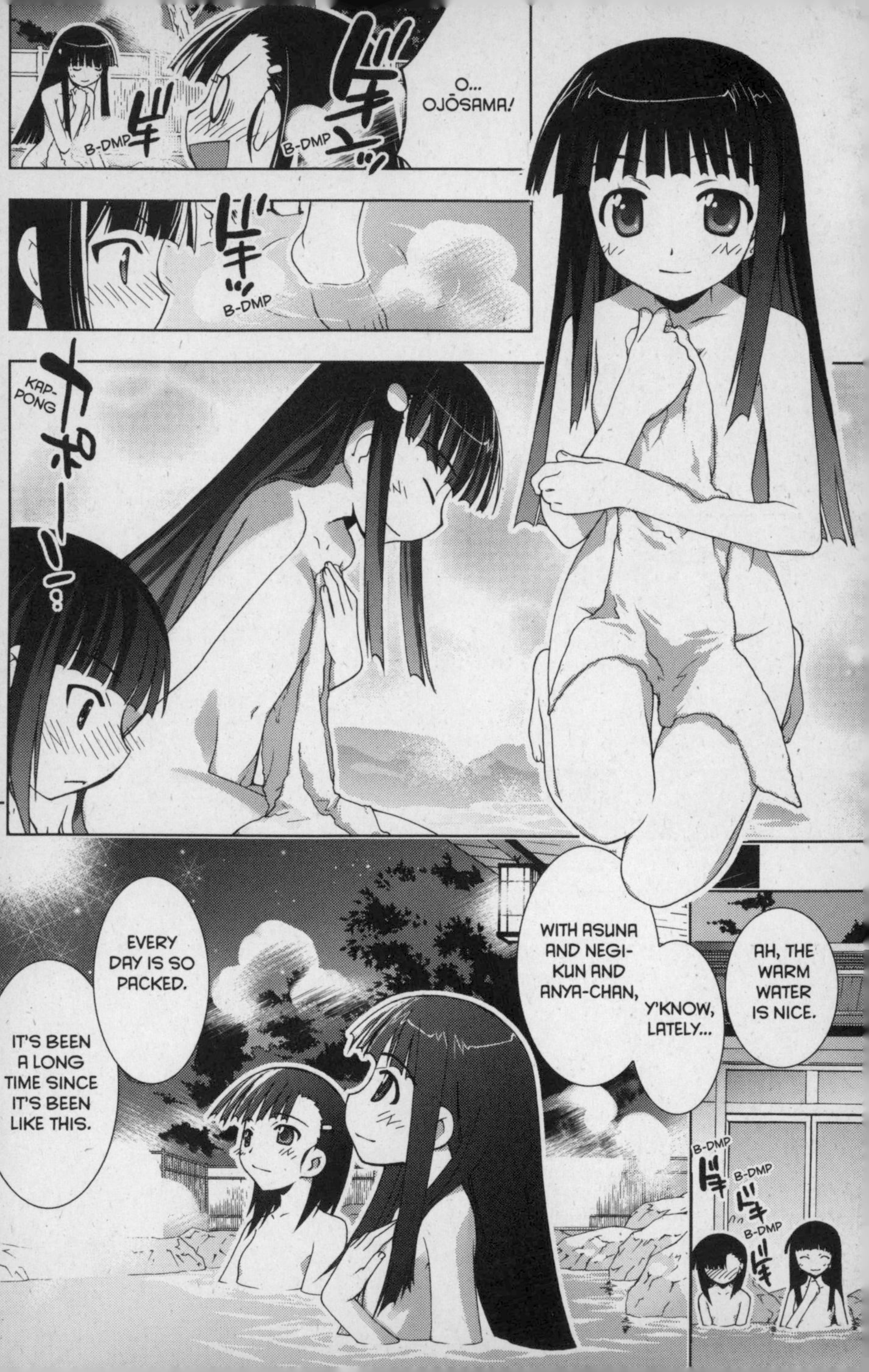
O... OJŌSAMA!
B-DMP
B-DMP
B-DMP
KAP-PONG
AH, THE WARM WATER IS NICE.
Y'KNOW, LATELY...
WITH ASUNA AND NEGI-KUN AND ANYA-CHAN,
EVERY DAY IS SO PACKED.
IT'S BEEN A LONG TIME SINCE IT'S BEEN LIKE THIS.
B-DMP
B-DMP
B-DMP

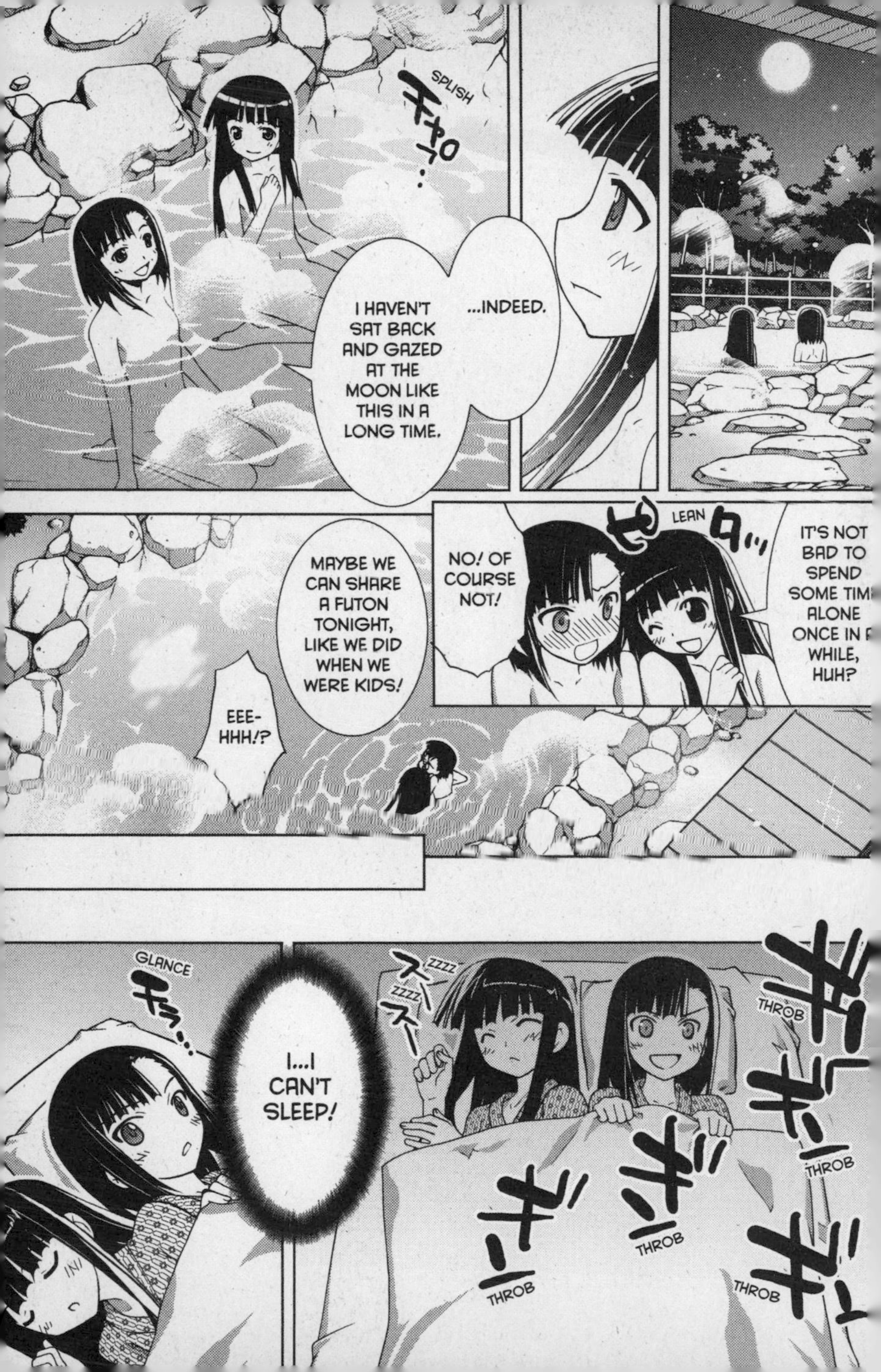
...INDEED.
SPLISH
I HAVEN'T SAT BACK AND GAZED AT THE MOON LIKE THIS IN A LONG TIME.
IT'S NOT BAD TO SPEND SOME TIM ALONE ONCE IN A WHILE, HUH?
LEAN
NO! OF COURSE NOT!
MAYBE WE CAN SHARE A FUTON TONIGHT, LIKE WE DID WHEN WE WERE KIDS!
EEE-HHH!?
THROB
THROB
THROB
THROB
THROB
ZZZZ
ZZZZ
GLANCE
I...I CAN'T SLEEP!

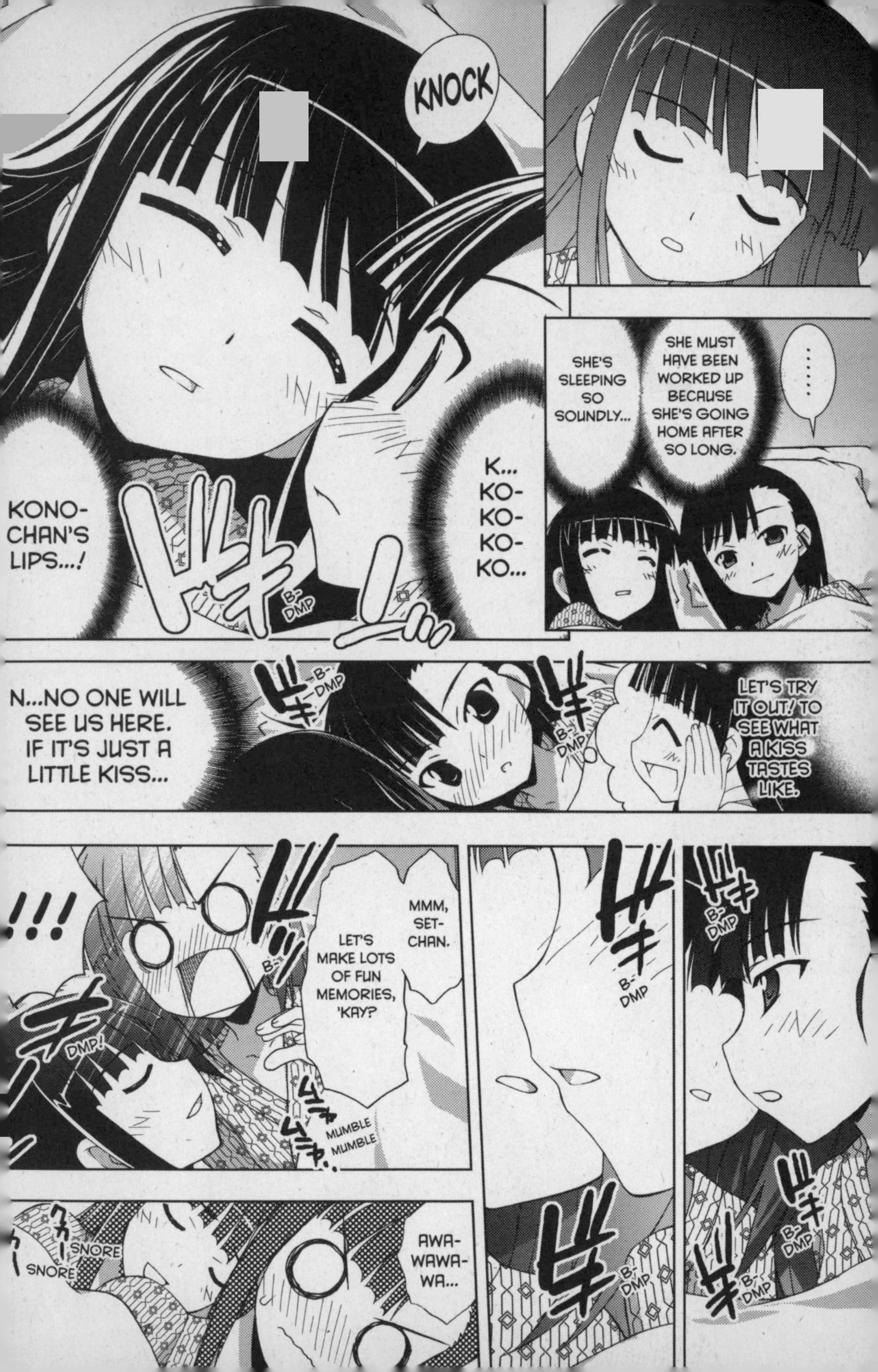

......
SHE MUST HAVE BEEN WORKED UP BECAUSE SHE'S GOING HOME AFTER SO LONG.
SHE'S SLEEPING SO SOUNDLY...
KNOCK
K... KO-KO-KO-KO...
KONO-CHAN'S LIPS...!
B-DMP
LET'S TRY IT OUT! TO SEE WHAT A KISS TASTES LIKE.
B-DMP
B-DMP
N...NO ONE WILL SEE US HERE. IF IT'S JUST A LITTLE KISS...
B-DMP
B-DMP
B-DMP
B-DMP
B-DMP
MMM, SET-CHAN.
LET'S MAKE LOTS OF FUN MEMORIES, 'KAY?
!!!
B-
DMP!
MUMBLE MUMBLE
AWA-WAWAWA-WA...
SNORE
SNORE

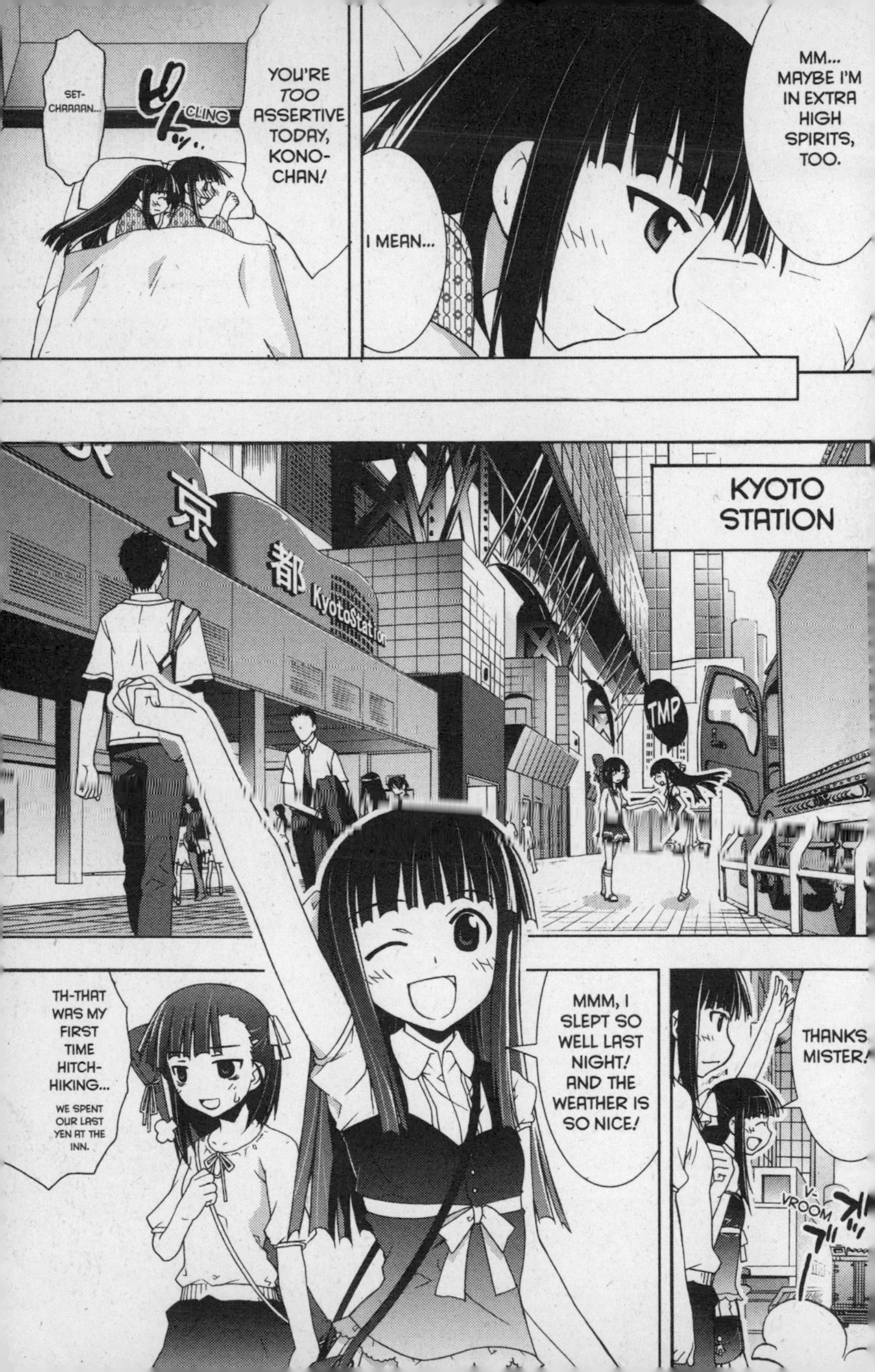
MM... MAYBE I'M IN EXTRA HIGH SPIRITS, TOO.
I MEAN...
YOU'RE *TOO* ASSERTIVE TODAY, KONO-CHAN!
CLING
SET-CHAAAAN...
KYOTO STATION
京都 KyotoStation
TMP
THANKS MISTER!
V-VROOM
MMM, I SLEPT SO WELL LAST NIGHT! AND THE WEATHER IS SO NICE!
TH-THAT WAS MY FIRST TIME HITCH-HIKING...
WE SPENT OUR LAST YEN AT THE INN.

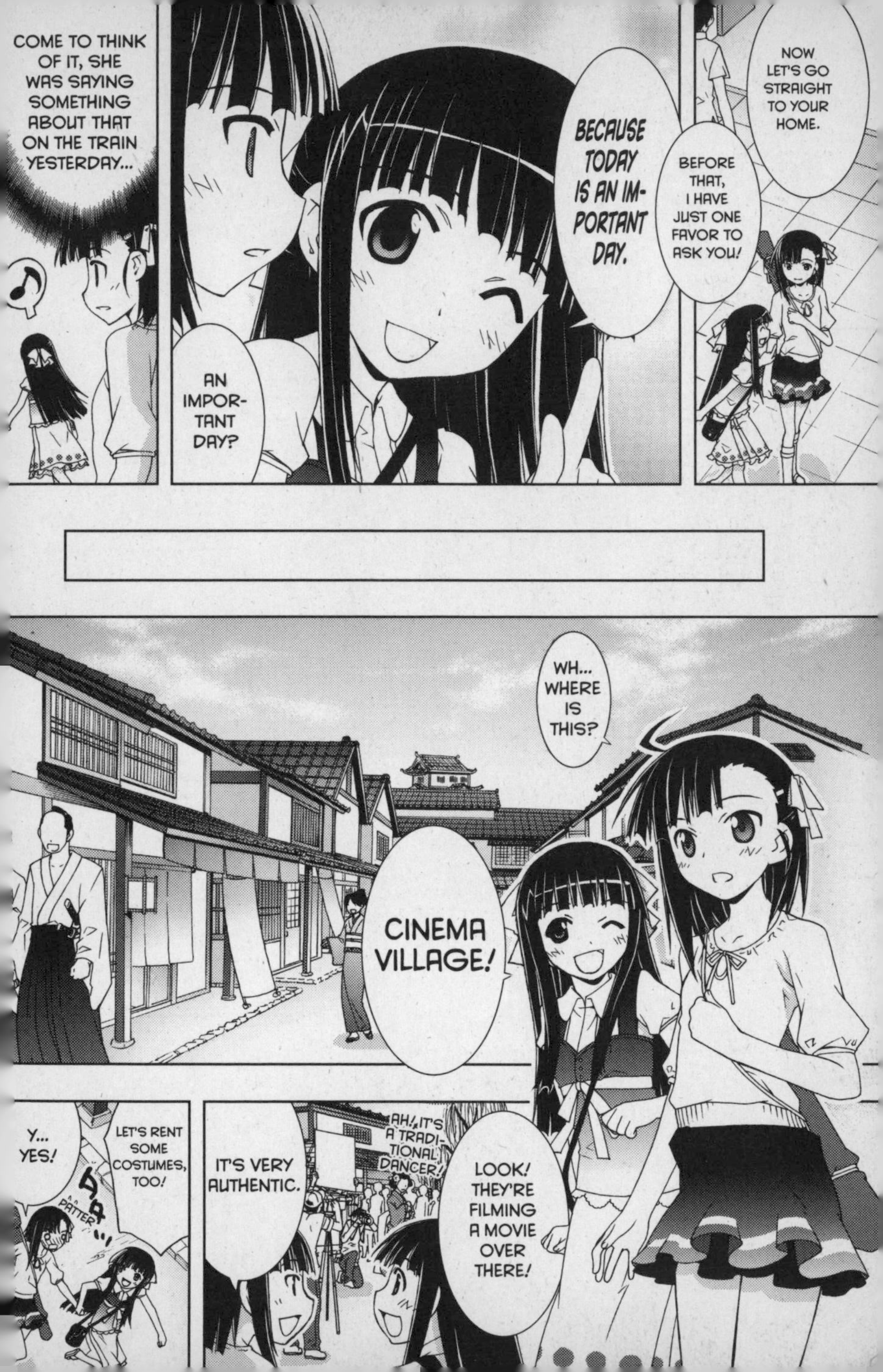
NOW LET'S GO STRAIGHT TO YOUR HOME.
BEFORE THAT, I HAVE JUST ONE FAVOR TO ASK YOU!
BECAUSE TODAY IS AN IMPORTANT DAY.
AN IMPORTANT DAY?
COME TO THINK OF IT, SHE WAS SAYING SOMETHING ABOUT THAT ON THE TRAIN YESTERDAY...
WH... WHERE IS THIS?
CINEMA VILLAGE!
LOOK! THEY'RE FILMING A MOVIE OVER THERE!
AH! IT'S A TRADITIONAL DANCER!
IT'S VERY AUTHENTIC.
LET'S RENT SOME COSTUMES, TOO!
Y... YES!
PATTER

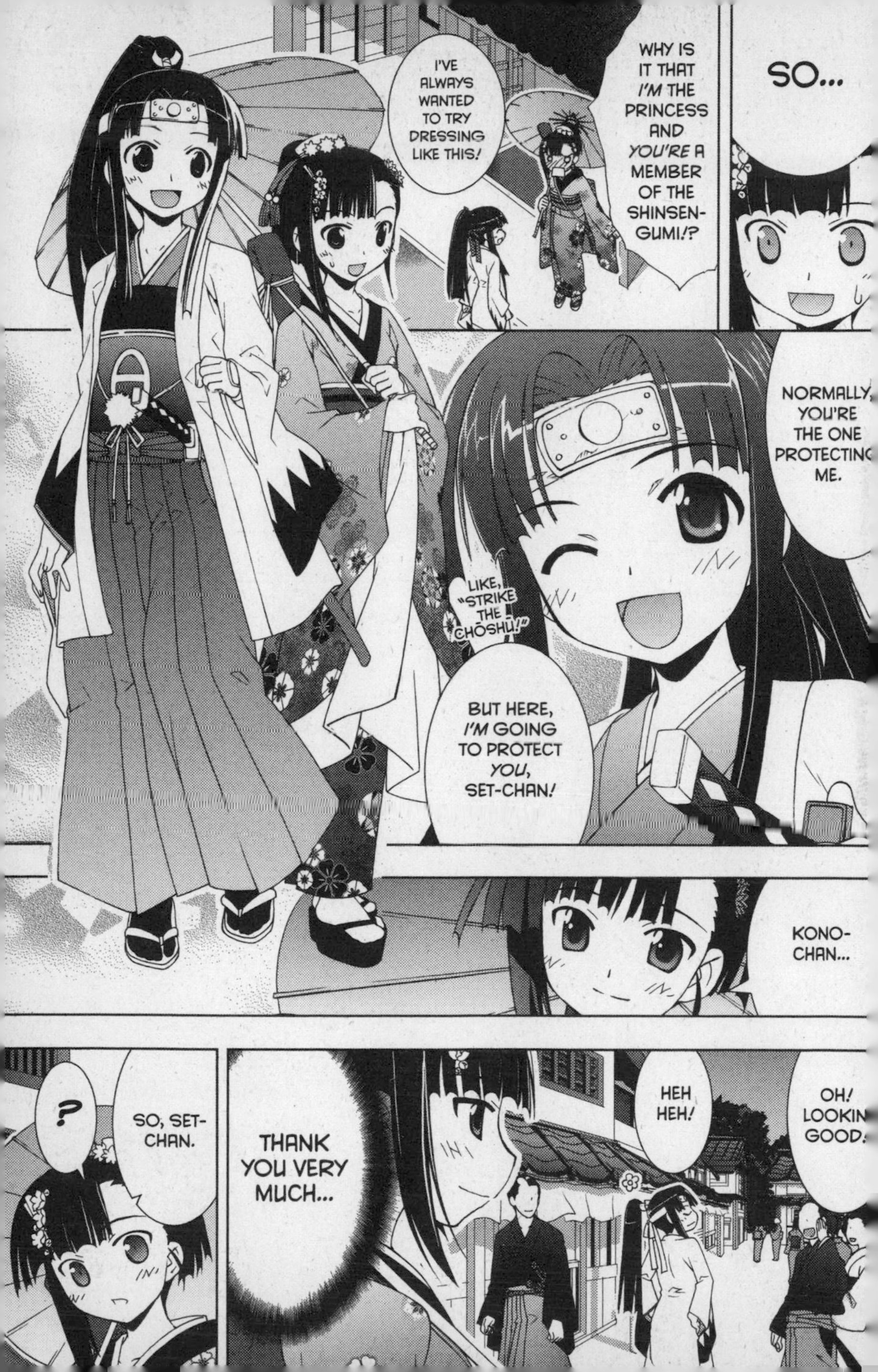
SO...
WHY IS IT THAT I'M THE PRINCESS AND YOU'RE A MEMBER OF THE SHINSEN-GUMI!?
I'VE ALWAYS WANTED TO TRY DRESSING LIKE THIS!
NORMALLY, YOU'RE THE ONE PROTECTING ME.
LIKE, "STRIKE THE CHŌSHŪ!"
BUT HERE, I'M GOING TO PROTECT YOU, SET-CHAN!
KONO-CHAN...
OH! LOOKIN GOOD.
HEH HEH!
THANK YOU VERY MUCH...
SO, SET-CHAN.
?

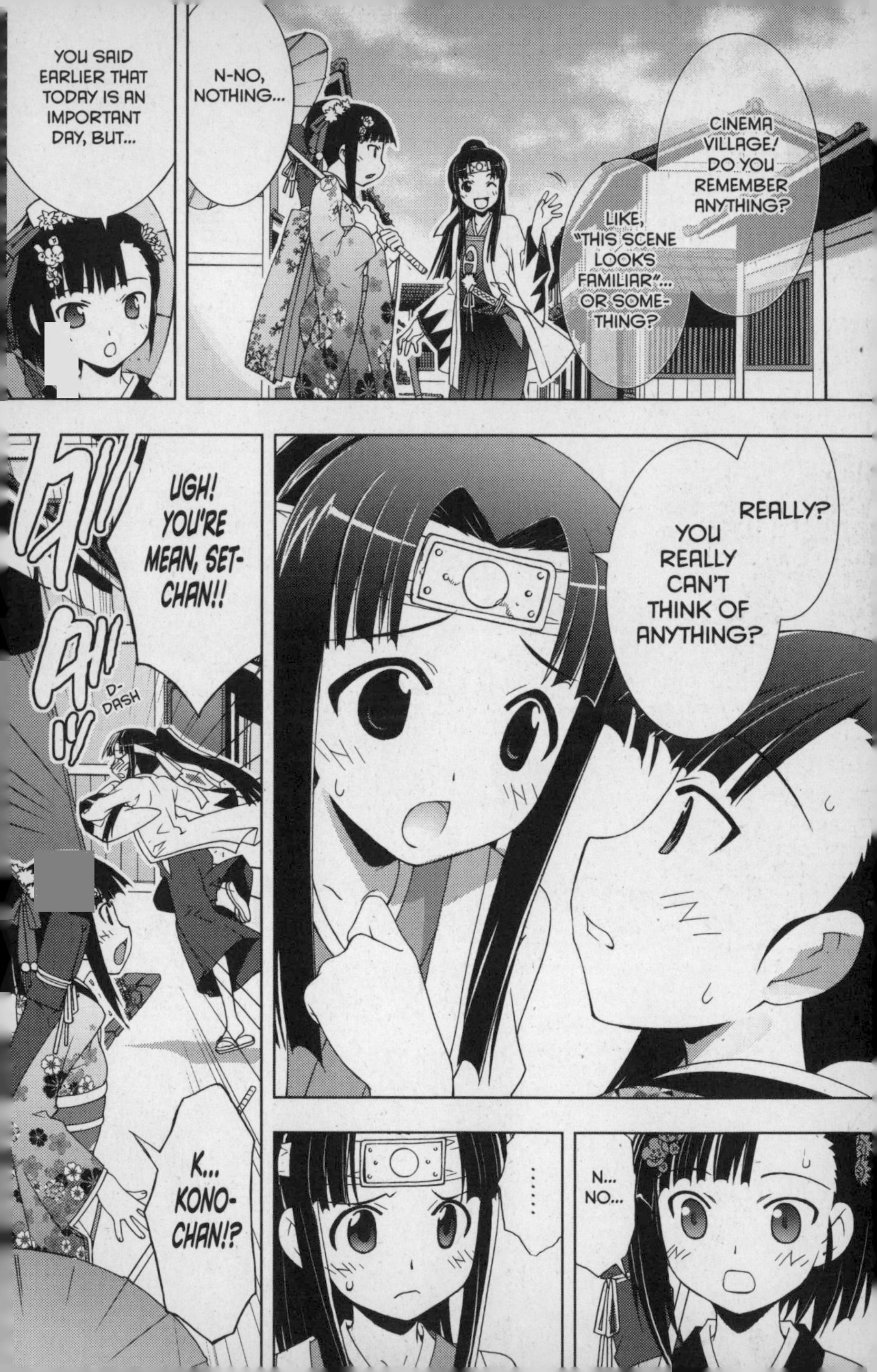
CINEMA VILLAGE! DO YOU REMEMBER ANYTHING?
LIKE, "THIS SCENE LOOKS FAMILIAR"... OR SOME-THING?
N-NO, NOTHING...
YOU SAID EARLIER THAT TODAY IS AN IMPORTANT DAY, BUT...
REALLY? YOU REALLY CAN'T THINK OF ANYTHING?
N... NO...
......
UGH! YOU'RE MEAN, SET-CHAN!!
D-DASH
K... KONO-CHAN!?

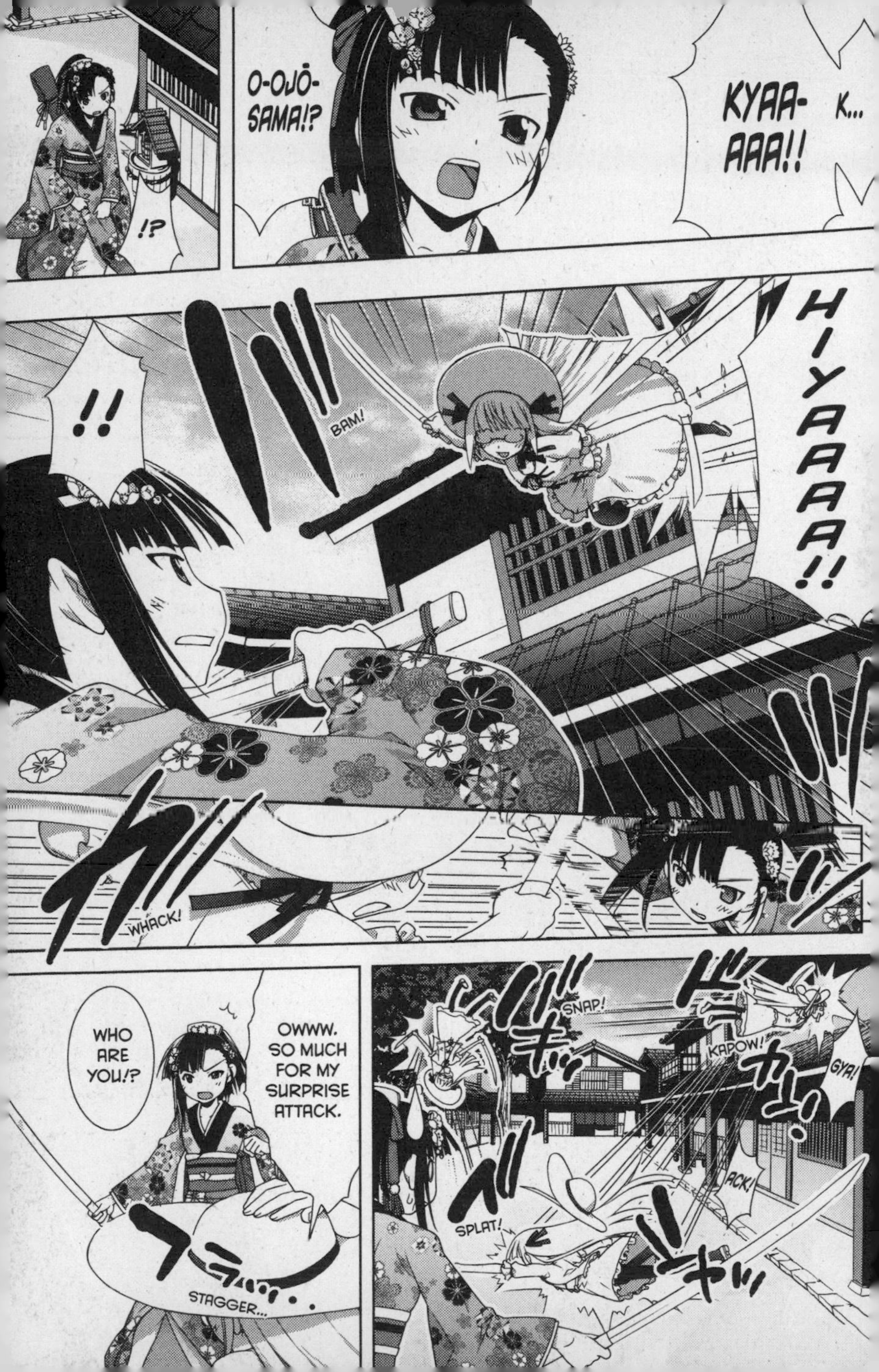
K...
KYAA-AAA!!
O-OJŌ-SAMA!?
!?
HIYAAAAA!!
BAM!
!!
WHACK!
GYA!
KAPOW!
SNAP!
ACK!
SPLAT!
OWWW. SO MUCH FOR MY SURPRISE ATTACK.
WHO ARE YOU!?
STAGGER...

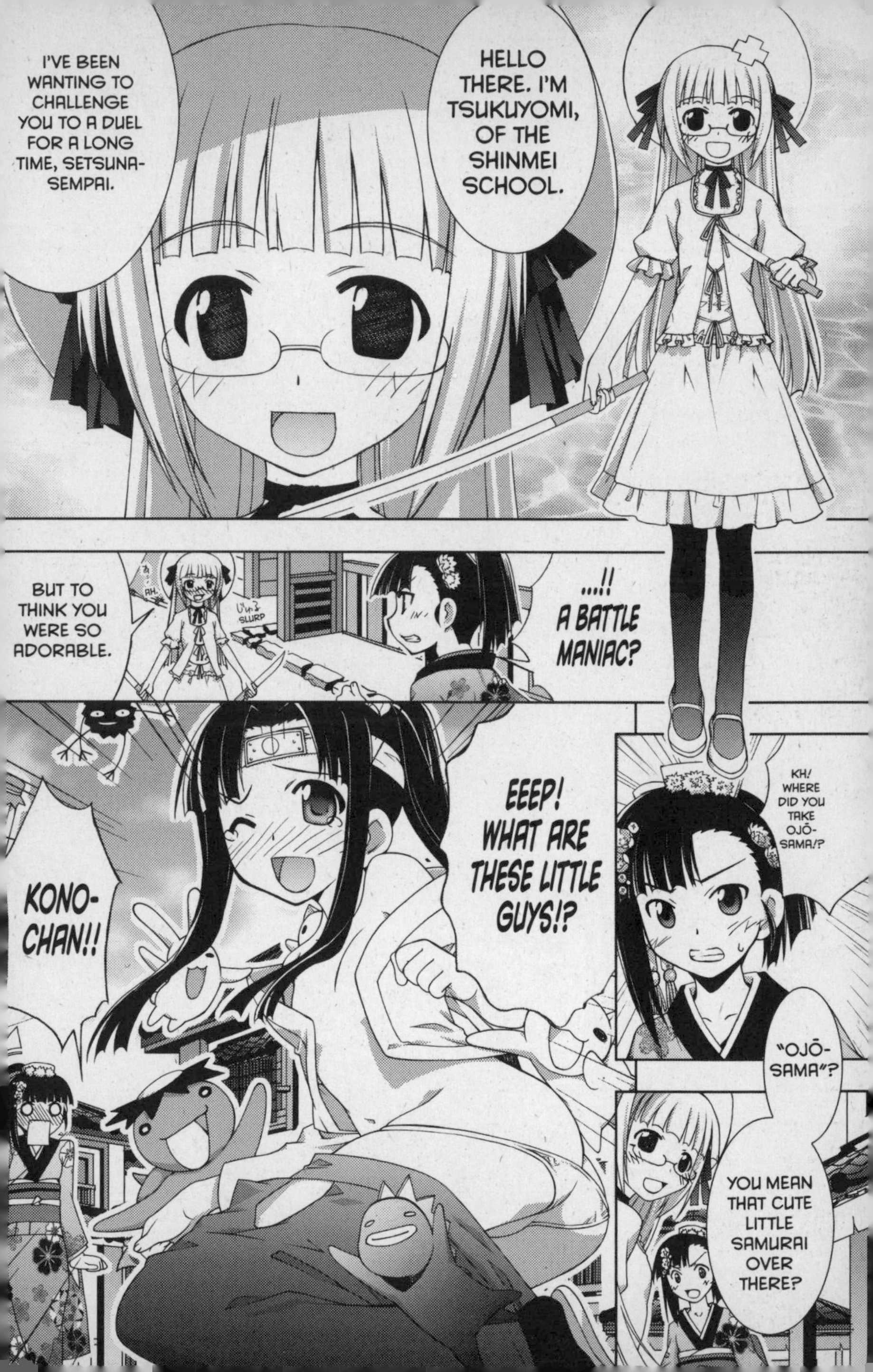
HELLO THERE. I'M TSUKUYOMI, OF THE SHINMEI SCHOOL.
I'VE BEEN WANTING TO CHALLENGE YOU TO A DUEL FOR A LONG TIME, SETSUNA-SEMPAI.
...!! A BATTLE MANIAC?
SLURP
AH.
BUT TO THINK YOU WERE SO ADORABLE.
KH! WHERE DID YOU TAKE OJŌ-SAMA!?
"OJŌ-SAMA"?
YOU MEAN THAT CUTE LITTLE SAMURAI OVER THERE?
EEEP! WHAT ARE THESE LITTLE GUYS!?
KONO-CHAN!!

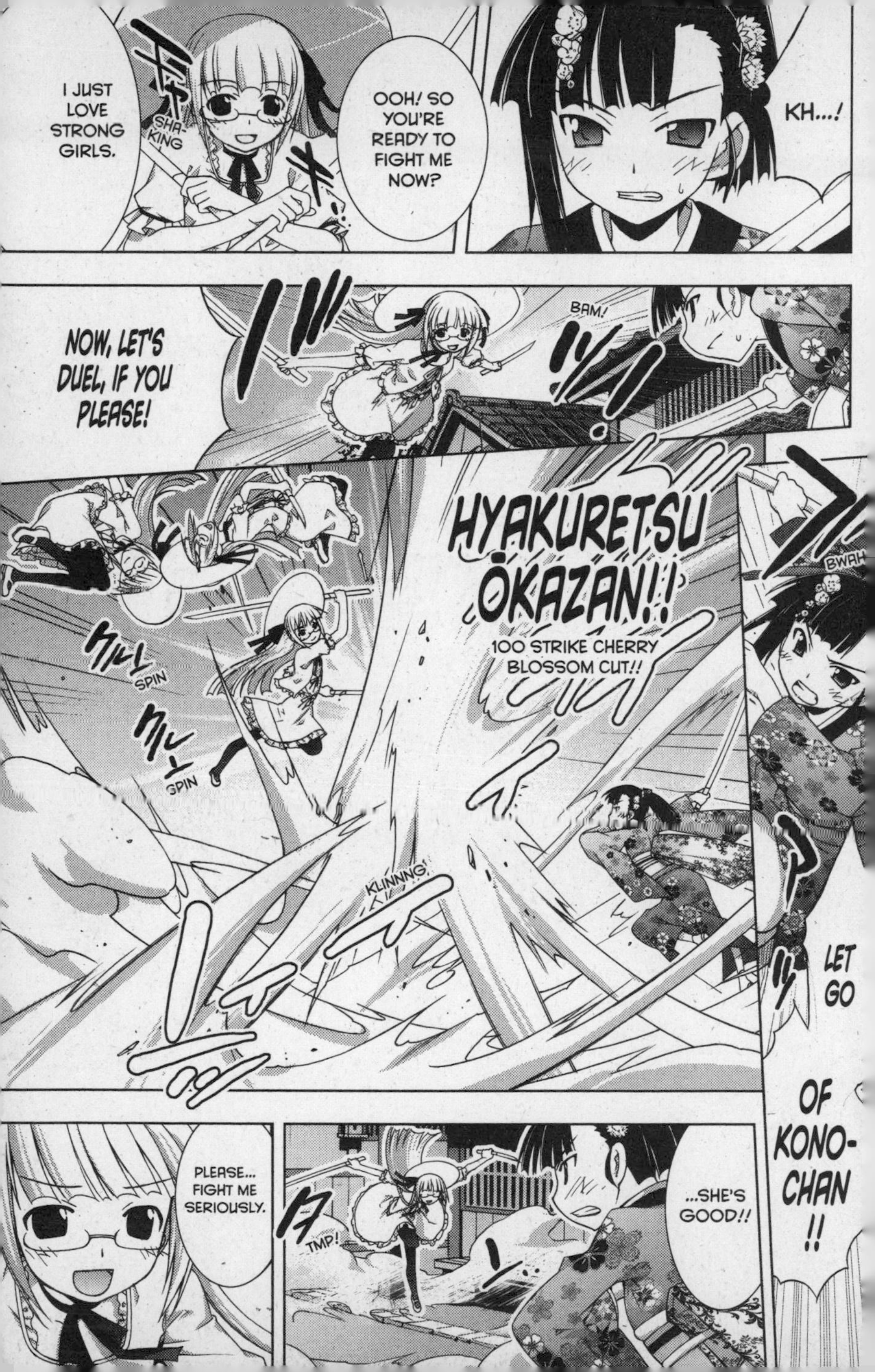
KH...!
OOH! SO YOU'RE READY TO FIGHT ME NOW?
SHA-KING
I JUST LOVE STRONG GIRLS.
BAM!
NOW, LET'S DUEL, IF YOU PLEASE!
BWAH
LET GO OF KONO-CHAN!!
HYAKURETSU ŌKAZAN!!
100 STRIKE CHERRY BLOSSOM CUT!!
KLINNING
SPIN
SPIN
...SHE'S GOOD!!
TMP!
PLEASE... FIGHT ME SERIOUSLY.

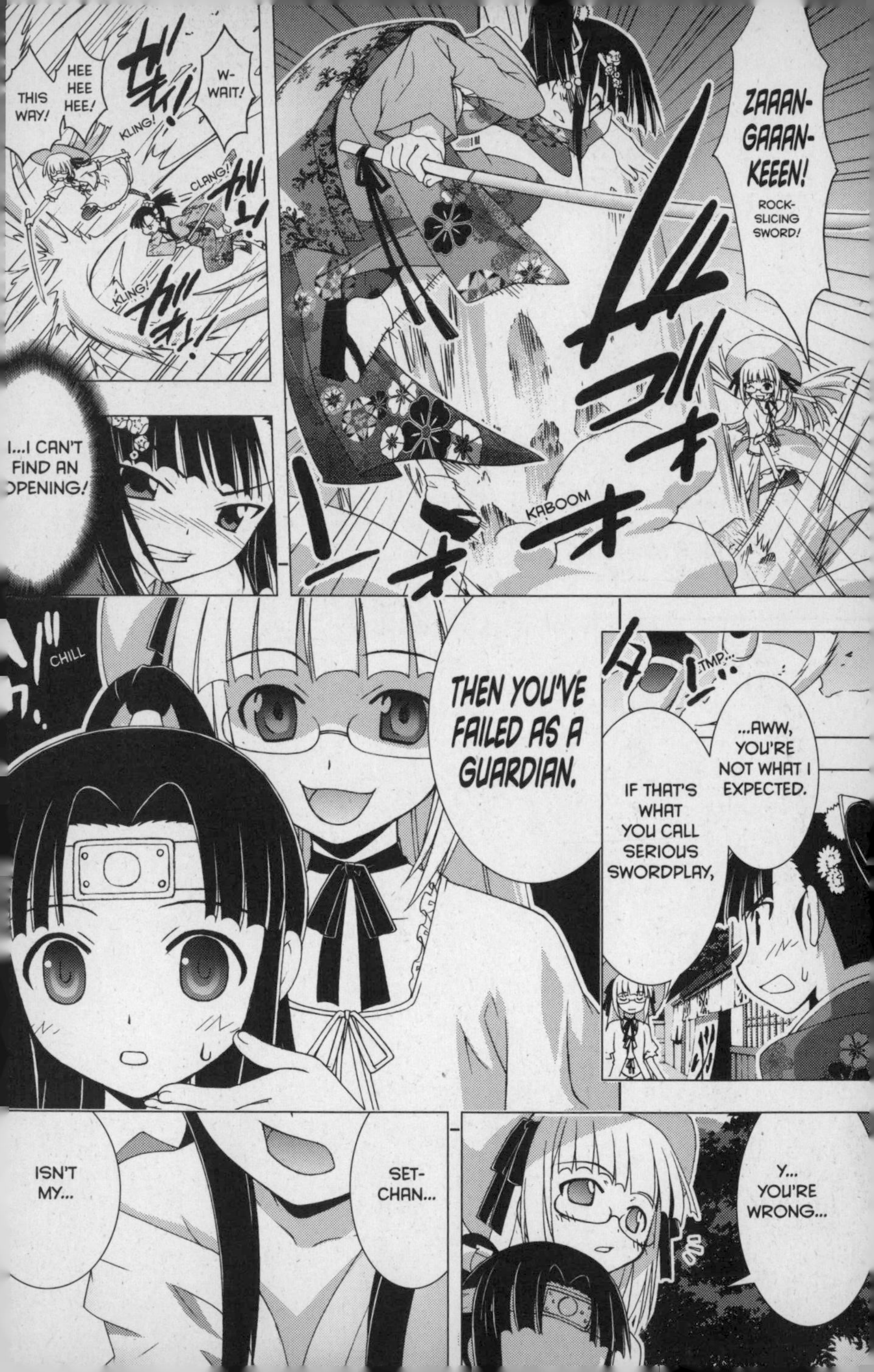
ZAAAN-GAAAN-KEEEN!
ROCK-SLICING SWORD!
KABOOM
W-WAIT!
HEE HEE HEE!
THIS WAY!
KLING!
CLANG!
KLING!
I...I CAN'T FIND AN OPENING!
TMP...
...AWW, YOU'RE NOT WHAT I EXPECTED.
IF THAT'S WHAT YOU CALL SERIOUS SWORDPLAY,
THEN YOU'VE FAILED AS A GUARDIAN.
CHILL
Y... YOU'RE WRONG...
SET-CHAN...
ISN'T MY...

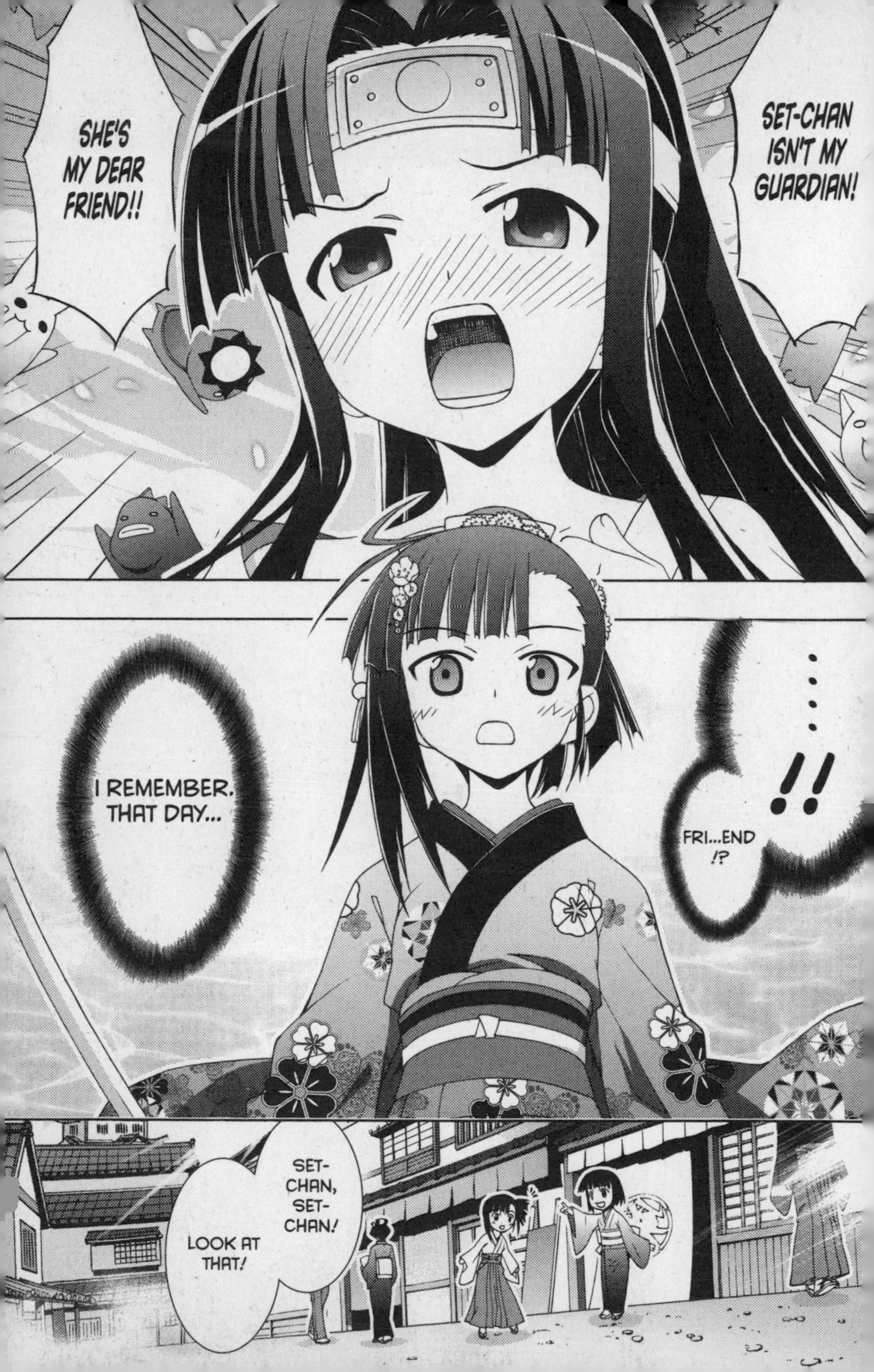
SET-CHAN ISN'T MY GUARDIAN!
SHE'S MY DEAR FRIEND!!
...
!!
FRI...END !?
I REMEMBER. THAT DAY...
SET-CHAN, SET-CHAN!
LOOK AT THAT!

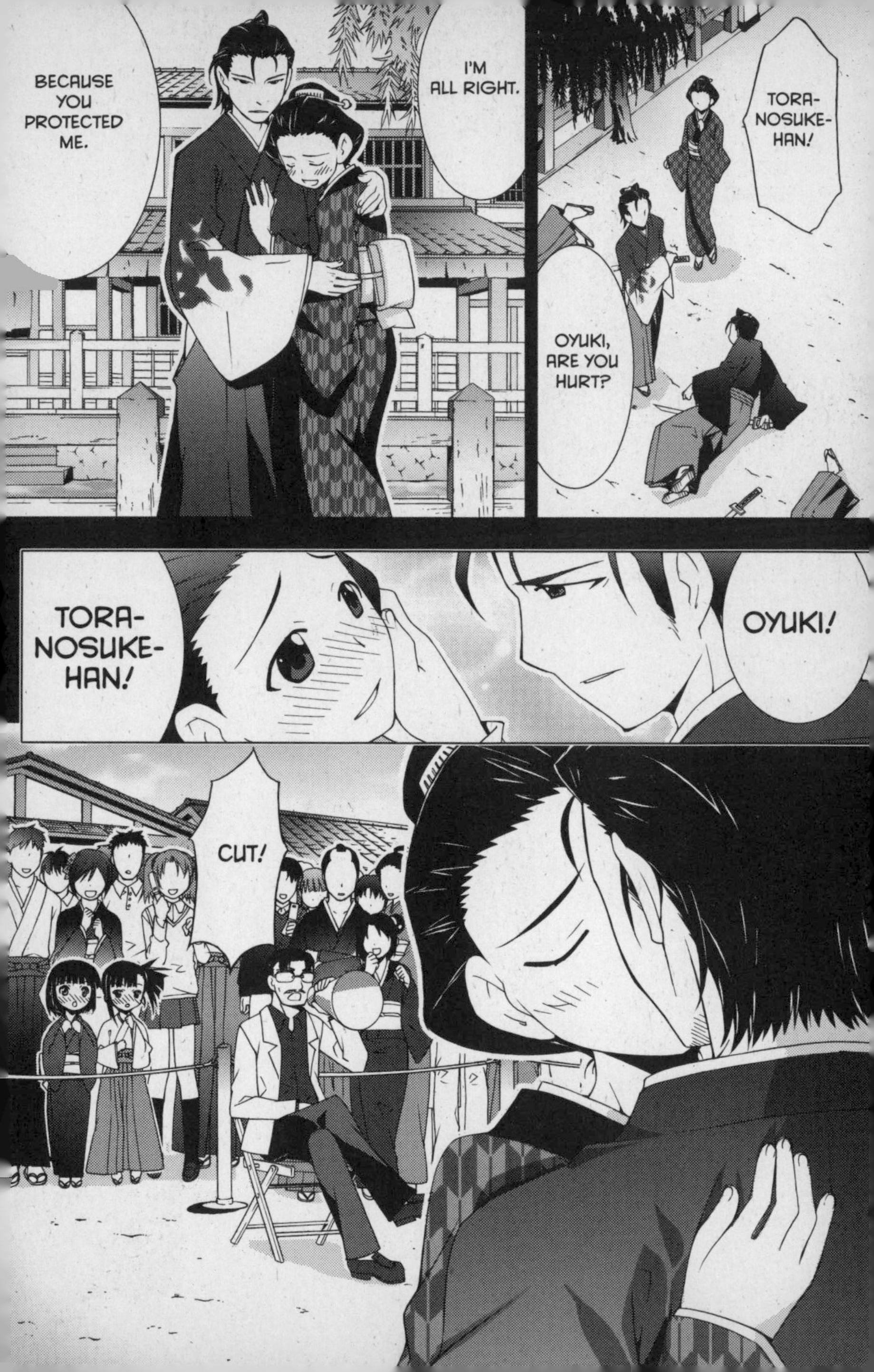
TORA-NOSUKE-HAN!
OYUKI, ARE YOU HURT?
I'M ALL RIGHT.
BECAUSE YOU PROTECTED ME.
OYUKI!
TORA-NOSUKE-HAN!
CUT!

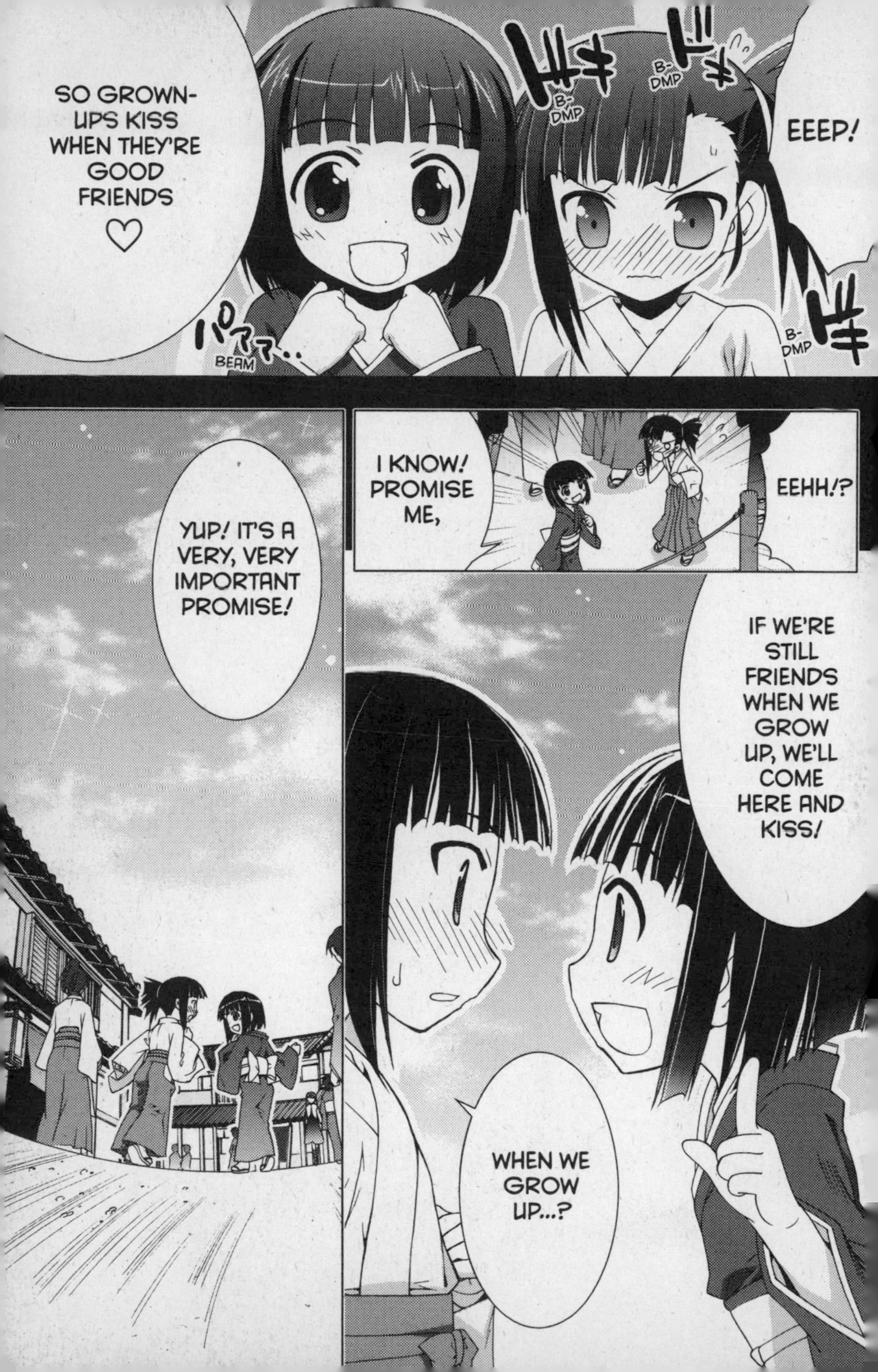
SO GROWN-UPS KISS WHEN THEY'RE GOOD FRIENDS ♡
EEEP!
B-DMP
B-DMP
B-DMP
BEAM
EEHH!?
I KNOW! PROMISE ME,
IF WE'RE STILL FRIENDS WHEN WE GROW UP, WE'LL COME HERE AND KISS!
WHEN WE GROW UP...?
YUP! IT'S A VERY, VERY IMPORTANT PROMISE!

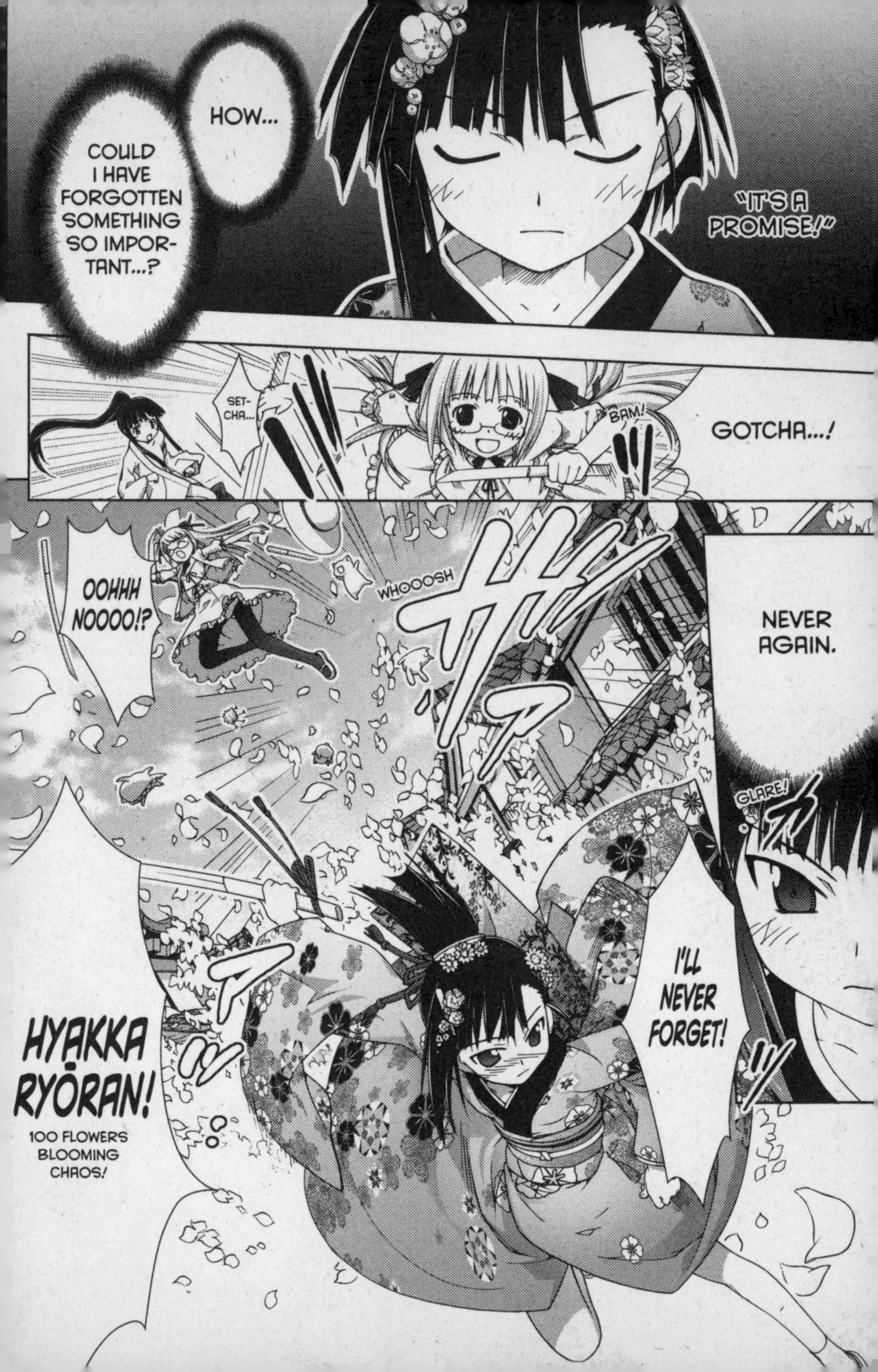
"IT'S A PROMISE!"
HOW...
COULD I HAVE FORGOTTEN SOMETHING SO IMPORTANT...?
GOTCHA...!
BAM!
SET-CHA...
NEVER AGAIN.
GLARE!
I'LL NEVER FORGET!
WHOOOSH
OOHHH NOOOO!?
HYAKKA RYŌRAN!
100 FLOWERS BLOOMING CHAOS!

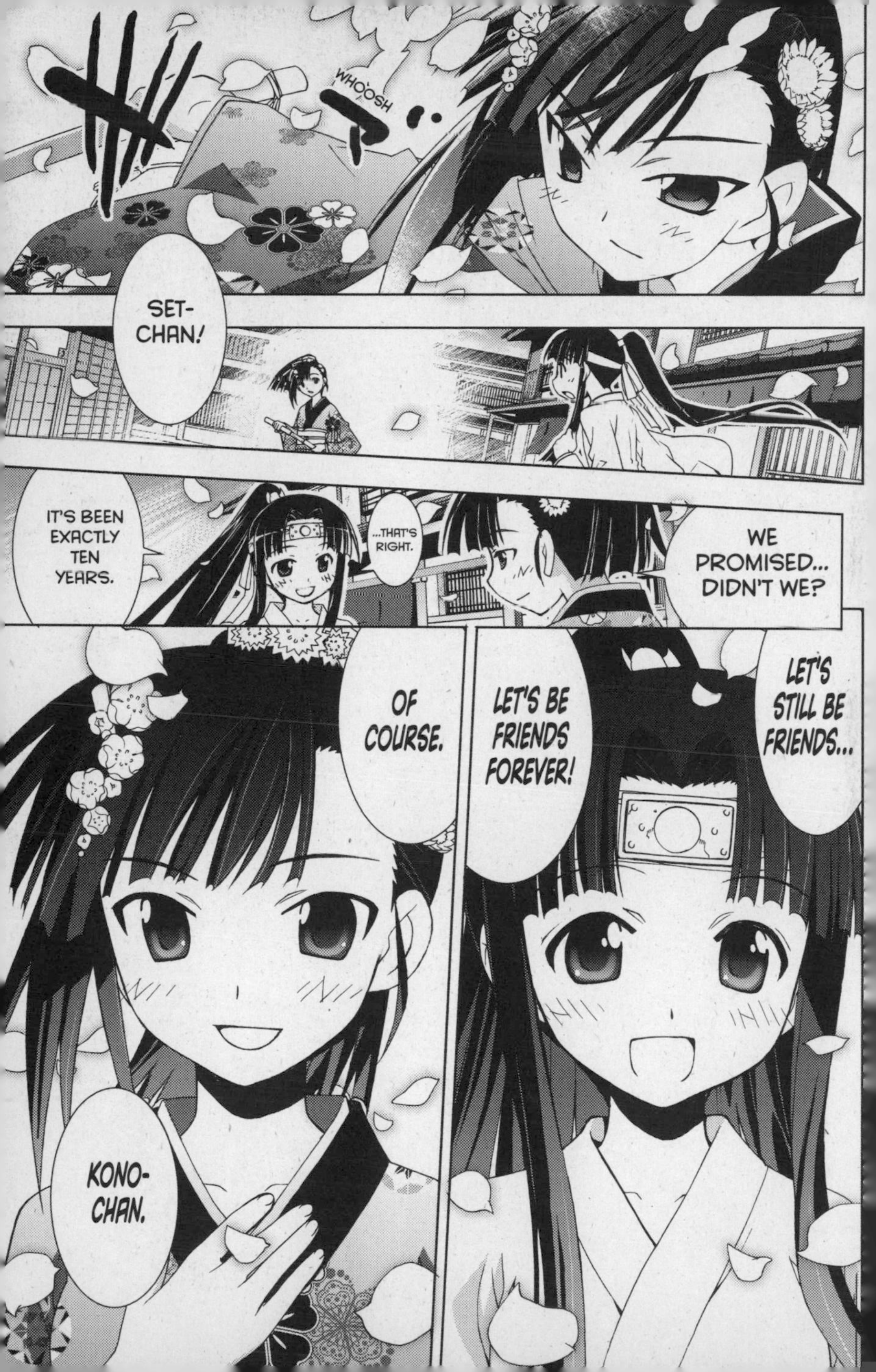
WHOOSH
SET-CHAN!
WE PROMISED... DIDN'T WE?
...THAT'S RIGHT.
IT'S BEEN EXACTLY TEN YEARS.
LET'S STILL BE FRIENDS...
LET'S BE FRIENDS FOREVER!
OF COURSE.
KONO-CHAN.

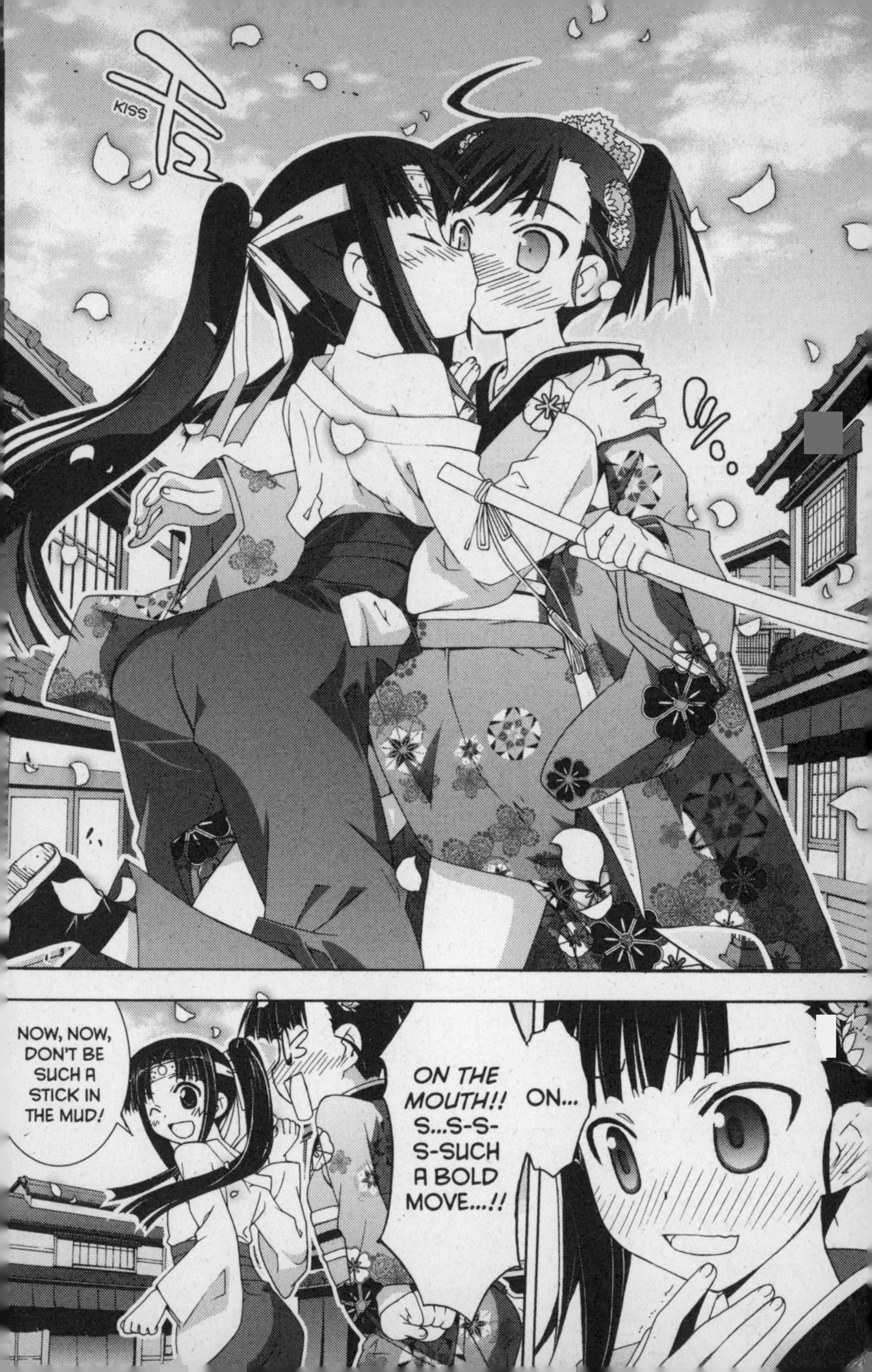
KISS
ON...
ON THE MOUTH!! S...S-S-S-SUCH A BOLD MOVE...!!
NOW, NOW, DON'T BE SUCH A STICK IN THE MUD!

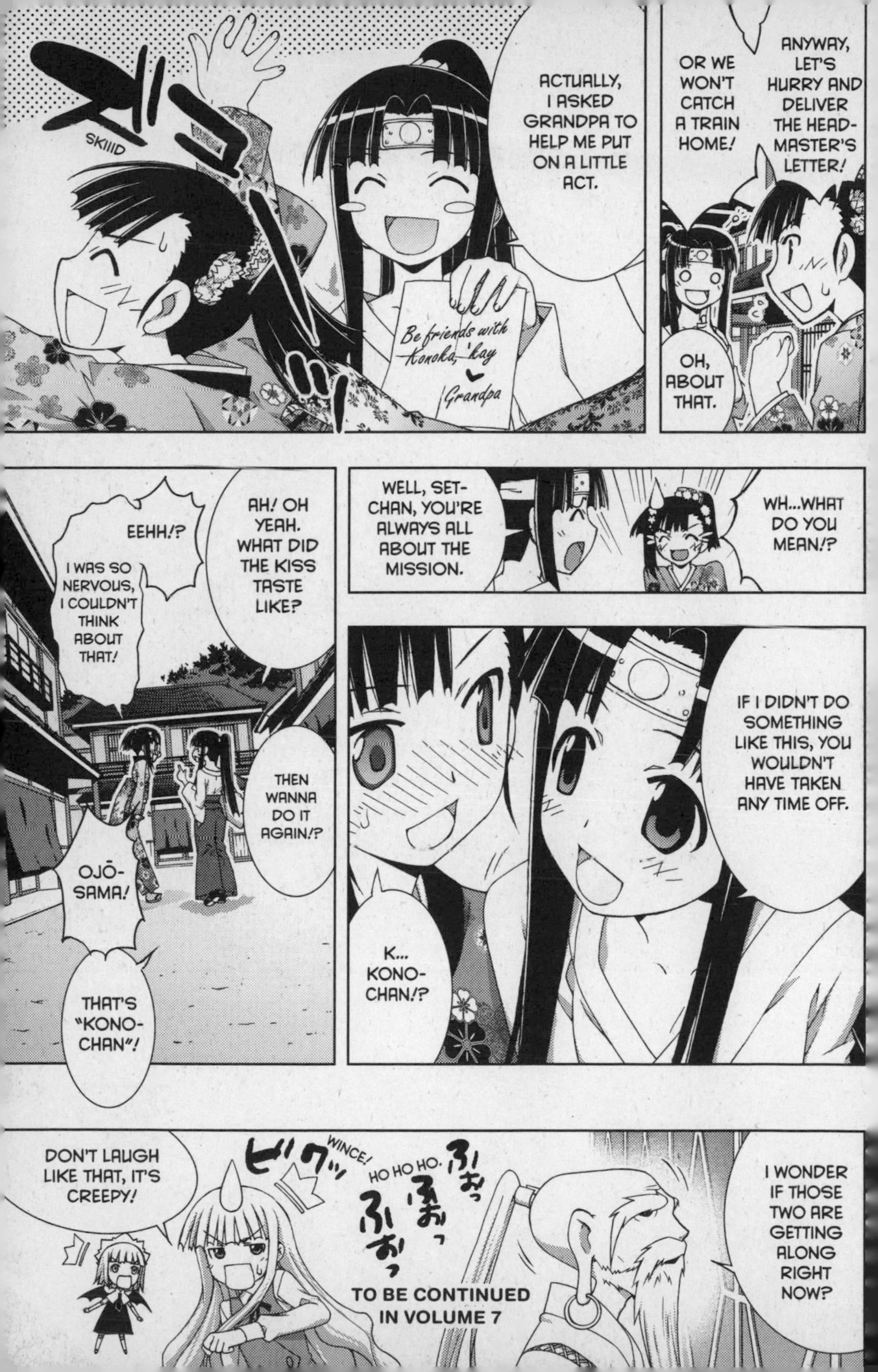
ANYWAY, LET'S HURRY AND DELIVER THE HEAD-MASTER'S LETTER!
OR WE WON'T CATCH A TRAIN HOME!
OH, ABOUT THAT.
ACTUALLY, I ASKED GRANDPA TO HELP ME PUT ON A LITTLE ACT.
SKIIID
Be friends with Konoka, 'kay ♥ Grandpa
WH...WHAT DO YOU MEAN!?
WELL, SET-CHAN, YOU'RE ALWAYS ALL ABOUT THE MISSION.
IF I DIDN'T DO SOMETHING LIKE THIS, YOU WOULDN'T HAVE TAKEN ANY TIME OFF.
K... KONO-CHAN!?
AH! OH YEAH. WHAT DID THE KISS TASTE LIKE?
EEHH!?
I WAS SO NERVOUS, I COULDN'T THINK ABOUT THAT!
THEN WANNA DO IT AGAIN!?
OJŌ-SAMA!
THAT'S "KONO-CHAN"!
I WONDER IF THOSE TWO ARE GETTING ALONG RIGHT NOW?
HO HO HO.
WINCE!
DON'T LAUGH LIKE THAT, IT'S CREEPY!
TO BE CONTINUED IN VOLUME 7

# Translation Notes

Japanese is a tricky language for most Westerners, and translation is often more an art than a science. For your edification and reading pleasure, here are notes on some of the places where we could have gone in a different direction or where a Japanese cultural reference is used.

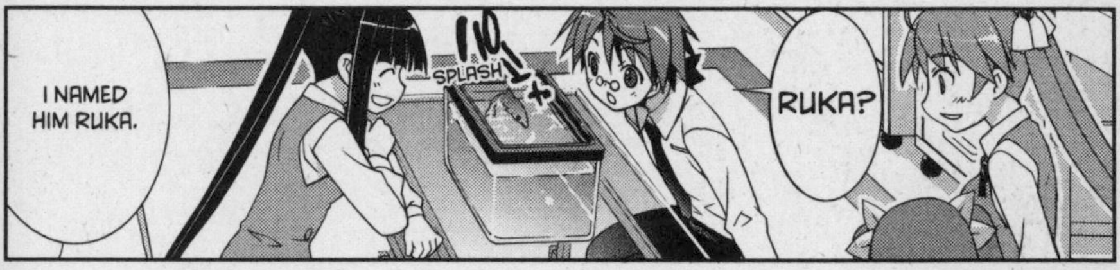
RUKA?
SPLASH
I NAMED HIM RUKA.

## Ruka, page 84

Ruka is a fairly obvious name for a dolphin in Japan, since the Japanese word for dolphin is *iruka*.

## Albatross of Mahora, page 106

While it's not entirely clear why, of all the birds in the world, Makie would be referred to as an albatross, it's fairly easy to guess. The Japanese word for albatross is *ahōdori,* or "idiot bird." And as Baka Pink, Makie, though graceful as a bird, would also be known for being dumber than a brick.

## Nova Kids tissues, page 127

Even in the United States, it's not uncommon to find people standing around handing out flyers to advertise a business or product. In Japan, they put the advertisements on packs of tissues and other useful things, so instead of throwing away a useless piece of paper, the recipient might keep it and use it later, thus reminding them of the business or product being advertised.

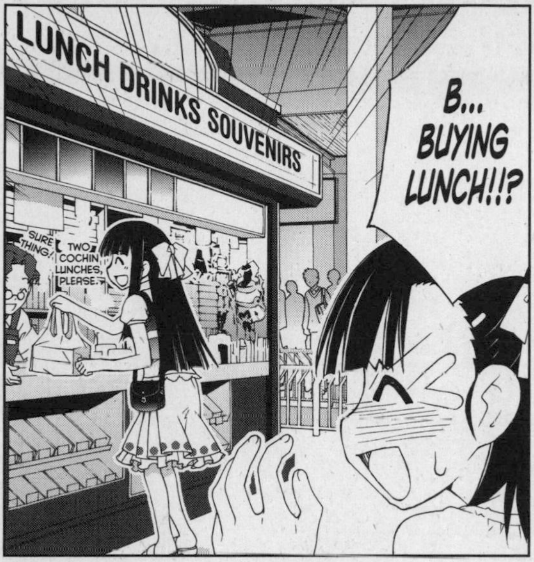
B... BUYING LUNCH!!?
LUNCH DRINKS SOUVENIRS
TWO COCHIN LUNCHES, PLEASE.
SURE THING!

## Cochin lunches, page 151

A cochin is a type of chicken, for which Nagoya is famous. Naturally, a lunch sold at a train station in Nagoya would feature the region's special breed of chicken.

## Nagano, Niigata, and Inaka, page 152

As can be surmised from their shock and Konoka's statement about going in the wrong direction, Nagano is in the opposite direction from Kyoto. In her attempt to get back on track, Konoka chooses another random train, taking them even farther in the wrong direction, to Niigata. They finally arrive at a place called Inaka, which basically means "the backwoods."

## *Yukata*, page 157

While a *yukata* is traditional Japanese summer wear, like a kimono, it is also typically worn while relaxing at Japanese inns.

## Shinsengumi, page 163

The Shinsengumi was a special police force from the late shogunate period. Members of the Shinsengumi show up frequently in Japanese historical dramas as well as anime. Their greatest enemies were the lordless samurai of the Mōri clan, also known as the Chōshū, hence Konoka's line about striking them down.

## Toranosuke-han, page 170

Here in Kyoto, the people use Kyoto dialect, which replaces *-san* with *-han*.

# Preview of
# *Negima!? neo*
## Volume 7

**We're pleased to present you a preview from volume 7. Please check our website (www.delreymanga.com) to see when this volume will be available in English. For now you'll have to make do with Japanese!**

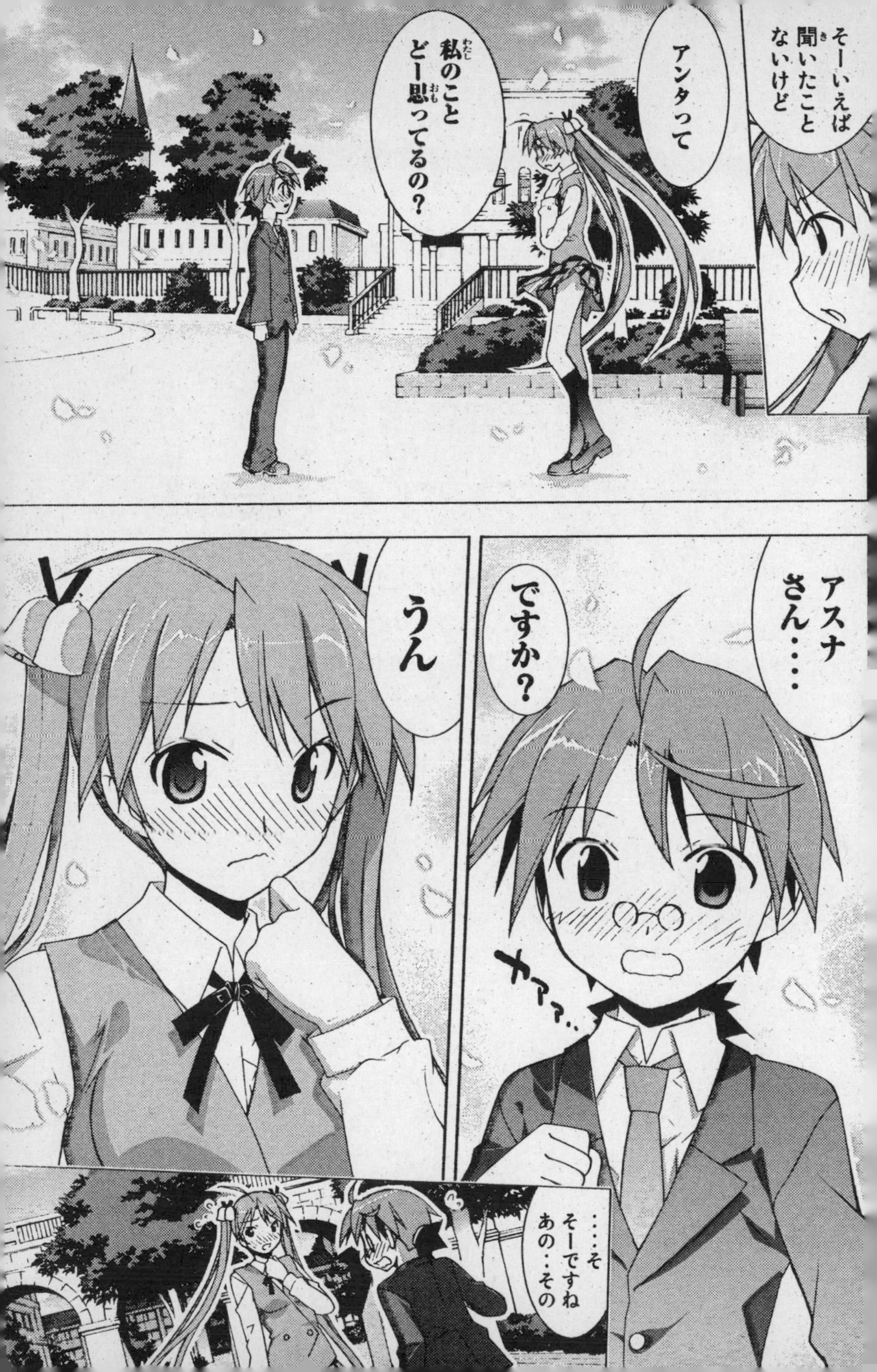
そーいえば聞いたことないけど
アンタって
私のことどー思ってるの?
アスナさん・・・・
ですか?
カァァ…
うん
・・・・そそーですねあの・・その

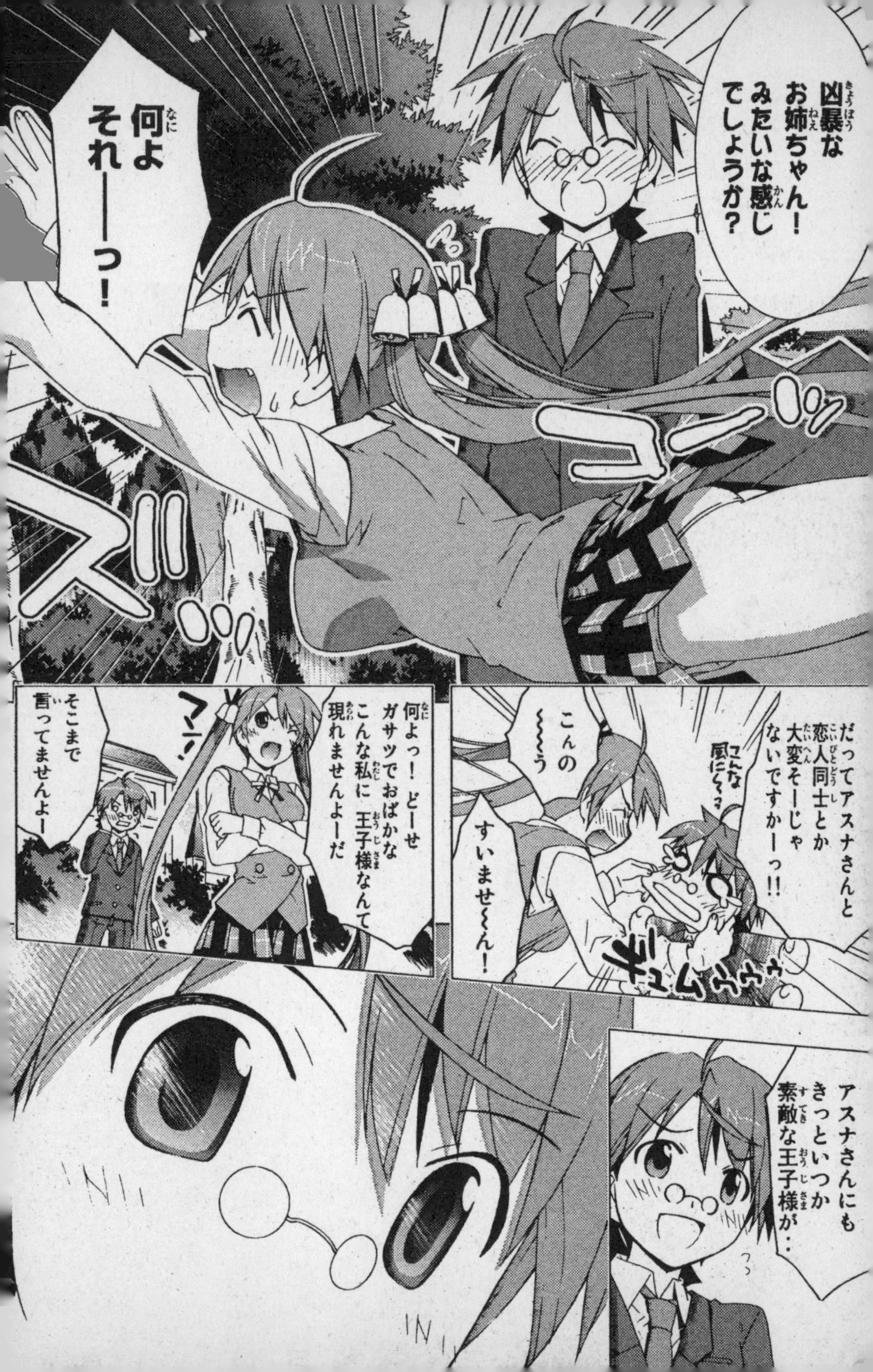
凶暴なお姉ちゃん！みたいな感じでしょうか？
何よそれーーっ！
だってアスナさんと恋人同士とか大変そーじゃないですかーっ!!
こんな風に〜〜
こんの〜〜〜う
すいませ〜ん！
何よっ！どーせガサツでおばかなこんな私に王子様なんて現れませんよーだ
そこまで言ってませんよー
アスナさんにもきっといつか素敵な王子様が‥

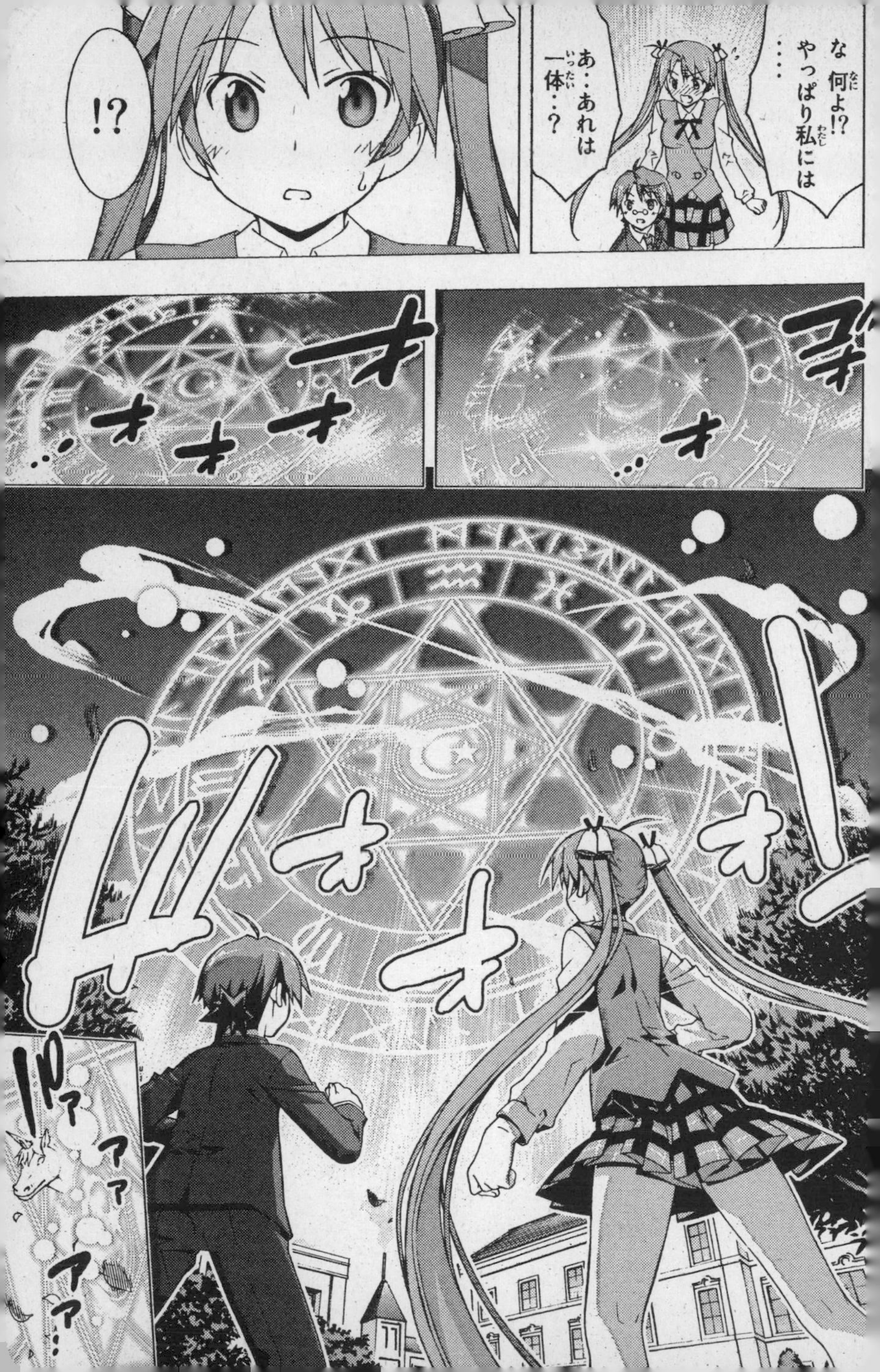

な 何よ!? やっぱり私には・・・・
あ・・あれは一体・・?
!?
ゴォ…オ
…オォォオ

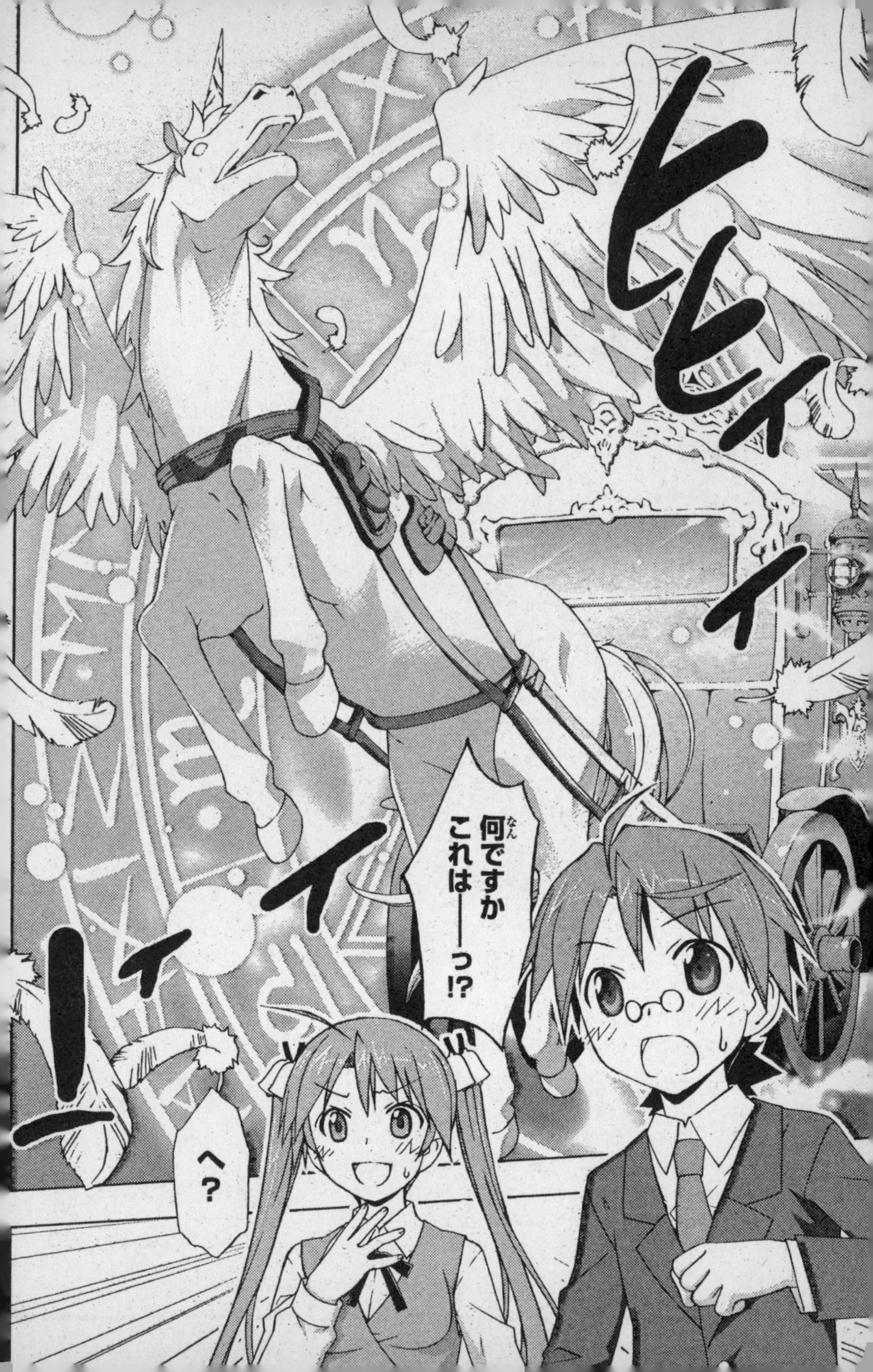
ヒヒイイイ
イイ
ィ
ー！
何ですかこれは――っ!?
へ？

# TOMARE!

STOP

## You're going the wrong way!

**MANGA IS A COMPLETELY
DIFFERENT TYPE
OF READING EXPERIENCE.**

**TO START AT THE BEGINNING,
GO TO THE END!**

## That's right!

Authentic manga is read the traditional Japanese way—from right to left—exactly the opposite of how American books are read. It's easy to follow: Just go to the other end of the book, and read each page—and each panel—from right side to left side, starting at the top right. Now you're experiencing manga as it was meant to be!